BEITRÄGE ZUR
GESCHICHTE DER BIBLISCHEN EXEGESE
Herausgegeben von
OSCAR CULLMANN, BASEL/PARIS · NILS A. DAHL, NEW HAVEN
ERNST KÄSEMANN, TÜBINGEN · HANS-JOACHIM KRAUS, GÖTTINGEN
HEIKO A. OBERMAN, TÜBINGEN · HARALD RIESENFELD, UPPSALA
KARL HERMANN SCHELKLE, TÜBINGEN

20

The Church and Racial Hostility

A History of Interpretation of Ephesians 2: 11—22

by

WILLIAM RADER

1978

J. C. B. MOHR (PAUL SIEBECK) TÜBINGEN

CIP-Kurztitelaufnahme der Deutschen Bibliothek

Rader, William
The church and racial hostility: a history of
interpretation of Ephesians 2, 11—22. —
Tübingen: Mohr, 1978.
  (Beiträge zur Geschichte der biblischen Exegese; 20)
  ISBN 3-16-140112-3
  ISSN 0408-8298

PREFACE

The present study was originally presented as a doctoral dissertation written under Prof. Oscar Cullmann at the University of Basel. I want to express my thanks to Prof. Cullmann for guiding and encouraging this project with patience and wisdom. I have conceived of it as an experiment in keeping with Prof. Cullmann's proposal that the concept of redemptive history has implications for Christian ethics which need to be more fully explored.

I am grateful also to the other members of the Basel faculty, especially Prof. Max Geiger and Prof. Jan Lochmann who were my advisors in Church History and Systematic Theology. Prof. Walter Neidhardt supplied some sermons on Eph 2: 11—22 from his files as professor of Practical Theology. Prof. Bo Reicke's careful correction of details is appreciated. In the initial stages, Prof. Karl Barth gave counsel and was always encouraging. I also want to thank the staff of the Basel University Library for their assistance.

Other libraries whose assistance in research I much appreciate are those of Yale Divinity School, Princeton Theological Seminary, Lancaster Theological Seminary and the Pennsylvania State University. The services of the computer at the Center for Patristic Analyses and Documentation of the Faculty of Protestant Theology at the University of Strasbourg were also helpful.

I am also indebted to professors of other universities: Prof. Paul Achtemeier then of Lancaster Theological Seminary helped in the early decisions on scope and method; Prof. Andrew Murray of Lincoln University shared his knowledge of the history of race relations in the United States; Prof. Markus Barth then of Pittsburg provided much inspiration and many suggestions out of his intensive study of Ephesians; Prof. Paul Schubert and Prof. Nils Dahl of Yale Divinity School both offered help in early stages. Prof. Dahl's thoughtful reading of the completed dissertation and his suggestions for alterations and additions before publication are especially appreciated. My thanks go also to Prof. Donald Englert of Lancaster, who was instrumental in guiding me to Basel for graduate study, and to Prof. Bela Vasady, my advisor in earlier explorations in theology and race.

IV

Very personal thanks go to the many friends who supported, encouraged, or criticized my work including Lidia Brefin, Eberhard Busch, Ruedi Brändli, Peter Barth, the staff of Agape Verlag, Martha Grosshans, Vroni Thurneysen, fellow residents of the Alumneum, Jörg and Kati Liechti, and the community of Missionhurst Seminary, Washington D.C. Finally, I am grateful for the support of my family and my wife's family, and above all for my wife's participation in every aspect of the work, including discussion, critical reading, and typing.

William Rader

TABLE OF CONTENTS

Chapter III

THE WESTERN MIDDLE AGES

Chapter IV

THE REFORMATION

Chapter V

THE SEVENTEENTH CENTURY

Chapter VI

THE EIGHTEENTH CENTURY

Chapter VII

THE NINETEENTH CENTURY

VIII

Chapter VIII

THE TWENTIETH CENTURY

Developments in New Testament Research Influencing
the Interpretation of Eph 2: 11—22

Developments within the Church and its Relation to the
World Which Have Motivated Attention to Eph 2: 11—22

INTRODUCTION

The following study of Eph 2:11—22 was prompted by a contemporary problem facing the church: the wall between blacks and
whites in the United States. More specifically, this study had its
origins in an inner-city church in Cincinnati whose once white
neighborhood had become predominantly black—a situation common to many city churches in the United States. The difficulties
our white congregation had in deciding upon its course and following it revealed how little we understood what the church is. We had
been so accustomed to congregations which reflected the divisions
in society that it was difficult to conceive that this might be a
denial of the very nature of the church.

Much helpful material on the problem of racial discrimination
was available to our inner-city congregation from church sources
and elsewhere. The material contained many insights from sociolo-
gy, psychology, and contemporary literature, but few contributions
from theology, least of all from biblical studies. In recent years
more efforts have been made to relate the findings of biblical
studies to the race problem, and it is hoped that this history of the
interpretation of one peculiarly relevant passage will be a contribution to such efforts.

The present study is based on the thesis that the uniting of Jew
and Gentile in the early life of the church has significance for our
understanding of the nature of the church today. That the uniting
of Jewish and Gentile ideas—or Hebraic and Hellenistic ways of
thinking—has shaped Christian theology is obvious, and has been,
and still is, the subject of a great deal of investigation and debate.
The significance of the uniting of Jewish and Gentile persons in
visible fellowship has not been so thoroughly explored: what have
been and what are the implications for the church that it is the
church out of Jew and Gentile? The general question originated for
me in the specific form: what are the implications of the reconciliation of Jews and Gentiles in the New Testament period for the reconciliation of blacks and whites today?

It may be objected that the question is not legitimate since the
Jews occupy a unique place in history; they are not just one people

among many, but the people chosen by God. This objection is important, and must be considered throughout the study. But is it not part of God's purpose for creating this people that they might represent all of mankind? And may not their relationship with Gentiles represent the relationships between all human groups? An affirmative answer seems to be implied in I Cor 12:13, Gal 3:28 and Col 3:11. Each of these texts speaks of the overcoming of human divisions in Christ: each begins with "Jew and Greek" and then lists other groupings—slaves and free, male and female, barbarian and Scythian. The letter to the Ephesians itself can be understood as pointing to the reconciliation of Jew and Gentile in the church as the first visible step in God's plan to "unite all things in Christ" (Eph 1:10).

Another objection which may be raised is that a method which goes from a specific biblical passage to contemporary issues is inadequate. C. F. Sleeper warns that "we should not try to discover in the Bible (particularly in the New Testament) answers to complex questions of social ethics, such as race relations"[1]. Sleeper's approach, therefore, is to derive a basis for social ethics from the entire biblical witness, thus avoiding the danger of proof-texts. This kind of work is very much needed. But close study of a particular text as it has interacted with the life and thought of the church can also contribute to the development of a biblical basis for social ethics. And in the meantime, a study of the interpretation of a particular text can be of help to the preacher who regularly attempts, in the light of the entire biblical witness, to open up the relevance of a particular text for today's problems.

C. H. Dodd opens up the relevance of Eph 2:11—15 for international relations in his *Christianity and the Reconciliation of the Nations*. The entire work is an exposition of the Ephesians passage, based on the conviction that the relation of Jews and Gentiles is paradigmatic for relations between nations. Dodd says of Eph 2:11—15: "In its historical aspect it refers to a particular event of considerable importance — the effectual overcoming of a long-standing and deep-rooted enmity, which we may fairly treat as a model of the process of reconciliation between nations."[2]

The "long-standing and deep-rooted enmity" of nations within a nation faces the church in the United States today. The present situation is in one way comparable to that of a century ago. Then concerned Christians actively participated in the struggle which culminated in the abolition of slavery. But their work was directed

[1] Black Power and Christian Responsibility, New York 1969, 148.
[2] Christianity and the Reconciliation of the Nations, London 1952, 25.

only to the political order and not to the church's own life. And the work of reconciliation which might have come from a church seeking to actualize the unity given in Christ was not accomplished. Barriers raised by the tensions of those times within the church itself remain to this day in the form of denominations founded because of racial differences. A historian has said of the role of the church a century ago: "The failure of the churches at this point in our history forced the country to turn to political action against slavery, and political action destroyed slavery as a system, but left the hearts of the slaveholders unregenerate and left oppression of the free Negro little less of an evil than slavery had been."[3]

Have there been times when the church has *not* failed in reconciling hostile groups within its own life? The reconciliation of Jews and Gentiles in the early church was the first. What were others? What part did the interpretation of scripture play in the ministry of reconciliation? When the church has failed, how has that failure been related to the interpretation of scripture? Are there insights in the history of interpretation that could help the church in its reconciling ministry?—Questions like these indicate that a history of the interpretation of Eph 2:11—22 could contribute to articulating the nature of the church with regard to racial questions.

It may be added that a historical study cannot help but reveal that the concept of race itself is not static. In the ancient world and until comparatively recent times a person's "race" was determined by his language, customs and religion, whereas today it is more often determined by physical characteristics. Despite the imprecision of the term "race", it is used here in order to deal with the actual problems and hostilities to which "race" and "racial" are daily applied.

The following study depends primarily upon commentaries. Since the particular interest is in how the passage has been applied to the problem of hostility between contemporary groups, treatments of it in other Christian writings, including sermons, are also considered. The material used spans the entire history of interpretation from the Apostolic Fathers to the present. Specific interest in the black-white problem provides one means of limitation. Since this problem has been primarily that of the western world, only works from this area are dealt with after the Middle Ages. Works in German, English, French, Dutch, Spanish and Italian[4] are dis-

---

[3] D. L. Dumond, Antislavery: The Crusade for Freedom in America, Ann Arbor 1962, 344.

[4] Translations of passages from modern as well as classical languages quoted in the text are my own unless otherwise indicated.

cussed with special attention to the United States and South Africa where the problem is markedly evident. An attempt is made to consider representative writings of a particular period or school and to include the chief varieties of interpretation.

The following questions shape the discussion of the material:

1. How have interpreters understood the middle wall of partition?— Where have they located it? between God and man? Jew and Gentile? elsewhere? How have they defined its nature? Is it legal? sociological? psychological? cosmological?
2. Have interpreters seen significance for the relation of the church to contemporary Judaism? Has the breaking of the wall been interpreted as God's rejection of Israel?
3. What is the nature and extent of the peace spoken of in vv. 14 and 15? Is it peace with God? peace of conscience? peace between Jews and Gentiles? peace within the church? peace in the world? Correspondingly, what is the nature and extent of the hostility referred to in vv. 14 and 16?
4. Who is the New Man (v. 15)? Is it the Christian? the church? Jesus Christ? Does the difference between Jew and Gentile have any continuing significance for the New Man? Do any other group differences have significance for the New Man?
5. What is the place and function of the Cornerstone (v. 20)?
6. Have interpreters looked at the passage in ways which militated against its application to group hostilities?
7. Have interpreters seen implications in the passage for divisions within church and society?

Chapter I

THE FIRST THREE CENTURIES

For the church fathers of the first three centuries the unity of Jews and Gentiles as proclaimed in Eph 2:11—22 is still an amazing fact. If they themselves have not seen members of these two hostile groups reconciled, this miracle is nevertheless real to them. It is a sign of Christ's work in the world which they can point to as encouragement for fellow believers, or as refutation of Gnostics.

Refutation of Gnostics is an urgent matter for the early fathers. They are convinced that Gnosticism represents an insidious threat to the life of the church. One of the key issues in the struggle is the question, "What method should be used to interpret scripture?" Gnostics claim that scripture must be interpreted symbolically, and that ordinary Christians make the mistake of reading only literally and historically.

When it comes to interpreting Eph 2:11—22, Gnostics and church fathers do share a basic conviction: the passage is crucial for understanding the unity of the church. However, the two groups differ a great deal about what unity means, what the threats to it are, and how it is realized.

The Apostolic Fathers and the Apologetes

The earliest Christian writings after the New Testament, those of the apostolic fathers and the apologetes, frequently display ideas and language about the unity of the church which parallel Ephesians 2. Although it is an open question to what extent they depend on Ephesians[1], their chronological priority and their interest in the reconciliation of Jews and Gentiles justify beginning with them.

---

[1] The New Testament in the Apostolic Fathers, Oxford 1905, regards Ignatius' knowledge of the New Testament Ephesians as almost certain. R. Grant (The Formation of the New Testament, New York 1965, 95) says that Ignatius derives some of his expressions about the unity of the church from Ephesians. H. Rathke (Ignatius von Antiochien und die Paulusbriefe, TU 99, Berlin 1967,

6

Ignatius

Ignatius of Antioch's letter to the Smyrneans parallels Eph
2:13—17 when he says that the Lord was "really crucified for us in
the flesh . . . in order that he might raise a standard forever,
through the resurrection, for his holy and faithful ones, whether
among Jews or among Gentiles, in the one body of his church"[2].
The fact that Ignatius uses the phrase "raise a standard" in connection with Jews and Gentiles probably indicates that he has in
mind the Old Testament prophecy of the calling of the Gentiles.
Isa 11:10, 12 in the Septuagint uses the same figure in prophesying
the calling of the Gentiles together with the dispersed Jews. Ignatius' allusion to Isaiah indicates the significance to him of the fact
that the church is made up of Jew and Gentile: this fact shows that
the church does fulfill the Old Testament promise.

Ignatius' concern for the unity of the church[3] is exemplified by
his comparison of Christians to the stones of a temple in language
much like Eph 2:20—22. Like "stones of the Father's temple" they
are "being prepared for the building of God the Father" by means
of the cross through the Holy Spirit[4].

The Shepherd of Hermas

Use of the figure of the temple to describe the church is quite
prominent in both *The Letter of Barnabas*[5] and *The Shepherd of
Hermas*. Similitude IX of the latter combines several parallels to
Eph 2:20—22. Stones in the foundation of the building represent
prophets and apostles[6]. Later, stones in the superstructure brought
from twelve different mountains represent believers from all nations who are united in the church[7], forming "one body"[8]. The
stones are at first many-colored, but become one color when they

---

65) concluded that Ignatius knew and used Ephesians. However, H. Schlier
(Religionsgeschichtliche Untersuchungen zu den Ignatiusbriefen, Gießen 1929,
177) and V. Corwin (St. Ignatius and Christianity in Antioch, New Haven
1960, 67) come to the opposite conclusion.

[2] Die Apostolischen Väter I, ed. K. Bihlmeyer, Tübingen 1956, 106. The
phrase "in the one body of his church" is cited by Rathke, 52, as dependent
on Eph 2:16; 4:4.

[3] Corwin, Chs. 3,4.

[4] Ign. ad Eph. IX, 1; Bihlmeyer, 85. Rathke, 50—51, finds that this passage
depends on I Peter 2:5, but may also have been influenced by Eph 2:21.

[5] IV, 11; VI, 15; XVI; Bihlmeyer, 14, 17, 29—31. Forms of the word
οἰκοδομέω (Eph 2:20—22) occur frequently in XVI.

[6] Simil. IX, 15; GCS 48, 89.   [7] Simil. IX, 16—17; GCS 48, 89—91.

[8] Simil. IX, 13, 5 and 7; 17, 5; 18, 3—4; GCS 48, 87 and 91.

are built into the tower. On the face of it, this suggests that members of the various nations lose all their distinguishing features when they become members of the church[9]. But this is not the case: the point of this part of the allegory is that peoples otherwise different from one another have "one understanding and one mind, one faith and one love"[10]. *The Letter to Diognetus* expresses the same idea when it says that the Christians follow the customs of the cities in which they live and yet are united in "their own commonwealth"[11].

Justin Martyr goes a step further when he points out in his Apology that the differences between various peoples often give rise to hostility. The fact that this hostility is overcome in the church is presented by Justin as a demonstration of the truth of Christianity: "Peoples who hate and kill one another and do not associate with those of different races because of their customs, now since the coming of Christ are becoming comrades."[12]

Justin Martyr

Willingness to live together as brothers with people of different groups is for Justin a criterion of Christian faith. The crucial case is that of Jewish Christians who want to continue observing the Mosaic Law. In his *Dialog with Trypho,* Justin says that they too will be saved so long as they do not pressure other Christians to conform to their ways and do not refuse to have fellowship with them: "If these people, because of weakness of understanding, wish to keep such of the laws of Moses as they now can ... along with hope in this Christ and the ways and piety which are right eternally and by nature, if they keep unity with Christian believers ..., not persuading them either to be circumcised like them or to keep Sabbath or other such things, and if they participate and fellowship with everyone as brothers, I declare my approval."[13]

---

[9] The question of whether national, racial and other group differences are abolished in the church becomes crucial in 20th century interpretation of Eph 2:11—22. See below pp. 219—220, 229—230, 248.

[10] Simil. IX, 17, 4; GCS 48, 91. A. von Harnack, The Mission and Expansion of Christianity, transl. J. Moffatt, New York 1961, 253 n. 2, says: "Hermas (Simil. IX, 17) brings forward one of the most important features of the Christian polity—its power to bring together to unity of attitude and way of life people who varied so in position and customs."

[11] V, 4; Bihlmeyer, 144.

[12] 14, 3; Die ältesten Apologeten, ed. E. J. Goodspeed, Göttingen 1914, 34.

[13] Dial. XLVII, 2—3; Goodspeed, 145. Theodoret of Cyrus's interpretation of Eph 2:11—22 bears some similarity to Justin's position on the relations be-

Justin argues that Gentile Christians are already circumcised, but with a spiritual circumcision, which he connects with Christ the Cornerstone (Eph 2:20). The connection is made by means of the word "stone"; Josh 5:2 tells of a "second circumcision" of the people of Israel with stone knives. This second circumcision is the type of Christian circumcision, since "through sharpened stones, that is, through the words of the apostles of the Cornerstone and without hands, it circumcises us from idolatries and all evils"[14]. Thus in his argument by typology, Justin relies on Eph 2:11—22 for showing how Jewish and Gentile Christians can live together.

Gnostics

Gnostics were apparently the first to comment explicitly on Ephesians[15], but their exegesis is far removed from the interest of men like Justin Martyr in the reconciliation of Jews and Gentiles. Gnostics hold that the relation of Jews and Gentiles not only is irrelevant to the needs of their day, but never was the basic issue with which Eph 2:11—22 dealt. According to them the basic issue for Paul is the relation of "the pneumatics" to "the psychics"[16].

"Pneumatics" is the term which Gnostics apply to themselves. They believe that they are filled with πνεῦμα, spirit, and that they are enabled to interpret scripture in its true spiritual meaning, that is, in a symbolic way. Ordinary Christians are "psychics" because they are led by the human psyche with its earthly emotions, which include slavery to the literal sense of scripture and lack of ability or interest to think beyond the material and historical realms.

---

tween Jews and Gentiles with respect to the law. Theodoret says that the law was only destroyed (2:15) insofar as it was a barrier between Jews and Gentiles. The laws which God "wrote into nature" (Theodoret cites the Ten Commandments as the prime examples) are not involved. See below, p. 35.

[14] Dial. CXIV, 4; Goodspeed, 231.

[15] Gnostic literature containing comments on Ephesians is dated as early as about 140 A. D. No Gnostic commentary on the whole letter is extant. Fragments are quoted by orthodox writers and brief comments exist in other Gnostic literature, such as the manuscripts from Nag Hammadi.

The question of Gnostic influence on the composition of Eph 2:11—22 is discussed in the chapter on the twentieth century, pp. 177—185.

[16] Gnostics claim to be the only legitimate interpreters of Paul. For a sympathetic investigation of this claim, see E. Pagels, The Gnostic Paul, Philadelphia 1975. Pagels says that recently discovered sources make possible a clearer picture of Gnostic writers than the traditional one, based as it was on anti-Gnostic writings of church fathers. Pagels believes this will help clear the way for a fresh understanding of Paul.

In Gnostic exegesis, then, the terms "near" and "far" in Eph 2:13 and 2:17 refer to the pneumatics and the psychics. Those near to God are the pneumatics; those far from God are the psychics[17]. In a striking reversal of the apparent sense of the passage, Jews, even after their conversion to Jesus as the Christ, are included among the psychics who are "far off" (2:13). This is because Jews are much concerned with what is material, historical and literal, as their attention to circumcision and other elements of ceremonial law attests. This is the "law of commandments in ordinances" abolished by Christ (2:15). A creation of the lesser God of the Old Testament, or demiurge as the Gnostics call him, this law actually served injustice[18].

For Gnostics, the "wall of partition" (2:14) refers to the barrier in the temple at Jerusalem separating the "outer court" from the "holy of holies". The temple symbolizes the whole church. The holy of holies is of course the place of the pneumatics, whereas the psychics are limited to the outer court. As to how this applies to the present condition of the church, there seems to be considerable divergence within Gnosticism. Theodotus indicates that Christ has done away with the temple barrier[19]. Heracleon, however, is clearly still waiting for the division between the two to be abolished[20]. That Gnostic exegesis runs into trouble at this point is not surprising. The severe distinction which Gnostics draw between pneumatics and psychics would naturally make it difficult for them to say in what way Christ has already "made both one" (2:14).

Church Fathers of the Second and Third Centuries

The church fathers of the second and third centuries react strongly against Gnostic exegesis. Their method of combatting Gnosticism is to exegete the same texts in a more thorough way to show how the Gnostics have erred. Combat is particularly intense over the Pauline letters.

---

[17] Hippolytus, Refut. omn. haer. V, 8, 22; GCS 26, 93; Origen, Comm. on Ephesians, JTS 3, 408.

[18] Epistula ad Floram 6, 6; SC 24, 68.

[19] Clement, Excerpta ex Theodoto 38, 2–3; SC 23, 140–142.

[20] Origen, Comm. in Io. X, 33; GCS 10, 206–207. Perhaps because Gnostics refer so often to the wall of partition in the temple in explicating Eph 2:14, orthodox writers avoid this identification. Not until the sixteenth century is the wall in 2:14 related to the Jerusalem temple again, see below p. 104, n. 14.

Irenaeus (d. ca. 202)

The first great anti-Gnostic theologian is Irenaeus of Lyon, who lived in the latter half of the second century. Irenaeus' major work, *Adversus Haereses,* is directed primarily against Gnosticism.

For Irenaeus, the unity of Jews and Gentiles in the church is the sign that Christ has healed the fundamental division of mankind. The very shape of the cross symbolizes this healing, since on it Christ died with outstretched hands: "Through the divine stretching out of hands he joined the two peoples in one God. For there were two hands because there were two peoples scattered to the ends of the earth."[21]

This understanding of the shape of the cross is not original with Irenaeus, who attributes it to "one of our predecessors"[22]. This strand of thinking has been traced to Jewish Christianity[23].

The difference between Irenaeus' use of the cross and that of the Gnostics is significant: whereas Irenaeus sees the shape of the cross as a symbol of Christ's uniting mankind, the Gnostics see it as a symbol of a basic separation. According to the Valentinian Gnostics' view of the cross, "the horizontal bar is the limit between the upper and the lower world over which Christos stretches himself out to reach the lower Sophia, while the vertical bar divides between the right and left areas of the lower world, i. e. pneumatics and psychics"[24].

In contrast to the divisiveness of Gnosticism, Iraeneus sees the uniting of different races in the church as an important demonstration that Jesus is the Messiah. He points to the prophecy in Isa 11:6—9 which pictures "unity, peace and concord between animals of different species who are by nature opposed and hostile to one another" to describe the peace which the Messiah will bring. Irenaeus observes that this prophecy has been interpreted to mean that "men of different races ... shall come together in unity and peace, thanks to the name of Christ". Then Irenaeus adds exultantly, "And now this very thing has taken place."[25]

Irenaeus considers it one of the important tasks of theology to explore the meaning of the fact that Gentiles are now part of the same body with the Jews. In a list of basic themes of theology,

---

[21] Adv. haer. V, 17, 4; Harvey II, 372; SC 152, 234.

[22] This interpretation appears again in Hippolytus (below, p. 13) and Athanasius (below, pp. 24—25).

[23] J. Danielou, "La croix cosmique", Théologie du Judéo-christianisme, Tournai 1958, 303—315.

[24] H. Jonas, The Gnostic Religion, Boston 1958, 186n.

[25] Epideixis 61; SC 62, 126—127.

Irenaeus says the theologian must "not be silent about how God has made the Gentiles, whose salvation was despaired of, fellow heirs, and of the same body, and partakers with the saints."[26] The use of phrases from Eph 2:19 indicates how formative this passage is for Irenaeus' theology.

Another concept from Ephesians 2:11—22 which plays an important part in Irenaeus' theology is that of Christ as the Cornerstone. He writes: "This man, appearing in very recent times, the chief Cornerstone, has gathered into one and united those who were far off and those who were near, that is, the circumcision and the uncircumcision, enlarging Japheth and placing him in the dwelling of Shem."[27] By referring to Japheth and Shem in this context, Irenaeus interprets the benediction upon them in Gen 9:27 as a prophecy of the uniting of Jews and Gentiles fulfilled in Eph 2:11—22[28]. Irenaeus holds that the Old Testament not only prophesies the uniting of Jews and Gentiles, but also presents a person who is a type of the Cornerstone uniting Jews and Gentiles: Abraham. Abraham unites in his own person the Gentile and Jewish believer because he had faith in God before he was circumcised, that is as a Gentile, and after he was circumcised, that is as a Jew. Irenaeus here follows Paul's argument in Rom 4 quite closely. Abraham is "the father of all who follow the Word of God and maintain a pilgrimage in this world, that is, of those from the circumcision and from the uncircumcision who are faithful, even as also Christ is the chief Cornerstone sustaining all things and gathering into the one faith of Abraham those from either covenant who are suited for the building of God"[29]. In speaking of Christ in this context as the Cornerstone sustaining all things, Irenaeus presents him as the uniting center who holds together the entire history of salvation. Christ not only unites the Jews and Gentiles in the first century, he also unites with them the faithful Israelites of Old Testament times.

The interpretation of Christ as the Cornerstone uniting people from both covenants will be taken up by later writers[30]. The high point of its influence is in Augustine, who uses it frequently and applies it to the controversies of the church in his time[31]. Because

---

[26] Adv. haer. I, 10, 2; Harvey I, 92.

[27] Adv. haer. III, 5, 3; Harvey II, 20; SC 34, 126.

[28] In this he follows Justin (Dial. CXXXIX, 3—5; Goodspeed, 261) who, however, did not specifically mention Eph 2.

[29] Adv. haer. IV, 25, 1; Harvey II, 233; SC 100, 705—707.

[30] See the discussion below on Origen's use of this figure with references to other Greek writers, p. 20.

[31] See below, pp. 47—51.

the interpretation recurs throughout the centuries, it should be noted that from the beginning it has a historical dimension. That is, it involves the historical continuity of the church with Israel.

For Irenaeus the historical continuity of the church with Israel is of the utmost importance in his battle against Gnosticism. It is an essential aspect of the οἰκονομία, Irenaeus's term for the history of God's dealings with man from the Creation onward. The Gnostics, in rejecting continuity with Israel, divide Creation from Redemption. For them the created world is inherently evil, and redemption can only be some form of release from the created world. The Gnostics therefore do not admit that the Redeemer actually became flesh. Irenaeus shows that the Gnostic Redeemer is not the same as the Christ of the New Testament, since many passages testify that Christ did have flesh and blood[32]. Among others, Irenaeus cites parts of Eph 2:13—15: "But now, by communion with himself the Lord has reconciled man to God the Father in reconciling us to himself by the body of his own flesh, and redeeming us by his own blood, as the Apostle says to the Ephesians, 'In whom we have redemption through his blood, the remission of sins'; and again in the same letter, 'You who formerly were far off have become near in the blood of Christ'; and again, 'Abolishing in his flesh the hostilities, the law of commandments in ordinances.' "[33] That Christ had flesh and blood means that he had a physical human existence which included being part of a particular historical community—Israel. Christ's relationship with men is therefore necessarily involved with Israel and with Israel's relationship to other people. This is the reason why Irenaeus speaks in passages on the cornerstone and the cross about Christ's joining Jews and Gentiles. In contrast to Irenaeus, the Gnostics are not interested in actual historical communities; they divide men into completely ahistorical groups[34].

---

[32] On the fundamental connection of the Incarnation with the οἰκονομία of God in Irenaeus's thought, see A. Bengsch, Heilsgeschichte und Heilswissen, Leipzig 1957, 79. Bengsch concludes: "In the bond between these two doctrines, Incarnation and Oikonomia Theou, lies the decisive Christian confession of Irenaeus against all Gnosis."

[33] Adv. haer. V, 14, 3; Harvey II, 362; SC 152, 190—193.

[34] S. Laeuchli, The Language of Faith, New York 1962, 87, offers one of the Gnostic writings as an example of the Gnostic loss of history and community: "The Gospel of Truth speaks nowhere about the earthly nature of the congregation as a vital matter of Christian faith. The whole meditation is an extensive elaboration of the perpendicular relation between God and man."

Hippolytus (d. 235)

Hippolytus, a pupil of Irenaeus who did most of his writing in the early third century at Rome, also devotes much of his energy to combating Gnostic ideas. Like Irenaeus, Hippolytus sees the two arms of the cross as symbolizing Jews and Gentiles. Hippolytus, however, carries the symbolism further. Commenting on Gen 27:9, he says that the skins which Jacob wore on his arms to impersonate Esau are types of "the sins of both peoples which Christ in stretching his arms on the cross fastened to it along with himself"[35]. Hippolytus' emphasis is less on the uniting of Jew and Gentile than on their common reconciliation with God. The same emphasis appears in Hippolytus' use of Eph 2:14—15a in his commentary on Daniel. Expounding the prophecy in Dan 9:24 about the future "blotting out of unrighteousness and atoning for sins", Hippolytus adds: "Who it is that has blotted out our unrighteousness, Paul the apostle teaches saying, 'He has become our peace who has made both one and has broken down the dividing wall, the hostility in the flesh, abrogating the law of commandments and ordinances and blotting out the bond of sins which was against us.'"[36] Since Hippolytus uses Eph 2:14—15a to describe atonement, he apparently locates the dividing wall between God and man. We might have expected that Hippolytus, as an anti-Gnostic writer, would have interpreted the wall in a more historical way; that is, as the hostility between Jews and Gentiles. But he apparently does not, and thus becomes the first orthodox writer we have found to interpret the dividing wall of Eph 2:14 as the barrier between God and men.

Tertullian (b. ca. 169, d. 220)

Whereas Hippolytus, like writers before him, makes only scattered references to Eph 2:11—22, Tertullian, an African theologian of the early third century, deals with the entire passage in the course of his refutation of the gnostic teaching of Marcion[37].

---

[35] Fragment on Gen, GCS 1, 2. 54.

[36] In Dan. IV, 31; GCS 1, 1. 268. It is interesting that "in the flesh" instead of "in his flesh" stands here. Hippolytus's teacher Irenaeus uses the reading "in his flesh" in his refutation of Gnosticism (above, p. 12) and Tertullian charges that Marcion dropped "his" in order to make the phrase favor his views (below, p. 14).

[37] Adv. Marc. V, 17; CSEL 47, 636—638. For a discussion of reasons for classifying Marcion as a Gnostic, see Jonas, Gnostic Religion, 137—138.

Tertullian uses Eph. 2:11—22 extensively in combatting Marcion's proclamation of a new Savior God opposed to the Creator
of the Old Testament. He points out that vv. 11—13 contradict
Marcion's assertion that Christ proclaimed a God other than that
of the Old Testament, since these verses say that Christ brought
the Gentiles to the God of the Old Testament. Furthermore, Tertullian quotes Isa 46:12—13 to show that the Old Testament itself
foretells that the Gentiles will come near to its God. On Eph 2:14
Tertullian says that the two whom Christ has made one are "plainly the Jewish race and the Gentile, the near and the far." On the
phrase, "having broken down the dividing wall of hostility in his
flesh" (v. 14), Tertullian notes that Marcion has deleted the word
"his", giving the reading "hostility in the flesh". Tertullian claims
that Marcion's motive for deleting the word "his" is to associate
flesh with hostility rather than with Christ[38].

Tertullian's task in v. 15 is difficult because the clause, "he made
void the law of commandments by decrees"[39] seems to confirm

---

[38] Although Tertullian says this deletion is Marcion's gnosticizing corruption of the text, such a decidedly anti-gnostic writer as Hippolytus can also
omit it, as we have seen above, p. 13. It is very unlikely, therefore, that
Marcion can be blamed for a corruption of the New Testament text. See Vetus
Latina 24, 1 Epistula ad Ephesios, ed. Hermann Frede, Freiburg 1962—64, 30*.

[39] "Legem praeceptorum sententiis vacuam fecit." Grammatically this clause
may be understood in two ways. If "sententiis" is connected with the last two
words, it is translated "he made void the law of commandments by decrees." If
"sententiis" is connected with the first two words, the clause means "he has
made the law of commandments in decrees void." The Nestle text reads τὸν
νόμον τῶν ἐντολῶν ἐν δόγμασιν καταργήσας. Modern commentators all agree
that ἐν δόγμασιν belongs with τὸν νόμον τῶν ἐντολῶν. Some of them note
that the fathers understood the clause wrongly when they connected ἐν δόγμασιν
with καταργήσας.

The common patristic understanding is that the δόγματα are Christ's, and
that by means of them he abrogated the law of commandments. This opinion
is apparently so firmly fixed that even those fathers whose text reads ἐν δόγμασιν
still take δόγμασιν instrumentally. The freedom of the fathers' interpretations
is thus restricted: they have to explain the δόγματα as Christ's. Some, like
Tertullian, say they are Christ's ethical teachings. The danger of this interpretation is that it may contribute to seeing the gospel as primarily a new,
more demanding law. — Tertullian's tendency in this direction was so strong
that he left the Catholic Church for Montanism. — Others, like Chrysostom,
say Christ's δόγματα means faith. The danger here is of regarding faith either
as intellectual formulation or as a work which takes the place of the works
of the law. Theodore of Mopsuestia tries to avoid the difficulties of both these
alternatives by interpreting them as Christ's deeds. Theologically his course is the
most profound, but it forces the language quite a bit. Severian and Theodoret,
the first to try to work out the idea that not all of the Old Testament law is
abrogated, would have had more support for their position if they had taken ἐν

Marcion's basic tenet, that the gospel is totally opposed to the law[40]. Tertullian holds, however, that Christ has made the law void by fulfilling it: "If he made the law of commandments void by decrees—it was certainly by fulfilling the law. For 'Do not commit adultery' is void when 'Do not look to lust' is spoken; 'Do not kill' is void when 'Do not curse' is spoken. You cannot make an adversary of the law out of its supporter."

Under the exigencies of refuting gnosticism, Tertullian's comments on vv. 15 and 16 focus sharply on the man Jesus Christ. When gnostics call Jesus "the new man", they explain his newness by denying his humanity[41]. Tertullian counters, "If he is truly new, he is also truly man, not a phantasm." Similarly, Tertullian sees the "one body" (v. 16) as Christ's body on the cross and holds that this is further testimony that Christ's body had flesh. In his treatment of both the "one body" and the "one new man", Tertullian's anti-gnostic purpose makes him neglect the word "one" in order to fight against false understandings of the new man which involved denials of Jesus' physical body. Therefore Tertullian does not consider the phrases in relation to the unity of the church.

Tertullian notes that in v. 20 Marcion has erased the phrase "and prophets". He suggests somewhat sarcastically that Marcion "has forgotten that the Lord has prophets as well as apostles in his church. But more likely Marcion is afraid to admit that our building stands in Christ on the foundation of the ancient prophets also." Tertullian alludes here to the two possible interpretations of "prophets": they may be either of the New or of the Old Testament. Marcion has obviously interpreted them as Old Testament prophets, and therefore erased the mention of them. Tertullian apparently also takes them to be Old Testament prophets, for he writes, "The Apostle himself does not cease to build us up everywhere from the prophets. For where did he learn to call Christ the chief cornerstone if not from the proclamation of the psalm, 'The stone which the builders rejected has become the head of the cor-

---

δόγμασιν as modifying "the law of commandments". They could then have maintained that the complicated expression of the law indicates that only one aspect of it is meant. H. Schlier develops such an interpretation, Der Brief an die Epheser, Düsseldorf 1968, 125—126.

[40] Tertullian, Adv. Marc. I, 19; CSEL 47, 314: "The separation of the law and the gospel is the unique and principal work of Marcion."

[41] Valentinus, for example, calls Jesus "the new man" because he is the result of the union of the Demiurge with Wisdom, unlike the descendants of Adam who are the creatures of the Demiurge alone; Mary was only the channel through whom Jesus came into the world (Hippolytus, Ref. omn. haer. VI, 35, 3—4; GCS 26, 164).

ner'?" In succeeding centuries the fathers with very few exceptions interpret "prophets" as the Old Testament prophets. Undoubtedly they are also influenced here by the early use of the passage in polemic, particularly against Marcion as well as against any attempt to renounce the Old Testament. Whether or not they are right in saying that the "prophets" of v. 20 are those of the Old Testament, it is one way of expressing their conviction that according to Eph 2:11—22 the Old Testament cannot be separated from the New Testament.

Clement of Alexandria (d. ca. 215)

Although it seems clear from his comments that Tertullian locates the dividing wall between Jew and Gentile, he does not discuss the matter. The first to do so is an eastern contemporary of Tertullian, Clement of Alexandria. Clement places the breaking down of the dividing wall in the context of the history of salvation:

There is essentially one saving covenant extending from the foundation of the world to us, the reception of the gift being different according to different generations and times. For it is fitting that there be one unchanging gift of salvation from one God through one Lord, serving "in diverse ways"; that is why the "partition wall" dividing the Greek from the Jew is broken down so that there might be a unique people. And so both come "to the unity of the faith" and the election of both is one[42].

Because of passages like this, Harnack concludes: "The religious philosophy of history of Clement of Alexandria is based entirely on the view that the two peoples, the Greek and the Jew, who have both been trained by God, are now (see Paul's letter to the Ephesians) raised to the higher unity of a third people."[43]

Clement is the first of the fathers to use the phrase "new man" to refer to the people formed out of Jews and Gentiles. He does so in a passage which depends on Eph 2:15, although it starts from consideration of Matt 18:20, "Where two or three are gathered together in my name, there am I in the midst of them."

The harmony of the many, inferred from the three with whom the Lord is present, might be the one church, the one man, the one race. Or was not the Lord legislating with the one, the Jew, and then prophesying by sending Jeremiah to Babylon? Moreover, through the prophecy, by calling people from the Gentiles, did he not join the two peoples, and was

[42] Stromata VI, 106, 3—107, 1; GCS 15, 485.
[43] Mission I, 248—249. See discussions below on "higher unity" pp. 171—172, and "third race" pp. 228—230, 246—247.

not the third one created out of the two into one new man, in whom he now moves, and dwells in the church itself[44]?

The above passage reiterates a characteristic theme of Clement: Christ is present with the Jew and Gentile as well as with the new man formed out of the two. He has been at work in the history of both groups even before they have joined to form the church. The fact that the new man is made up of Jew and Gentile means that the unity of the church has a specific history and thus a specific character; the fact that it is Christ who holds the two together means that the new man depends completely on him. Clement's historical conception of the new man contrasts to that of some later interpreters who simply equate the new man with "the Christian people" or "the church"[45].

Origen (b. 185, d. 253)

The successor of Clement as head of the Catechetical School in Alexandria was Origen, the most influential exegete of the early centuries[46]. Origen's world-view, developed from a Neo-platonic perspective on scripture, makes his interpretation of Eph 2:11—22 resemble Gnostic views at points and causes some difficulties which he himself admits. Origen believes that in the beginning God created only spiritual rational beings with free will. Depending on how they have exercised their free will, these beings have either remained near to God, or have gone far from him. Those who have gone farthest have become involved in the material world. Matter

---

[44] Stromata III, 70, 1—2; GCS 15, 227—228.

[45] Another passage, Stromata V, 1—4; GCS 15, 390—391, where Clement discusses the three groups of mankind may be the source for one of Chrysostom's illustrations on Eph 2:15 (below, p. 33). Clement speculates that Plato's three groups of men—iron, silver, and gold (Republic III)—may signify Greek, Jew and Christian.

[46] Origen's three-volume commentary on Ephesians is no longer extant, although there are comments in catenae on most of Eph 2:11—22 (J. F. Gregg, JTS 3 [1902] 405—408). Another source for knowledge of Origen's commentary is Jerome's commentary on Ephesians. In his introduction, PL 26, 472, Jerome says that he has relied chiefly on Origen, as well as on Didymus and Apollinaris; nothing remains of the commentaries of the latter two on Eph 2:11—22. Comparison of portions of Jerome's commentary with the parallel fragments of Origen shows that Jerome does indeed depend very heavily on Origen, often simply paraphrasing him. On the degree of Jerome's dependence on Origen and the extent to which he preserves Origen's material, see Gregg, 234, and Harnack, "Der Kirchengeschichtliche Ertrag der Exegetischen Arbeiten des Origenes", TU 42, Leipzig 1920, 4. 155.

itself is not evil, but is a symptom or expression of wills that have chosen evil[47].

It is easy to see how vv. 13 and 17 which talk about "the near" and "the far" invite interpretation in terms of Origen's world-view. Referring to the parallel passage, Col 1:20, which he para-phrases as "making peace by the blood of his cross of things on earth and in heaven", Origen concludes:

These things tell about the superior powers and those of mankind who are being saved; of the superior powers as near and of men as far ... of the superior powers that they were friendly toward God, of men that they were hostile toward him. And this hostility was the middle wall of separation preventing the nature of men from being capable of the blessedness of the superior beings. This middle wall of separation then, the hostility, was broken down by our Savior's becoming man, and therefore is said to be broken down in his flesh[48].

Origen finds that the abrogation of the law of commandments (v. 15) fits very well into this picture. The superior beings serve God according to the true spiritual law which is identical with the δόγματα by which Christ abrogates the law of commandments. When the middle wall is broken down, the higher spiritual law, which had previously been limited to the superior powers, becomes available to men. Although Origen sounds like a Gnostic when he describes the wall as separating superior from inferior beings, he differs from the Gnostics in that he does not posit a fundamental division of mankind. The wall is broken down for all men, not just for some.

Origen cannot explain the new man (v. 15) so easily in his Neo-Platonic terms. He makes an attempt: "He brought both the superior powers and the believers among men together into one new man. The new man is recognized by the 'daily renewal' and will be made at home in a new cosmos, for 'heaven and earth will be new.'"[49] At this point Origen admits that his interpretation

---

[47] R. A. Norris, God and World in Early Christian Theology, New York 1965, 139—156, treats this aspect of Origen's thought.

[48] Referring to Eph 2:14—15 in his commentary on Rom 4, Origen says that turning again to sin after Christ has made peace "without doubt we build up hostilities again and construct a wall of dissension and by this destroy the work of Christ and make vain the cross of his passion". (MPG 14, 989) This comment is in a more existential and pastoral vein compared to the primarily theoretical treatment in his Ephesians commentary.

[49] Jerome's commentary repeats Origen's interpretation of the new man as the unity of superior beings and men. Since Jerome does not reject this inter-pretation, Rufinus accuses him of teaching that men and angels have the same nature (Apologia I, 38—39; MPL 21, 576—78). The church in Jerome's time

may not fit the text so well as it fits his world-view. He says candidly, "The matter about becoming one new man will seem to oppose the interpretation." On v. 20 he becomes even more explicit: "Inferences from 'built upon the foundation of the apostles and prophets' will seem to agree with the interpretation about 'the near' being Israel and 'the far' being the Gentiles."

In his comments on other verses Origen stays much closer to tradition. He says that v. 12 refutes "those who think that believers in Christ are not members of the commonwealth of Israel but of some other new commonwealth, and that they have nothing in common with the former." The verse makes clear that "now they are not only no longer without Christ, but they are also not separated from the commonwealth of Israel"[50]. However, Origen speaks of Israel in a way that again suggests Neo-Platonic influence: "Membership in the commonwealth of Israel belongs to all who observe the spiritual law and live according to it even more than to physical Jews." Nevertheless, Origen's interpretation is more friendly toward the Jews than Jerome's. On v. 11 Jerome departs from Origen to say pointedly: "Jews are Gentiles in spirit, and in the flesh Israelites."[51] Jerome's attitude is one often expressed by the church fathers: we Christians, *rather than* the Jews, are the members of the commonwealth of Israel.

Origen regards "He is our peace" (v. 14) as one of the most important designations of Christ: "He who does not have peace does not have Christ." The phrase "He is our peace" appears often in Origen's works. It means that a believer cannot support factionalism[52] or war[53]. Origen quotes it when he discusses Solomon as a type of Christ[54], because Solomon brought peace between Israel and the Gentiles. The Gentile Queen of Sheba, who came to Solo-

---

condemned this and other ideas of Origen as heresy. Jerome claimed that he agreed with the church's decision, but Rufinus gave Jerome's commentary on Eph 2:11—22 as evidence to the contrary.

[50] Tertullian used Eph 2:11—13 to make a similar point against Marcion, above, p. 14. In a dialog by an unknown writer around the end of the third century, the orthodox Christian also uses Eph 2:11—13 against a Marcionite. (De Recta in Deum Fide XVIII; GCS 4, 96)

[51] This seems to be an example of a shift in attitude toward the Jews on the part of the church fathers. It is the only one of Jerome's comments on Eph 11—22 which expresses a different position than that found in extant comments of Origen. On Origen's concern for the Jewish people, see K. Schelkle, Paulus, Lehrer der Väter, Düsseldorf 1956, 420—421.

[52] Comm. Io XIX, 23; GCS 10, 325. See also XX, 37; GCS 10, 378.

[53] In Lib. Iesu Nave hom. XIV, 1; GCS 30, 375 and Comm. Matt. ser. 121; GCS 38, 256.

[54] Comm. Cant. II; GCS 33, 119.

mon, is for Origen a type of the Gentiles who come to the King of Israel, Jesus Christ.

Like Tertullian, Origen interprets "prophets" (v. 20) as Old Testament prophets and argues that the building of which they and the apostles are the foundation symbolizes the unity of the Old and New Testaments. Therefore Origen sees in vv. 19—22 another weapon against "those who divide divinity and think the prophets belong to one god and the apostles to another", the Gnostics: "For if those who are no longer strangers and sojourners but fellow citizens of the saints and members of the household of God are built on the foundation of the apostles and prophets, Christ Jesus himself being the chief cornerstone, . . . then there is one God of one building and temple."

Origen's commentary almost certainly interpreted the cornerstone (v. 20) as joining the two walls representing Jews and Gentiles. Although the interpretation is not preserved in the catenae, it appears twice in Jerome's highly derivative commentary, and also in other commentaries of Origen. In a fragment on Matt 21:42, Origen says: "A corner is the joining of two walls; the stone which is Christ, the Truth, joining 'the Remnant' of Israel and 'the fullness of the Gentiles' into one, makes the corner."[55]

The concept of Christ as Cornerstone uniting Jews and Gentiles had its beginnings in Irenaeus[56]. From Origen on it appears with great regularity, not only in comments on Eph. 2:20, but on other passages which mention a cornerstone or foundation stone, such as Job 38:6, Ps 118:22, Isa 28:16, Matt 21:42, I Pet 2:7. Early writers such as Irenaeus see the two walls primarily in historical terms: the wall of the Jews refers to the Jews of Old Testament times and the wall of the Gentiles refers to Gentile Christians. Another way of expressing this view is to say that the walls are the old and new covenants, as Origen does in a comment on Matt 21:42[57]. For Origen the cornerstone is overwhelmingly a symbol of the continuity of the church and Israel. Even when he lets the walls stand for Jewish and Gentile Christians only, Origen calls the wall of Jewish Christians "the Remnant" in a way that suggests he sees them as representatives of all Israel.

---

[55] Fragm. 428; GCS 41, 1. 178.   [56] See above, p.. 10—12.

[57] Comm. Matt. XVII, 12; GCS 40, 616. This historical view is very pronounced in a writer from the end of the third century, Eusebius, who enlarges upon the figure: "For he set up the building of Moses to last until His coming, and then joined to one side of it our building of the gospel. This is why he is called Cornerstone." (Demonstr. ev. I, 7, 15—16; GCS 23, 37) For other instances of two buildings see Origen, Comm. Matt. IX, 17, 6; GCS 23, 443, and Didymus of Alexandria, Expos. Ps. 117, 22; MPG 39, 1561.

Cyprian (d. 258)

Less irenic in his attitude toward the Jews is Cyprian, a younger contemporary of Origen. One of the few references Cyprian makes to Eph 2:11—22 is in a work which is largely directed against Jewish disbelief[58]. It is possible that Cyprian's predominantly negative attitude toward the Jews prevented him from seeing the help he could have received from Eph 2:11—22 in his efforts toward maintaining unity in the church in Africa[59]. It is tempting to speculate on how the cause of unity in Africa—where the variety of ethnic and social groups was a divisive factor[60]—might have been helped if Cyprian had worked on the significance of Eph 2:11—22 for the unity of groups within the church.

Summary

Study of Eph 2:11—22 in the writings of the early church fathers shows that in combatting Gnostic views, the fathers emphasize two themes above all: the flesh-and-blood manhood of Jesus Christ, and the continuity of the church with Israel.

To show that Jesus Christ had flesh and blood was necessary in order to refute the Gnostic belief that he only seemed to have a human body. To describe their views, the Gnostics sometimes used the term "new man" which occurs in Eph 2:15[61]. In combating this Gnostic interpretation, the fathers accepted the Gnostics' simple identification of the new man with Jesus, overlooking the context which indicates that the new man is the unity of Jews and Gentiles.

Origen and Clement, however, do not identify the new man simply as Jesus; they recognize that the context speaks of a new unity. Origen, after proposing a unity between men and superior

---

[58] Ad. Quir. II, 27; CSEL 3, 1, 94. Cyprian quotes Eph 2:17—18 as proof "that it is impossible to attain to God the Father except by his Son Jesus Christ". In the introduction to this work, Cyprian says that he wants to show that the Jews have been rejected by God and the Gentiles have taken their place, deserving it because of their faith.

[59] Cyprian's most influential writing is on the unity of the church. See J. Quasten, Patrology, Westminster, Maryland 1962², II, 349.

[60] See S. L. Greenslade, Schism in the Early Church, New York 1953.

[61] Some contemporary scholars say that the Gnostics may have used the term before Ephesians was written, and that Ephesians itself combats Gnosticism by transforming the meaning of this and other Gnostic terms. The problem of the relation of Gnosticism to our passage will be discussed in the chapter on twentieth century interpretation, see below, pp. 177—185.

beings, intimates that the passage may instead speak of unity between Jews and Gentiles. Clement definitely holds that the new
man is the unity of Jews and Gentiles. He speaks of the church as
a third people, which suggests that he may have regarded the difference between Jews and Gentiles as obsolete, at least within the
church. The problems which are entailed in such a view will be
discussed in the final chapter[62]. Clement's interpretation of the
new man looks back to God's working with Jews and Gentiles
before the coming of Christ, and thus emphasizes historical continuity between Old Testament and New Testament times.

This continuity plays a more important role in anti-Gnostic
interpretation of Eph 2:11—22 than does the insistence on the
reality of the flesh and blood of Christ. To refute the Gnostic
claim that the God of the New Testament is a different being from
the Jahweh of the Old Testament, the fathers cite Ephesians's
portrayal of the inclusion of the Gentiles as the continuation of
God's redeeming work in the history of Israel. As evidence of this
continuity, Irenaeus especially presents Old Testament prophecies
and types of the unity of the Gentiles with Israel. The most important symbol for this unity is the cornerstone, which Irenaeus is
the first to interpret as signifying the unity of Jews and Gentiles.
One of Tertullians's arguments for the bond between New and
Old Testaments is that the Old Testament is the source from which
Ephesians got the cornerstone symbol.

Irenaeus sees the unity of Jews and Gentiles primarily in historical terms: it is the continuity of the Church with Israel. But this
view is closely related to the more sociological one according to
which the two different groups, Jews and Gentiles, are united in
the present. Whether the cornerstone is understood as uniting all
Jews and Gentiles or only those within the church is difficult to
determine.

It is virtually certain, however, that when the fathers speak of
the cross uniting Jews and Gentiles they refer to all men. The two
arms united in one cross symbolize the uniting of all Jews and Gentiles in the death of Christ for both groups. But this concept appears only rarely; after its clearest expression at the beginning of
the fourth century by Athanasias it is no longer mentioned. Pos-
sibly one reason for this is the increasing tendency to think of the
Jews as the people who sent Christ to the cross—a tendency which
crowded out the understanding of the cross as reconciling Jews and
Gentiles.

---

[62] See below, pp. 228—230, 246—247.

The destruction of the dividing wall is also spoken of in universal terms. For some interpreters the wall was between men and God; now that it has been broken down the way is open for all men to have fellowship in the church. Each of these interpretations will continue in later centuries with increasing detail and variation.

In the earliest period, no commentators discuss Eph 2:11—22 in terms of relationship with contemporary Jews, although Origen may imply this when he speaks of Jewish Christians as the Remnant. Though he sometimes speaks of peace in individual terms, Origen shows that he does not limit it to inner peace when he says that it is opposed to factions and war. Origen is thus the first to say directly that Eph 2:11—22 involves the reconciliation of other hostilities besides the fundamental one between Jews and Gentiles. This conviction is developed by several later fathers, especially by Augustine.

Chapter II

FROM THE FOURTH CENTURY TO THE CLOSE OF
THE PATRISTIC AGE

Beginning with the fourth century there is an abundance of material on Eph 2:11—22 since this is a time of great productivity in all areas of theological work. Origen's influence affects both East and West, and may be partly responsible for the fact that the earliest interpreters in both East and West locate the dividing wall (v. 14) between earth and heaven. The view which later predominates in the West is that the wall is between Jews and Gentiles. This view is also represented in the East, but is overshadowed by the tremendous influence of Chrysostom who locates the wall between God and man. In both East and West, Eph 2:11—22 is used in connection with attempts to heal divisions within the church.

Athanasius (295—373)

A key figure in the life of the church at the beginning of this period is Athanasius, bishop of Alexandria. He is an Eastern theologian who also knows the Western Church very well, and is highly regarded in both East and West. In this respect he resembles Irenaeus, who bound in himself the Eastern and Western Christianity of his day. Like Irenaeus, Athanasius knows the tradition that the two arms of the cross symbolize Christ's uniting Jews and Gentiles. Athanasius expresses this idea in connection with Christ's breaking down the dividing wall (v. 14): "If the death of the Lord is a ransom for all, and by the death of this man the dividing wall is destroyed and the calling of the Gentiles comes about, how would he have called us if he had not been crucified? For only on the cross does someone die with outstretched arms. Therefore it was fitting for the Lord to endure this too, and to stretch out his arms in order that he might draw the ancient people and those of the Gentiles and join both together in himself."[1] For Athanasius, as

---

[1] De incarn 25, 3—4; MPG 25, 140.

for Irenaeus, the cross symbolizes not only the reconciliation of the individual with God, and not only the reconciliation of individuals with one another, but the reconciliation of different groups with one another.

After Athanasius this understanding of the symbolism of the cross no longer appears. Perhaps it does not because the number of Jewish Christians in the church is dwindling to an extremely low point and therefore the uniting of Jews and Gentiles in the church is no longer part of experience or living memory. The fact that this idea was not retained in the history of interpretation is a sad loss, for it certainly could have been helpful against temptations for the church to let racial hostility violate its unity.

Eastern Writers

Eastern writers are responsible for most of the new developments in the interpretation of Eph 2:11—22 in this period. Usually their comments are longer and more detailed than those of Western writerrs; Eastern writers are often more involved with theological speculation—in keeping with the tradition of the first great Eastern exegete, Origen.

Ephraem of Syria (b. ca. 306, d. 373)

The earliest extant commentary on Ephesians, that of Ephraem of Syria, apparently inherits some of Origen's ideas about the dividing wall and the law. According to Ephraem, the dividing wall was "the madness of idols which was hidden above everyone and did not allow the mind of men to go beyond the heavens"[2]. Because of the wall, men lived by "the law of earthly mandates" until Christ abrogated the law "by his spiritual decrees". Ephraem contrasts the earthly legal mandates with the heavenly spiritual decrees in much the same way as Origen did[3].

But in the rest of his interpretation Ephraem differs from Origen. Whereas Origen preferred the view that the united groups are men and angels, Ephraem holds that they are Jews and Gentiles. Ephraem's comment on v. 19 summarizes his position. Speak-

---

[2] Comm. in epp. D. Pauli, Venice 1893, 145. The fact that this Latin edition is a translation of an Armenian translation of Ephraem's original Syriac accounts at least in part for the strangeness of the language. Perhaps he has in mind Eph 2:2, "the powers of the air".

[3] See above, p. 18.

ing of the Jews he says: "For they lumped us together and segregated us from themselves because of their law; now, however, there is access for us in one Spirit to the Father of all. That is, through the Spirit which we have received from baptism itself; so that within Him there is no longer Jew and Gentile, since Christ is all in all." The preceding sentence is a conflation of ideas and phrases from I Cor 12:13 and Col 3:11. Both these verses say that belonging to Christ rules out divisions between various groups, beginning with the basic division of mankind into Jews and Gentiles. Ephraem's is the only commentary on Eph 2:11—22 in the patristic period to connect the passage explicitly with baptism. It is interesting to note that several scholars have in recent years proposed that baptism is the key to the interpretation of the passage[4].

Pseudo-Basil

A similar connection of Eph 2:11—22 with baptism and with Pauline passages about the unity of various groups in Christ appears in a treatise on baptism attributed to Basil the Great[5]. This work, probably written about the end of the fourth century, deals primarily with the ethical implications of baptism. It quotes the whole of Eph 2:14—22 in a passage which explains that baptism means breaking fellowship with people devoted to fornication, drunkenness and other unworthy practices, and on the other hand keeping fellowship with people of various social groups in the church. The author says that St. Paul "hands down wisely and firmly with whom and with what kinds of people we are to live in saying 'He is our peace who has made us both one'." The quotation of Eph 2:14—22 follows, after which the author quotes from Gal 3:27 and Col 3:11: "As many of you as are baptized into Christ have put on Christ. It is not possible that there be Greek and Jew, circumcision and uncircumcision, barbarian, Scythian, slave and free; but Christ is all in all."[6]

Linking Eph 2:11—22 with Gal 3:27—28, I Cor 12:13 and Col 3:11 is a significant step in the history of the passage's interpretation. It indicates an awareness that unity between Jews and Gentiles is related to the unity of other groupings in the church. Ephraem's brief comment can hardly be called more than a hint of this

---

[4] See below, pp. 189—190, 199.
[5] De bapt; MPG 31, 1513—1628. O. Bardenhewer, Geschichte der altkirchlichen Literatur, Freiburg 1912, III, 144, inclines to the view that Basil outlined the work, but had someone else do the actual writing.
[6] De bapt I, 22; MPG 31, 1564.

relation, but Pseudo-Basil establishes it more definitely. In the twentieth century, a number of scholars hold that because the unity of Jews and Gentiles as portrayed in Eph 2:11—22 is basic to the unity of the church, Paul always places Jews and Gentiles first when he lists various groupings in order to make clear that unity in Christ overcomes all human divisions[7].

Other Eastern commentaries do not link Eph 2:11—22 with these passages. One reason for this may be that the major questions in their world are "Who is Jesus Christ?" and "What is salvation?" rather than "What is the church?". Nevertheless, Eph 2:11—22 does call forth discussion of some aspects of the nature of the church. One of these is the relation of the church to Israel.

Epiphanius (b. ca. 315, d. 403)

Epiphanius, fourth century Bishop of Salamis, struggles with the problem of the relation of the church to Israel in his *Panarion*, which deals with the Marcionite heresy. Marcion's contention, as we have seen, was that there is the sharpest discontinuity between the church and Israel: the church has no roots in Israel, and the Old Testament is to be rejected. Epiphanius argues that there is a continuity between the church and the people of the Old Testament. And yet the church is not simply a continuation of Judaism: it does not make Gentiles into Jews. How this is so Epiphanius believes to be demonstrated by Eph 2:14—15, since it says that Christ has made both Jew and Gentile one (v. 14) and also that they are now "one new man" (v. 15):

If he has made both one, and has not ended the one in order to establish the other, then he has not changed the former (the Jew) into something else. Nor has he kept the second separate from the first; but he has brought the two together into one; not simply, not seemingly, but manifestly in his blood[8].

Probably the most significant feature of this statement by Epiphanius is that it insists on the presence of difference within the new unity. This is a dimension which commentators often overlook.

The School of Antioch

In the city of Antioch was a school of exegesis whose fame was established under the leadership of Diodore, who taught there for many years before becoming Bishop of Tarsus in 378. Diodore

---

[7] See below, pp. 215, 220.   [8] Pan 42, 12, 3; GCS 31, 179.

28

taught his students to concentrate on the historical sense of scripture and to analyze words and grammar with care. Antioch produced the greatest Greek exegetes of antiquity. Severian of Gabala[9] was followed by Theodore of Mopsuestia and John Chrysostom, who studied there together under Diodore from 369 to 371[10]; Theodoret of Cyrus was there a generation later. Although all four men employ the Antiochene method, each of their commentaries has its own unique character.

Severian of Gabala (d. ca. 408)

The close attention to words and grammatical construction stressed by the Antiochene School is demonstrated in Severian's exegesis of Eph 2:11–22[11].

Severian approaches the passage by analyzing the words used for the wall between Jew and Gentile (2:14). Why are there two words when one would have sufficed? Severian's solution is that the middle wall, μεσότοιχον, refers to something distinct from the separation, φραγμός. The φραγμός is "the protection of the Spirit"[12]. This has not been broken; only the μεσότοιχον, "the segregation from the Greeks", has been broken.

Severian argues that while the segregation of Jews from Greeks had depended on the law, the protection of the Spirit depends upon grace. Since the law was subordinate to grace, its abrogation did not end the effectiveness of grace. Correspondingly, the dividing wall, which depended on the law, was broken down, while the protection of the Spirit, which depends on grace, is maintained. It is not clear whether Severian thinks that the protection of the Spirit serves to maintain the identity of the Jewish people even after their law has been abrogated, or whether the Spirit maintains the identity of the Christian church—or both. At any rate, Severian's insistence on the on-going protection of the Spirit throughout the whole history of God's dealings with his people serves to emphasize the continuity of the church with Israel.

[9] K. Staab, Pauluskommentar aus der griechischen Kirche, Münster 1933, xxxi.

[10] B. Altaner, Patrologie, Freiburg 1966, 322.

[11] Although Severian's commentary has been lost, fragments including Eph 2:11–22 have been gathered by K. Staab, 308–309.

[12] Severian cites Isa 5:5b as the source of his interpretation of φραγμός; Chrysostom cites the same passage, see below p. 32. Both Chrysostom and Severian say that φραγμός means protection, but Chrysostom says it is the protection of the law. The divergence in their interpretations may well go back to different interpretations of φραγμός in the story of Tamar (Gen 38:29).

According to Severian's view of history, God instituted the law as part of his plan for the salvation of the world. Far from being antithetical to the Spirit, the law served as a temporary auxiliary of the Spirit. However, "since the law is what divided Jews from Greeks, according to fore-ordination the law was going to end. But it did not end in any other way than that the Lord rose from the dead."

Severian writes about the law so exclusively in terms of its function of dividing Jews from Greeks that one wonders why other functions of the law should not continue even after Christ's resurrection. Severian seems to have struggled with the same question and to have attempted an answer. He makes a distinction between the two parts of the phrase, "the law of commandments" (v. 15), in much the same way as he distinguishes between the dividing wall and the separation. The law is custom or tradition; the commandments are the Mosaic commandments, the foundation behind the tradition. "He abrogated the law of commandments—not the commandments as out of place, but the tradition as no longer useful." Although this distinction between "tradition" and "commandment" as two different senses of the word "law" is common among the fathers[13], Severian is the first to suggest it for Eph 2:15.

Severian gives several examples of the teachings by which Christ has abrogated the traditions: "'Not what goes in defiles a man' nullified 'Eat this and do not eat that'; 'Do not give a bill of divorce' is against divorcing a wife for any cause." According to Severian, although the traditions were abrogated by Christ's teachings, the commandments were not. However, Christ's death and resurrection have altered the status of the commandments: "the commandments are honored even if they do not have power."

Severian's comment on the new man (v. 15) serves as a kind of summary of his interpretation of the whole passage: "After Greeks have been taken away from idolatry because it is irreligion, and Jews from the law because it is no longer useful, they are rebuilt into another newness of religion." It is characteristic of Severian's emphasis on the continuity of the church with Israel that he says "newness of religion", and not "a new religion".

---

[13] See Schelkle, 431.

Theodore of Mopsuestia (d. 428)

Like Severian, Theodore pays considerable attention to the actual community of the Jews[14]. Theodore concentrates specifically
on circumcision as the distinguishing mark of Jews: "The law,
through circumcision, distinguished them from aliens, whence there
could not be any fellowship of Gentiles with Jews; and by circumcision they had a certain power." In elaborating on the important
role which circumcision played, Theodore calls "that separation
which arose from circumcision 'the dividing wall'" and emphasizes
how completely it prevented fellowship between Jews and Gentiles[15]. For him the unique theme of Eph 2:11—22 is the ending of
this separation: "Now the death of Christ joins you who were widely separated, since it has given resurrection and introduced another life for the present one."

The contrast between "another life" and "the present one" plays
an important role in Theodore's theology. He sees God's plan for
the world as consisting of two stages: the present life of change,
decay and death; and the future life of resurrection, changelessness
and immortality—which has already come in the life of Christ.
Using the categories of this plan, Theodore explains how the separation of Jews and Gentiles is overcome and how the law is abrogated.

Since Christ presented to us immortality through the resurrection, he
abolished this separation; for in immortal nature circumcision would not
exist. If it does not exist, no distinction will appear between uncircumcision and circumcision. But also in doing this he ended the law of commandments, for the entire structure of the law is superfluous. He took
away this hostility not only by taking away circumcision, but also by
ending the law itself through his own decrees—that is, of resurrection,
incorruptibility, and immortality. He calls these things decrees as existing
in acts by which the divine grace works in us so that we do not need
ordinances and a commandment which wants us to do this or not to do
that[16].

A difficulty in Theodore's interpretation arises from the over-
lapping of the present and future ages. The present age is still here:

[14] Theodore of Mopsuestia on the Minor Epistles of Paul, ed. H. B. Swete,
Cambridge 1880, I, 148—154.

[15] Ishoda'ad of Merve (ca. 850), who depends heavily on Theodore, writes:
"The hedge was the law which stood between the Nation and the Gentiles,
and prevented them from mixing in love with one another." (The Commentaries of Ishoda'ad of Merve, ed. and transl. M. D. Gibson, Cambridge 1916,
V, 2, 67).

[16] On the fathers' interpretations of Christ's "decrees", see above, p. 14.

the difference between Jews and Gentiles still exists; the law is very much in evidence. Does this mean that the dividing wall is not completely broken down, the law not fully abrogated?

Although Theodore does not deal with this problem in his commentary on our passage, he wrestles with the difficulties inherent in his idea of the two ages in his commentaries on other Pauline texts[17]. Relevant for this study is Theodore's conclusion that Christians live in both the present and the future ages. Since the future age is determinative, Theodore sees evidence of it in historical events. One of these events is the reconciliation of Jews and Gentiles in the church[18].

That hatred and separation, then, which arose out of circumcision he made to cease, along with all law, making us two—that is, he who was of the Gentiles and he who was of the Jews—one new man by the resurrection which makes us immortal, between whom no difference of circumcision and uncircumcision is possessed. For thus he made us into that one immortal body, constituting us in peace, granting us each that familiarity to God which is here.

For Theodore, the difference between peoples marked by circumcision has been important as part of God's plan for the present age. The future age where circumcision means nothing has already begun in the resurrection, but is not yet fully here. While recognizing the different roles of Jew and Gentile, Theodore sees their unity based on their common destiny.

John Chrysostom (b. ca. 350, d. 407)

For Chrysostom the primary issue dealt with by Eph 2:11—22[19] is the separation of humans from God. Contrasting himself to Theodore and Severian[20], he writes:

Some say that the dividing wall is the law, and that this is why he mentioned the law; because it did not allow the Jews to mix with the Greeks. But to me it does not seem to be this; rather, "dividing wall" means "the hostility in the flesh" in that it is a common barrier separating us from God.

[17] See especially his discussion of Gal 2:15—16 (Swete, 24—32).

[18] Some recent writers say that Eph 2:11—22 portrays the reconciliation of Jews and Gentiles in the church as the foretaste of the future unity of the church and synagogue, see below, p. 231.

[19] Hom. Eph 5 and 6; MPG 62, 37—44.

[20] Exact dates for their respective commentaries are not known, but Chrysostom could have known Theodore and Severian's position from personal discussion.

To substantiate his view of the dividing wall, Chrysostom cites Isa 59:2, which speaks of Israel's sins as having made a separation between them and God. Chrysostom is well aware that in the Septuagint φραγμός usually designates the law in its function as a protective hedge around Israel[21]. But Chrysostom argues that because the law was disobeyed "it became a dividing wall no longer establishing them in security but cutting them off from God." In and of itself, the law is not a wall between man and God, but "by being disobeyed it caused hostility."

The difference between Chrysostom's interpretation and those of Severian and Theodore involves more than just the location of the dividing wall. It has to do with their understanding of Israel and its relation to the church. Chrysostom assumes that "the commonwealth of Israel" (v. 12) is not the empirical Jewish community, but a "heavenly commonwealth". Thus he can assert flatly: "the Jews were outside the commonwealth." Severian and Theodore take the "commonwealth of Israel" to be the historic Jewish community; they take seriously the history of the Jewish people in which God not only speaks, but works.

Although the historical community of the Jews is of comparatively little importance for Chrysostom, he cannot avoid the fact that the promise was specifically to the Jewish people. He admits that God "made the promise to the Israelites", but immediately adds, "they were unworthy". Although they were outside "not as aliens, but as indifferent", they were nevertheless outside.

---

[21] The law as a hedge or separation (φραγμός) between Jews and Gentiles is seen by many early exegetes as being pre-figured in Gen 38:29 in the account of the birth of the twin sons Perez and Zerah. Chrysostom talks about this interpretation in a sermon on Matt 1 which attempts to explain why Perez and Zerah are included in the genealogy of Jesus (Hom. Matt 3, 3:MPG 57, 34—35).

Chrysostom says that the word φραγμός in Gen 38:29 is connected by exegetes with Eph 2:14. In the Septuagint, Tamar's midwife says at the birth of Perez, "Why was a separation cut through because of you?" Therefore the two sons are seen as types of the Jewish nation and the church. The appearance of Zerah's hand first represents the preliminary appearance of grace before the giving of the law. Perez represents the Israel of the law. Chrysostom says that some interpret Gen 38:29 to mean that for the Jewish nation a temporary break was made in the reign of grace; others say it means that for the church a break was made in the reign of law.

Although Chrysostom does not name any interpreters, we know that Irenaeus (Adv. haer. IV, 25, 2; SC 100, 706—708) sees Tamar's sons as types of Israel and the church. Other writers who connect Eph 2:14 with the Tamar story include: Eusebius (Quaest. ev. ad Steph. VII, 1—3; MPG 22, 905—909), Theodoret (Quaest. Gen. 96; MPG 80, 204—205) and Cyril of Alexandria (Glaph. Gen. VI; MPG 69, 320).

Because for him Jews and Gentiles were equally separated from God by the dividing wall, Chrysostom repeatedly emphasizes that in Christ the Gentile is not joined to the Jews, but that both are lifted to a new status. Thus he comments on v. 14: "He made us one, not by joining us to them, but by joining both them and us into one." Most of the homily's illustrations apply to this point: it is as though two statues, one of silver, the other of lead, were melted down and miraculously became one gold statue[22]; or as though an adopted son and a slave, both of whom had offended the master, were made full sons and heirs; or as though people divided into two rooms in the first floor of a house should come to one large undivided second floor. In all these illustrations, the uniting of the two is accomplished by completely removing the difference between them. For Chrysostom both Jew and Gentile become a third entity—the Christian. This is in sharp contrast to Epiphanius who says flatly that the Jew "is not changed into something else"[23]. Chrysostom, in order to emphasize the newness of the Christian's status, minimizes the continuity between the church and Israel. For Epiphanius, by contrast, unity does not depend on a new nature or status, but on a new relationship established by Christ's death.

Since Chrysostom has denied at such length that the Greek is joined to the Jew, it is noteworthy when he cooly asserts the converse: "For the Jew is joined to the Greek at the time when he becomes a believer." As well as suggesting that he thought of the church as the church of the Gentiles, this contradiction probably reflects some of the antipathy toward the Jews which was expressed in much more direct and harsh fashion in his sermons against the Jews[24]. There are signs of strong tension between this antipathy and the desire to be faithful to the text. For example, on v. 13 Chrysostom writes:

"Is this then a great thing", says one, "that we have come into the commonwealth of the Jews? What are you saying? He has summed up all things in heaven and on earth, and now do you talk about Israelites?" "Yes", is the reply. For those things must be received by faith, but these by the deeds themselves.

It is difficult to understand exactly what Chrysostom means by the last sentence above, but one senses the disillusionment as the view shifts from the exciting prospect of universal reconciliation to

---

[22] A parallel in Clement of Alexandria is noted above, p. 17n.

[23] See above, p. 27.

[24] Adv. Iud. hom.; MPG 48, 843—944. On the harshness of Chrysostom toward the Jews in his commentary on Romans, see Schelkle, 421—422.

the strange small minority called Jews. Nevertheless, Chrysostom seems to acknowledge that whatever his own and his congregation's feelings may be, universal reconciliation begins visibly and concretely in the reconciliation of Jew and Gentile.

On v. 16, "He has reconciled both in one body to God through the cross, killing the hostility in himself", Chrysostom asks how, if Christ has killed the hostility between God and men, is it possible for that hostility to arise again? His answer is that it does not, but from "our great wickedness" we create new hostility. At this point he adduces Rom 8:7, "For the mind of the flesh is hostility against God", and gives an extended interpretation of this verse. This lengthy digression shows very clearly that Chrysostom's interest in Eph 2:11—22 lies overwhelmingly in the relationship of the individual with God, and not the relationship between Jews and Gentiles.

To be sure, Chrysostom does make some references to the uniting of Jews and Gentiles. For example, in common with most of the fathers he connects v. 14 with v. 20 because he reasons that Christ as the cornerstone unites the two walls of Jews and Gentiles: "When he says 'He created them in Himself into one new man', he clearly shows that by Himself He binds together both walls." In his commentary on Ps 118:22 Chrysostom shows how he understands this traditional Cornerstone idea. Whereas earlier writers like Irenaeus and Origen thought of it as emphasizing the continuity of the Church with Israel, Chrysostom regards it in a more sociological way: the two walls represent not the Israel of history and the Gentiles, but only Jewish Christians and Gentile Christians[25]. Looking at the Cornerstone in this way, Chrysostom can see it as a symbol of *discontinuity* between the church and Israel: "the stone rejected by the builders" (Ps 118:22, Matt 21:42). Chrysostom elaborates further on the symbol when he says that the wall of the Jews rejected the Cornerstone because the Jews wanted to be the only wall; they would not accept the Gentiles[26]. Apparently this idea originates with Chrysostom. It never appears in any commentary on Eph 2:11—22 itself.

Our study of Chrysostom's interpretation of Eph 2:11—22 shows that an unfriendly attitude toward the Jewish people affected his approach to the passage. Consequently he treats it in a way which allows it little relevance for the relation of Jews and Gen-

---

[25] The walls are "the believers from the Jews and from the Gentiles", Exp. Ps 118 (117):22; MPG 55, 335. So also the noted fifth century exegete, Theodoret of Cyrus, Interp. Ps 118 (117):22; MPG 80, 816.

[26] This idea is stated somewhat later by a Latin father, Arnobius the Younger, Comm. Ps 118 (117):22; MPL 53, 506.

tiles, which is a sore subject for him. If we ask why it took until modern times before interpreters found relevance in Eph 2:11—22 for the relation of Christians to Jews[27], we must answer that one of the reasons is the direction Chrysostom's exegesis of the passage took. Chrysostom's influence has continued down through the centuries[28].

Theodoret (d. ca. 466)

Theodoret is the first commentator to say explicitly that the passage is about both the reconciliation of man with God and of Jew with Gentile[29].

He ended the law, which, resembling some wall, separated you from one another. But first he destroyed the hostility toward God, giving his own body as a sacrifice for us.

All previous commentators assume that the hostility was a concomitant of the middle wall. Theodoret parts the two, thereby agreeing with Severian and Theodore that the dividing wall was between Jews and Gentiles and with Chrysostom that the hostility was between man and God.

Theodoret breaks fresh ground in handling the problem of the abrogation of the law. As his guide he uses the gospel account of Jesus' encounter with the rich young man (Mark 10:17—22). Since Jesus points to the Ten Commandments in response to the request for the way to eternal life, Theodoret reasons that they are not to be ended. Theodoret believes that the Ten Commandments express what God included in man's nature at creation: "He makes laws those things which He wrote into nature when He created it from the beginning."

The same gospel account guides Theodoret to his interpretation of the δόγματα, by which, according to the traditional patristic interpretation, Christ abrogated the law. Like his appeal to the young man to sell all, give to the poor, and follow him, Christ's δόγματα go beyond the law in the sense that they deal with a person's intention or purpose. Theodoret says that Christ's "evangelical teaching" is called δόγματα, "since in the choice of purpose lies

---

[27] See below, p. 117 and pp. 222—234.

[28] Perhaps Theodore of Mopsuestia, whom many scholars today consider the greatest Greek exegete, might have had at least an equal influence if he had not been branded as unorthodox in the fifth century, with the result that his works were practically inaccessible to later exegetes.

[29] Interp. ep. ad Eph.; MPG 82, 521—525.

the key to perfection". Unlike the law which was in force regardless of the individual's attitude toward it, Christ's teachings "are
of self-accepted purpose". Theodoret's position is thus made fairly
clear: Christ has ended only that part of the law which separated
Jews from Gentiles, the cultic law; in its place he has put his "evangelical teaching". After Theodoret, there are no further advances
by Eastern writers in the interpretation of Christ's abrogation of
the law.

Cyril of Alexandria (d. 444)

Although Eastern commentaries on Eph 2:11—22 usually concentrate on the problem of the relationship of law and grace, the
fifth century theologian, Cyril of Alexandria, connects the passage
with a discussion of the unity of the church. Cyril uses Eph 2:14
to interpret a key passage on the unity of the church, John 17:20—
21. In this passage Cyril sees Christ praying for the unity of two
groups, the one Jews and the other predominantly Gentiles: "I do
not pray for these only, but also for those who believe in me
through their word, that they may all be one; even as thou, Father,
art in me, and I in thee, that they also may be in us, so that the
world may believe that thou hast sent me." Cyril concludes that
Eph 2:14 describes what Christ is expressing in his prayer: the uniting of Jew and Gentile is the demonstration of Christ's intention
for the church.

Taking the essential unity which the Father has with him and he has
with the Father as an image and type of undivided love, harmony and
unity, of thinking in one spirit, Christ wants us to mingle with one
another in some such way—in the power of the holy and consubstantial
Trinity. He wants the whole church to be regarded as one body, through
the meeting and joining of the two peoples into a union of one complete
people, growing up in Christ. For as Paul says, "He is our peace who has
made us both one and has broken down the dividing wall of the hostility,
in himself." And this is brought to fulfillment as the believers in Christ
have the same spirit among themselves and receive, as it were, one
heart[30].

Cyril argues that just as there is unity in the diversity of the
Trinity, so there is unity in the diversity within the church. In this
sense the church is to reflect the Trinity. Cyril's argument is based
on the understanding that in the New Testament the most significant diversity among men is that between Jews and Gentiles. The

---

[30] Comm. Io. XI; MPG 74, 557.

uniting of these two is fundamental to the unity of the church. It is the visible type of all other expressions of unity, all other movements for the realization of unity.

A dramatic illustration of how important Eph 2:14 is for Cyril's thinking about the unity of the church is the beginning of his letter containing the Formula of Union of 433. The letter marks the end of the fierce controversy between groups led by Cyril and by John of Antioch over the nature of Christ, which reached its climax at the Council of Ephesus in 431. Two years of difficult negotiations toward unity resulted in agreement. Cyril's thankfulness and joy are evident in the opening words of his letter to his former antagonist, John: "Let the heavens rejoice and the earth be glad, for the dividing wall is broken down."[31]

Later Eastern Commentaries

Later Eastern commentaries rely very heavily on Chrysostom, with only occasional changes or additions.

John of Damascus (b. ca. 675, d. ca. 749)

John of Damascus differs from Chrysostom by applying Pauline statements about circumcision in Rom 2 and Col 2 to the exegesis of Eph 2:11—22[32]. The breaking down of the dividing wall is described in the language of circumcision: "He cut off from between us the separation, which is the flesh because of the sin in it." This identification of the dividing wall with the flesh itself marks an intensification of Chrysostom's position, where the wall was only "the hostility in the flesh". John of Damascus seems to have in mind Col 2:11, "In him also you were circumcised with a circumcision made without hands, by putting off the body of flesh in the circumcision of Christ." His comment on v. 16, where he uses a form of the verb meaning "to circumcise", reveals even more clearly that the idea of circumcision is the key to his interpretation: "Since the cross has put an end to the present life, and cut off, περιτεμόντος, the flesh, everyone who is characterized according to Christ is designated as one man, whether in circumcision or in uncircumcision, according to the new life." No one until the twentieth century interprets the dividing wall with such consistent reference to circumcision[33].

[31] Acta Conciliorum Oecumenorum, ed. E. Schwartz, Berlin 1928, I, 1, 4, 15.

[32] In ep. ad Eph. comm.; MPG 95, 831—834.   [33] See below, p. 189.

The Oecumenius Commentary

In the commentary labelled Oecumenius[34] the attitude toward
the Jews seems to be more critical than Chrysostom's, for it height-
ens and adds to the negative comments of Chrysostom. Thus on
v. 12, where Chrysostom says "the promise was to the Jews, but
they were unworthy", Oecumenius says, "The Jews, even if they
failed because of great unworthiness, still had hope from the promise." And on the same verse Oecumenius comments, "For the
Jews, even if they struck him, still knew God." Similarly, while
Chrysostom at one point admits that the Gentiles have in some
sense come into the commonwealth of Israel, however spiritualized
the concept may be, Oecumenius refuses to admit this much. He
declares: "This does not mean that he brought us into the commonwealth of the Jews, but that having unyoked us from the customs
and traditions of the fathers, and having yoked us to one another,
Christ led us into his faith."

Theophylact (b. ca. 1050, d. ca. 1108)

Theophylact, on the other hand, seems to display a more fa-
vorable attitude toward the Jews than does Chrysostom. Close to
the beginning of his interpretation of the passage[35] he remarks,
"For great was the dignity of these people", and a little later he
adds, "the Israelites because of their worship of God were honored
and most noble." Consonant with this attitude is the fact that
Theophylact, while repeating Chrysostom's opinion that the primary theme of the passage is peace with God, pays more attention
to the unity between Jew and Gentile than Chrysostom does. His
comments on the new man (v. 15) are illustrative of this:

> For no longer are this man and that man characterized by their own
> marks, but the marks of the one man formed according to Christ cha-
> racterize both. You will come closer to what is meant if you understand
> the Lord as the Cornerstone, and these two men as walls, created into
> one in him.

Here is a clear example of the sociological use of the cornerstone
concept: the cornerstone unites two different groups in the present.
Thus Theophylact's comment seems to imply that though Jews and
Gentiles are no longer characterized by their respective marks,
these marks are not lost. There is diversity, joined by a more fun-

---

[34] Comm. in ep. ad Eph.; MPG 118, 1193—1200.
[35] Comm. in ep. ad Eph.; MPG 124, 1231—1236.

damental unity, as the figure of the walls joined by the cornerstone suggests[36].

Photius of Constantinople (b. ca. 820, d. 891)

Photius of Constantinople attempts to combine the basic ways in which the dividing wall has been understood among Eastern interpreters:

Two-fold was the hostility, and two-fold the dividing wall, even rather three-fold; for the human realm was also at war with the angels. But now, for the time being he has two in mind: the one which those of the Gentiles had against those of the Jews, and the one which both had against God. But Christ our God broke down each hostility and each dividing wall[37].

Thus he has included the interpretations of Origen, Theodore and Severian, and finally Chrysostom.

Western Writers

The majority of Latin writers interpret Eph 2:11—22 in terms of the relationship between Jews and Gentiles, locating the dividing wall between these two groups. However, where the influence of Origen, the Alexandrian method of exegesis, or Neoplatonism is strong, other interpretations appear.

Marius Victorinus (d. ca. 362)

Neoplatonism is especially evident in the earliest of the extant Latin commentaries, that of Marius Victorinus[38], a fourth century African theologian who taught in Rome. Victorinus' philosophy is not so well tempered by a thorough biblical perspective as is Origen's, perhaps because Victorinus was a professional philosopher converted to Christ late in life. Neoplatonic influence can be seen in Victorinus' interpretation of the wall (v. 14), which he says is "between kingdoms divided, since souls born from the fount

---

[36] Zigabenus (twelfth century) also uses the cornerstone symbol to interpret the new man, and indicates that the unity of the new man includes diversity when he says that the Jew and Gentile are made one "by placing upon both one new form of citizenship—the gospel form" through baptism (Comm. in epp. S. Pauli et cathol., ed. N. Kalogeras, Athens 1887, 20).

[37] Staab, 615. [38] In ep. Pauli ad Eph. comm.; MPL 8, 1256—1262.

of God are held, or rather were held, in this world because a dividing wall came between like a hedge or fence through pleasures of the flesh and worldly desires." Christ has destroyed the dividing wall "by conquering flesh and teaching that it must be conquered, and by destroying the desires of the world and teaching that they must be destroyed."

Generally speaking, Victorinus uses the term "flesh" to mean "that which is opposed to God's will". Flesh has gained control of the human soul and stamped it with its character.

The "new man" (v. 15), by contrast, is the spiritual man. Victorinus's account of the formation of the new man out of two is essentially the one previously given by Origen[39]. But whereas Origen puts forward his interpretation that the new man is the unity of humans with "superior beings" rather hesitantly, admitting at several points that to interpret the "two" as Jews and Gentiles would fit the context better, Victorinus elaborates the idea without reservation.

Victorinus sees little in the passage about the relation of Jews and Gentiles—indeed less than any other commentator. However, he does say that in v. 17 the "far" and the "near" to whom Christ preached peace are the Gentiles and the Jews. But his interpretation displays here the very attitude which, according to many twentieth century scholars, the writer of Ephesians wanted to combat: pride on the part of Gentile Christians expressed in disrespect of the Jews. Victorinus claims that the Gentiles are referred to first because "the Savior himself received the gospel that he might proclaim God to the Gentiles ... for those from the Gentiles who come to faith are called better sons than those of the Jews." This anti-Jewish comment marks a significant difference of Victorinus from Origen. Another difference is that whereas Origen wavers between two interpretations of the dividing wall (v. 14), Victorinus interprets it as a wall between this world and the world above. Origen's wavering is evidence of a tension between his philosophy and the text; Victorinus, on the other hand, presents a highly unified interpretation which seems basically dominated by his philosophy.

---

[39] Undoubtedly Victorinus knew Origen's writings, although his commentary does not appear to depend directly on Origen's commentary on Ephesians. (Souter, 27).

Jerome (b. ca. 347, d. 419)

Jerome's commentary[40] contains both of Origen's interpretations of the dividing wall (v. 14): that it is between men and angels,
and that it is between Jews and Gentiles. Jerome explains that the
Jew-Gentile interpretation is the literal one and the other interpretation the spiritual one[41]. He further suggests that the two interpretations are harmonized quite well in the concept of the new man
(v. 15). For in Jerome's view, the new man will have the same
form which the angels have. This will be completely fulfilled only
in the world to come. But the newness begins in this world when a
person, be he Jew or Gentile, is reconciled with God. This interpretation of the new man sees the reconciled man as having ultimately
the same nature as the angels. Yet it has in common with other interpretations, particularly those of Eastern writers, that it puts all
the emphasis on the new nature of the individual Christian rather
than on unity among men of different groups.

But the note of unity among men of different groups is not completely lacking in Jerome's commentary. He links Eph 2:11—22
with John 10:16, "There will be one flock and one shepherd." The
"other sheep who are not of this fold" are, according to Jerome,
"we who are to be gathered from the Gentiles." Christ "transmuted
the legal precepts by his evangelical teachings" so that Jewish and
Gentile believers might have "peace and concord".

Ambrose of Milan (339—397)

Like Jerome, Ambrose the Bishop of Milan offers two interpretations of the dividing wall. Besides locating it between Jews and
Gentiles, Ambrose says that it is within the individual. Both interpretations appear in the following passage from his exposition of
Luke:

For he abolished that barrier which divided the unity of mind and body
and thus of a pure life, and "he is our peace who made both one, destroying the dividing wall." This wall the Apostle explains as "the hostilities in the flesh". These hostilities then the Lord bore away, restored
peace, and "abolished the law of commandments in decrees that he might
establish the two in one new man." By this he indicates not only the

---

[40] Comm. in ep. ad Eph.; MPL 26, 502—508.

[41] It is quite possible that Origen himself gave this explanation of the two
interpretations, since it is completely in accord with Origen's exegetical method.
Here, as elsewhere, it is difficult to estimate what comments in Jerome's commentary are original with him and what is Origen's. See above, p. 17n.

4*

outer and inner man, but also the Jew and the Greek, that Christ may be all in all[42].

Ambrose apparently interprets "the hostilities in the flesh" to mean hostilities in the human sphere. Within the human sphere he sees two basic categories of hostility: hostility between various parts of one man, and hostility between various parts of mankind. Since Ambrose subscribes to the Alexandrian method of interpretation which allows or even expects more than one sense for any given passage, he does not hesitate to adopt both senses[43]. Because as a pastor he is deeply concerned about the struggle of the individual divided against himself, he speaks more frequently of the dividing wall within the individual. He terms it the division of the soul from the flesh or of the soul from the spirit[44] as well as the division of the mind from the body and the inner man from the outer man, as quoted above.

It seems to be Ambrose's assumption that the unity which Christ brings within the individual is a parallel on a small scale of the unity which Christ has brought within human history by breaking the wall between Jew and Gentile.

In explaining the abrogation of the law (v. 15), Ambrose emphasizes that it is the law as literally understood which is abrogated. This way of solving the problem follows quite naturally from the Alexandrian method. Whereas the Antiochene school found their solution in a distinction between the ritual law and the basic moral law, rejecting the former, the Alexandrian found it in allegorizing the entire law. Allegorically interpreted, or as the Alexandrian school put it, "spiritually" interpreted, the law remains valid, good and necessary for all[45].

---

[42] Exp. Luc. III, 26; CSEL 32, 4, 117. The view that the dividing wall is within the individual was suggested by Gregory of Nyssa (Contra Eunom. II, 13; MPG 45, 548) in connection with Christ's healing miracles which saved both mind and body. Jerome also speaks of the uniting of the inner and outer man (Tract. de Ps. CXL, 4; CCSL 78, 304).

[43] The text Ambrose uses has the plural "hostilities" in v. 14 as opposed to the Greek fathers and the best manuscripts; this may have suggested to him that more than one kind of hostility is meant.

[44] Exp. Luc. VII, 138—141 and 193; CSEL 32, 4, 343—344 and 370.

[45] Exp. Luc. III, 27; CSEL 32, 4, 119.

Ambrosiaster[46]

In contrast to the foregoing writers, the Ambrosiaster commentary interprets Eph 2:11—22[47] consistently in terms of the relation between Jew and Gentile. Ambrosiaster says that Christ opposes the group pride which made Jews and Gentiles reject one another. In breaking down the dividing wall Christ gives "a law that the Jew might not rely on his circumcision and thus reject the Gentile, nor the believing Gentile from uncircumcision—that is from paganism—despise the Jew; but that both, renewed, might follow the faith of one God in Christ." This faith is therefore not only an individual matter. It has to do with the ending of group hostility. Ambrosiaster contrasts faith which depends on Christ's teaching, with the temporary ritual law which had separated Jew and Gentile. Whereas "everything which the Savior taught he confirmed when he rose from the dead", the ritual law was destined to end. For Ambrosiaster the temporary nature of the ritual law is signified by the word "maceria", which he takes to mean a temporary partition or fence, as distinguished from a permanent solid wall. Viewed from the other side, the fence signifies the instability of paganism, since paganism is man's invention.

Ambrosiaster further stresses the temporary character of the fence when on v. 16 he says that fundamentally all people are "men of one nature". Although "they had been divided through error", Christ "has killed the hostility in himself, since he has died for all, both Jews and Gentiles." Ambrosiaster underscores his conviction that the ending of hostility applies to all men by adding, "For the death of the Savior has benefitted all."

The importance which Ambrosiaster attributes to the reconciliation between Jews and Gentiles is reflected in his saying that in removing the dividing wall, "Christ first reconciled the peoples to one another, then made them peaceful toward God the father." Ambrosiaster is the first commentator to specify this sequence, which gives more importance to the reconciliation of the two groups than when it is seen—as it usually is—as coming after reconciliation with God.

In emphasizing the reconciliation of the two groups, Ambrosiaster by no means minimizes the importance of personal faith. On v. 17 he says that Christ ordained that there should be preaching so

---

[46] The actual identity of the author is unknown. Ambrosiaster is the name given by Erasmus to the author of a set of commentaries on Paul's letters which had been commonly attributed to St. Ambrose of Milan.

[47] Comm. in ep. ad Eph.; CSEL 81, 3, 82—86.

that Jews and Gentiles "might receive the faith of Christ, through which they would be made one." This seems to contradict Ambrosiaster's comment that Christ already has reconciled the two peoples. But Ambrosiaster believes that there is one sense in which Christ has already given unity to all men, and another sense in which this unity is yet to be fulfilled. Its fulfillment depends on faith, which for Ambrosiaster is not only a matter of a man's relationship to God; it has to do also with incorporation into God's community made up of Jews and Gentiles. Ambrosiaster illustrates this by an analogy from political life: "As when any people wanted to follow the peace of the Romans, they were received when they had offered a gift, that they might become Roman citizens (as the people of Tarsus in Cilicia, whence the Apostle calls himself a Roman citizen) so also anyone who by faith associates himself with Christians becomes a fellow citizen of the saints and a member of God's household."

Members of God's household are "built upon the foundation of the apostles and prophets" (v. 20), which Ambrosiaster interprets as the Old and New Testaments[48]. The foundation is outlined by the Old Testament prophets[49] and laid by the New Testament apostles. Ambrosiaster notes that Christ also prophesies his church before building it when he says, "On this rock I will build my church." (Matt 16:18) This "rock" Ambrosiaster interprets as "the confession of catholic faith which is a faithful foundation for life." He explains this interpretation with its noteworthy expression, "confession of catholic faith", by returning from Matt 16:18 to Eph 2:20: "The sense of the Lord's saying, 'Upon this rock I will build my church', is this: the Savior received the two peoples into himself and made them one in the Lord, just as the cornerstone contains two walls which hold the house in unity." Thus Ambrosiaster's interpretation suggests that the basis for the church's catholi-

---

[48] Ambrosiaster's is the first commentary to do this. Ephraem may have meant the same thing by "the preaching of the prophets and apostles". Pelagius interprets the foundation as Christ, Victorinus as "Christ and his precepts". Chrysostom says that the apostles and prophets themselves are the foundation. Earlier commentators saw the phrase chiefly as evidence against Marcion's rejection of the Old Testament, and therefore probably thought of the apostles and prophets primarily in terms of their writings; but they do not make this distinction.

[49] Although Ambrosiaster considers the possibility that New Testament prophets may be meant, as in I Cor 12:28 "God has placed in the church first apostles, then prophets", he rejects it because he finds that I Cor 12:28 is about the organization of the church, whereas Eph 2:10 is about its foundation.

city is its creation by Christ out of the "two peoples", Jews and Gentiles.

Pelagius (d. ca. 420)

Several features of Pelagius' interpretation of Eph 2:11—22[50] testify to the influence of Ambrosiaster: the dividing wall is between Jews and Gentiles[51]; the ritual law, not the moral law, is abrogated; no allegorical interpretations are offered; the importance of faith is emphasized.

But Pelagius differs from Ambrosiaster by making everything depend on faith. He does not, as Ambrosiaster does, speak of the unity Christ has already brought, the acceptance of which belongs to faith. Pelagius' comments make the validity of the passage's statements about Christ's work depend on the faith of the individual. For example, the statement that the Gentiles are "brought near in the blood of Christ" (v. 13) means for him "by believing in his blood and passion you are freed." The phrase "through the cross" (v. 16) means "through the faith of the cross alone, which deters no one for it is not burdensome or difficult; even the robber fixed on the cross could have it." These comments are typical of the way Pelagius makes faith rather than Christ's deed central to the passage. And accordingly, Pelagius makes lack of faith rather than God's decision responsible for the ritual law: "Circumcision and the rest ... were caused not so much by the will of God as by the circumstances of the time or the hard-heartedness of the people."

Thus, while ostensibly discussing the relation of two groups, Jews and Gentiles, Pelagius actually focuses on the faith of the individual. An example of the consequence of Pelagius' interpretation is his comment on v. 21: "In the holy temple unholy stones cannot be placed." This presupposes that the individual can be made holy in isolation from the people of God. Basically Pelagius is interested in the relationship of the individual to God and not in God's working with groups. His view precludes any serious consideration of God's election of a people as fundamental to the work of reconciliation.

[50] Pelagius' Expositions of Thirteen Epistles of St. Paul, ed. A. Souter, Cambridge 1926, II, 353—356 (Texts and Studies, ed. J. A. Robinson, IX).

[51] The Pseudo-Primasius commentary, an orthodox revision of Pelagius' commentary in the sixth century by Cassiodorus and his school (Souter, Earliest Latin Commentaries, 210) reverts to the view that the hostilities are between man and God: "Surely actual sins and original sin which separates from God are called hostilities." (MPL 68, 613).

Pelagius' moralism resembles in some respects that of the Donatists, who flourished in North Africa through most of the fourth century and the beginning of the fifth. The Donatists claimed as the basis for their separation from the Catholic Church the principle that only persons who live a truly Christian life should be allowed in the church.

Augustine (354—430)

In his efforts to show that the Donatists misunderstand the nature of the church, the great African theologian Augustine makes frequent use of Eph 2:11—22. For example, he takes v. 14 as the scriptural basis for his exposition of Ps 120:7, "Among those who hated peace I was peaceful." Augustine maintains that in the Donatists' attempt to insure their own goodness they are actually guilty of the grave evils of "hating peace" and "tearing unity apart"; he argues that peace and unity are valid Christian aims, while separation from bad people is not. Augustine concludes with Eph 2:14 as his authority for the exhortation to peace:

Love peace, love Christ. For if they love peace they do love Christ... How is that? Because the Apostle says about Christ, "He is our peace who has made both one." If then Christ is peace because he made both one, why have you made two out of one? How are you peaceful when, while Christ makes one out of two, you make two out of one[52]?

According to Augustine's interpretation of Eph 2:14, the two who are made one are Jews and Gentiles. That the church is formed out of Jew and Gentile is such a basic element in Augustine's view of the church that he sees many types of the uniting of the two peoples throughout the Bible. So in a sermon on John 10 he says:

Did not the Lord come for this purpose: to found the church ... and to make one wall of the circumcision to which another wall from the uncircumcision of the Gentiles would be joined—so that he himself would be the cornerstone of the two walls coming from different directions? Did not the Lord therefore say about these two peoples who were to be one, "I have other sheep who are not of this fold"? Furthermore, he said to the Jews, "I must bring them that there may be one flock and one shepherd." For this reason there were two boats out of which he called his disciples.

---

[52] Enn. in Ps. 119, 9; MPL 37, 1605. Augustine draws the contrast between Christ, who makes one out of two, and the Donatists, who make two out of one, elsewhere: Enn. in Ps. 94, 8; MPL 37, 1222—1223; Enn. in Ps 124, 10; MPL 37, 1655—1656; Contra Litt. Petil. II, 70; CSEL 52, 101.

After pointing out several other types of the two peoples joined in Christ, such as the two wives of Jacob and the two blind men in Matt 20:30, Augustine concludes: "If you look closely at the scriptures you will find the two churches signified in many places. For the cornerstone serves this very purpose: to make one out of two."[53]

The cornerstone of Eph 2:20 is Augustine's favorite symbol for Christ who is peace because he unites two into one[54]. As noted above, this is a traditional concept of the fathers, with its beginnings in Irenaeus and its full statement in Origen[55]. Nor is Augustine the first to use it in efforts to heal schism in the church. Optatus of Mileve used it in his work against the Donatists, providing Augustine with starting points for his refutation of Donatism. Optatus asserts: "One wall cannot have the cornerstone which is Christ who, receiving the two peoples in himself, one from the Gentiles, the other from the Jews, joins both walls in the bond of peace."[56] Optatus also quotes Eph 2:14 as his reason for calling the Donatists "brothers", which he consistently does. Christ is peace for both the Donatists and the Catholics, he says; therefore, the Donatists remain brothers even though they refuse to accept the name or participate in the peace[57]. As we will see, Augustine also calls the Donatists "brothers".

Augustine develops Optatus's interpretation of the cornerstone and concludes that the church, by its very nature, is a corner:

"The stone which the builders rejected has become the head of the corner? (Ps 118:22; Matt 21:42) ... What stone did the builders reject? ... Of what corner has the stone become the head? ... The stone of the corner is Christ; the head of the corner is the head of the church. Why is the church a corner? Because to it He has called Jews and Gentiles. Coming like two walls from different directions (de diverso) and meeting, he has joined them in himself by the grace of his peace, "For he is our peace who has made both one"[58].

[53] Ser. 137, 6; MPL 38, 757. Jerome also links Eph 2:11—22 with John 10, see above, p. 41.

[54] Augustine uses this figure in at least 37 sermons and five other works. For lists of occurences of the figure in Augustine, see B. Blumenkranz, Die Judenpredigt Augustins, Basel 1946, 174, and A. Lauras, "Deux images du Christ et de l'Église dans la prédication augustinienne", Augustinus Magister (Études Augustiniennes) Paris 1954, II, 671—675.

[55] See above, pp. 11—12, 20.

[56] Contra Parmen. Donat. III, 10; CSEL 26, 95. On Optatus as a source for Augustine's thought on the church, see J. Ratzinger, Volk und Haus Gottes in Augustins Lehre von der Kirche, Munich 1954, chap. 4.

[57] Contra Parmen. Donat. IV, 2; CSEL 26, 103.

[58] Serm. 89, 4; MPL 38, 557.

This implies that it belongs to the nature of the church to unite groups of people as different from one another as Jews and Gentiles. Augustine emphasizes this point by his repeated use of the phrase "de diverso", or "ex diverso", to describe the walls. The phrase could be translated simply "from diversity". And that is certainly one of the ideas Augustine wants to convey: there not only can be, there *must* be differences within the church, differences united in Christ. This point certainly needed to be made in the Africa of Augustine's time, where differences between landowners and tenants, town and country dwellers, African and Roman, Punic-speaking and Latin-speaking, were powerful factors in the Donatist schism[59]. Augustine reminds his hearers that no difference between human groups was ever so great as that between Jews and Gentiles, yet it was precisely they who were united in Christ the Cornerstone.

What was so different as the circumcision and the uncircumcision, having one wall from Judah, the other from the Gentiles? But they are joined together by the cornerstone, for "the stone which the builders rejected has become the head of the corner." There is no corner in a building unless two walls coming from diversity (ex diverso) join in one[60].

The phrase "ex diverso", or "de diverso", can also have the connotation "from antagonism or hostility", and this suggests a further meaning which Augustine sees in the figure of Christ as cornerstone. Augustine notes: "Circumcision and uncircumcision were hostile ... The Apostle has shown the two walls coming from a diversity of hostilities and the Cornerstone, the Lord Jesus, to whom they have both come from diversity, and in whom they both have concord."[61]

As Christ reconciled the hostile Jews and Gentiles, so Augustine prays that he will reconcile the hostile Donatists and Catholics in North Africa. Augustine begins a sermon in the presence of the recalcitrant Donatist bishop Emeritus, who had just accepted Augustine's request to come and listen, with the quotation of Eph 2:14: "We rejoice in our Lord God, of whom the Apostle says, 'He is our peace, who has made both one'."[62] A few minutes later, in the midst of urgent pleading for Emeritus to unite with the Catholic

---

[59] On social, economic and national factors in the Donatist schism, see Greenslade, Schism in the Early Church.

[60] Ser. 88, 10; MPL 38, 545.   [61] Ser. 204, 2; MPL 38, 1037.

[62] Serm. Caes. eccl. 1, 4; MPL 43, 689—98. On Augustine's relations with Emeritus, see G. Bonner, St. Augustine of Hippo, Philadelphia 1963; and G. Willis, St. Augustine and the Donatist Controversy, London 1950.

Church, Augustine again uses Ephesians: "I speak plainly to my Lord. O Christ, who art our peace, who hast made both one, make us both one that we may rightly sing, 'Behold how good and pleasant it is for brothers to dwell in unity.'" The fact that Augustine probably delivered this sermon impromptu testifies all the more strongly to the importance the Ephesians passage held in Augustine's thought about the unity of the church.

Augustine contends that the Donatists misunderstand the nature of the church because they try to limit the church to Africans. The Donatist party consists only of Africans, whereas the Catholic Church includes all nations. Augustine shows that he regards the unity of Jews and Gentiles as basic, because it includes the unity of all groups of men: "Scripture mentions these two peoples and it omits no race of men when it says, 'circumcision and uncircumcision'; in these two names you have all nations."[63] The church is formed out of Jews and Gentiles; therefore it is the church for all groups of men.

Although Augustine relates Eph 2:11—22 most frequently to the Donatist schism, he also relates it to other contemporary problems. One of these is the heresy of Manicheism. Augustine tells Faustus the Manichean that by rejecting the Old Testament, Manicheism rejects the wall of the Jews and thereby rejects Christ the Cornerstone: "You occupy an unhappy position in a building of which Christ is not the cornerstone. For you do not belong to the wall of those who like the apostles, belonging to the circumcision believed in Christ; nor to the wall of those who, belonging to the uncircumcision like all the Gentiles, are joined in the unity of faith as in the fellowship of the Cornerstone."[64] Here Augustine sees the cornerstone as symbolizing the historical continuity of the church with Israel. By virtue of their rejection of the wall of the Jews, the Manicheans have read themselves out of the church.

Augustine also sees relevance in the Ephesians passage for the relationship between the church and the contemporary synagogue. In the sermon *Adversus Judaeos* he uses the familiar image of the cornerstone: "The peoples of the circumcision and the uncircumcision, like walls which come from different directions, are joined together in the corner as in a kiss of peace. Therefore the Apostle

---

[63] Tract. Io. IX, 17; MPL 35, 1466.

[64] Contra Faustum XII, 24; CSEL 25, 352. The context is Augustine's demonstration of the fulfillment of Old Testament prophecies in the New Testament. Augustine introduces Eph 2:14—20 as the fulfillment of the blessing on Shem and Japheth in Gen 9:26, 27. See above, pp. 11—12.

says, 'He is our peace who has made both one.'"[65] A thorough
study of this sermon in the context of Augustine's thought about
the Jews shows it to be "the most conciliatory expression of
Augustine about the Jews"[66]. To be sure, Augustine recognizes
that only a minority of Israel has accepted the Cornerstone. Thus
the majority does not experience the unity which Christ has
brought; they "are building a ruin and rejecting the Cornerstone"[67]. Augustine nevertheless continues to hope that the people
of Israel will accept the Cornerstone:

> Many from that Judea believed and will believe; for the apostles were
> from there and many thousand who were associated with the apostles in
> Jerusalem . . . This is the reason why the Lord is called the Cornerstone in
> the psalm: because he joins the two walls in himself . . . That prophet
> speaks rightly who lets the sons of Judah stand for the Jews and the sons
> of Israel for the Gentiles; and they will be gathered, he says, the sons of
> Judah and the sons of Israel equally, and will place themselves under
> one head[68].

The prophet to whom Augustine refers is Ezekiel. Ezekiel 37:15
—28 speaks of a future reconciliation between the Northern and
Southern Kingdoms. Augustine sees a wider meaning in Ezekiel's
prophecy: God will unite Jews and Gentiles. By connecting this
hope with the symbol of the Cornerstone, Augustine shows once
again that in his view Christ continues to work as Cornerstone.
This is not simply a part of his work that lies in the past; it has
present and future relevance for the unity of the church.

Augustine is more concerned with the cornerstone as a symbol of
unity than he is with a problem of interest to exegetes of later centuries: the relation of the cornerstone to the building as a whole. In
his commentary on Ps 86, however, he does discuss the problem[69].
He begins with the question which will become acute during the
Reformation[70]: what is the relation of the cornerstone to "the

---

[65] Adv. Iud. VIII, 11; MPL 42, 60.

[66] B. Blumenkranz, 174. Blumenkranz calls this formulation of Eph. 2:14—20
"Augustine's favorite idea", and compares the attitude it expresses to that of
Augustine's sermon on the prodigal son, in which the Gentiles are the prodigal,
Israel the older brother. Augustine cites Eph 2:17 as authority for his interpre-
tation of the parable: the Jews are "near", the Gentiles "far". (Ser. 2, 8—11,
Sancti Augustini sermones post Maurinos reperti, Miscellanea Augostiniana, ed.
G. Morin, Rome 1930, I, 260—262.).

[67] Adv. Iud. VIII, 11; MPL 42, 60.

[68] Contra Faustum XXII, 89; CSEL 25, 696.

[69] MPL 37, 1102—1103. The link with Eph 2:20 is the word "foundations"
in Ps 86:1.

[70] See below, pp. 70—78.

foundation of the apostles and prophets"? Someone could object, says Augustine, that the apostles and prophets support Christ rather than Christ the apostles and prophets "if they are in the foundation, while he is in the corner". But the objector "should consider that the corner is also in the foundation. The corner is not only there where it is seen as it rises toward the apex, for it begins from the foundation." So Augustine finds the Ephesians account of the foundation in harmony with I Cor 3:11, "No one can lay a foundation besides that which has been laid: Christ Jesus." Christ is "the foundation of foundations", just as he is "the shepherd of shepherds". Augustine stresses that the spiritual truth bursts the limits of the figure: "In earthly buildings the same stone cannot be at the bottom and at the top ... but divinity is everywhere present." Augustine's concluding suggestion is that the foundation of the church is really in heaven, and is thus, in contrast to earthly buildings, at the top rather than at the bottom[71].

Summary

For the fathers of the first three centuries, Eph 2:11—22 witnessed primarily to the continuity of the church with Israel. But from the fourth century onward, commentators begin to put more weight on discontinuity with Israel. What are the reasons for this shift? The one which we can see in the texts themselves is the changed situation with regard to Gnosticism. From the fourth century on, few writers regard Gnosticism as a viable threat; consequently they do not feel the same urgency about stressing continuity with Israel. A second reason is undoubtedly the fact that the presence of Jews and Gentiles together in the church is, in the main, no longer part of living experience or memory. The church tends to understand itself as "the church of the Gentiles" rather than as "the church out of Jew and Gentile". A third, more general reason, is probably the increase of anti-Judaic sentiment in the church. To analyze the causes of this lies beyond the scope of this work, although the beginning of the Constantinian Era certainly is a factor; the anti-Judaism of many pagans comes with them when they find themselves suddenly part of the church.

---

[71] Augustine seems to conclude that in the terms of the figure in Eph 2:20 the cornerstone is at the top of the building. Twentieth century scholars are divided on the philological question of whether "cornerstone" meant a foundation stone or a capstone. For a discussion of research on this question, see R. J. McKelvey, The New Temple, Oxford 1968, Appendix C.

Chrysostom's commentary, more than any other, stresses discontinuity between the church and Israel. And it is his interpretation which dominates in the East. Discontinuity with Israel is expressed most vividly in Chrysostom's explanation of how the Jew and Gentile are made one. He emphasizes a break with the past: the Gentile is not joined to the Jew but both become something else. The illustrations he uses involve a new nature, and a new status. For Chrysostom the one new man takes the place of the Jew and the Gentile. Significantly, Chrysostom applies the passage to the struggle within the soul of the Christian, and not to the tensions between various groups in the church.

In contrast to Chrysostom, Epiphanius and Severian emphasize the element of continuity in the church's relation to Israel. They consider peace between Jews and Gentiles as the primary emphasis of the passage. Consequently they tend to see the new man as the church, rather than as the individual Christian. Yet for most Eastern commentators, peace between Jew and Gentile in the church depends on the disappearance of their difference. According to Theodore, the difference between them belongs to the present age which is displaced by the future age; since the future age has not yet completely replaced the present age, the discontinuity is not so abrupt as that posited by Chrysostom.

In Western interpretation of Eph 2:11—22, above all in Augustine, the continuity of the church with Israel is more often emphasized than the discontinuity. Augustine is the only writer of this period for whom the continuity is so important that he applies Eph 2:11—22 to Jews of his own time. Other commentators speak simply of the Israel of the Old Testament or of Jewish Christians. However, Athanasius and Ambrosiaster, by the way they interpret the unity created in the cross, imply that it includes all Jews and all Gentiles. Therefore at least in the eyes of these interpreters, the passage proclaims not only the unity of the church, but the unity of mankind.

This emphasis on unity does not mean for the Western writers the abolishing of differences, as in the typical Eastern interpretation of the new man. On the contrary, Augustine underscores the importance of diversity within the unity of the church, and therefore finds Eph 2:11—22 relevant to the problem of the Donatist schism in which national, ethnic and social differences were involved. For Augustine, the Cornerstone symbolizes the fact that an essential mark of the church is its inclusion of different groups. More than any previous writer, Augustine emphasizes the fact that Christ as the Cornerstone not only unites different groups but that he brings peace where there was racial hostility. Undoubtedly Augustine's close acquaintance with group hostility in the Donatist schism made him especially aware of this aspect of Eph 2:11–22.

In the East also, some appeals for maintaining unity are based on this passage. These are by writers who are either earlier than Chrysostom or who do not accept his basic thesis that the wall was between men and God. Pseudo-Basil holds that to be baptized means to be prepared to live with people of all ethnic and social backgrounds. Cyril points out that the joining of Jew and Gentile is the primary historical analogy to the unity of Christ with the Father, and thus the basis for Christians, with their differences, to live together. And in his letter accompanying the Formula of Union of 433, Cyril uses Eph 2:14 in an expression of thanks that a division in the church because of theological differences has been overcome, and unity restored.

Both Eastern and Western writers, then, in the patristic period, relate Eph 2:11–22 to problems of church unity, in view of not only theological differences, but also economic, social and racial differences.

Chapter III

THE WESTERN MIDDLE AGES

As the Roman Empire collapsed, its citizens became subject to the conquering Germanic peoples. For a long time these two groups had as little to do with one another as possible. However, after the victory of Catholic Christianity over the Arianism to which the Germanic tribes had originally been converted, a gradual merging of peoples began to take place[1]. Conceivably this confrontation of two different peoples might have affected the way scholars approached Eph 2:11—22. With the exception of Gregory the Great, however, they make no reference to it. Early medieval commentators for the most part limit themselves to conserving the work of the great scholars of the past.

Gregory the Great and the Cornerstone (b. ca. 540, d. 604)

Before the period in which virtually all commentaries consist of quotations from the fathers stands Gregory the Great at the end of the sixth century. Although Gregory depends very much on the biblical scholarship of the past, he is creative in expounding scripture in light of the present needs of the church.

Gregory did not write a commentary on Ephesians, but his *Morals on the Book of Job* refers to Eph 2:11—22 in the course of interpreting the word "cornerstone" in Job 38:6[2]. The scriptural context is a series of questions about the creation of the world. Gregory's allegorical method of exegesis invites him to see these as questions about the creation of the church. On the question, "Who laid the cornerstone?", Gregory comments:

But since many things are now being related concerning the building of the Holy Church, the mind seeks to hear with what power hostile nations are united, that is, with what skill the different buildings of this house are fitted together. There follows: "Or who laid its cornerstone?"

---

[1] K. Heussi, Kompendium der Kirchengeschichte, Tübingen 1960[12], 140.

[2] Earlier commentators have often connected Job 38:6 and Eph 2:20, see above, p. 20.

Christ is the Cornerstone in whom Jews and Gentiles come together. Now it is clear to all by divine grace who it is that Holy Scripture would call the Cornerstone: surely he of whom it is written, "He has made both one": since he took into himself from one direction the Jewish people, from the other the Gentiles, and joined them in the one building of the Church like two walls[3].

By using the general term "hostile nations", Gregory brings out the relevance of the passage for the situation of his day when hostilities among nations had begun to be overcome by a sense of common participation in the Catholic Church. Gregory himself contributed to the realization of unity among nations in his work as Pope[4].

Gregory points out another sense in which Christ is the Cornerstone: "He unites the active and the contemplative life in himself."[5] By Gregory's time the differences between those Christians who practiced the monastic-contemplative life and those who led an active life in the world had become a problem. This may well be the reason why Gregory names the two as joined in the cornerstone.

In their comments on Eph 2:20, all of the medieval writers share the conception that the cornerstone unites the two walls of Jews and Gentiles[6]. Most of them, following the lead of Augustine, treat the cornerstone as both at the base and at the top of the building[7]. They usually explain that Christ is both the foundation and the consummation of the church[8].

---

[3] Exp. in lib. Iob 28, 7–8; MPL 76, 458–459.

[4] The Oxford Dictionary of the Christian Church, ed. F. L. Cross, London 1963, 583.

[5] Exp. in lib. Iob 28, 13; MPL 76, 467.

[6] Sedulius Scotus (MPL 103, 200) is the only commentator who mentions in addition an alternative: the two walls symbolize the heavenly and earthly realms.

[7] See above, p. 51.

[8] Some variants of this interpretation are: faith is begun and completed in him (Haymo of Auxerre; MPL 118, 712); he is the deepest stone as regards faith and the highest stone as regards the fulfillment of righteousness (Herve of Bourg-Dieu; MPL 181, 1249); just as Christ is the highest fulfillment of righteousness, so he is also the ground of righteousness (Bruno; MPL 153, 329).

G. B. Ladner, "The Symbolism of the Biblical Corner Stone in the Medieval West", Mediaeval Studies, Pontifical Institute, Toronto 1942, IV, 43–60, is chiefly interested in locating the position of the stone. He finds: "The identification of the stone-at-the-head-of-the-corner with a cornerstone or foundation stone is undoubtedly predominant. The interpretation of that stone as exclusively a coping stone is rare and represents a special trend, different from the main current of biblical exegesis and of liturgical symbolism; a trend which through

However, commentators on Eph 2:20 rarely go beyond the mere statement that the cornerstone unites Jews and Gentiles. They do not indicate whether they think of the cornerstone as symbolizing the historical continuity of the church with Israel, or the sociological unity of Jews and Gentiles in the early church[9]. The brevity of their comments reflects a way of thinking for which historical questions were not very important. A study of the attitude of medieval authors toward Jews finds that the cornerstone has an eschatological value[10]. This is certainly true in Augustine's writing, and in turn in medieval writers insofar as they are influenced by him. The fact that medieval commentaries speak of the cornerstone as the consummation of the church as well as its foundation may also be an indication of the belief that Christ will unite Jews and Gentiles in the church at the end of time. Although the belief that the Jews will be saved at the end of time is often mentioned by medieval writers, there are no statements based on Eph 2:20 which make this hope explicit.

Rabanus Maurus (780—856)

Commentators of the early Middle Ages are usually content to quote the Latin fathers. Typical is the ninth-century commentary of Rabanus Maurus[11] whose stated aim is to gather what he considers the best exegetical ideas of the past. The comments he chooses on Eph 2:11—22 are from Jerome and Ambrosiaster from whom Maurus alternately reproduces long excerpts. On v. 16, for example, he begins with Ambrosiaster's explanation that the two whom Christ reconciled are first Jews and Gentiles and then God and men; then comes the passage from Jerome's commentary which says the reconciliation is between Jews and Gentiles and also between angels and men[12].

For the next two centuries, scholars often use parts of the patristic material reproduced by Maurus, at times adding comments from other fathers[13]. But besides writers whose aim is to preserve the scholarship of the past, there are, even in earlier centuries, some whose work shows independent thought.

---

the medium of the medieval Rabbins ultimately goes back to the era of Hellenistic, Jewish, and Christian syncretism."

[9] An exception is Bruno, see below, pp. 57—58.

[10] B. Blumenkranz, Les Auteurs Chrétiens Latins du Moyen Age sur les juifs et le judaïsme, Paris 1963, 207.

[11] MPL 112, 406—411.   [12] See above, pp. 41 and 43.

[13] After Ambrosiaster and Jerome, the father they quote most often is

Haymo of Auxerre (d. 855)

As early as the first half of the ninth century, Haymo of Auxerre's[14] comment on the abrogation of the law (v. 15) points toward the exegesis which commentators from the Reformation onward will almost unanimously agree upon: the means by which Christ abrogated the law is his death. For the fathers, however, the means by which Christ abrogated the law was his "decrees"[15]. Formally, Haymo abides by the opinion of the fathers, but the content of his comment shows the new direction: "In the decrees of the gospel he has abrogated the law in mysteries, since he has not commanded either Jew or Gentile to offer sacrifice and to circumcise, after he himself has suffered, who was prefigured in those sacrifices."

Haymo finds support in the silence of Jesus about the continuation of the ceremonial law for his idea that the ceremonies, which Haymo calls "mysteries", were types of the crucifixion of Christ: this made them superfluous.

Bruno, Founder of the Carthusian Order (b. ca. 1030, d. 1101)

Bruno[16] is the first major commentator on Eph 2:11—22 in a new period of medieval exegesis which begins in the latter part of the eleventh century. As we might expect of a man with the originality to found a new order, he is not content merely to repeat traditional material. Bruno is more analytical than previous commentators, presaging the method of the Scholastic commentators; he remarks about the way in which the apostle Paul unfolds his

Augustine. Sedulius Scotus (MPL 103, 199—200) in the ninth century does not name his sources but draws primarily on Pelagius as well as on Jerome; Pelagius's material circulated, in revised versions, under the names of Jerome and Primasius. Atto of Vercelli (MPL 134, 553—556) in the tenth century uses all the early Latin commentaries except Ambrosiaster. Lanfranc (MPL 150, 291—293) in the eleventh century can use material from a Greek father, Theodore of Mopsuestia, because a Latin translation of Theodore's commentary on the Pauline epistles circulated in the West. It was ascribed in some manuscripts to Ambrose and in others to Hilary of Poiters.

[14] Exp. in ep. ad Eph., PL 117, 709—712. Until recently this commentary was attributed to Haymo of Halberstadt. In discussing the independence from tradition which Haymo displays, B. Smalley (The Study of the Bible in the Middle Ages, Notre Dame, 1964², 40) concludes that "he stands on the line that divides the compiler of select extracts from the author of a commentary."

[15] See above, p. 14. Of the fathers, Theodore came closest to the position of modern scholars. However, for him the law was abrogated not so much by the death of Christ, as by the resurrection life which Christ gives to his followers.

[16] Exp. in ep. ad Eph., MPL 153, 327—329.

ideas. At the end of v. 15, Bruno notes a transition: up to this point
Paul has shown that the Gentile has been brought near to the Jew;
now he treats the reconciliation of man and God. After v. 16 Bruno
explains that the author adds material about preaching, since all
these matters would have had little effect had they not been made
known.

According to Bruno's analysis of the structure of the passage,
the statement about the one new man (v. 15) belongs to the uniting
of Jews and Gentiles, rather than to the reconciliation of man with
God. Yet Bruno describes the new man as the man of grace. This
indicates that for Bruno grace has significance for relations between groups of men, as well as for man's relationship with God:
"He is the man of grace, and therefore new; if he were the man of
law he would be opposed to the Gentiles; if he were the Gentile, he
would be opposed to the Jew and neither of the two would consent
to unite because of his hostility."

In contrast to other medieval commentators who simply state
that the cornerstone (v. 20) joins the two walls of Jews and Gentiles, Bruno elaborates on the concept. First he admits his inability
to answer the philological question about the architectural meaning
of the cornerstone: "We have no certainty about where that stone
literally was." Then Bruno makes a comment which suggests that
he would locate the cornerstone in terms of history:

We believe that the stone could not be placed rightly until it was
placed as the completion of both walls; but he has fused both walls in
a marvelous unity at the summit. Here the stone signifies Christ, joining
Jew and Gentile in the perfection of faith.

Bruno's statement refers to the Incarnation "in the fullness of
time". Jesus of Nazareth is the cornerstone who fulfilled the histories of Israel and the Gentiles, symbolized by the two walls.

Peter Abelard (1079—1142)

Peter Abelard and his school are even less dependent on the
fathers than Bruno. The heart of Abelard's interpretation of
Eph 2:11—22[17] is a discussion of the dividing wall in the light of
the biblical doctrine of election. Abelard's is the most extensive
effort up to his time to put the broken wall in the context of the
history of salvation.

---

[17] Comm. in epp. Pauli, ed. A. Landgraf, Notre Dame 1939, II, 398—402.
This commentary was not actually written by Abelard himself, but by his
school.

"Who has made both one", that is, who caused both peoples to unite into one church. And this by first "breaking down the dividing wall", that is by removing the law which, placed like a fence between them, had aroused hostilities between them. Had this fence not been removed, the Gentiles would never have come to have faith along with the Jews. For, as we remember in the letter to the Romans, when God wanted to establish as it were his city in this world, he did not immediately choose the whole world, but a certain part—since every wise person begins from the smallest so that he may arrive at the greater—expecting the general conversion of all to faith at the coming of his son.

Abelard goes on to trace the beginning of "God's city" with Abraham, and the separation of Abraham's people from others both geographically and by laws, so that they would not fall back into unbelief. Since the influence of other people would be most powerful through marriage and through eating together, circumcision and food laws were instituted to hinder intermarriage and common meals.

But Christ abrogated the law so that the Gentiles could come to faith. He thereby made it impossible for the Jews to use the law as a privilege, refuge, or cause for pride. Jews and Gentiles are both thrown upon the mercy of God. To illustrate the situation of Jews and Gentiles, Abelard uses the story of the city of Carthage and the Roman general, Marius. Both are defeated, and having no more grounds for pride, are forgiven by the gods. Marius, exiled from Rome, in his need seeks refuge with the Carthaginians, formerly his enemies. Carthage, humble in defeat, accepts him. As Carthage is defenceless after its wall is destroyed, so the Jews are defenceless after their ceremonial law is destroyed; as Marius, exiled from Rome, is a stranger and sojourner, so the Gentiles are strangers and sojourners. Neither has room for pride. At this point Abelard speaks of the destruction of Jerusalem, including the temple, because Jewish confidence in these hindered them from recognizing the true church.

Abelard departs from all previous exegesis when he translates the phrase ἐν δόγμασιν (v. 15) as a further definition of "the law of commandments" rather than as the means by which Christ abrogated the law. Modern exegesis agrees with Abelard on this point. Abelard defines decrees as "those dispensations which were temporary because they obviously taught about external matters." The moral precepts, on the other hand, God did not abrogate since they are "natural for all men".

Abelard's careful attention to details together with his understanding of biblical and secular history make his interpretation of

Eph 2:11—22 one of the clearest and most interesting of the Middle Ages.

Thomas Aquinas (1225—1274)

The upsurge of biblical scholarship in the twelfth century, of which Abelard's commentary is an example, reaches its culmination in the Scholastic commentaries of the thirteenth century. Thomas Aquinas's commentary[18] is the outstanding representative of Scholastic exegesis of Ephesians. It gathers much of the best of earlier commentaries, adds some new ideas, and arranges it all in typical Scholastic fashion by means of a very detailed outline. For example, on v. 14 Thomas says:

> Having recalled in general terms the benefits which have come to the Ephesians through Christ, he here recounts them more specifically in two parts. First he shows how they have come near to the Jewish people, second how they have been brought close to God ... Again, the first part is in three subdivisions, since he first shows the cause of the coming near, second the means, and third the end.

The analysis goes on to explain that Christ is the cause, the broken wall the means, and the new man the end.

Thomas's interpretation of the broken wall (v. 14) is important because it explicitly says that the unity declared here includes the entire world. There is no possibility in this commentary of an implicit limiting of the unity to Jewish and Gentile Christians, as is the case in many earlier commentaries whose language may sound universal.

> To understand the literal meaning we ought to imagine one great field and many men congregated there. Through their midst stretches and rises one wall dividing them so that not one people is seen, but two. Whoever therefore would remove the wall would unite those men into one crowd, and they would be made one people. This is how what is said here must be understood. For the world is like a field. Matt 13:38 says, "The field is the world." This field, the world, is full of men. In this field is a wall, since some are of one party, some of the other. The wall can be called the old law—observances according to the flesh ... Christ removed this wall, and since no barrier remains, the Jewish and Gentile people have been made one.

---

[18] Super epistolas S. Pauli lectura, ed. P. R. Cai, Rome 1953, II, 27—33. Thomas's commentary on Ephesians consists of notes taken on his lectures by Reginald of Piperno. See C. Spicq, Esquisse d'une histoire de l'exégèse latine au Moyen Age, Paris 1944, 305 f.

Thomas names several means by which Christ removed the wall of the old law: by his sacrifice, since it made obsolete the ceremonies which prefigured it[19]; by his teaching, since it summed up the multiplicity of laws in the commandments to love God and your neighbor.

In the course of his careful treatment of the abrogation of the law, Thomas raises the question of how this can be reconciled with Matt 5:17: "I have not come to destroy the law, but to fulfill it." His response is that the Old Testament law consists of a ceremonial part, which is no longer valid, and a moral part, which not only remains valid but is expanded by Christ.

But why is it called the law of *commandments*? It cannot be in order to distinguish it from the new law, says Thomas, because the new law also has commandments (John 13:34). It may be because of the multiplicity of commandments in the old law (Acts 15:10, Job 11:6). Or—and here is Thomas's most original contribution on the question of the law—"the law of commandments" may mean "the law of works" as Paul calls it in Rom 3:27: "The old law is called the law of works, since it taught only what they ought to do, but did not confer grace by which they would be helped to fulfill the law. The new law guides by teaching what is to be done and helps in its fulfillment by conferring grace." Thomas's interpretation is new in the history of exegesis of our passage because it does not regard "the law of commandments" as some specific body of laws, whether ceremonial or moral, nor simply as the letter of the law as opposed to its spirit. Rather, Thomas says that a particular aspect of the law is meant: its demanding, merciless aspect; its lack of grace. Thomas's interpretation of the law of commandments points the direction which many Reformation commentaries will pursue.

Thomas notes that v. 16 marks the transition from the reconciliation of groups of men to the reconciliation of men with God. He emphasizes the importance of the sequence of reconciliation:

It must be understood that love of neighbor is the way to the peace of God: since as I John 4:15 says, "Whoever does not love his brother whom he has seen, how can he love God whom he has not seen?" And Augustine says that no one should think he has peace with Christ if he has discord with a Christian. Therefore he puts the peace between men made by Christ first, and then the peace of man with God.

---

[19] This idea appears first in the commentary of Haymo of Auxerre, see above, p. 57.

Thomas is not the first Latin commentator to assert that Eph 2:11—22 regards Christ as making peace first between men and then between men and God: Ambrosiaster made this point also[20]. The Greek scholar Theodoret took the opposite position[21]. This difference reflects the respective tendencies of Latin and Greek theology: the Latin tends to stress the horizontal dimension, the Greek the vertical.

Herve of Bourg-Dieu (1080—1150)

Besides the main stream of Western exegesis, which sees the dividing wall between Jew and Gentile, there is a stream of mystical interpretation which is chiefly concerned about the wall between man and God. An early representative of the mystical interpretation of Eph 2:11—22 is Herve of Bourg-Dieu in the twelfth century[22].

Although Herve gives several explanations of the dividing wall, the one which obviously claims his greatest interest locates the wall between man and God:

The wall was the obscurity of the law and the prophets, obstructing the way of life for us and forming a barrier between us and God. Christ by his flesh and passion broke down the dividing wall and the hedge, that is the obscurity of the old prophets, and every ancient law has revealed a sacrament. By sweeping aside the barrier to our going forward he revealed the way to the eyes of all, so that whoever wants to advance to God is hindered by no barricade and frightened by no darkness of obscurity. Wherefore when he gave up his spirit on the cross the veil of the temple was split in the middle and the holy of holies was opened to all. For that veil signifies the same thing as the wall.

This interpretation resembles that of Chrysostom in locating the wall between man and God. But whereas for Chrysostom the dividing wall between man and God was sin, for Herve it is lack of understanding. Furthermore, Herve adds the characteristic mystical idea of the ascent of the soul to God[23].

Herve's use of the torn veil of the temple (Mark 15:38) as an equivalent for the broken wall is new in the history of the interpretation of our passage. Many subsequent commentaries, including

---

[20] See above, p. 43.   [21] See above, p. 35.

[22] Comm. in ep. ad Eph., MPL 181, 1224—1230.

[23] The interpretation of Eph 2:11—22 by Dionysius the Carthusian (Enn. in ep. B. Pauli ad Eph, Opera omnia, Monstrol 1901, XIII, 305—308) is similar to that of Herve. He calls the dividing wall "the obstacle against ascending to God".

some in the twentieth century, use the torn veil to interpret the broken wall.

Summary

If the commentators of the Middle Ages had had first-hand contact with Chrysostom's interpretation, the exegesis of Eph 2:11 —22 may well have taken a different course. As it was, their lack of knowledge of Greek meant that if Chrysostom had any influence at all, it was late, indirect, and then only in commentaries with a mystical leaning. On the whole, medieval commentaries interpret the passage along the lines set down by the Latin fathers. Though earlier commentaries say that the dividing wall was between men and angels as well as between Jews and Gentiles, later commentaries speak only of Jews and Gentiles[24]. Despite the fact that the allegorical method would have allowed several interpretations, there is actually a process of narrowing down to the historical sense which medieval authors take on the authority of Ambrosiaster and Augustine: they hold that the dividing wall was between Jews and Gentiles.

Although scholars of the Middle Ages often quote Augustine on Eph 2:11—22, they do not discuss the unity of the church on the basis of this passage as Augustine does. An important exception is the brief comment of Gregory the Great that hostile nations are united in the church, a statement which he bases on the idea of Christ as Cornerstone uniting Jews and Gentiles.

Interpretations of Eph 2:11—22 in this period contain no comments which plainly concern the relationship of the church to the synagogue. Here again, Augustine's suggestions do not seem to have met with response. Thomas Aquinas, however, elaborates on the figure of the broken wall in his interpretation of the phrase "He has made both one" in a way which shows he regards both parts of the human race, Jew and Gentile, as having been united. Thus he definitely considers that Christ has brought a new unity of all mankind although he says nothing explicit about the relation of Christians to Jews. The figure of the cornerstone uniting the walls of Jews and Gentiles sometimes seems to be understood to include all men, especially when it is identified with the cornerstone

---

[24] An example is the Glossa Ordinaria (MPL 114, 592), a standard commentary until the Reformation; it is now accredited to the school of Anselm of Laon in the twelfth century.

of the whole world (Job 38:6) as in Gregory. Yet most commentators apparently assume that only Christian believers are united by the cornerstone. A few say this explicitly, sometimes adding that the cornerstone was rejected by the leaders of Israel.

Considering their heavy dependence on the fathers, the medieval commentators, particularly the later ones, make a surprising number of contributions to the exegesis of Eph 2:11—22. The more significant among them are: Abelard's connecting the phrase "in decrees" with "the law of commandments" which is the construction later argued for by Erasmus and generally accepted today; Haymo of Auxerre's finding that Christ abrogated the ceremonial law by fulfilling in his death that which the ceremonial law prefigured, an idea often elaborated in the Reformation period; Thomas's portraying the broken wall in a way that clearly shows he sees in it a new unity for the whole world. We can seldom be certain, of course, that any given idea in the Middle Ages is new; it may come from an earlier source which has since been lost. But preserving material from earlier sources is also an important contribution of medieval commentators. Thus the commentaries of the Reformation do not ignore medieval commentators, considering only the fathers as aids in the interpretation of scripture. Rather, they look at the Bible in company with the medieval exegetes as well, disagreeing with them often, but at the same time learning from them.

Chapter IV

THE REFORMATION

Two parallel developments take place in the interpretation of
Eph 2:11—22 during the Reformation period. One is that new
philological tools are being forged as a result of the Renaissance
which make possible a more accurate and detailed understanding of
the text than ever before. The other is that the passage is more
closely related to current events than it has been at any time since
Augustine. This is so not only because of the powerful renewal of
all biblical studies connected with the Reformation, but also because of the particular content of this passage: it speaks about the
unity of the church at a time when a tremendous struggle is dividing the church and Christian Europe.

Catholics

Erasmus (1469—1536)

An early representative of both these developments is Erasmus
of Rotterdam. Erasmus refers to Eph 2:11—22 in his appeal for
peace among the nations of Europe, *Querela Pacis*[1]. Christ as the
Cornerstone who contains and unites both walls is one of the
images Erasmus chooses in order to show that war is against the
will of Christ: war tears apart people whom Christ has united.
This use of the cornerstone-figure is in keeping with the tradition
of the fathers and medieval writers that takes the primary reference of the figure to be Christ's uniting of Jews and Gentiles[2]. Erasmus does not however specifically mention Jews and Gentiles[3]. For
his argument the more general implication of the passage is important: Christ unites people of different nations.

---

[1] Opera omnia, IV, Leyden 1703, 631—632.

[2] Erasmus's point recalls Gregory's: Christ is called the Cornerstone because
he unites hostile nations (see above, p. 55). Both Erasmus and Gregory assume
that the nations are Christian, or that they are in some sense within the church.

[3] In Paraphrases in Nov. Test., Opera omnia, VII, Leyden 1706, 978, Erasmus also says simply that the cornerstone "joins and embraces both walls".

In the notes to his edition of the Greek New Testament[4] Erasmus discusses grammatical questions in greater detail than ever done before in the history of exegesis. Erasmus's notes on philological questions were highly respected, especially by Protestant scholars. On v. 15 he gives philological arguments which support the construction of Abelard[5] against the otherwise unanimous exegetical tradition that Christ abolished the law by his teaching (δόγματα)[6]. Erasmus argues that Paul uses the word δόγματα only when referring to the law, as in Col 2:14, and never when speaking of Christ's teachings. Therefore the meaning must be that Christ abolished the law of commandments which consisted of ordinances (δόγματα). Erasmus's conclusion, though opposed for quite a while by some Roman Catholic interpreters[7], has since been commonly accepted.

Besides his notes on the Greek text, Erasmus also evaluates the Vulgate translation. He remarks that the use of the word "maceriae" to translate φραγμός (partition, separation) in v. 14 is fairly good. He points out that the comic poet Terence of the second century B. C. uses the word in a similar context: "maceriam dirui, ut fiat una domus" (I have destroyed the partition, that there may be one house). Although this note by Erasmus was not intended to shed light on the meaning of the Greek original, it nevertheless influences many subsequent commentators who either refer to Terence or at least say that the dividing wall was like a partition in a house. For some, this provides a link to the building image in vv. 20—22 which represents the church. The end result is that the dividing wall is viewed as a partition within the church between Jewish Christians and Gentile Christians. Thus the breaking of the wall is seen as a strictly inner-churchly event and does not apply to all Jews and Gentiles.

---

[4] Nov. Test. iuxta Graec. lect, Opera omnia VI, Leyden 1705, 839—840.

[5] See above, p. 59.

[6] See above, p. 14. Erasmus tries to claim support from the fathers: he reports that Ambrose (Ambrosiaster) and Jerome omit saying that by Christ's teachings the law is abrogated. But Erasmus quotes from Ambrosiaster only the comment on v. 15; the comment on v. 14 makes it probable that Ambrosiaster shares the traditional view (MPL 17, 400). From Jerome, Erasmus quotes a passage in which Jerome explains that the law of commandments is abrogated when it is spiritually understood. But Jerome makes explicit elsewhere that he shares the traditional view (MPL 26, 473).

[7] Zegerus, for example, speaks disparagingly of the "modern writers" who read "legem mandatorum in decretis sitam"; "none of the old scholars expound it this way", says Zegerus (Critici Sacri, V, 586). Sasbout cites many of the fathers in an extended attack on Erasmus's translation (In omnes D. Pauli ... epp. explicatio, Antwerp 1561, 235—236).

Jacob Faber Stapulensis (b. ca. 1450, d. 1536)

In contrast to Erasmus's close textual analyses, the commentary of another humanist, Jacob Faber Stapulensis, speaks primarily to the contemporary situation[8]. On the basis of Eph 2:11—22 Faber vigorously proclaims the unity of the church in all its dimensions. "Christ is our peace" means that he is "the peace of angels and men, the peace of Gentiles and Jews, who has made both covenants one." This affirmation is followed by a fervent appeal against discord among Christians:

How would you make a common body with heavenly angels, holy souls, apostles, prophets, peace-making martyred sons of God, and all the blessed, while sowing some discord or other? How would you belong to Christ your head, the peace-making king, who came and preached peace for all, the Gentiles who were far from God as well as the Jews who by the election of God and the preparation of the law were close, if you do not have peace? If you are not a member you are not made alive by his Spirit, which is the Holy Spirit; for a member cut off from the body, torn away, separate, no longer lives by the life of the body ... Nor should you think that the churches in heaven and on earth are two churches. They are not two but one.

By affirming the unity of the heavenly and the earthly church, Faber does not intend a simple identification of the visible ecclesiastical organization with the true church. Official membership in the visible organization is not the essential qualification for belonging to the church. It is essential, however, to be at peace with the visible church, and not to foment discord. Undoubtedly the position reflected here is largely responsible for the fact that in later years, despite his great sympathy for the Reformers, Faber did not break with the Roman Church.

Thomas Cajetan (1469—1534)

Most Roman Catholic interpreters of Eph 2:11—22 in the Reformation period are strongly influenced by Thomas Aquinas. They do not follow him slavishly, however, and are usually open to the philological proposals of Erasmus. A minority oppose both Thomas and Erasmus in favor of commentaries of the early centuries.

The influence of Aquinas is very evident in the commentary of the Thomist scholar, Cardinal Cajetan[9]. However, Cajetan can go

---

[8] In omnes D. Pauli epp., Cologne 1531[3], V. The first edition was published before the Reformation, in 1513.

[9] Epp. Pauli, Paris 1540, 262—264.

a step further in clarifying the abrogation of the law (v. 15) because he accepts the grammatical construction of Erasmus according
to which Christ abrogated the law not by his teachings but by his
death. Cajetan is now in a position to resolve in a new way the
apparent contradiction between Eph 2:15 and Matt 5:17, "I have
not come to destroy the law." Matt 5:17 applied during Jesus's
earthly life only; his death abrogated the law. The same explanation holds for the related saying of Jesus, "I am sent only to the
lost sheep of the house of Israel" (Matt 15:24). This does not apply
after Jesus's death, for then the apostles are sent to the Gentiles
also. In order that the Gentiles be included in the people of God,
the Mosaic law had to be abrogated.

Alfonso Salmeron (1515—1585)

Alfonso Salmeron[10], a Jesuit biblical scholar of Spain, also follows the basic lines of Thomas Aquinas's commentary. But Salmeron's chief concern is not the problem of the abrogation of the
law, but the problem that group hostility poses for the church.
Using material from both Old and New Testaments, Salmeron
depicts the hostility which existed between Jews and Gentiles. He
finds that hostile attitudes arose not only because of religious difference, but because of racial pride. The problem presents itself
then not only between people of different faiths, but also between
people of different races. Salmeron sees Christ's work proclaimed
in Eph 2:11—22 as the creation of unity among races, both in the
first century and in the sixteenth century.

He has made them brothers of one another and participants of his
heavenly inheritance. He has bound them each to the other in such a
way that what Christ is for us, any neighbor is also, whether he be
Gentile or Jew; since as the Lord says, "Inasmuch as you have done it
to one of the least of these my brothers, you have done it to me." Therefore anyone who abhors another nation or race from his own is immature
and has not yet put away the old man.

Salmeron evidently believes that Eph 2:11—22 speaks of the
unity of all men, not just those who believe in him. As the last
sentence above implies, this does not mean that hostile attitudes
have ceased.

Salmeron condemns the neglect by contemporary Christians of
the teaching that Christ "has killed the hostilities" (v. 16) between
Jews and Gentiles: "Those people gravely neglect this precept who

---

[10] Disput. in epp. D. Pauli, Cologne 1604, III, 201—208.

are hostile toward certain nations which have been called to Christ from Jewish or Mohammedan blood, and who, so far as they can, not only persecute them with evil talk but also deprive them of every public right, whether of state or church or marriage." Since the Jews and Mohammedans referred to have been "called to Christ", Salmeron's charge is levelled not against religious bigotry but against racial discrimination. It is because of their "blood", that is, their physical descent, that Jewish and Mohammedan converts are denied rights in both church and state.

Salmeron's comments are the first in the history of the passage's interpretation which openly say that there is hostility and discrimination against Christians of Jewish (and Mohammedan) descent: for the first time race is named as the grounds for discrimination within the church. This is not a question of schism or heresy which may have some racial concomitants[11]. Jewish Christians are not being discriminated against because of their beliefs, but because of their Jewish descent.

When Salmeron writes against racial hostility and discrimination in his interpretation of Eph 2:11—22, he writes out of personal experience. It has been shown that "racial antisemitism" reached especially severe proportions in Spain[12]. By the late fifteenth century religious orders had begun adopting a "statute of pure blood". This meant that "a future priest, kneeling with his right hand on the crucifix, had to swear that he was not a descendant of either Jews or Moors. Then he had to give the names of his parents and grandparents and their places of birth." Only one religious order openly opposed this racial discrimination: the Jesuits, founded by Ignatius Loyola with the assistance of Alfonso Salmeron and James Laynez. So strong was the Jesuit's stand on this issue that Loyola's successor as General of the order was himself of Jewish descent, James Laynez.

Parallels between the situation of Jewish Christians in Salmeron's time and in Nazi Germany are obvious. Salmeron is the forerunner of twentieth-century authors who interpret Eph 2:11—22 as God's word against the racial hostility of anti-semitism[13].

It is noteworthy that Salmeron first discusses racial discrimination and only afterward mentions the breakdown of the organizational unity of the church which comes from "heretics and schismatics and those who, because of worldly laws about nobility and

---

[11] This was very likely the case in the Donatist schism, see above, p. 47.

[12] R. Pfisterer, Im Schatten des Kreuzes, Hamburg 1966, chap. VI.

[13] See below, pp. 213—221.

more worldly passion, dissent in order to gain political prestige, ecclesiastical honors, and marriages." Foremost in Salmeron's mind as destroyers of the unity of the church are surely the Reformers. Yet Salmeron's moderation is evidenced by the fact that this is the closest he comes to polemic against them.

Clarius (1495—1555)

Although the majority of Roman Catholic commentators hold that Eph 2:11—22 is primarily about the relation of Jews and Gentiles, a few maintain that its emphasis is on the relation of man to God. One member of this group, Clarius[14], says that the word "wall" (interstitium) denotes the hostilities between man and God; the word "separation" (maceriae) denotes the law. By law is meant not only the Mosaic law, but also the law "engraved in the minds of the Gentiles and comprehended in the books of the philosophers." Christ abrogated both the Jewish law and the Gentile law, "if one can speak of two and not rather of one", adds Clarius. Since for him the difference between the Jewish law and the Gentile law is negligible, he does not put much stress on the law as a barrier between Jews and Gentiles. Much more important is that the law separates men from God, because men do not keep it. Therefore Christ abrogated both Jewish and Gentile laws, "not by another law, which would prescribe more things to be done by weak men than these two laws, but by the law of faith."—Clarius obviously rejects Thomas Aquinas's view that the abrogation of the law does not involve natural law. In his radical position on the law Clarius stands closer to Luther.

The Reformation Conflict over the Interpretation of Eph 2:20

The point at which Roman Catholic commentaries differ most decidedly from those of the Reformers is v. 20, which says that the Gentiles are "built on the foundation of the apostles and prophets, Christ Jesus himself being the cornerstone." The importance which this verse assumes in the controversy of the Reformation period allocates to it a central position in this chapter, between the discussions of the Catholic and Protestant commentators. In their interpretations of Eph 2:20 the contrast between the Roman Catholic concept of the church and that of the Reformers is most evident. The Roman Catholic commentators believe that the verse author-

---

[14] Critici Sacri, ed. N. Gürtler, Frankfurt a. M. 1695[2], V, 585.

izes a particular form of organization which is necessary for the unity of the church. The Protestants maintain that the church's unity is in Christ alone, and can only be realized through faith in him, and consequently by the mutual sharing of faith in the personal association of believers.

Eph 2:20 is treated by many Protestant commentators as a key argument against the Roman Catholic concept of the church structure, specifically against the belief in the primacy of the Roman Church. The Protestants hold up the Ephesians verse particularly against the Roman Catholic interpretation of Matt 16:18, "You are Peter, and on this rock I will build my church." Eph 2:20, say the Protestants, shows that Christ alone is the cornerstone of the church; therefore, the "rock" of Matt 16:18 cannot be Peter himself[15]. Thus after quoting Eph 2:19–22, Martin Luther writes:

> This is all to be carefully noted, so that we can despise the boasting tomfoolery that the popes carry on about their Roman church, which separates itself from the common Christendom and from the spiritual building which is thus built on this stone, and fabricates for itself a fleshly, worldly, empty, deceptive, vicious, idolatrous authority over all Christendom. For of these two one must be true: if the church at Rome is not built on this stone together with all other churches, then she is the Devil's church; but if she, together with all other churches, is built on this stone, then she cannot be lord and head over the other churches. For Christ, the Cornerstone, does not know of two kinds of churches, but only of *one*, as the faith of all Christendom speaks: "I believe in one holy *Christian* church." For the Roman church is and must be a piece or member of the holy Christian Church, not the head, which is appropriate to Christ alone, the Cornerstone[16].

Luther does not mention that Roman Catholic commentators have already "carefully noted" Eph 2:20, and have interpreted it in a way which not only does not conflict with their interpretation of Matt 16:18, but even to a certain extent supports it. Their interpretation of Eph 2:20 is sketched by John Calvin when he writes about the cornerstone: "Those who transfer this honor to Peter, so as to assert that the church is founded in him, are so shameless that they even misuse this testimony as a pretext for their error. For they claim that Christ is called the primary stone with respect to

---

[15] As patristic testimony that Matt 16:18 must be interpreted in the light of Eph 2:20, Zwingli and Zanchius quote Ambrosiaster on Eph 2:20 where he says that "this rock" of Matt 16:18 is "this confession of catholic faith". (Zwingli, Auslegen und Begründen der Schlußreden, Hauptschriften, IV, 176; Zanchius, Comm. in ep. S. Pauli ad Ephesios, I, 219.).

[16] Wider das Papstum zu Rom, WA 54, 245–246.

others, since there are many stones by which the church is supported."[17] Calvin's brief criticism oversimplifies the matter. However, the idea that Christ is the "primary stone" and that the apostles and prophets are the secondary foundations is actually what most Roman Catholic commentators of the sixteenth century hold, following Thomas Aquinas. Thomas uses the distinction between primary and secondary foundations to solve the problem posed by the apparent conflict of Eph 2:20 with I Cor 3:11, "No other foundation can be laid than that which is laid, Jesus Christ." Thomas believes that Eph 2:20b confirms his view: "Christ Jesus himself being the chief cornerstone" was included by Paul precisely to remind his readers that the apostles and prophets do not replace Christ as the foundation, but are subordinate to him[18]. In this way Thomas presents in greater detail the solution suggested earlier by Augustine[19].

Calvin himself, like most other Protestant commentators, solves the same problem by saying that "the foundation of the apostles and prophets" is not to be understood as the foundation which *is* the apostles and prophets, but rather their foundation, that is, the "doctrine" of the apostles and prophets. The distinction between the apostles and their doctrine, which is crucial for Calvin, is not made at all by Thomas; after saying that the secondary foundation is the apostles and prophets, he adds, "that is, their doctrine". This identification of doctrine with the apostles themselves has important consequences in later Roman Catholic interpretation of Eph 2:20, as the following brief survey shows.

Cajetan, even though he avoids calling the apostles and prophets a foundation, comes out very close to Thomas: we are built on Christ, but not on him immediately, only "insofar as he sustains the apostles and prophets . . . since the mediating doctrine is administered through apostles and prophets"[20]. In the commentary of Jacob Naclantius there is more emphasis on the apostles and prophets as privileged persons, than on their doctrine: "They are grander living stones, having been first made near to that living stone . . . and especially the apostles, who furthermore are joined to Christ, so that with him they become the foundation of the church. And among all primarily Peter, who by virtue of his singular faith and his outstanding confession truly has become the rock on which the church is founded, as Jerome teaches."[21] Here

---

[17] Comm. in ep. Pauli ad Eph., CR 51, 175.
[18] Super epp. S. Pauli lectura, ed. P. R. Cai, Rome 1953, II, 32.
[19] See above, pp. 50—51.   [20] Epp. Pauli, Paris 1540, 264.
[21] Ennar. in D. Pauli epp. ad Eph. et Rom., Venice 1567, 115.

Peter is singled out and spoken of almost as though his faith were his own achievement. Adam Sasbout does not even feel the need to qualify his statement that the apostles and prophets themselves are the foundation. As he sees the verse, Christ as the Cornerstone connects the foundation of the apostles and prophets with the Gentile believers, and so consummates and perfects the church[22].

Alfonso Salmeron says that I Cor 3:11 means that no foundation "diverse from and contrary to" Christ can be laid. But this allows apostles and prophets to be the foundation, since they are not "diverse from and contrary to" Christ, but continue his work. The way is open now for the claim that there can also be successors of the apostles who in continuing Christ's work are the present foundation of the church.

> In him and under him are apostles and prophets, and especially the vicar of Christ and successor in the apostolic seat of Peter, to whom the Lord said, "On this rock I will build my Church." The apostles therefore are foundations, but under Christ the foundation in whom most clearly the apostles themselves are built, and by whose power and place they support the fabric of the church[23].

As evidence for this interpretation Salmeron cites Rev 21:14 which says that the heavenly Jerusalem is built on twelve foundations which bear the names of the twelve apostles. Perhaps because of this reference, Salmeron speaks of the apostles as the foundation without mentioning the prophets in the final sentence above.

Thus, starting from a view which does not distinguish between the persons of the apostles and their unique witness, Roman Catholic commentators increasingly emphasize the exalted position of the apostles in ruling the church. From there it is a short step to the idea that their positions must exist in the church down through history and be filled by men who stand in personal succession to the apostles. The Roman Catholic commentators take the metaphor of the foundation more literally than the Protestants, and see it as authority for the present structure of the church. The Protestants see the metaphor as describing not the present structure, but the historical origin of the church. It is interesting to note that each of the above Roman Catholic commentators repeats the idea of Augustine that whereas in a material building the foundation is at the bottom, in this spiritual building it is at the top[24]. No Protestant commentator mentions this idea. The reason is not difficult to conjecture: it fits too well with the hierarchical structure which

[22] In omnes D. Pauli ... epp. explicatio, Antwerp 1561, 237.
[23] Disp. in epp. D. Pauli, Cologne 1604, III, 206.   [24] See above, p. 51.

6*

the Roman Catholics increasingly tend to see confirmed by Eph 2:20.

In contrast to the Roman Catholics, the Protestants make a sharp distinction between the apostles and prophets themselves, and their doctrine or testimony. Nicolas Hemming reflects this distinction when he says that the apostles are "connected to that foundation (Christ) in order to be saved", but that they are mentioned here "much more with respect to doctrine. For the apostles built the church on this foundation"[25]. The distinction may be stated thus: like all Christians, and equally with them, the apostles are built on Christ so that they may be saved and in this respect they have no unique position; only their "doctrine", that is their preaching, is unique because of their relationship to the historical Jesus. Megander underscores their inability to be a foundation by saying that the apostles and prophets themselves are sand[26].

All Protestant commentators agree: the apostles and prophets are not themselves the foundation of the church. Almost all say that the "doctrine" of the apostles and prophets is the foundation[27]. This position is best presented by Calvin[28], who reasons that if the men themselves had been intended, other categories of leaders would have been mentioned as well: "He does not mention patriarchs or pious kings, but only those who have the function of teaching, and whom he had appointed for the building of his church. And so Paul teaches that the faith of the church must be founded on this doctrine." Calvin resolves the apparent conflict with I Cor 3:11 by explaining that Eph 2:20a deals with a particular aspect of the basic truth that Christ alone is the foundation of the church.

The way of its founding must be noted; for strictly speaking the single foundation of the church is Christ, since he alone sustains the entire church, and he alone is the rule and measure of faith. But in Christ the church is founded by the preaching of doctrine. For which reason the prophets and apostles are called architects.

---

[25] Comm. in omnes epp. Pauli, et al., Leipzig 1571, 411.

[26] In ep. Pauli ad Eph. comm., Basel 1534, 70.

[27] A notable exception is Bucer, who believes that apostles and prophets simply represent faithful Israel as a whole, on which the Gentiles are founded; Israel in turn is founded on Christ. "He names the most illustrious of the Jews by whom he means also the rest who were founded on Christ... He commends throughout the dignity of the Jewish people, from whom the apostles are given to us, and indeed Christ the foundation himself." (Praelect. in ep. ad Eph., Basel 1561, 74.).

[28] Comm. in ep. Pauli ad Eph., CR 51, 174—176.

The word "architect", by which Paul describes himself in I Cor
3:10, is appropriate to denote the unique and unrepeatable function
of an apostle, as the Protestants understand it. Although the teaching of doctrine continues in the church, this teaching is dependent
on the doctrine laid down by the apostles and prophets. Because of
this conviction, Protestant commentators hold that "the foundation
of the apostles and prophets" means, concretely, the New and Old
Testaments. This view has good precedent in the history of interpretation since, as the late sixteenth century Reformed theologian
Zanchius notes, Ambrosiaster holds it[29].

Among Protestant commentators, doctrine as the foundation of
the church is increasingly emphasized to the point where right doctrine in the sense of correct systematic presentation of scripture
tends to become the sole mark of the church, or even more extremely, doctrine itself virtually becomes the church. Georg Maior
seems to be close to this extreme when in interpreting the foundation of the house or city of God as the doctrine of the apostles and
prophets he says: "If you ask where this house or city is, Paul re-
sponds, 'It is where the foundation of the apostles and prophets is.'
Therefore they are not the church or house of God who subvert
this foundation and teach another doctrine than that which is
handed down from the Son of God by prophets and apostles."[30]

Against such an exclusive emphasis on doctrine stands Philipp
Melanchthon's insistence that to call Christ the foundation is to
speak

> not only about doctrine, but about redemption and power as well.
> First he is the foundation in the sense that he gives the one word of the
> gospel, by which the whole church from beginning to end is united, as it
> is said, "No other foundation can be laid than that which is laid, Christ
> Jesus." Second the Messiah is the foundation not only because of
> doctrine, but also because of redemption and power[31].

Melanchthon wants it to be remembered that the church depends
not only on words, but on the events which stand behind them.

But Melanchthon is in agreement with the Protestant position:
Eph 2:20 dare not be interpreted to mean that the apostles and prophets themselves are foundation stones of the church nor that Christ
as the cornerstone is only one stone among others, even though the
primary one. The Protestants must then face the objection of the

---

[29] Zanchius, Comm. in ep. S. Pauli ad Eph., ed. de Hartog, Amsterdam
1888, I, 219. For Ambrosiaster's interpretation, see above, p. 43.

[30] Ennar. ep. Pauli ad Eph., Wittenberg 1561, 65.

[31] Comm. in Ps. (118:22), CR 13, 1185—1186.

Roman Catholics: why does Paul call Christ the Cornerstone if he does not mean that other stones besides him are essential parts of the church's foundation? Calvin[32] replies:

The solution is easy. For the apostles use various metaphors according to the circumstances, yet with the same meaning. It remains firm that no other foundation can be laid. Therefore he does not mean here that Christ is only one corner or part of the foundation; for then he would contradict himself. What then? He wants to join Jews and Gentiles into one spiritual structure. For they were like two diverse walls. Accordingly he places Christ in the corner as mediator who unites both walls.

Calvin says v. 21 shows us clearly enough that Christ is not limited to any one part of the building, for it speaks of the entire building growing in Christ. Since, according to Calvin, the unity of the church depends on Christ alone and not on a hierarchical structure, Christian unity is realized by common discussion and adaptation: "First a fitting together is required, so that the believers may care for one another and accommodate themselves to one another by mutual communication; otherwise it would not be a building, but a confused mass."

Calvin can also say that Christ is called Cornerstone because he unites the Old and New Testaments[33]. For Calvin, this function of Christ is very closely related to his function of uniting the church:

St. Paul has not wished to place him in rank as one part in order to put other stones with him which also have mastery and authority. Rather, he has wished simply to declare that there is no more diversity between the law and the gospel as far as the substance is concerned, but that our Lord Jesus Christ is the end of all, and that through this means we are all so joined and united that we are all made the true temple of God ... St. Paul here puts the two completely together, as in fact they are inseparable things, that Christians should be purely instructed in the word of God, and then that they should receive in one heart and spirit what is there proposed to them, that they should have a fraternal concord among themselves[34].

Some Protestant commentators avoid the dangers and difficulties of metaphorical language by saying simply that no further meaning beyond "foundation" is intended by the term cornerstone. "Cornerstone", "Foundation", "Head", are all ways of saying the

---

[32] Comm. in ep. Pauli ad Eph., CR 51, 174—176.

[33] A closely related meaning of the cornerstone is found in Zwingli ("De peccato originali declaratio", CR 92, 385): Christ as Cornerstone joins the *church* of the Old Testament with the *church* of the New Testament.

[34] Serm. XV on Eph, CR 51, 431, 432.

same thing: that the church depends completely on Christ. Calvin's successor in Geneva, Theodore Beza, is perhaps the most important exponent of this view. He points out that in Ps 118:22 and elsewhere the Hebrew term for cornerstone, ראש פּנה , simply means "that on which the rest depends". Beza warns of the logical inconsistency to which too close interpretation of the metaphor can lead: "I want this noted, so that no one imagine a building of more corners, and consequently philosophize more subtly on this similitude, since for an angle, two walls must come together, but a building cannot be built out of two walls."[35]

In denying any special significance at all to the term "cornerstone", Beza rules out the interpretation commonly held since the earliest Christian commentaries that the cornerstone represents Christ's uniting of Jews and Gentiles[36]. This interpretation of the cornerstone also appears in most Reformation commentaries, both Protestant and Roman Catholic. However, the implications of this interpretation are expounded only by Calvin, whose comments were considered above, and by his contemporary in Berne, Wolfgang Musculus.

Musculus sums up in a unique way the strengths and weaknesses in both the Roman Catholic and Protestant views of Christ as Cornerstone. He begins by stating that the uniting of Jews and Gentiles in the cornerstone is the basis of the church's unity, and then proceeds to discuss the contemporary split between Protestants and Roman Catholics.

The two peoples of the Jews and Gentiles ... just like two walls are joined in the cornerstone Christ ... and so they constitute the unity of the building. There is moreover a double aspect of this unity. One, that the whole building is united ... by the cornerstone ... The other, that ... the individual believers are joined into one body and held together. Neither without the other is possible in Christ. For it is impossible that we be joined to Christ if we are divided from one another in sects, since it is not possible that Christ be divided ... The latter part of this proposition the Papists urge, since they contend that the unity of the church must not be torn. About the former, on which the latter depends however, they do not reflect. Rather they transfer this to the Roman Simon in whom they want to require the whole building of the church to be held together.

We who profess evangelical doctrine easily understand and reprehend this error of theirs. Yet I cannot conceal the daily and unremitting sorrow of my heart which is caused by that yen for individualism, yes even a spirit zealous for contention, which disturbs the whole harmony of the

---

[35] Annot. in Nov. Test., Geneva 1594, II, 362.   [36] See above, pp. 11—12.

building of God. I sense that in this very matter Satan labors in extremity, and that it is a fatal thing that those who rightly hold the former part of unity—between Christ and his members—and clearly expound it to the churches, are unthinking and dissenting in the latter, which must also be kept[37].

Musculus's description of the dilemma of church unity in the age of Reformation underscores the fact that the strength of each side's argument has its corresponding weakness. The Roman Catholics' insistence on the church's unity does not emphasize strongly enough that unity is not the church's possession or achievement, but Christ's gift, and that therefore unity must continually be reexamined to see if it truly comes from Christ. On the other hand, the Protestants' insistence on unity with Christ alone does not emphasize strongly enough that unity with Christ involves unity with one another.

Differences Among the Reformers

The chief disagreement among the Reformers themselves in their interpretation of Eph 2:11—22 is on the abrogation of the law (v. 15). Although most of them agree that the law is what the metaphor of the wall signifies, and that the wall was between Jews and Gentiles, they differ about whether the entire law is abrogated or only a part of it. The characteristic Lutheran position is that the entire law is abrogated; the characteristic Reformed position is that only the ceremonial law is abrogated. The divergence of opinion about the abrogation of "the law of commandments in decrees" is of course only part of a much larger discussion about the relationship of the law and the gospel, which became central in the Reformation period. We are concerned here with the difference the two views of the abrogation of the law make in the interpretation of the dividing wall.

Those commentators who say the entire law is abrogated tend to emphasize the moral pride of the Jews resulting from their possession of the law. When the law is abrogated, say these commentators, moral pride has no basis, and thus genuine fellowship between Jews and Gentiles is possible. By contrast, those commentators who say that only the ceremonial law is abrogated tend to emphasize what may be called racial pride: a feeling of superiority and exclusiveness based on the idea that being chosen by God gives privileges to one's own people not to be shared by other peoples.

---

[37] In ep. Pauli ad Eph., Basel 1561, 72—73.

These commentators tend to see the actual conversion of Gentiles and their inclusion in the Messianic community as the means by which racial pride is broken. This gives the actual fellowship between Jews and Gentiles a more central place in their interpretation. But of course moral pride and racial pride usually appear together and cannot be so easily separated in the individual commentaries. At most, analysis can show only a difference in emphasis. We will consider first those scholars who say that the entire law is abrogated.

Martin Luther (1483—1546)

Although Luther nowhere interprets our entire passage, he does have a note on it in his German translation of the Bible of 1522. That note is on the clause, "abrogating the law of commandments in ordinances" (v. 15):

Christ did not abrogate the law so that one need not keep it, but rather he gave the Spirit, which freely does everything so that one does not need the written law (which the fleshly carry out) and is not driven by it. The Jews boasted of the written law and its works against the Gentiles, but since one Spirit has been given to both, the boasting about the law ceases, and they become friends in Christ[38].

According to this comment, pride in the moral achievement of keeping the law divides Jews from Gentiles. The solution to the problem is the giving of the Spirit. Since the keeping of the law is the work of the Spirit and not a moral achievement, there is no basis for pride. This note, written shortly after the beginning of the Reformation in 1519, reflects Luther's personal discovery at that time.

In a sermon a decade or so later, Luther seems to suggest racial pride and exclusiveness as factors in the Jewish rejection of Jesus Christ the Cornerstone:

The Jewish people are God's church and people, and the Gentiles are also his church. Now comes the cornerstone, on whom both churches are built, and binds Jews and Gentiles together. That vexed the Jews terribly, so that to this day they are not content with it. Yes, they have been broken on this, as we will hear afterwards, because the cornerstone is a stone of offense; that has been demonstrated by the Jews and today by the Pope and his followers[39].

Luther does not develop further the idea of racial exclusiveness as a reason for Jewish rejection of the cornerstone, probably be-

---

[38] WA Deutsche Bibel, VII, 196.
[39] Matt 18—24 in Predigten ausgelegt 1537—1540, WA 47, 425.

cause he is primarily impressed by the parallels he sees between
Jewish rejection of Christ and what he believes to be Roman Catholic desertion from Christ. In the case of the Jews, race is a factor, but in the case of the Roman Catholic Church it is hardly so.
What both do have in common, as Luther describes it, is their primary concern for their own survival and justification against criticism rather than with the will of God revealed in Christ.

John Bugenhagen (1485—1558)

John Bugenhagen, Luther's confessor in Wittenberg, whose commentary discusses in detail only those passages he regards as particularly important or difficult, singles out in our passage the abrogation of the law[40]. The whole law is abrogated, says Bugenhagen,
not the law "of ceremonies alone, as some interpret". According to
Bugenhagen, "it was the law which he calls 'the hostilities in the
flesh' of Christ, that is, the Jews." Here is a new interpretation of
the phrase "in his flesh" (v. 14). Most earlier commentators have
taken it to describe the way in which Christ broke down the dividing wall. A few have said it refers to the flesh as that part of man
which is hostile to God[41]. Bugenhagen takes "in his flesh" to mean
"in his people", and attributes the hostility to the Jews alone. Bugenhagen's comment accents Jewish responsibility for the hostility
without corresponding mention of Gentile responsibility. The same
emphasis can be noted in Luther's sermon and seems to follow
from his association of Jews with Roman Catholics in the interpretation of this passage.

Bugenhagen's way of understanding how the hostility was resolved is consonant with his Lutheran position: when Jews "came
to understand that the works of the law do not justify", then "they
saw that they were no better than the Gentiles", and fellowship
with them was possible[42].

Philipp Melanchthon (1497—1560)

Bugenhagen refers the reader of his commentary to Philipp Melanchthon's *Loci Communes* for a fuller treatment of the abrogation of the law. "The Abrogation of the Law" is the subtitle of

---

[40] Annot. in epp. Pauli ad Gal., Eph., et al., Basel 1525, 67.

[41] See especially Victorinus, p. 40.

[42] Georg Maior expresses the matter similarly: "Christ took away the hostility ... since now the Jews do not believe in decrees or works of the law."
(Ennar. ep. Pauli ad Eph., Wittenberg 1561, 63.).

one of Melanchthon's loci[43], entitled "On the Difference between the Old and New Testaments". Rather surprisingly, Melanchthon does not refer to Eph 2:15 here. His discussion of the matter is careful and differentiated, but leans toward a fairly negative understanding of the law. His conclusion is that the whole law is abrogated in the sense that the Christian is free from it and may now use it "to mortify the flesh". Forty years later, in the final edition of *Loci Communes* in 1559[44], Melanchthon drops the subtitle, "The Abrogation of the Law" and attributes a more positive role to the law. The anti-legalist mood which was part of anti-Roman Catholicism has been modified, partly because of the experience of the extremes to which some of the anti-legalistic Anabaptists have gone.

In an earlier section of the *Loci Communes*, where he gives due weight to Christ's deepening and widening of the law, Melanchthon cites Eph 2:14 as an extension of the command to love your neighbor. In the course of explicating Jesus's saying, "You have heard that it was said, 'You shall love your neighbor and hate your enemy' but I say to you, 'Love your enemies'", Melanchthon comments that he can find no place where the Old Testament commands us to hate our enemies. He suggests that Jesus may be alluding to Ex 28, where God commands the Israelites to drive out the Canaanites. If so, then Jesus is talking about a new attitude toward Gentiles: "If this is true, what else do we say Christ wanted than at the revealing of the gospel and the breaking down of the dividing wall ... and the dissolving and overcoming of the distinction between Gentiles and Jews, that, just as previously there was a mandate for the Jews to love Jews, whether friends or enemies, so now we should love both Gentiles and Jews, whether friends or enemies."[45] Melanchthon's interpretation of the breaking of the wall between Gentile and Jew has implications not only for relations between different groups of Christians, but also for relations of Christians to Jews as well as others. This is strong emphasis on the horizontal, ethical implications of Eph 2:14 which is exceptional among early Lutheran writers.

---

[43] Loci Communes of 1521, Melanchthons Werke in Auswahl, ed. R. Stupperich, Gütersloh 1952, II, 1, 125—137.

[44] Werke, II, 2, 440—460.   [45] Werke II, 1, 72—73.

Johannes Brenz (1499—1570)

The interpretation of Eph 2:11—22 by Johannes Brenz[46], reformer of Württemberg, illustrates the chief difficulty in holding that "the law of commandments in ordinances" (v. 15) refers to the entire law. Although Brenz can explain how the entire law is a barrier between man and God, he cannot show how the entire law is a barrier between Jews and Gentiles. Most commentators who say that the entire law is the barrier try to meet this difficulty by saying that the abrogation of the entire law takes away the moral pride of the Jews which prevented their fellowship with Gentiles. In Brenz's commentary, however, we do not find this explanation. Brenz maintains vigorously that the entire law is abrogated; yet when he comes to explain what separated Jews and Gentiles, he does not speak of the entire law but only of certain ceremonial and political laws: "Gentiles and Jews differed by circumcision, sacrifices, land, kingdom and priesthood. For all these were the dividing wall by which they were separated from one another." Here Brenz has shifted his ground. First the dividing wall was the entire law; now it is the ceremonial law. This problem of inconsistency in their interpretation of the dividing wall faces all commentators who say the entire law is abrogated; in Brenz we see it in extreme form. This tendency accounts for commentators of this group giving less attention to the uniting of Jews and Gentiles than those who hold that only the ceremonial law is abrogated.

Ulrich Zwingli (1484—1531)

The key difference between exegetes of the Lutheran tradition and those of the Reformed on Eph 2:11—22 is that Reformed exegetes say only the ceremonial law is abrogated. This leads to a greater emphasis by Reformed writers on the continuity of the people of God and on the shared life of the community.

Although Ulrich Zwingli did not expound Eph 2:11—22 in a commentary or in any of his collected sermons, he did quote the passage in its entirety to support his arguments against the spiritualism of the Anabaptists[47]. Through his controversy with the Anabaptists Zwingli is led to emphasize the continuity of the church with Israel so strongly that he says his readers will probably

---

[46] Kommentar zum Brief des Apostels Paulus an die Epheser, ed. W. Köhler, Heidelberg 1935.

[47] In catabaptistarum strophas elenchus, CR 93, 166—167.

object, "You want to make us Jews!"[48] Zwingli strenuously rejects any suggestion that there are two peoples of God, or two covenants, one of the law and the other of the spirit. There is only one people of God, one covenant, one church. Summarizing Eph 2:11—22, Zwingli concludes: "In these words Paul teaches throughout that which we want to say about the question at hand: one people has been made out of the two through the one Christ Jesus, who has joined together in one both those who first were near, and us who for a long time were far."

Caspar Megander (1495—1545)

In interpreting Eph 2:11—22, Zwingli's co-workers in Zurich find various ways to emphasize the continuity of the church with Israel. Megander[49] connects the unity of the new man out of Jew and Gentile with Peter's preaching on Pentecost when he said that the promise was to his Jewish hearers, their children, and "to all who are far off" (Acts 2:19). Megander sees in this verse proof for infant baptism. Since the covenant with the Jews is the same as that with the Christians, it must include the Christian children just as it included the Jewish children. This, says Megander, refutes the Anabaptists who hold that children are not members of the covenant until they make their own confession of faith.

Heinrich Bullinger (1504—1575)

Heinrich Bullinger, also of Zurich, is a particularly vigorous spokesman for the unity of the covenant[50]: "Unless you ponder this diligently it will seem most obscure to you, not only in this passage (Eph 2:11—22), but in this whole letter of Paul. We gather from this passage that the church of the Jews and the church of the Gentiles is one and the same."

Because Bullinger is convinced that God's covenant is one and his church one, he says that the Jewish people as such are not rejected[51]. However, membership in the church now means for both Jews and Gentiles giving up their old ways:

---

[48] For documentation of this, see G. Schrenk, Gottesreich und Bund im älteren Protestantismus, Gütersloh 1923, 36—49.

[49] In ep. Pauli ad Eph., Basel 1534, 47—73.

[50] In omnes apost. epp., Zurich 1537, 417—422.

[51] J. Staedke ("Die Juden im historischen und theologischen Urteil des Schweizer Reformators Heinrich Bullinger", Judaica 11, 1955, 236—256) shows that Bullinger was more sympathetic than most Christian writers to the Jews both of Bible and contemporary times.

For nothing is changed in it except the decrees: the dividing wall is removed and the Gentiles are admitted. Nor are the Jews thrown out, except those who by opposing the removal of the middle wall do not want to be new men in the fellowship of a renewed church.

The Jewish ceremonies and the Gentile superstitions "are both to be cast down at the bare cross of Christ." Membership in the church also means that both Jews and Gentiles be willing to fellowship with one another, since Christ "first re-united both races into one, then reconciled the one people to God."

Rudolf Gwalther (1519—1586)

The commentary of Rudolf Gwalther, another Zurich theologian, is especially interesting because it contains a direct appeal against racial and national discrimination. In this important respect, Gwalther is the Protestant counterpart of Salmeron[52]. Gwalther sums up the consequences of Eph 2:11—22 for the contemporary unity of the church in the face of racial pride in these words: "If the church of all races is one, then the religion of all races who are in it must be one. Nor dare we, because of differences of race or nation, spurn those whom God has joined to us by this bond."[53]

Martin Bucer (1491—1551)

Because the dispute among Protestants about the meaning of the abrogation of the law becomes increasingly vexed, Martin Bucer, the reformer of Strasbourg, devotes more than three-fourths of a lengthy treatment of Eph 2:11—22[54] to an attempt to clarify the issues. Bucer explains that the abrogation of the law does not mean that the letter of the law is done away with.

The opinion is false that "only the letter was given to the people of the Old Covenant, but to us what the letter contains." Both are given to them and both are given to you. But even the gospel is only the letter for you if you do not embrace the Christ promised in the gospel ... If the law is read by faith and is accepted, it is a minister of life ... But without faith and without Christ it is a minister of condemnation.

Bucer insists that when we read Paul's strong statements against the law, we dare not forget the situation in which Paul is writing:

[52] See above, pp. 68—70.
[53] Archetypi hom. in epp. S. Pauli ad Gal., Eph., et al, Zurich 1609, 175—176.
[54] Prael. in ep. S. Pauli ad Eph., Basel 1561, 72—91.

he is combatting the claim that Gentiles must submit to the ceremonial law in order to belong to God's people. Paul was not speaking against the Jewish observance of the ceremonial law before Christ's Incarnation. In that time it was God's will that the ceremonial law be kept, for Christ was then working in the ceremonial law.

But Christ has now abrogated the ceremonial law. He has done so not because the ceremonial law was merely literal, but because a new period in the history of salvation has begun in which God's people are not only Jews but also Gentiles. In this new period the Spirit is more fully given, so that the varied and complex discipline of the ceremonial law is no longer necessary.

Even after the Incarnation, however, it is not sinful to use the ceremonial law "as education and discipline, for God does not condemn the use of the law as such, but slavery to it." Bucer points out that Paul used the ceremonial law when he circumcised Timothy, when he shaved his own head, and so forth. The important point is that the ceremonial law dare not keep Jews and Gentiles from living together. Bucer is very conscious of the practical matters of living in community. Jews and Gentiles are reconciled "in one body" (v. 16)

so that we may live together in true faith and love with one another as members of the one body of Christ. For we are one body, not natural, not even political, but more than political, so that among us may be the best of mutual understanding and knowledge, community of goods, the height of love, peace, agreement and planning together toward the Kingdom, and obedience to God. Since the civil and ceremonial laws given to the Jews were not useful to all nations, he abrogated them so far as their outer form is concerned.

The fact that Bucer puts great emphasis on life in community may help to explain why, despite his stress on the continuity of the church with Israel, he felt it would be best if Jews did not live in the same community with Christians. As Bucer saw it, when Jews lived in the same city with Gentiles, their practice of the ceremonial law aroused hostility because it endangered the faith of simple Christians; this in turn sometimes led to violence against the Jews. Rather than have a city divided into two groups, Jews and Gentiles, Bucer found it better for Jews to leave[55]. Bucer believes that true Jews accept Gentiles; that is, they become Jewish Christians. "Those who were of the elect people did not hate the Gentiles but

---

[55] "Judenratschlag", Opera omnia I, 7, ed. R. Stupperich, Gütersloh 1964, 321–361.

loved them. So today there appear among us those who are marked by the name of Christ."—In the context of his time Bucer is relatively tolerant, although people of a later era would see his rationale for the exclusion of the Jews as coercion.

John Calvin (1509—1564)

Calvin moves beyond Bucer by pointing out the universal implications of the reconciliation of Jews and Gentiles. "Inasmuch then", says Calvin, "as through faith we are made children of Abraham, there is a spiritual parentage among all."[56]

Because he believes that Christians have been made children of Abraham, Calvin treats the Christian sacraments of baptism and the Lord's Supper as analogous to the Jewish ceremonies of circumcision and the Paschal meal. The Christian sacraments are also symbols of God's setting apart a people for his own. But they differ in an extremely important respect: they are not limited to any one race or nation. On the contrary, they serve to unite people of all kinds.

Note that baptism and the Lord's Supper (which are the sacraments that Jesus Christ has instituted) do not make a division similar to that of the forms of the law. Because as much as we would be separated from the unbelieving and those who have never entered into the church of God, the fact remains that there is no one certain nation that God has preferred today in the world, but he wishes that his grace be scattered through the whole ... And baptism and the Lord's Supper are today to unite all the world, because if the most barbarous come, they will be accepted by God; baptism will be bestowed upon them, for it belongs to all those who are united in the body of the only Son of God[57].

Calvin is well aware how difficult it was for the Jews to give up the ceremonies[58] which had been given them by God, and thus to surrender their separate existence: "They thought that all communication with the Gentiles was inconsistent with their prerogatives. To beat down such pride, Paul says that both they and the Gentiles

---

[56] Serm. 13, CR 51, 406.　　　　　　[57] Serm. 13, CR 51, 406.

[58] To illustrate why the ceremonies had to be given up, Calvin compares them to political symbols, such as the white cross of France and the red cross of Burgundy, which serve to distinguish one people from another. When a prince unites two peoples who were formerly divided, he commands that the symbols of the former division be done away with. Calvin holds that only the ceremonies are to be given up because "the moral law is not a wall of partition separating us from the Jews, but includes teaching which concerns us no less than the Jews". (Comm., 171).

have been united in one body."[59] According to Calvin, pride is precisely what Paul is trying to combat in vv. 11—22. In vv. 11—13 he attacks Gentile pride, and in vv. 13—15 he aims to break down Jewish pride[60]. Calvin sums up his analysis of the situation of the Jews in a syllogism which expresses clearly that racial pride is an enemy of Christian faith:

Now put all these things together, and you will form this syllogism:
If the Jews want to have peace with God, they must have Christ as mediator.
But Christ will not be their peace in any other way than by making one body of them and the Gentiles. Therefore the Jews have no fellowship with God unless they grant fellowship to the Gentiles[61].

Calvin emphasizes the essential connection between fellowship with God and fellowship between different groups of men.

Since he sees pride, not only in its racial form, but in all its forms, as a barrier to unity, Calvin presses home his conviction that the passage indicates how pride is overcome:

Here then is the means to unite us as is required: it is that each one in his estate recognize that it is a poor and miserable condition. And after he shall have attributed everything to the pure grace of God, then he should recognize that it is today scattered through all, and that it is not for us to impose on it law and bound: but inasmuch as he has chosen us we should also accept those whom he has put in our rank and company[62].

When he speaks of "accepting those whom God has put in our rank and company", Calvin may have in mind the problem of hostility between some old-line citizens of Geneva and the French Protestant refugees.

Calvin sees important implications for the unity of the church in the uniting of Jews and Gentiles. Does he see any implications for the relationship of the church and the Judaism of his day? There is one comment which may refer to contemporary Judaism: "From this passage we can refute the error of some, that circumcision and all the ancient rites, though not binding on the Gentiles, still remain today for the Jews. On this principle there would still be a dividing wall between us, which is proved to be false."[63] By "Jews" Calvin may mean contemporary Jewish Christians. Yet it hardly seems

---

[59] Comm., 171. [60] Serm. 13, 401.
[61] Comm., 170. [62] Serm. 13, 402.
[63] Comm., 171. For evidence of Calvin's openness to dialog with Jews and of a sense of solidarity with them, see G. Locher, "Calvin spricht zu den Juden", ThZ, Basel, 23, 3, 180—196.

probable that anyone in this period would argue for the keeping of the ceremonial law by Jewish Christians. More likely some people argued that God keeps the Jews under the burden of the law as a punishment for their rejection of Christ. According to this view, the breaking of the wall would be an event within the Christian church only. It is probably such a view that Calvin opposes here, and in so doing asserts that the wall is broken down between all Gentiles and Jews, and hence for the whole world, not just for the church.

Wolfgang Musculus (1514—1581)

Like Calvin, Wolfgang Musculus focuses on contemporary church unity. Musculus, leader of the Reformation in Berne, goes from the problem of Jewish-Gentile relationships to the problem of Protestant-Catholic relationships[64]. The dividing wall of the Jewish ceremonial law becomes very quickly for him the dividing wall of Roman Catholic ceremony, organization, and practice, above all the papacy. Just as the unity of Jew and Gentile was not accomplished by making Jews out of the Gentiles, as the false apostles whom Paul opposed wanted to do, so unity between Protestants and Roman Catholics is not to be accomplished by making Roman Catholics out of Protestants, but only by both becoming one in Christ.

Musculus emphasizes that the hostility between Jew and Gentile was open and destructive, much like the contemporary religious hostilities, except that the latter are not only between people of different nations, but between people of the same nation as well.

We today experience more than enough what sharp hostilities dissension in religion breeds, not only in diverse peoples such as Jews and Gentiles, but in people of the same race, nation, religion and language. Who can express how hostile Frenchman can be against Frenchman, Spaniard against Spaniard, Italian against Italian, German against German because of religious dissidence? Unless these hostilities be resolved, no reconciliation of the dissenting parties can be hoped for. That is the reason why Christ abolished those which rankled between Jews and Gentiles, and thereby reconciled the two into one.

The above quotation shows that Musculus recognizes the need for religious tolerance before reconciliation can take place[65]. This becomes even more apparent in the following sentences, which

---

[64] In ep. Pauli ad Eph., Basel 1561, 53—74.
[65] See P. Schwab, The Attitude of Wolfgang Musculus toward Religious Tolerance, Scottdale, Pennsylvania, 1933.

show Musculus's understanding of some of the prerequisites for religious dialog: "We are so inclined by nature that when we have hostile feelings we neither hear him whom we hate, no matter how truly he may teach, nor do we accept being joined with those whom we detest as impious, even though not they, but we are impious. If these hatreds can be dispelled or at least lessened, arrival at reconciliation will become easier." Musculus perhaps has in mind here primarily differences among Protestants. But even in his controversy with Roman Catholicism, communication is more important than attack. He opposes the ideas and practices of the Roman Church, not any specific persons. For example, in commenting on v. 20 he says, "I believe that among them (the Roman Catholics) there are not a few who are so built upon this foundation of apostles and prophets by faith that by the grace of God they are saved." Throughout his language is temperate, not abusive.

Musculus's sensitivity to religious dissension leads him to formulate more clearly than anyone before him the question about the inclusiveness of the phrase "who has made both one" (v. 14).

Did he not rather make two out of one instead of making one out of two peoples? For out of the people of the Jews, who previously were united in Judaism, he made two, since he divided it into Jews and Christians. Furthermore, he also made two out of the Gentile people, that is heathen and Christians. And this division remains to this day in the world. How therefore did he make one out of two?

Musculus's answer is that Paul says Christ is peace for Christians only.

He did not say, "He is the peace of the world", but "He is our peace", and he adds "who has made both one"; which is not to be understood as if he made all the Jews and Gentiles in the universe one people, but that out of both peoples, of Jews and Gentiles he himself, the one shepherd of his sheep, constitutes one flock, that is the elect; as can be seen in John 10. As far as the world is concerned, he did not come to bring peace and gather the reprobates into one, but rather to cause a separation. (Matt 10) Those out of Jews and Gentiles who truly believed in him he made one people.

But this answer stands in apparent conflict with his interpretation of the reconciliation spoken of in v. 16:

For when he says, "that he might reconcile both to God", speaking about Jews and Gentiles, he includes the whole world. This is what II Cor 5 says: "God was in Christ reconciling the world to himself." And the Baptist said, "Behold the Lamb of God, who takes away the sins of the world." In Adam the world is separated from God, in Christ it is reconciled. Observe that in this reconciliation there cannot be people dissenting and hostile among themselves, but they must be one in Christ.

According to Musculus's argument so far, all men are one in Christ. And yet suddenly Musculus speaks as though he had been talking all along about the church.

When he says, "in one body", he means that he is not talking about some unity or other, which would consist in externals, but about that kind of unity which is like the unity and coordination of the members which belong together in one body and are given life and movement by one and the same spirit. Because of this unity the church is called the body of Christ.

The paradox of a world reconciled and not yet reconciled calls forth many patient attempts on Musculus's part to make clear his understanding of the peace of Christ. In his comments on Christ's proclaiming peace to the far and the near (v. 17) Musculus's own solution to the problem is most apparent. There he says that this peace truly is prepared for all men, even though all men do not accept it. It would be ridiculous, says Musculus, to proclaim peace to someone to whom the promise did not apply. But not all men accept the peace, and thus do not live in it and cannot say, "He is our peace." Musculus ends with a series of illustrations of his point; for example, when a king proclaims peace to rebellious subjects, the peace applies to all, but those who persist in rebellion will not be at peace.

If Musculus can speak about the whole world's being in some sense reconciled to God, even though some men do not accept this reconciliation, we could hope that he might also say something about all men's being reconciled to one another, even though they do not accept this reconciliation. Although he does not expound this idea, it seems to be the underlying basis of his desire for unity and tolerance. Musculus advocated a greater measure of toleration for Jews than other Protestant leaders of his time. He not only opposed forced baptism, but also objected to limiting Jews to usury as a means of livelihood; he was not in favour of requiring Jews to imitate the Christian religion or attend its services. And while Christians should have nothing to do with the worship of Jews, Turks and heathens, they may associate with these people in personal and group life[66].

As far as the unity of Christians is concerned, Musuculus is quite specific about the implications of the passage for his times:

---

[66] Schwab, 52—53.

As many as are Christians are members of the body of Christ, and though they are many in number yet in Christ they are not many, since they are not dissenting, but the same, according to the new creation which makes all one new man, in which there is neither Jew nor Greek, nor Frenchman nor Englishman nor German, nor male nor female, nor slave nor free, but Christ is the same in all.

The fact that he places Frenchmen, Englishmen and Germans alongside Jews and Greeks in quoting St. Paul on the unity of the church reflects Musculus' desire to see the problems of his time in the light of the Bible.

Shortly after Musculus' commentary was published the decrees of the Council of Trent were confirmed in its concluding session. This crucial event in church history marks a hardening of the Roman Catholic position. Reaction to it is partly responsible for the development of Protestant orthodoxy, which is reflected in commentaries published less than a decade after that of Musculus. These commentaries tend to treat the passage as a piece of material useful for the construction of a more or less carefully developed doctrinal system and consequently do not give enough consideration to the context and uniqueness of the passage.

Matthias Flacius (1520—1575)

This tendency can be seen in the commentary of Matthias Flacius[67], leader in the development of orthodox Lutheran hermeneutics. Apparently wanting to include as many aspects of doctrine as possible, he says that the dividing wall was between man and God as well as between Jew and Gentile[68]. Whereas the Reformers all held that the dividing wall was between Jews and Gentiles, Flacius sees the picture in a more complex way. The wall represents the entire law, which in its moral part separated man from God and in its ceremonial and judicial parts separated Jews from Gentiles. Flacius qualifies this position further by adding that while it was primarily the ceremonial and judicial law which separated Jews from Gentiles, the moral law was also involved, since Jews and Gentiles differed about morals as well.

---

[67] Glossa comp. in Nov. Test., Basel 1570, 929—932.

[68] Flacius's interpretation of the dividing wall recalls that of Photius of Constantinople, see above, p. 39.

Hieronymus Zanchius (1516—1590)

In orthodox Reformed commentaries the doctrinal system often plays an even more obvious role. Hieronymus Zanchius[69] deduces four doctrinal propositions from the clause in v. 16, "that he might reconcile us both to God in one body through the cross": 1. Outside Christ no one is reconciled to God. 2. All the elect were reconciled at one time. 3. There is no hope for anyone who was not reconciled at that time. 4. Since the elect were reconciled not as individuals, but as one body, the church, and since the church cannot perish, none of the elect can perish.

When he is not deriving doctrine from single verses but considers the actual historical situation of the first century, Zanchius sees that the unity of the church is not abstract but requires personal fellowhip. Among the reasons why the ceremonial law had to be abrogated, Zanchius lists first the fact that Jews and Gentiles "could not be one body without being friends."

Zanchius wonders how the divided Christians of his own day can become one body. Again there are walls, but they are not of God's making as the Mosaic law was. If the wall which God had erected was broken down, says Zanchius,

How much more then should human walls be torn down — traditions, ceremonies, customs and many other human things for the sake of the joining of the churches. All are crying that we must strive for the unity of the churches, and that all must be united in one. O may it be! But what is the true way of uniting? Here the apostle teaches what it is. Above all, hostilities must be given up. What do these really come from? From human laws, decrees, mandates, canons; about such things as rites and ceremonies which disagree with the word of God, or at least have no testimony from it. And all the while consciences are burdened with them beyond measure.

Zanchius' words testify to the importance the question of church unity held in the thought of his time. However, he does not contribute a great deal toward unity, since his chief point is the common Protestant criticism of Roman Catholic rites and ceremonies. Although Musculus likewise compared Roman Catholic ceremonies to the Jewish ceremonial law, he also spoke of religious dissension generally as a cause of hostility. Musculus counselled laying aside hostility in order to understand those who disagree with you and to see the faults in your own position; Zanchius puts all the blame on the other side.

---

[69] Comm. in ep. S. Pauli ad Eph., ed. de Hartog, Amsterdam 1888, I, 182—226. The first edition was published in 1594.

Robert Rollock (1555—1599)

Another orthodox Reformed commentator, Robert Rollock[70], puts the propositions he derives from the text in separate paragraphs labelled "doctrines". Less theological and systematic than Zanchius, Rollock devotes more attention to contemporary problems[71]. His "doctrines" on Eph 2:11—22 include:

1. Christ is the arbiter of religious disputes. As he ended the religious strife between Jew and Gentile, so he will end the religious strife which rends Europe today. But he will not do so until he comes again at the end of time. And then he will not abrogate ceremonies, but will shut out the adversaries and give peace in heaven to his own.
2. There are two steps to Christian peace: the first is the abolition of the human traditions of the adversaries, and the second is the actual uniting of Christians.
3. As the Jewish ceremonies were given by God to separate them from the Gentiles, so our religion is given to us as a wall to separate us from our adversaries. If the Jews supported their wall until Christ's coming, how much more should we support our wall until Christ's second coming.

Rollock shifts his terms at will, so that at one time the middle wall can represent the traditions of his "adversaries", the Roman Catholics, and at another time "our religion", Protestant Christianity. Pushed by the hostility of the contemporary religious situation, Rollock actually tries to defend a dividing wall on the basis of our passage, despite the fact that the passage proclaims that the wall has been broken down. Rollock's procedure demonstrates the pitfalls of making contemporary applications without careful attention to the text: he obviously uses scripture to defend his own position.

Although he has no hesitation about separating from other Christians on doctrinal matters, Rollock says clearly that non-doctrinal matters, such as race or nation, dare not separate Christians. Here where the need to defend his position is not so great, Rollock comes closer to the text. In the new man which Christ created in himself (v. 16) these fleshly matters no longer pertain; as II Cor 5:16 says, "We no longer regard anyone according to the flesh." Rollock concludes: "If there be a Christian who concerns himself

---

[70] In ep. S. Pauli ad Eph., Geneva 1593², 110—141.

[71] An anonymous sixteenth century writer was also prompted by the hostility between Jew and Gentile to reflect on contemporary strife: "The Jewish rites were the causes of hostility *per accidens*, just as now the cause of most wars is religion." (Annot. in Vet. Test. et in Eph., Franeker 1704, 736.).

unduly about these fleshly matters which divide men from one another, who can say that he is a member of this new man?"

Rollock also notes that the preaching of peace to those who are far (v. 17) means that Christians must reach out to those who are outside the church and different from themselves. They must not be like the Jews who were jealous of the converted Gentiles. That is the false religion which Paul combatted, as when he

asserted against them that reconciliation applies to both peoples, and likewise the preaching of reconciliation, that is the gospel. Note therefore the difference between true members of the body of Christ and false. The false neither enter into the kingdom of heaven themselves nor do they allow others to enter. Those who are true members of the body of Christ both want to enter themselves and are very desirous of the salvation of others.

Rollock does not recognize the inconsistency of urging Christians to reach out to other people while calling upon them to guard the wall around themselves.

Summary

Early Orthodox commentators are no longer so painfully aware of the problems of church unity as were the Reformers. They evidence the beginnings of a withdrawal behind the walls of their own positions, be they Lutheran or Reformed. The Reformation commentators, however, feel the sharp contrast between the church united out of Jews and Gentiles as portrayed in Ephesians, and the divided Christendom of their own day. This is one reason why their interpretation of our passage is more intense than that of any earlier period.

Because the chief factor dividing Christendom is a difference in the understanding of the gospel itself, commentators wrestle with the problem of theological differences. The point in Eph 2:11–22 where theological differences between Roman Catholics and Protestants are most clearly revealed is v. 20, which says that the Gentile Christians are "built on the foundation of the apostles and prophets, Christ Jesus himself being the cornerstone." Development in Roman Catholic interpretation leads to the exposition of the verse as support for the doctrine of apostolic succession. Protestants take the same verse as evidence that Christ alone upholds the church's unity through his word witnessed to by scripture.

Because of their belief in the authority of the Bible, Protestants often claim that the Roman Catholic insistence on traditions which are not clearly based on scripture erects another dividing wall in the church, in defiance of our passage. Roman Catholics, on the other hand, sometimes say that the Protestants do not take the unity of the church seriously enough, and put personal considerations above it.

Roman Catholic interpretation of our passage, however, is far less polemic than that of the Protestants. Nor do Catholics use Eph 2:11—22 to launch a direct appeal to the Protestants to return to the unity of the Roman Catholic Church. We might have expected that Catholic interpreters would have borrowed from Augustine's use of Eph 2:11—22 during the Donatist schism. It may be a sign of the different nature of the Reformation controversy that they do not. Whereas the Donatist controversy involved primarily the question of the order and discipline of the church, the Reformation involves primarily the question of the nature of the gospel itself.

For the commentators of the Reformation period, the hostility between Jews and Gentiles (v. 14) had a double aspect. In one aspect it arose from a difference of conviction about religious law: therefore some commentators draw parallels to the hostility between Roman Catholics and Protestants. In the other aspect the hostility between Jews and Gentiles was based on difference in physical descent; in this sense, on racial difference. Consequently some commentators draw parallels to the national and racial hostilities of their times: since the church began with the uniting of two hostile peoples, it is a denial of the unity of the church to accept national and racial discrimination in the church at any time. Thus Erasmus speaks of wars between nations as a denial of the unity symbolized by Christ as the Cornerstone. Specific condemnations of discrimination within the church on the basis of race or nationality are made by Rollock, Musculus, Gwalther, and especially Salmeron.

Commentators who give attention to the contemporary unity of the church particularly with regard to racial and national differences invariably understand the dividing wall as the ceremonial law and tend to emphasize the continuity of the church with Israel. One Protestant and one Roman Catholic speak about the relationship of contemporary Jewish and Gentile Christians: Bucer joyfully acknowledges the presence of some Jewish Christians in the church of his day, and Salmeron records that Jewish Christians are sometimes discriminated against, which he brands as flagrant violation of our passage. From the comments of these two theologians and others we can draw several inferences about Christian attitudes toward the Jews at that time. The interpreters of Eph 2:11—22 saw very clearly that any polemic against the Jews must be only against their beliefs, not against their race. When a Jew became converted, he was to be fully accepted. But there were members of the church, and even established policies in some areas of the church, which discriminated against Jews after they had become Christians. This was clearly racial discrimination.

Although no commentator in this period reflects about the possible implications of Eph 2:11—22 for the contemporary relation of church and synagogue, Calvin rejects the idea that the ceremonial law, although abrogated for the church, is still in effect for the Jews. He does so on the grounds that the dividing wall between all Jews and Gentiles is broken down.

Especially Protestant commentators emphasize pride as the chief element of the hostility between Jews and Gentiles in New Testament times. The group which sees the dividing wall as the entire law stresses moral pride, the group which sees the wall as the ceremonial law stresses racial pride. Both groups proclaim that God's grace alone is able to take away pride and thus make unity possible. More than anywhere else, this idea is developed in Calvin's sermons on our passage. Protestants tend to give more attention than Roman Catholics to the motivation for overcoming hostilities and accepting fellow Christians of whatever background, since according to Protestants the unity given by Christ is to be realized by fellowship, discussion and common understanding rather than by a church structure with apostolic authority. Although both Protestants and Roman Catholics agree that the church is one, they disagree about the way unity is realized in practice.

About the relevance of Eph 2:11—22 for the unity of all mankind, little is said directly. Insofar as he holds that the dividing wall between all Jews and Gentiles is broken down, Calvin believes that a certain unity has been accomplished for all men. Musculus begins by limiting Christ's peace to the church, but his later comments have a more universal thrust. The only clear statement is that of Melanchthon, who says that because of the broken wall Jesus' command to love our enemies refers to our relations with people of other races and nations.

Chapter V

THE SEVENTEENTH CENTURY

In the seventeenth century the interpretation of Eph 2:11—22 is not so often related to the events of the times as it was in the previous century. Sixteenth century commentaries reflect, and sometimes make explicit, a tension between two loyalties: loyalty to the church's unity and loyalty to the truth of the gospel. In the seventeenth century, however, the respective doctrinal positions of Catholic, Lutheran and Reformed have been hammered out, and people tend to think in terms of three churches rather than of one church. This does not mean that men have forgotten the unity of the church, but they think in terms of a unity which has been lost and must now be regained. A few outstanding men devote much thought and energy to the quest for unity[1]. Several of them write commentaries on Ephesians, but these commentaries say little directly about the contemporary unity of the church. Rather, precisely because they want to emphasize what all Christians have in common, they tend to minimize the amount of doctrinal reflection—even about the doctrine of the unity of the church.

Most orthodox Protestant commentators work within the horizon of their doctrinal positions and are not primarily concerned about the unity of the church; consequently they say little about it in their interpretation of Eph 2:11—22. For Roman Catholic commentators it is the tendency to rely on the tradition of the centuries which keeps them from discussing contemporary problems of unity. Of Roman Catholic commentaries those of the Dutch scholar Willem Estius and the Flemish Jesuit Cornelius a Lapide are probably the best representatives on our passage. Like the sixteenth century Roman Catholic commentators, they differ from the Protestants in their greater reliance upon the medieval tradition, above all Thomas Aquinas, and specifically in their interpretation of the "foundation of apostles and prophets".

---

[1] The Lutheran scholar George Calixtus is an important proponent of church unity, but does not contribute anything new in his comments on Eph 2:11—22 (In ep. Pauli ad Eph., Braunschweig 1653, 23—30).

Willem Estius (1542—1613)

Of the two, Estius[2] is closer to the Protestants. He does repeat the traditional Catholic idea on v. 20 that Christ is the primary foundation, the apostles and prophets the secondary foundation. But he makes a clear distinction between the function of apostles and prophets, and that of later church leaders when he says, "even if through other prelates and doctors the faith can and must be explained, it cannot be increased or changed." Estius's way of arguing that the "prophets" of v. 20 cannot be those of the early church is worth noting. According to I Cor 14:26—33 what contemporary prophets say must be weighed and judged; this is not true of the Old Testament prophets, who are authorities by whom later prophecies must be judged. In this interpretation Estius supports the position that all teaching in the church must be subordinate to scripture.

On v. 21 Estius comments that the church is constructed and grows by love. He then poses the question whether those who do not love do not belong to the church. His answer suggests that he does not simply equate "the whole building" with the organizational church: "'Whole' does not include all those who are in any way members of the church, but only those who fully participate in the language of members in this way: that they respond to their name and profession." According to Estius this response involves a serious attempt to follow the teaching of Jesus, especially his command to love one another.

Cornelius a Lapide (1567—1637)

Cornlius a Lapide[3] is more typically Roman Catholic than Estius in that he draws support for the view that Peter is the foundation stone of the church from "the foundation of apostles and prophets". After a review of the various types of interpretation of the dividing wall given by commentators through the centuries, a Lapide concurs with Erasmus that the wall is the mutual contempt between Jews and Gentiles. According to a Lapide, Gentiles hated Jews "as the other birds hate and persecute the owl".

---

[2] Comm. in omnes D. Pauli et cath. epp., Biblia Maxima, Paris 1660, XVI, 118—125.

[3] Epp. D. Pauli, Antwerp 1614, 604—609.

Hugo Grotius (1583—1645)

An important figure who saw himself as a kind of mediator be-tweeen Roman Catholics and Protestants was the Dutch jurist and theologian Hugo Grotius. Although Grotius lived among Roman Catholics for some time and was increasingly influenced by them, as his interpretation of Eph 2:20 indicates, he never officially left the Reformed Church. Because one of his chief goals was the uni-fication of the church, Grotius wanted his commentary to contain only material which all Christians could accept. Therefore he inclu-des a great deal of philological material and a minimum of theolog-ical discussion. Grotius's commentary holds a unique place in the history of interpretation because its philological contributions in-fluence subsequent exegesis and because it is a forerunner of ration-alist commentaries.

In his interpretation of Eph 2:11—22[4], Grotius minimizes theo-logical discussion by avoiding as far as possible the theme of re-conciliation between men and God. Even the statement, "He has reconciled both in one body to God" (v. 16), Grotius interprets to mean that Christ has reconciled Jews and Gentiles among them-selves "so that they may serve God". Grotius' idea of the unity between Jew and Gentile is predominantly that of equality before the law. Whereas the law of Israel contained a "dividing wall" which prevented Gentiles "not only from gaining honors, but even from being citizens, ... now the pact which Christ has brought makes you equal to the Jews".

Grotius denies that the covenants made with Abraham, Isaac, Jacob and Moses have any relevance for the Gentiles. As evidence for this view he offers Ps 147:20: "He has not dealt thus with any other nation; they do not know his ordinances." Grotius does not dispense with the Old Testament, but as here often uses it to inter-pret the New Testament[5]. In connection with "He is our peace" (v. 14), Grotius calls attention to Mic 5:4, telling of "one who shall be ruler in Israel" and of a time when "the rest of his brethren shall return to the people of Israel ... for he shall be great to the ends of the earth, and this shall be peace". Yet in his view the Old Testa-ment only foretells the church; he would never say that the church is already present in the Old Testament because the church does not appear until Christ brings its constitution.

---

[4] Opera omnia theologica, Amsterdam 1679, II, 2, 889—891.

[5] Like Augustine, see above p. 50, Grotius holds that Ezek 37:17 in its allegorical sense is fulfilled by Eph 2:14, "who has made both one". This is also found in Estius, Comm., 120.

Grotius' conviction that the church is united by Christ's doctrines seems to determine his interpretation of the breaking down of the dividing wall. According to Grotius, Christ broke the wall by his doctrines; that is, through the apostles he taught that the ceremonial laws were no longer obligatory. Here Grotius reverts to the way in which all the pre-Reformation commentators except Abelard construed the phrase ἐν δόγμασιν. As justification for his decision Grotius says that the Syriac version supports this construction. He further explains that "δόγματα is a Greek word which frequently denotes doctrines of philosophy. Paul uses this word here in writing to men acquainted with the writings of philosophers. Thus the Greek fathers often called Christian doctrine by the name δόγματα"[6]. For Grotius, Christian doctrine is not doctrine about Christ, but the doctrine which Christ himself taught. Thus the phrases "in his flesh" (v. 15) and "through the cross" (v. 16) are not related to the doctrines of Incarnation and Reconciliation, but simply mean that Christ's doctrines were so important that he was willing to die for them; as such they should be highly valued by Christians.

Grotius explains that the church is called "a new man" because "it does not use those old laws, but the new ones" which Christ taught. The church is a new body in the sense that an association or guild in ancient Rome was called a body. The members might not be together in one place, but they still form a body since they are organized by law. So the church can also be called a republic because it is "an association, not of areas, but of laws"[7]. Since laws, in Grotius' view, are the basis of the church's unity, Christ can be said to be the maker of unity, but he is not the unity itself. Thus "He is our peace" means "Christ is the cause of concord between converts out of Jews and Gentiles". Grotius consistently renders "in Christ" and similar phrases by "through Christ". For although Christ is the means by which it comes, unity depends ultimately on the principles implied in and derived from Christ's doctrine, which Grotius calls laws. Grotius presupposes a natural law with which Christ's laws are in agreement. One of these laws

---

[6] Grotius may give this elaborate explanation because he departs at this point from the philological conclusions of Erasmus, see above p. 66, whom he much admired.

[7] "non locorum, sed legum consortio". Grotius may intend more than one meaning. The word "locus", aside from its literal meaning "place" or "area", was used in theology to mean a subject of doctrine. Since Grotius strove for organizational rather than confessional unity, he may be saying here that theology is not the basis of the church's structure, but rather legal structure.

is that every person has equal opportunity to gain honors in the church. This principle is crucial for Grotius because he holds that the church's unity depends on its legal structure, and that this must be a hierarchical structure: "In a structure some stones are closer to the foundation, others more remote, and there are many grades. In a body there is the head, there are arteries, veins, muscles, nerves. So in the church there are and must always be grades through which the Spirit of God flows even to the lowliest part."

Prior to Grotius, commentators have differed as to whether "in one body" (v. 16) refers to the earthly body of Christ or to the church. But they all recognize that the church's existence and the crucifixion are inseparable. Grotius, however, goes a long way toward dissolving the relationship between the two when he considers the body of Christ as simply one human organization among others. Grotius thereby does not see the unique nature of the church implied in its being the body of Christ: it does not, like purely human associations, owe its existence and unity to the agreements men make with one another but is gathered by Christ and united by him. In this context it is significant that Grotius does not speak of Christ the Cornerstone as uniting the two peoples in himself. Undoubtedly he does not because he believes men become part of the church by accepting a legal pact. This pact, guaranteeing equal rights to all, Grotius sees as the basis of harmony. But he overlooks the fact that equality, though important, is not the same as reconciliation, nor is structural unity the same as actual fellowship. Grotius underestimates the depth of the hostility among men, which is not basically overcome only by a just legal structure. Equal opportunity to "rise through all the grades of honor" can itself be an invitation for men of similar background or opinion to form alliances in order to gain positions of honor and keep others from them.

Ironically, Grotius' commentary, in its attempt to help the cause of unity by avoiding controversial theological issues, itself provokes theological controversy. Orthodox commentators such as Cocceius even claim that Grotius takes ideas from the Socinians, whom orthodox theologians violently opposed because of their rejection of the doctrine of the Trinity. Although Grotius was too original to depend on the Socinians for his material, his interpretation does have some similarities to theirs. The Socinian Joannis Crell[8], for example, has the same interpretation of the phrase,

---

[8] Opera omnia exegetica, Bibliotheca fratrum Polonorum, Amsterdam 1656, I, 479—480.

"that he might reconcile both in one body to God": it means that Christ unites Jews and Gentiles "so that they may serve God". Another similarity to Grotius' interpretation is the important position Crell gives to natural law as contrasted to the will of God. This is particularly apparent in his comment on the abrogation of the law (v. 15). He says that the part of the law which is abrogated consists of precepts drawn "not out of nature itself" but "from the free will of the Legistor". Another Socinian, Jonah Schlichting[9], asserts that these precepts "do not have a foundation in natural honesty and justice". Like Grotius, Schlichting interprets the phrase "through the cross" (v. 16) to mean simply that Christ's death is a sign. However, it is a sign of God's love, rather than of Christ's teachings, as Grotius has it.—In the ideas of the Socinians and Grotius are some of the early signs of the Enlightenment.

Abraham Calov (1612—1686)

Because he believed that these ideas were all the more dangerous in a scholar of such repute as Grotius, the orthodox Lutheran theologian Abraham Calov[10] combats them by reproducing Grotius' comments on each verse in small print before giving his own. He indicates his polemic purpose in the subtitle of his book, announcing that "the Grotian depravation and false interpretations are placed under just examination and exploded".

Calov's chief objection to Grotius' interpretation is that it omits the reconciliation of men to God, which Calov holds to be the absolute prerequisite for reconciliation between Jews and Gentiles. He accuses Grotius of willfully altering the clear sense of v. 16 which speaks not of the reconciliation of Jews to Gentiles, but of the reconciliation of both to God. Calov insists that the hostility between Jews and Gentiles can only be overcome when the hostility between men and God is overcome.

The hostility ... here (v. 16) is not the hostility between Jews and Gentiles, but ... between both of them on the one hand and God on the other. For the extinction of that primordial hostility was necessary in order that true peace be established among men, since its foundation is union with God. Those who are united to him can also experience solid peace among themselves. For there is no solid peace except in God.

---

[9] Comm. posthuma, Bibliotheca fratrum Polonorum, Amsterdam 1656, II, 155—156.

[10] Biblia Nov. Test. illustr., Dresden and Leipzig, 1719, II, 687—685. First published 1672.

Calov therefore maintains that both the vertical and horizontal dimensions of peace are implied in the words "He is our peace": "There cannot be true and solid peace among men, much less among peoples separated, unless Christ be our peace. We had to come together in God; therefore we first had to be reconciled to God through Christ the Mediator."

Although Calov agrees with Grotius that the dividing wall is the ceremonial law which separates Jews and Gentiles, he does not agree that Christ's doctrines are the means by which the ceremonial law is abrogated. Rather, it is taken away "in his flesh" (v. 15), that is, by his death which fulfills what the ceremonies typified. Calov charges that by making Christ's doctrines the means for abolishing the ceremonial law Grotius not only fails to understand that Christ himself is the mediator between Jew and Gentile, but he makes Christ into a new lawgiver: "'Grace and truth have come' through him, not law, that 'was given through Moses' (John 1:17) ... The new man is new not because of new laws, since new laws do not make or constitute the new man, but because of the renewal of the Spirit."

Frederick Balduinus (1520—1573)

Another Lutheran commentator, Frederick Balduinus[11], relates the passage to a practical theological question: if the wall is broken down, "then does it not follow that all men have equal access to the church?" Balduinus explains that he raises this question "because of those who think that Jews and Turks should be admitted to our churches, and their children, without distinction, be snatched for baptism, since there is no longer any distinction between Jews and Gentiles in Christ." The policy which Balduinus refers to is one often practiced by the church until it was discouraged by the influence of the Enlightenment. Disturbed by the presence of Jews and Moslems within the bounds of Christendom, the church tried to baptize them. It used many measures, often involving various kinds of force, including taking Jewish children away from their parents[12]. Balduinus staunchly opposes this policy. He argues that although there is no longer a distinction between Jews and Gentiles, "there is a distinction between those who are born in the church and those who are outside". He explains that unbelievers are not simply excluded; they can come into the church when they are

---

[11] Comm. in epp. Pauli, Frankfurt a. M. 1691, 884—891.
[12] See R. Pfisterer, Im Schatten des Kreuzes, Hamburg 1966, VI.

called by God. Balduinus' list of ways in which God calls people
expresses in rather interesting fashion the prevailing attitude toward church membership in Protestant Orthodoxy. God calls not
in mysterious ways, but in ways revealed in the Bible: by reading
of scripture, by slavery, by captivity as a result of wars, by miracles, and by all other circumstances in which Christians have responsibility for unbelievers.—Thus, in contrast to Grotius, Balduinus warns against the consequences of over-emphasizing the church
as a human institution rather than as those chosen by God. But it
is noteworthy that he accepts uncritically as "biblical" the human
institutions of slavery and captivity as a result of war, whereas
voices have been raised against war and will soon be raised against
slavery on the basis of Eph 2:11—22.

Ludwig Cappellus (1585—1658)

While Calov and Balduinus devote most of their attention to
questions of dogmatic and practical theology, the Reformed commentator Ludwig Cappellus[13] investigates the source of the figure
of the dividing wall as the way to understand the original meaning
of the passage. Cappellus finds that the "dividing wall" (v. 14) is
an allusion to the walls in the Jerusalem temple which separated
the Gentiles from the Jews and both from the Holy of Holies[14].
He acknowledges that other commentators believe "the metaphor
is taken from the dividing wall which customarily separates and
distinguishes connected houses and keeps apart the families living
in them"[15]. But Cappellus holds that the double wall of the temple
gives the key to the entire passage: the Apostle Paul is contrasting
the Jerusalem temple with the temple "not made with hands" in
which Jew and Gentile are united and in which all may have access

---

[13] Critici Sacri, Frankfurt a. M. 1695, ²V, 590—591.

[14] The sixteenth century commentator Salmeron suggested among other
possibilities that the figure of the dividing wall may be taken from the construction of the Jerusalem temple (Disput. in epp. D. Pauli, III, 202). According
to W. Schmidt (Brief an die Epheser, KEK, Göttingen 1875⁵, 122) Anselm
held this view, but I have not been able to find it earlier than Salmeron, with the
exception of Gnostica, see above p. 8. To my knowledge, Capellus is the first to
cite extra-biblical sources about the temple wall and the first to see it as the key
to the passage; many subsequent commentaries agree.

[15] This view is frequent from Erasmus onward, see above, p. 66. Earlier
writers located the metaphor in the Old Testament, either in the story of
Tamar interpreted allegorically, or in the idea of the law as a protective hedge
around Israel, or in the idea of sin as a wall between man and God. Chrysostom discusses all three of these views, and decides for the last, see above
p. 32.

to the Father. Citing Josephus, Cappellus gives full details of two walls within the temple, one separating Jews from Gentiles, the other separating both from the Holy of Holies. According to Cappellus, both these walls symbolize the ceremonial law. The ceremonial law is called "hostility" for the following reasons: the observance of the ceremonial laws was very difficult; the laws were reminders of God's hatred of man's sinfulness; hostility between Jew and Gentile arose because of them.

Johannes Cocceius (1603—1669)

Like Cappellus, the Reformed theologian Johannes Cocceius[16], father of "Covenantal Theology", says that the metaphor of the wall alludes to the temple in Jerusalem and stands for separation both between God and men and between Jews and Gentiles. But for Cocceius the veil of the temple rather than its walls provides the key to the passage. The veil enables Cocceius to interpret Eph 2:14—16 by Heb 10:20, which speaks of the new way Christ "opened for us through the veil, that is his flesh". The breaking of the wall is the breaking of Christ's flesh, since that is where the separating hostility was located.—But what was the hostility and why can it be said to have been in the flesh of Christ? Cocceius goes to great lengths, with much discussion of other scripture passages, to answer these questions.

The hostility was a double one. Primarily it was God's hostility toward sinful man[17]. This is what Eph 2:3 means when it says we were all "children of wrath". Consequently God allowed men access to himself only on the condition that a future event would make amends for their sins. The sign that this reconciling event had not yet taken place was the ceremonial law. The second part of the hostility consisted in God's decision "to exercise severity toward the Gentiles" and therefore not to tell them of the future reconciling event, but to let them continue in their sinful ways.

In explaining what it means that the hostility was in Christ's

---

[16] Exerc. de princ. ep. ad Eph., Opera omnia, Amsterdam 1673, IV, 56—100.

[17] Cocceius says the hostility arose because man broke the original law, of whose precepts Gal 3:12 says, "He who does them shall live by them." In his systematic works Cocceius says this law was that of a "covenant of works" God made before the Fall with Adam. (See G. Schrenk, Gottesreich und Bund im älteren Protestantismus, vornehmlich bei Johannes Cocceius, Gütersloh 1923, 85 ff.). The fact that Cocceius does not mention the covenant of works in his interpretation of our passage even though it might have helped him expound "hostility" suggests that his exegesis is more biblical and less dominated by his theological system than is sometimes supposed.

flesh, Cocceius says that Isa 53:6 tells of God's charging to Christ "the sins of us all" and that in Ps 40 Christ "calls our sins his". For Cocceius these passages mean that already in Old Testament times Christ stood in our place as the object of God's hostility against sin[18]. Yet the actual execution of the penalty for sin and thus the ending of the hostility had to wait until Christ came in the flesh and was crucified. In this sense Cocceius says the hostility was in the flesh of Christ: it was charged against the flesh of Christ.

Until Christ paid the debt by his death, the presence of the hostility was expressed in two ways: the disinheritance of the Gentiles, and the ceremonial law of Israel. The ceremonial law was necessary because satisfaction had not yet been made for sin, as well as because the people of Israel were still to a large extent childish and in need of strict discipline. The ceremonial law served to foretell the future reconciliation, to show that guilt was not yet absolved, and to hold the people of Israel together until Christ's appearance. When Christ died, he made the ceremonial law superfluous, for he absolved the guilt which the ceremonies expressed; his people are held together not by laws but by whole-hearted acceptance and praise of him.

Cocceius' unique interpretation of the dividing wall as the hostility in the flesh of Christ expresses both the eternal background and the historical unfolding of salvation. It reflects Cocceius' theology of redemptive history. This theology represents a departure from the scholastic methods of Protestant orthodoxy. It makes possible some of the emphases which will later be found in Pietism: the usefulness of the Bible as a whole and not just certain passages; the importance of God's plan of salvation, and thus, the place of eschatology as a living hope for the future and a spur to evangelistic activity.

As applied in his interpretation of our passage, Cocceius' theology of redemptive history presents a coherent picture of God's active relationship with men, but does not have much room for the relationships of men to one another. Despite his statement that the separation between Jews and Gentiles was one aspect of a two-fold hostility, Cocceius' exposition really emphasizes instead the hostil-

---

[18] In his systematic works Cocceius speaks of a pact between the Father and the Son made before all time in which the Son promises to be obedient to death as the punishment for sin and the Father promises in return to give him those who are to be saved; this is the eternal background of the covenant of grace (see Schrenk, 91 ff). Again Cocceius does not introduce material from his theological system into his exegesis, but refers to other biblical passages instead.

ity between God and the Gentiles. He speaks of "the hostility which was between God and the Gentiles, on account of which the Gentiles were alienated from God and from his people". As the alienation of Gentiles from God's people appears here only as a by-product of the alienation from God, so the reconciliation of which Eph 2:11—22 speaks is for Cocceius primarily between man and God. Reconciliation between Jews and Gentiles is only a minor concomitant.

Paul Bayne (d. 1617)

Anglo-Saxon writers in the seventeenth century refer more frequently than those on the continent to contemporary problems of disunity. The commentary of Paul Bayne[19], for example, is in continual dialog with the first century and the seventeenth. A Scottish Puritan, Bayne insists that unity demands the acceptance of Christ as head. "The papists therefore, the Jew and the Turk, not holding Christ the head, cannot be one with us." Bayne warns that the unity of the church with Israel does not include contemporary Jews: "Therefore we are one, not that the Jews and we now go hand in hand, but that the ancient church and we do conspire."

Bayne highlights the call to unity which Eph 2:11—22 gives to the church of his day: "Mark, first, how highly the peace of the church is to be rated. God letteth all his own institutions be repealed, that this may be procured. It is plain, from the argument in the text, that the union of the faithful is highly rated with him." If God's institutions can be repealed for his purposes, how much more readily should we be prepared to repeal human institutions.

Samuel Sewall (1652—1730)

At the end of the seventeenth century, more than fifty years after Bayne's commentary was published, the reading of it stimulated a Massachusetts judge, Samuel Sewall, to challenge the human institution of slavery. In one of the earliest anti-slavery pamphlets in America, *The Selling of Joseph*[20], Sewall cites Eph 2:14 as grounds for his position. Since Christ has broken down the wall

---

[19] An Entire Commentary upon the Whole Epistle of St. Paul to the Ephesians, Edinburgh 1866, 150—163. First published posthumously in 1643.

[20] Reprinted in American Issues, ed. W. Thorpe et al., Chicago 1944, I, 66—67. The connection of Bayne's commentary with The Selling of Joseph is documented by D. B. Davis, The Problem of Slavery in Western Culture, Ithaca, N. Y. 1966, 341—345.

between Israel and the nations, Christians are to act toward all nations as the Israelites were commanded to act toward Israelites[21]. Israelites were not allowed to keep other Israelites permanently as slaves. "Since the partition wall is broken down", says Sewall, "inordinate self-love should likewise be demolished." By self-love Sewall means love of one's own people, not individual self-love. Today instead of "inordinate self-love" we would say "racial pride" or "ethnocentrism".

GOD expects that Christians should be of a more Ingenuous and benign frame of spirit. Christians should carry it to all the World, as the Israelites were to carry it towards one another. And for men obstinately to persist in holding their Neighbors and Brethren under the Rigor of perpetual Bondage, seems to be no proper way of gaining Assurance that God has given them Spiritual Freedom. Our blessed Saviour has altered the Measures of the ancient Love-Song, and set it to a most excellent New Tune, which all ought to be ambitious of Learning. Matt 5. 43,44. John 13. 34. These Ethiopians, as black as they are: seeing they are the Sons and Daughters of the First *Adam*, the Brethren and Sisters of the Last *Adam*, and the offspring of GOD, They ought to be treated with a Respect agreeable.

Robert Boyd (1578–1627)

While people of European background felt the difference between themselves and people of Africa very keenly, Robert Boyd's commentary[22] maintains that the difference between Jews and Gentiles was greater than that between any other peoples. It was easier to distinguish a Gentile from a Jew in the ancient world, says Boyd, than "it is for us to distinguish the most diverse peoples, whether by difference of facial characteristics, dress, manners or languages". If Christ could unite peoples so different as Jews and Gentiles, then he is able to be the source of the church's unity today.

Christ himself, like a cornerstone, was abundantly sufficient for the binding and uniting of the parts of his church among themselves, though they were extremely diverse in manners, education, language, laws, and whole way of life. Such was the condition of the Jews and Gentiles whom Christ joined very aptly and firmly into this one building.

For Boyd, the most serious differences of his time were religious. Nothing causes "greater hostilities or moves peoples more to wound

---

[21] This argument is essentially the same as that of Melanchthon, see above p. 81.

[22] In ep. Pauli ad Eph., London 1652, 290–342.

and tear apart, not only different peoples, but even fellow tribes-
men, fellow citizens, blood relatives, than diversity of religion and
divine worship".

So Boyd is moved by the passage to look for a deeper unity,
based not on man's religions but on God's working: "Hence our
spirits are brought and formed to mercy and patience toward
others that we may have mercy on them and tolerate with gentle-
ness and patience of spirit those who till now live in error and
misery, who till now wallow in the same filth from which the kind
hand of God has drawn us." Earlier commentators often say that
we should be moved to thankfulness by remembering that we have
been brought from the miserable condition described in v. 12. Boyd
goes beyond them to say that this thankfulness should issue in
patience with others.

In the same vein is Boyd's assertion that the only proper response to Christ's making peace between men and God and between
Jew and Gentile is for us to be peaceful toward all men, so far as
it is possible, and to practice genuine peace with our brothers to
whom we are bound in the same faith. Since we are united into one
new man (v. 16), says Boyd, our bond with one another is stronger
than any external differences. We have as it were a new fatherland,
new parents, new relatives.

Boyd is anxious that the "new man" (v. 15) be understood in
such a way as not to endanger the important truth of the church's
continuity with Israel. The new man is not a Jew insofar as he is
not bound by the law of Moses. This was the truth Paul had to
struggle for against the Judaizers. On the other hand the Gentiles
can be said to be joined to the Jews insofar as "the church of God
and its covenant, promises, worship, and word" belonged only to
the Jews.

Thomas Goodwin (1600—1679)

In a thorough, scholarly expository sermon on Eph 2:14—16[23]
Thomas Goodwin, like Boyd, expresses his faith that Christ can
make peace among the churches as he made peace between Jews
and Gentiles. Goodwin acknowledges that the hostilities between
various parties within the church of his time are so strong that no
resolution of them seems humanly possible. But he quotes extensively from biblical and classical sources to show that the hostility

---

[23] An Exposition on ... part of ... the Epistle to the Ephesians, London
1681, Appendix 1—28.

between Jew and Gentile was stronger still. Since the very founding
of the church involved Christ's overcoming this hostility, the unity
of the church is a given reality and is not dependent on human
achievement. It is part of the gospel itself. On this ground Goodwin
rests his hope for the realization of unity.

According to Goodwin, reconciliation among the people of God
is the primary theme of the passage. This is not to minimize the
importance of reconciliation with God, for the Apostle Paul deals
with that in many other places. And even though the passage focuses upon reconciliation between Jews and Gentiles, it shows that
this cannot be separated from reconciliation with God. For both
reconciliations were accomplished by one and the same act. The recognition of this fact keeps us from understanding the passage as
making reconciliation with God dependent on reconciliation among
men, even though the syntax of vv. 14—16 seems to suggest this,
insofar as Christ is said to end the hostility among men (v. 15)
"*in order that* he might reconcile them ... to God". (v. 16)[24]
Goodwin argues that Paul does not intend in v. 16 to state a consequence of v. 15, but rather begins here to speak of Christ's deed
under a different aspect, that of reconciliation with God. Thus v.
16 is parallel to, not subordinate to, vv. 14 and 15. That is the
reason why the same or apparently equivalent words and phrases
are repeated: "hostility" in vv. 14 and 16; "in his flesh" in v. 15
and "in himself" in v. 16.

In his treatment of the reconciliation of God's people, Goodwin
makes a distinction between two senses of reconciliation. The first
is the reconciliation made by Christ on the cross; the second is the
working out of the reconciliation in the life of the church, which
waits to be completed. This distinction is important for Goodwin,
since it enables him to proclaim the reconciliation of God's people
as already made in Christ, despite the difficult breaches within
God's people at the present time. The distinction is based not on
dogmatic considerations alone, but on an analysis of the text. The
tense of the participles ποιήσας and λύσας indicates accomplished
fact: Christ *has* made both one; he *has* broken down the wall. On
the other hand, the verb κτίσῃ is subjunctive in a purpose clause:
"that he might create the two in him into one new man." The tenses
of the verbs therefore clearly require two aspects of reconciliation:
"the first antecedent and already done; the other consequent, and to

---

[24] This may have disturbed copyists of the text of Ephesians, for instead of
the subjunctive, ἀποκαταλλάξῃ, "that he might reconcile", some manuscripts
begin v. 16 with the indicative, ἀπεκατάλλαξει, "he reconciled". (So K, L, P
and others, according to Tischendorf, II, 674.)

be accomplished; the latter distinguished from the former as the consequent or effect from its cause."

Goodwin illustrates this distinction by the parallel distinction within the reconciliation between God and man. Here too the reconciliation is in one sense already accomplished by Christ on the cross, yet in another sense remains to be worked out in each person. Therefore Paul can say, "God was in Christ reconciling the world to himself" (II Cor 5:19), yet add in the next verse, "We beseech you to be reconciled to God."

In describing how the reconciliation of Jew and Gentile was accomplished on the cross, Goodwin says that Christ ended the mutual hostilities of Jews and Gentiles by taking them upon himself. Christ thereby took a place analogous to that of the sacrifice customarily offered at the making of a covenant between two groups of men, as in Jer 34:18. This is why Christ is called "the covenant of the people" in Isa 42:6 and 49:8. In connection with the covenant sacrifice, Goodwin also cites biblical occurrences of eating and drinking together, especially after a covenant sacrifice, as further confirmation of reconciliation: Laban and Jacob (Gen 31:44), Isaac and Abimelech (Gen 26:28), David and Abner (II Sam 3:20). He also refers to accounts of the practice among other peoples. Finally he points out the parallel of the covenant meal to the Lord's Supper, and its consequent significance for the reconciliation of Christ's people. At the Lord's Supper, which is "to show forth his death", Christ's people are to be together as one. It is a terrible irony, says Goodwin, that the Communion, intended to express and confirm unity, should become a focal point for disunity because of disagreements about its nature.

Henry Hammond (1605–1660)

The covenant sacrifice as the background for Christ's reconciliation of Jews and Gentiles is also put forward by Henry Hammond[25]. He introduces this idea in his comment on v. 13, "You . . . have been brought near in the blood of Christ." Unlike most commentators, who assume that this verse tells of coming near to God, Hammond maintains that it refers to reconciliation with the Jews. Reconciliation with the Jews takes such a primary place in Hammond's interpretation that he also considers "saints" in v. 19 to

---

[25] A Paraphrase and Annotations upon the New Testament, London 1689[6], 60–61. In the twentieth century J. A. Robinson finds the covenant idea an important part of the passage's background (Epistle to the Ephesians, London 1928[2], 63).

refer to the Jews. Hammond reasons that the Jews are called saints because they were descendants of the patriarchs. The French scholar John Clericus, who translated Hammond's commentary into Latin, notes his disagreement with this opinion, adding that the Jews are called saints because they are holy to God, not because of any special qualities of their forefathers[26].

Summary

Although the seventeenth century, unlike the Reformation period, does not bring much that is radically new to the interpretation of Eph 2:11—22, there is one new direction which is particularly significant. That is the concept of the unity of the church expressed in Grotius' interpretation. Previous commentators had all assumed that the passage proclaims a unity given in Christ which continues to the present—even though the Reformers differed from the Roman Catholics about the nature of this unity. But Grotius sees unity as something to be achieved by men: their efforts must be based on the principles of Christ, and they must follow his example, but basically the church is a human organization among others. Although this view of the church is particularly characteristic of the Enlightenment, after Grotius it can be found in some commentaries in every period. It is an essentially individualistic view of the church, since it begins from the faith of the individual who then enters into covenant with other believers.

The concept of the covenant plays an important role in other interpretations of Eph. 2:11—22 as well as in Grotius'. But there are important differences in the way the covenant is understood. For Grotius, covenants are agreements which depend for their validity on their acceptance by the parties concerned. Therefore the unity of the church exists only when men make a covenant with one another. By contrast, Cocceius sees covenants as instituted by God and maintained by him regardless of men's response, because God's various covenants are the stages of the plan by which he redeems men. In Cocceius' view, covenants are almost entirely concerned with the reconciliation of men to God, rather than with the reconciliation of men to one another. An intermediate position between Grotius and Cocceius is that of Goodwin. For him, Christ is the covenant given by God between Jews and Gentiles. Of the

---

[26] Nov. Test. c. paraphr. et adnotat. H. Hammondi, Amsterdam 1698, II, 192.

three, Goodwin's view seems most nearly in accord with the sense of the passage.

In contrast to Grotius, Goodwin affirms that the unity of the church is given by God. But Goodwin takes very seriously the fact that in his time this unity is not expressed by Christians. Unlike Protestant commentators of the sixteenth century, he does not lay the blame on the Roman Catholic Church for erecting a new dividing wall; he recognizes that the problem is more difficult. But he also believes that Christ will bring the church to visible unity, for according to Goodwin's interpretation, Eph 2:11—22 speaks explicitly of a unity which is already given but whose fulfillment will be given in the future. While the beginnings of this interpretation can be seen in sixteenth century commentators, it is first stated explicitly in the seventeenth century.

The conviction that visible unity is a goal toward which God is working is expressed by Paul Bayne when he says that according to Eph 2:14 God overthrows his own institutions in order to gain the unity of the church. Bayne thus suggests the revolutionary element of the passage. It may have been this element in Bayne's commentary that helped Samuel Sewall to make the move, revolutionary in its time, of opposing the institution of slavery, which common opinion held to be divinely ordained.

Literary and historical criticism begins to assume a more important role in the seventeenth century interpretation of Eph 2:11—22. The investigation of the sources of the image of the wall (2:14) as a key to the meaning of the passage is the chief concern of Cappellus. Erasmus had made some contributions in this area, but he looked to classical sources, whereas Cappellus looks to Jewish sources.

References to Jewish Christians, infrequent in commentaries of the sixteenth century, do not seem to be present at all in seventeenth century commentaries. Perhaps the religious differences among Protestants, not to mention those between Protestants and Catholics, absorbed all the attention of interpreters. Balduinus and Bayne refer to contemporary Jews but only in order to deny that the passage includes them in its scope. The affirmation that Eph 2:11—22 is relevant for the Christian's attitude toward his Jewish neighbor awaits Pietist commentaries of the eighteenth century.

Chapter VI

THE EIGHTEENTH CENTURY

Although orthodoxy, whether of Catholic, Lutheran, or Reformed variety, dominated the interpretation of Eph 2:11–22 in the
seventeenth century, some commentaries of that century contain
evidences of two new movements which characterize the commentaries of the eighteenth century. In the commentary of Cocceius
were some ideas which presage the development of Pietism[1]. And
the commentaries of Grotius and the Socinians expressed viewpoints characteristic of Rationalism[2]. Both these movements challenged the orthodoxy of the institutional church, with its emphasis
on the acceptance of an authoritative system of doctrine[3].

Pietism

The Pietists insist that doctrine means nothing if it makes no difference in the way an individual feels and acts in daily life. Therefore in their commentaries they aim to give help for the daily life
of the individual Christian. This aim largely accounts for two formal characteristics of Pietist commentaries. The first is a tendency
to see the text as a series of statements each of which can be used
to gain rules for faith and life, with a corresponding slackening of
interest in explaining the passage as a whole. The second is the
practice of listing "applications" in a section separate from the
exegesis. Since the connection between application and exegesis is
not explained, it is often not clear how the application was arrived
at.

The method of including a section of "applications" appears in
the treatment of Ephesians by Johann Reinhard Hedinger, one of

---

[1] See above, pp. 105–107.   [2] See above, pp. 99–102.

[3] Although Pietism and Rationalism may be distinguished from each other
as movements and therefore serve as divisions for the following discussion, in
the case of individual interpreters the lines are often less clear.

the forerunners of Pietism[4]. Hedinger applies the statement of
Eph 2:12 about the hopeless condition of the Gentiles to contem-
porary Christians: "What can be more miserable than life without
God! Is it the heathen only whose souls are not saved? No! also the
Christians who live like heathen."

Philipp Jakob Spener (1635—1705)

The inclusion of lax Christians in the hopeless condition of the
Gentiles described in Eph 2:11—12 is a characteristic of Pietist
commentaries. It is listed as one of the "rules of life" drawn from
vv. 11—12 by the Lutheran Philipp Jakob Spener[5], who gave decisive impulse and form to the Pietist movement and has therefore
been called "the father of Pietism".

Such people as serve Satan, the world, and the flesh are also in this
condition without Christ, whose true faith they do not have. They are
outside the fellowship of the true invisible church, and strangers to the
covenants, even though they claim them for themselves. For they have in
practice rejected the covenant of God.

Spener holds that simply to be a member of the institutional
church is to be in a position comparable to that of the Jews. They
belonged to the visible people of God and had the sacrament of
circumcision. But these gifts, though good, were not enough for
salvation; salvation depended on their personal decision for Christ.
In the same way, Christians do not gain salvation only because they
have the Word and sacraments, even though these are great gifts.

What is necessary according to Spener is a conversion of heart
and life—a rebirth. On the exhortation to the Gentiles to remember
their former condition (vv. 11—12) Spener specifies attitudes to be
avoided when one remembers his life before conversion. He warns
against secret delight or even pride in the audacity of one's former
sinful life, and on the other hand against depression because of the
gravity of former sins. This illustrates the Pietist shift of emphasis
from earlier commentators, who saw the same verses purely as reason for giving thanks for the grace of God. The Puritan commentator Boyd added that remembering one's lost condition should
motivate patience with other people who are not converted[6]. Spener makes the same point, adding that the converted man is always

---

[4] Die Epistel an die Epheser, in Das Neue Testament... mit Summarien
etc., Bremen 1707[2].

[5] Erklärung der Episteln an die Epheser und Colosser, Halle 1706, 43—55.

[6] See above p. 109.

so close to the lost condition that he should continually examine himself to make sure he has not fallen back into it.

On v. 14 Spener comments, "He is our peace, who has made peace between Jews and Gentiles, and upon whom this peace yet stands." In the context of self-examination and conversion, Spener's comment seems likely to mean individual peace for those in contact with Christ. Yet one of Spener's "rules for life" indicates that his intention may be to speak of Christ as the peace between all Jews and Gentiles, i. e. all men: "We should love one another without distinction of nations, for the Lord has made peace among all men."

Peace among all men, according to Spener, has been made by Christ's abrogation of the law, which means the entire law, moral as well as ceremonial. However, it was particularly the ceremonial law which formed the dividing wall between Jews and Gentiles. Since this wall has been broken down, Spener says, "All distinctions of peoples are abrogated, because Christ abrogated the law. Therefore all laws which make a distinction as regards the grace of God between persons according to their outward condition can no longer be valid." It is important to note that Spener does not qualify or limit his statement that "all distinctions of peoples are abrogated". Christ has brought about a new unity of all mankind, "as regards the grace of God".

But Spener does not mean that all mankind is the "new man" (v. 15). Only those who experience the grace of God in Christ form the "new man" or the church. Thus, there is an inner distinction among men though all outward distinctions are removed. Spener's position might be described as holding that Christ created two levels of unity. The lower level, which includes all men, he formed by breaking down the dividing wall. This lower level is intended as a stepping stone to the higher level, which is the new man, for Christ has "broken the dividing wall ... *in order that* he might create" the new man. The ultimate purpose of the removal of outward distinctions therefore is that each individual may have equal opportunity to experience the grace of God in Christ, and thus participate in the new man. As Spener puts it, there is "no distinction among men and peoples as though some had more right than others to Christ, who has made all equal".

Constitutive for the new man as Spener describes him is that he "no longer is attached to outward regulations but the upright inner being is a new creature". The stress on inner righteousness as opposed to outer law holds first place in Spener's view of the new man: "The people, or the man, in whom the spiritual body of Christ exists must be a new man, and so must not operate with outward commandments . . . The Christian people shall be a new man who has no law except the law of faith and love." It is clear that Spener tends to individualize the passage. His interpretation of "the one new man" emphasizes newness in such a way that oneness is neglected. Spener's attention is drawn so strongly to the removal of earthly distinctions, individual rebirth, and "the inner being" that he gives hardly any consideration to the positive significance of the uniting of Jew and Gentile. For Spener, the reconciliation of Jews and Gentiles, and therefore the reconciliation of hostile groups generally, does not really seem to be an essential aspect of the new man.

Christoph Starke (1684–1744)

The compilation of exegetical material by the Swiss scholar Christoph Starke depends heavily on Spener, although it includes material from many post-Reformation commentators and adds some ideas of his own[7]. One of his "applications" of v. 14 is particularly important:

Let us not hate the Jews, nor seek to restore the hostility which has been taken away. Much rather, in merciful love let us pray for them, and with a holy life make Christianity dear and precious to them.

Here is the first explicit assertion in the history of the exegesis of Eph 2:11–22 that the hostility not only between Jews and Gentiles of New Testament times, and not only between Jewish Christians and Gentile Christians, but between contemporary Jews and Gentiles has been taken away. John Calvin did say explicitly that the wall between all Jews and Gentiles is broken, but he did not go on to base a call for friendship with contemporary Jews on this[8]. Previous commentaries have not considered the question of the implications of our passage for the relation of church and synagogue. Although the language of some would allow the inference that Christ's peace also includes Jews who remain in the synagogue, most commentators indicate that the peace includes only Jewish and Gentile converts to Christianity.

Regrettably, however, Starke does not explain how he arrived at this important affirmation. There is a gap, typical of Pietist commentaries, between the exegetical comments and the applications. Nevertheless, it is noteworthy that the statement has been made.

---

[7] Synop. bibl. exeg. in Nov. Test., Biel 1748[3].   [8] See above p. 87.

The Pietists' stress on experience and attitude as contrasted to doctrine, and their tendency to consider Jews as in a situation comparable to that of church members who have not experienced rebirth, as well as missionary efforts among Jews nourished by renewed eschatological hope—all helped to make possible Starke's affirmation.

Joachim Lange (1670—1744)

Except for isolated affirmations such as Starke's, the general trend in Pietist commentaries on Eph 2:11—22 is toward concentration on the vertical dimension and disregard of the horizontal dimension. This trend is already evident in the commentary of Joachim Lange[9], a younger associate of Spener, who holds that the theme of the passage is peace with God to which the uniting of Jews and Gentiles is only incidental. Lange says that central to the passage is the contrast between "peace" (vv. 14, 15, 17) and "hostility" (vv. 14, 16) and maintains that both always refer primarily to the relation between man and God. Paul links hostility with the ceremonial law because the latter was an expression of hostility, a reminder that God required satisfaction for man's sin. At this point Lange is close to Cocceius, who also put heavy emphasis on this negative aspect of the ceremonial law[10].

Lange's shift of emphasis away from peace between Jews and Gentiles apparently allows him to make a harsh judgment on the Jews: God punished their insistence on the ceremonial law by the destruction of the temple in 70 A.D. This seems to indicate a change in attitude toward the Jews from that of Spener. Spener was irenic in accord with his conviction that "we should love one another without distinction of nations" for according to Eph 2:14 Christ "has made peace between Jews and Gentiles". But for Lange, there is no peace between Jews and Gentiles until the peace which has been made with God "is accepted in the right order of salvation".

Nikolaus von Zinzendorf (1700—1760)

A homily by Zinzendorf on Eph 2:14—15[11] illustrates how strong the tendency is among Pietists to interpret the passage almost

---

[9] Apostolisches Licht und Recht, Halle 1729, 619—624.

[10] See above p. 105.

[11] Hauptschriften, Hildesheim 1963, II, 41—52. This is the fifth of seven homilies which Zinzendorf delivered in Herrnhag in the summer of 1741 before his voyage to America.

exclusively in terms of man's relation to God. "He has made both one" (v. 14) means that "the Savior has made two completely diverse and almost uncombinable things into one: God and man, the Spirit and the flesh." The sermon makes no reference at all to the hostility between Jews and Gentiles, but is concerned entirely with the hostility between the flesh and the Spirit.

Philipp Matthäus Hahn (1739—1790)

In some later eighteenth century Pietist commentaries, the hostility between flesh and spirit tends to be conceived as hostility between the material world and the spiritual world. This appears to be the case with Philipp Matthäus Hahn's interpretation[12]. Like Cocceius[13], Hahn construes v. 14 to read "the hostility in his flesh", and sees this represented by the veil in the temple. But whereas Cocceius works in a context of redemptive history, Hahn works much more with the difference between flesh and spirit[14]. For Hahn "the hostility in his flesh" means that Jesus took upon himself our intractable flesh and had to struggle against it just as we. The flesh is "that part of us which is from the earth, and because of its coarseness is the opposite of the spirit. It is the earthly intractable being, or the animal life, the floor of the spiritual, higher life, which cannot and will not follow the spirit's way and flight". According to Hahn, the resistance of the flesh against the spirit is "hostility" (vv. 14, 16). Such language suggests a simple identification of flesh with the physical world, which is considered if not the source, at least the primary locus of sin.

Although Hahn interprets Eph 2:11—22 almost completely in terms of man's relation to God, he does give some attention to unity among men. The man who believes that Christ has broken the veil of flesh separating him from God and has in himself

the beginning of new life from the Annointed, is by this united again with God and has become close to Him. And he who is in the Annointed and has received of his Spirit is also united in the Spirit with another who has received this Spirit, whether he has been Lutheran, Catholic, Turk, Jew or heathen.

But Hahn understands unity in Christ as a unity of individuals, not of groups. He says practically nothing about Christ's making

---

[12] Erbauungs-Stunden über den Brief an die Epheser, Stuttgart 1845, 61—79. First published in 1779.

[13] See above p. 105.

[14] So also another Pietist, Christian Fende, Des hocherleuchteten Apostels Pauli vortrefflicher Brieff an die Ephesier, Frankfurt a. M. 1727.

peace between two groups, Jews and Gentiles, undoubtedly because his negative attitude toward the flesh makes him disregard concrete historical communities. Consequently for him Christian unity has nothing whatsoever to do with the national and religious communities to which the individual belongs.

Johann Albrecht Bengel (1687—1752)

The commentary of the great Swabian Pietist Johann Albrecht Bengel is in a category of its own[15]. As the title, *Gnomon*, indicates, Bengel intended it to be a pointer which would prompt the student to carry on his own individual dialog with the New Testament. Therefore it does not contain a developed interpretation or the typical Pietist applications for everyday life. Instead, Bengel offers a careful outline of vv. 14—18, which as he observes, "by the tenor of their words and a kind of rhythm resemble a song". He thus is the first to anticipate the view developed in the twentieth century on the basis of form criticism that these verses are an early Christian hymn[16]. Like Goodwin in the previous century[17], Bengel divides this section into two parts: one describes the uniting of the Gentiles with Israel, the other the uniting of both Jews and Gentiles with God. Bengel's analysis is more detailed than Goodwin's. He says vv. 14—15a are about Jews and Gentiles, vv. 15b—18 about man and God. There is symmetry because each part tells first of the ending of hostility (vv. 14 and 16) and then of the proclamation of the gospel (vv. 15 and 17—18). Bengel can posit this symmetry, however, only because he reverts to the pre-Reformation way of construing ἐν δόγμασιν[18]. By proclaiming "the decrees of universal grace", says Bengel, Christ has abrogated the ceremonial law.

Although Pietists draw many applications from Eph 2:11—22, none of them is directed against the disunity of the visible church. This is in contrast to commentaries of the previous two centuries which frequently lament the disunity of the visible church and discuss how our passage speaks of true unity. But for the Pietists the invisible church has become so important that they are no longer distressed by the disunity of the visible church.

One Pietist commentator, Christoph Starke, does apply our passage to the relation with contemporary Jews. His is the first direct

---

[15] Gnomon Novi Testamenti, Tübingen 1742, 772—775.
[16] See below pp. 196—199.   [17] See above p. 110.
[18] So also Calmet, Commentaire littéral, Paris 1726, VIII, 431.

appeal for friendship with Jews based on our passage. For this the irenic attitude of Spener's commentary surely prepared the way. In Spener's view doctrinal differences do not divide men as they did in earlier Christian thought. However, a new dividing factor takes their place—the experience of the new birth. Yet Spener and the early Pietists at least wanted to avoid letting this factor cause hostility. Because they hoped for every man that he would experience the new birth, they counselled patience and understanding toward all outsiders.

Rationalism

While Pietism devoted its energies to the renewal of life among church members, another movement assumed major proportions. Developments in the intellectual world, most strikingly in the natural sciences, fostered the rise of Rationalism. The stimulation which Rationalism or the Enlightenment gave to all areas of human thought benefitted biblical study also.

Christian Schoettgen (d. 1751)

For example, new impetus was given to philological studies. One of the leading philologists who contributed to biblical studies was Christian Schoettgen. Schoettgen's *Horae Hebraicae* is a kind of commentary on the New Testament composed of Jewish materials. On our passage[19], Schoettgen proposes a new source for the figure of the dividing wall (v. 14). He thinks that it is based on the practice of Jews to live in a part of the city separated from the rest by a natural or man-made barrier. He finds only one piece of evidence for this practice before the time of Christ: a remark of Philo according to which the Jews lived on the other side of the Tiber. But Schoettgen can produce more evidence for later centuries, and finally can point to the Jewish ghettos of his own time. He explains that the rabbis, out of fear that their people would become Christian, added regulations to the law in order to make living together with Gentiles more difficult. These regulations were called "a fence". According to Schoettgen, they made it a virtual necessity for Jews to live in a closed community, and this is the reason for the ghetto wall.

Despite his observations about contemporary Jews, Schoettgen

---

[19] Horae Hebraicae, Dresden and Leipzig 1733, 761–769.

gives no indication of what bearing Eph 2:11—22 has, in his opinion, on the relations of Christians and Jews. The fact that he makes the Jews completely responsible for the ghetto wall, without a word about Christian discrimination against the Jews, plus the fact that at one point he calls the Jewish rites "superstition", indicates that his attitude toward Jews is not very cordial. His view about the origin of the dividing wall-figure receives little attention, and that mostly negative, from later commentators.

Johann Jakob Wettstein (1693—1754)

Johann Jakob Wettstein's edition of the Greek New Testament contains much philological material on Eph 2:11—22 gathered from a variety of sources[20]. For example, Wettstein quotes more than a dozen rabbinic passages which use the terms "near" and "far" in the same way as vv. 13 and 17. To be brought near usually means to become a convert to Israel and thus to the God of Israel. Wettstein's material is sometimes used and more often referred to by commentators, but it does not lead to any new interpretations of our passage.

John Locke (1632—1704)

Not only philologists like Schoettgen and Wettstein, but also philosophers like John Locke apply their methods to the interpretation of the Bible. Locke shows his desire to free the interpretation of Paul from systematic theology—and thus to let reason operate on it directly—when in the introduction to his commentary on Paul's letters he says that they must be interpreted by Paul's own system of thought, and not by the creed of any church or the philosophy of any school. This conviction is undoubtedly one of the reasons why Locke chooses the form of a paraphrase with notes[21], a form used by many eighteenth-century scholars. This form, it was thought, allowed the scripture to speak for itself; it need only be freed from dogmatic wrangling and antiquated language to let its clear and distinct ideas shine through to modern man.

By consulting primarily Paul's letter to the Galatians as well as Acts, Locke concludes in his opening synopsis of Ephesians that the central issue is Gentile inclusion. Paul's purpose in writing is to

---

[20] Η ΚΑΙΝΗ ΔΙΑΘΗΚΗ N.T. graecum ... opera et studio J. J. Wettstenii, Amsterdam 1752, 243—246.

[21] A Paraphrase and Notes on the Epistles of St. Paul, London 1707.

strengthen the Gentiles in Ephesus against the pressure of those who insist that Gentiles must keep the entire Mosaic law in order to be included in the Christian community.

Paul's radical opposition to the Judaizers is expressed in his assertion that Christ has abolished the law (v. 15). To explain this assertion, Locke offers a lengthy note. The Israelites came to be the people of God "by a voluntary Submission to him, and Acknowledgment of him to be their God and supreme Lord". Locke's rationalist orientation is particularly evident at this point: since human reason dictates that a valid covenant must be mutual, obviously Israel must fulfill certain conditions in order to be God's "Kingdom in this world"[22]. When they refuse the Messiah, says Locke, the Israelites are rejected. If we ask how Locke reconciles this opinion with Paul's statement in Romans 11:1 that God has by no means rejected his people Israel, Locke's answer is that there is a sharp distinction between God's dealings with nations and his dealings with individuals[23]. God has rejected Israel as a nation, but Israelites as individuals can become members of his Kingdom on the same terms as the Gentiles. It is about the Jews as individuals, about his "brothers according to the flesh" that Paul writes in Rom 9—11.

For Israel as a nation, maintains Locke, the Mosaic law is still valid, but it is no longer the law of "the Kingdom of God in this world". Although Locke usually speaks about the Mosaic law without qualification, he does specify at one point that he has in mind the ceremonial law. Locke does not want his readers to forget that there is another kind of law in the Old Testament—natural, or moral law.

There were, besides these, contained in the Book of the Law of Moses, the Law of Nature, or, as it is commonly called, the Moral Law, that unmovable Rule of Right which is of perpetual Obligation: This Jesus Christ is so far from abrogating, that he has promulgated it anew under the Gospel, fuller and clearer than it was in the Mosaical Constitution, or anywhere else[24].

Although the moral law is in force in the Kingdom of the Messiah, while the Mosaic ordinances are no longer obligatory, Jewish Christians were not forbidden to observe the latter: "they were indifferent things, which the converted Jews might or might not

---

[22] Locke's concept of the covenant is essentially the same as Grotius', see above, p. 101.

[23] See Locke's introduction to Rom 9—11 in the same work.

[24] Here again the similarity to Grotius is apparent, see above p. 100.

observe, as they found convenient." It was however contrary to the Gospel to make these ordinances binding, as the Judaizers did: "And accordingly we see (Gal 2:11) that what St. Paul blames on St. Peter was compelling the Gentiles to live as the Jews do: Had not that been the Case, he would no more have blam'd his Carriage at Antioch, than he did his observing the Law at Jerusalem."

Locke does not mention that the specific act of Peter which Paul critized was his withdrawal from table fellowship with the Gentiles. Paul's argument is based on the conviction that the unity of the church expressed in the concrete fellowship at the table dare not be broken. First of all, therefore, the Antioch incident had to do with the unity of the church. We might have expected that Locke would discuss this aspect of the incident, since the theme of church unity is so evident in Eph 2:11—22. But Locke is interested in the freedom of the individual from the Mosaic law rather than in the unity of the church. In his view the church of the Kingdom of God in this world is the place where the individual who aims for heaven prepares himself for his goal.

Although more and more commentators tend toward Locke's view of the covenant as a kind of contract[25], not all of Locke's ideas on Eph 2:11—22 met with approval on the Continent. Jacob Bruckner, who edited much of Locke's material for the so-called *Englisches Bibelwerk*[26], is quite critical of Locke's interpretation:

Locke's whole exposition of the covenants of God lacks thorough insight into the work of reconciliation of the human race: Locke is far from sufficiently discovering the covenant of works, and man's obligation, punishment and ruin. Thus it was not possible for him to see clearly enough the necessity of a universal Mediator, the means of reconciliation for blotting out transgression, and the purposes of the varied economy of God to this end.

Yet Bruckner himself seems to want to rationalize the mystery of God's covenant with Israel by explaining that the line of Abraham earned the right to the covenant because it was the only group to keep pure the teaching of Gen 3:15 about the Mediator to come— all other peoples garbled the doctrine by lies and phantasies.

---

[25] S. Baumgarten, who influenced many theologians of the period, comments on the term "covenants" (v. 12): "This is what every contract is named: a mutual agreement and requirement about a matter. This God has instituted with men." (Auslegung der Briefe Pauli, ed. J. S. Semler, Halle 1767, 223.)

[26] Die Heilige Schrift des Alten und Neuen Testaments, Leipzig 1762, IV, 837—845.

Siegmund Baumgarten (1706—1757)

Siegmund Baumgarten[27] is one of the few rationalist commentators to relate Eph 2:11—22 even in a general way to the issue of church unity in the eighteenth century. On the phrase, "He is our peace" (v. 14) he notes: "With this is indicated that the teaching about Christ, his reconciling sacrifice and its effect, is the right means for uniting us one with another." Baumgarten states categorically that the creation of one new man out of Jew and Gentile (v. 15) is not simply a side-effect but rather is the purpose of Christ's work. His ground for this position is the fact that the creation of one new man out of the two is announced in a purpose clause introduced by ἵνα (in order that):

ἵνα indicates that it was not an accidental result, but rather the real purpose of the actions of Christ; consequently it would be an insult to Christ and derision of all these struggles of his to oppose their purpose or to maintain the opposite by one's deeds.

Baumgarten goes on to say that according to v. 16 Christ's actions have a still deeper purpose than the reconciliation of Jew and Gentile; that is, reconciliation with God. "The highest and final purpose goes thereby to God, to effect and restore the separated unity of man with God." Baumgarten concludes that the passage shows the inseparability of the vertical and horizontal dimensions of reconciliation:

The Apostle wants to say: the true source and the strongest motivation for this uniting of men with one another is the recognized and accepted reconciliation of God, the taking away of his hostility against us, and his restored friendship. The peace of God and men hangs together so exactly with the peace of men with one another that neither can take place without the other.

Samuel Chandler (1693—1766)

Baumgarten, like most other commentators of the time, both Pietist and Rationalist, mentions that Christ as the cornerstone (v. 20) unites the walls of Jews and Gentiles. Baumgarten does not offer any further elaboration of the idea. Samuel Chandler does; he comments on the power of Christ to use the very different materials of Jews and Gentiles to build his temple[28].

---

[27] Auslegung, 220—235.
[28] A Paraphrase and Notes on the Epistles of St. Paul to the Galatians and Ephesians, London 1777, 104—109.

126

The materials of a building, in their original form, are shapeless and disagreeing, and could never constitute an edifice, ... till wrought and fashioned by the art of the workmen, fitted in size and shape for their proper places, and formed to conjunction; and what more unlikely, than that Jews and Gentiles would ever be brought to coalesce and join in one society, and constitute one church, between whom there had been so long and inveterate an opposition and hatred; and who seemed at the utmost distance from agreement and mutual friendship? But in Christ they were fitly framed; his gospel and doctrine and spirit so altered and fashioned them that they became capable of settling and joining together and in their several places, of contributing to the harmony, strength and beauty of this sacred temple, which it pleased God to erect out of them.

Johann David Michaelis (1717—1791)

Johann David Michaelis brings the resources of an excellent Orientalist to the interpretation of our passage[29]. He points out that the figure of a dividing wall is not uncommonly used by Eastern writers to describe hostility between groups of men, or the cause of such hostility. Michaelis quotes several instances of such usage by Ephraem of Syria. In the case of Jews and Gentiles, the cause of the hostility was the "law of commandments in ordinances" (v. 15) which Michaelis, like Locke, Baumgarten and Semler, interprets as "arbitrary decrees". The word δόγματα, he says, is used like the Hebrew word חֹק which usually stands for the cultic laws of the Jews.

Gotthilf Traugott Zachariae (d. 1777)

The disagreement which we have noted in earlier centuries, especially in the time of the Reformation, about whether the entire Old Testament law or only part of it is abrogated, continues in the eighteenth century. Gotthilf Traugott Zachariae[30] differs from earlier rationalist commentators by saying that the entire Mosaic law is abrogated. The phrase "in his flesh" means for Zachariae that Christ accomplished this "in his lowly condition on earth" by keeping the law and by taking in our place the punishment which the law threatens.

In a review of Zachariae's work[31], Johann August Ernesti says

[29] Paraphrases und Anmerkungen über die Briefe Pauli an die Galater, Epheser ..., Bremen und Göttingen 1769², 88—93.
[30] Paraphrastische Erklärung der Briefe Pauli, Tübingen 1781, 572—579.
[31] "Fortsetzung des Artikels: D. Zachariae paraphrastische Erklärung paulinischer Briefe", Neueste Theologische Bibliothek, Leipzig 1772, II, 1, 31.

he does not understand how Zachariae can so interpret "in the flesh". What Paul speaks of, according to Ernesti, is simply the abrogation of the ceremonial law by the death of Christ which fulfilled what the ceremonial law prefigured.

Johann Benjamin Koppe (1750—1791)

Johann Benjamin Koppe[32], Zachariae's successor at Göttingen, shows no signs of being disturbed by Ernesti's criticism and maintains that the entire Mosaic law is abrogated. He says that the Hebrew language is accustomed to join several synonyms together simply to express completeness; he refers to Neh 9:14, Deut 6:1, II Chron 33:8 where various terms are used together to denote the entire Mosaic law.

Friedrich Krause (1767—1827) and Carl Friedrich Bahrdt (1741—1792)

Perhaps the reason Rationalist commentators pay increasing attention to the question of the law's abrogation and less to the unity of the church is that Rationalism limits its interest more and more to the moral aspect of the Bible. There is growing scepticism about the possibility of gaining knowledge from the Bible. Scripture's role is to give encouragement for man's moral struggle and guidance for individual conduct.

The use of moral categories to interpret our passage is exemplified in Friedrich A. W. Krause's comment[33] on "the circumcision made in the flesh with hands" (v. 11). Krause says this circumcision is to be contrasted with "the circumcision with respect to morals—the circumcision not made with hands (Col 2:11); that is, with moral improvement".

A radical Rationalist like Carl Friedrich Bahrdt[34] minimizes the historical significance of the crucifixion in order to explain it as a sign of an eternal truth: "This image of his Being bled on the cross, in order to assure the world which is accustomed to bloody sacrifices that God without further sacrifice also forgives the past sins of him who does not want to sin any more." Bahrdt's language, especially his use of the phrase "image of his Being", has a Docetic ring; it suggests a kind of unreality in the crucifixion.

[32] Nov. Test. Graece perpetua annotatione... epp. Pauli ad Gal., Eph., Thess., Göttingen 1791, 49—60.

[33] Der Brief an die Epheser, Frankfurt und Leipzig 1789, 53—59.

[34] Briefe von Paulus, Die neuesten Offenbarungen Gottes, Riga 1773, III, 297—299.

Summary

With the exception of Baumgarten, Rationalist commentators say little about the significance of Eph 2:11—22 for the contemporary unity of the church. Only John Locke gives a clear answer to the question: does the breaking of the dividing wall apply only within the church or in the entire world? In his view the wall still stands between the nation of Israel and the rest of the world. Other commentators do not discuss the question. There seem to be no statements about the relationship between the church and the synagogue. This may strike us as unexpected since the Rationalists appeal to reason as common to all men. Yet perhaps just because they do so, they are not likely to speak about a unity which contrasts so strongly with the empirical evidence.

We have seen that in both Pietist and Rationalist interpretations of Eph 2:11—22 there is remarkably little interest in the unity of the church. In their own ways both Pietist and Rationalist commentaries focus on the individual and the equality of all individuals before God. Of the reconciliation of hostile groups there is scarcely a trace. Only in going outside of the categories of Pietist and Rationalist to the outstanding Catholic commentator Augustine Calmet[35], do we find that this aspect of interpretation has not been forgotten. For Calmet Christ's death is the sacrifice which seals the covenant between the Jews and the Gentiles. The sacrament of the Eucharist sustains the union: "in order to hold them in a love most perfect, he nourishes them with his own flesh."[36] But for Pietists and Rationalists this unity of the church is relatively unimportant, since they see the church primarily as a means by which the individual comes to salvation. Thus the great majority of the nineteenth century New Testament scholars are predisposed by their immediate heritage to regard unity as a secondary, organizational and outward matter, not as an essential part of the gospel.

---

[35] Commentaire litteral, Paris 1726, VIII, 430—432.

[36] This line of interpretation was taken in the seventeenth century by Goodwin, see above p. 111.

Chapter VII

THE NINETEENTH CENTURY

In the nineteenth century historical questions come strongly to the fore and affect in a particularly important way the interpretation of Eph 2:11—22. Who really wrote Ephesians? To whom did he write? What was the situation to which he wrote? What did he want to accomplish in this situation? What can be learned from the passage about the history of early Christianity? Whereas the study of Paul's writings had traditionally been pursued above all for doctrinal and practical purposes, the outstanding book of the nineteenth century on Paul is subtitled "a contribution to a critical history of early Christianity".

Under this approach, earlier boundaries in the discussion of Ephesians are disregarded. For example, the primary context of interpretation had always been the letters of Paul seen in the historical background provided by Acts. But in the nineteenth century a large group of scholars reject Pauline authorship and propose other contexts for the letter. Further, Acts is no longer accepted by all scholars as a completely reliable source for early church history. A critical use of it—as of all New Testament literature—is therefore demanded. The posing of historical questions in a critical way, which might serve as an elementary definition of the historical-critical method, is the outstanding development in biblical interpretation in the century.

Not all nineteenth century scholars are completely governed by the historical critical method, but almost all exegetes of any importance are influenced by it. In the following discussion, interpretations of Eph 2:11—22 are roughly categorized as placing primary emphasis on either a historical-critical, or a philological, or a theological, or a practical approach to the passage.

130

Ferdinand Christian Baur (1792—1860)

The historical-critical approach itself fosters strong interest in what Eph 2:11—22 says about the relation of Jews and Gentiles. This is so because the pioneer of the historical-critical method in biblical studies, Ferdinand Christian Baur, was convinced that New Testament writings must be understood in light of their position in the struggle between a particularistic Jewish Christianity and a universalistic Paulinism—a struggle which Baur saw as the leading dynamic of early church history.

In Baur's portrayal of a long struggle between Jewish Christianity and Paulinism which was finally resolved in the early Catholic Church, Ephesians is one of the writings which mediates between the two parties. Together with Colossians, it is a product of the Paulinist party, written at a time when the two parties are overcoming their differences and moving closer to one another[1].

According to Baur, "the actual practical purpose of these letters is the uniting of Jews and Gentiles into one and the same religious fellowship"[2]. Both letters aim to show that unity is necessarily involved in the principle on which the church is founded: Christ as head. The strongest common emphasis of both letters is the death of Christ as the event in which Jews and Gentiles are reconciled to one another and to God. To illustrate this, Baur relies chiefly on a summary interpretation of Eph 2:11—22:

It belongs to the unique character of both letters that they see the death of Christ as an event accomplished by God for the purpose of abolishing the wall between Gentiles and Jews, and through the peace made between them to reconcile both with God. Nothing else is lifted up unanimously with greater emphasis by both letters than this general εἰρηνοποιεῖν (peace-making) and ἀποκαταλάττειν (reconciliation) through Christ. Eph 2:14f; Col 1:20f. All difference between Jews and Gentiles is ended. The elaborate advantage which Judaism had over Gentilism is taken away, since through the death of Christ the Mosaic law, which is the handwriting of the law consisting of absolute commands and rules, is destroyed. Because in this way all national differences and oppositions, including whatever separates men from one another in the various relationships of life, are ended in Christianity by means of the death of Christ, there appears in Christianity a new man[3].

---

[1] Paulus, der Apostel Jesu Christi, Leipzig 1867[2], II, 40.

[2] Das Christentum und die Christliche Kirche der drei ersten Jahrhunderte, Tübingen 1860, 117.

[3] Paulus, II, 42.

Baur considers the passage to make reconciliation of Jews and Gentiles the means to reconciliation of men with God. He believes the passage proclaims unity "in the various relationships of life", and therefore not a unity "in spirit only".

But Baur sees an inner contradiction in Eph 2:11–22, a strain of thought which runs counter to the idea of unity on the basis of equality. According to this strain, "the Gentiles ... are the ones granted admission, the latecomers ... They merely take part in something on which the Jews have immediate and unique claim"[4]. According to Baur, this is a concession to Judaism which Paul never would have made. It gives Jews a privileged position, and on such an unequal basis genuine unity between Jews and Gentiles would be impossible. The letter must of course contain concessions, since it aims to conciliate between the Paulinist and Jewish Christian parties. But when the author of Ephesians writes as though "the substantial content of Christianity is Judaism itself", then Baur says he reveals that he has not really understood Paul's theology.—To understand this judgment of Baur, a brief sketch of Paulinism and Jewish Christianity as he sees them is necessary.

Jewish Christianity considers Christianity to be essentially Judaism. Therefore it believes the Jews remain God's chosen people; the law remains the revelation of God's will for his people, and the ceremonies and regulations contained within it are still valid. On this basis Jewish Christianity affirms the need for a theocratic, hierarchic form of government. Of course, Jewish Christians expect that the coming of the Messiah will entail some changes in their way of life. They are not so rigid that they cannot find ways of compromising with Paulinism. For example, most of them eventually come to accept the inclusion of Gentiles by means of baptism, which serves as a substitute for circumcision[5]. However, they stubbornly maintain their conviction that Christianity is enlarged Judaism and therefore that the literal keeping of the law, ritual purification, ceremonies and organization are essential. In short, they think in terms of the visible, outer forms of religion. For Baur, the word "outer" implies at least superficiality, if not hypocrisy. From concern for outer form, he believes, came the hierarchic government of the early Catholic Church, and later the increasing preoccupation with organization and outward form of the Roman Catholic Church.

It is important to note that Baur considers church unity to be a Jewish Christian idea: "Striving for unity belongs to the original

---

[4] Paulus, II, 45.   [5] Das Christentum, 101.

132

character of Judaism ... Everywhere this striving for unity has at
the same time an anti-Pauline tendency."[6] Paul had the task of
fighting for the right of Gentiles to become Christians and thus
labored for the universality of the church, whereas the unity of the
church—the merging of the Gentile Christians with the Jewish
Christians—is a later task. Baur makes a sharp separation between
these two tasks. Universality is Paul's cause, unity the cause of Jewish Christianity[7]. By unity Baur almost always means organizational unity.

Antithetical to Jewish Christianity, according to Baur, is Paulinism and its proclamation that Christianity is not a form of Judaism but is radically new. It does not depend on Judaism or on
any other religion, although these may have some elements of truth.
Paul considers Christianity the "absolute religion". Other religions,
and chiefly Judaism, have been shown by Christianity to be fundamentally bankrupt. They are related to Christianity only as
historical stages which must be rejected in order that the "absolute
religion" may be accepted. Thus in Paul's theology Judaism, like
Gentilism, has only a "negative relation to Christianity". For Paul,
Judaism is essentially law[8]. He declares a complete break with the
law because it stands opposed to Christian faith which is "an inner
process of consciousness, whose essential element is one's own experience and conviction of the impossibility of justification by the
law"[9].

The author of Ephesians, says Baur, apparently has not had this
experience and therefore does not understand Paul's concept of
faith. Since he does not, he can treat the object of faith—the death
of Christ—as an outward event which does not involve the Christian's personal existence. When the author speaks of Christ's death
abolishing the law (Eph 2:15), he means only that Christ's death
has made void the outward, physical, distinguishing mark of circumcision which is what he calls "the law of commandments in

---

[6] Das Christentum, 282. Although Baur makes this statement in his treatment of the pseudo-Clementine literature, the statement is relevant here because Baur believed that the pseudo-Clementine literature can be used to
illuminate the struggle already going on in Paul's lifetime.

[7] A. Schwegler (Nachapostolisches Zeitalter, Tübingen 1846, 381—382) puts
the attitude of his teacher Baur in sharpened form: "So long as Paul had to
fight for the universality of the church, he could not press for its unity. Only
when on the basis of the Pauline ideas a Catholic Church had been built,
could the idea of unity be set alongside the idea of universality. But the idea
of unity came not from the Paulinists; rather this thought of centralization in
doctrine and organization is a Petrine thought."

[8] Das Christentum, 111.   [9] Paulus, II, 45—46.

ordinances". According to Baur's interpretation of Ephesians, the abolition of circumcision is the means by which Jews and Gentiles are united.

It is obvious, says Baur, that merely abolishing a physical difference can produce only a very superficial unity. The unity which Ephesians proclaims is really only an "outward coalition" of Gentiles and Jews because it "does not rest on the deep fundamental concept of the religious anthropology of the Apostle Paul"[10]. This fundamental concept in Baur's view is justification by faith. Since this is not mentioned in Eph 2:11—22, Baur considers the unity portrayed here as without real foundation. So long as Jewish Christians believe that Christianity is essentially Judaism, and therefore means keeping the law, while Gentile Christians believe that Christianity is a new religion, they do not really hold the same faith.

In Baur's opinion, the theme of unity in Ephesians, as in Colossians, is elaborated in a way which shows strong Gnostic influence. Baur writes: "Just as the Gnostic systems rest on the basic idea that all spiritual life which has gone out from the highest God must return into its original unity, must be taken up again into the absolute principle, and every disharmony must be resolved into harmony, so also in these letters the activity of Christ is primarily a restoring, returning, uniting one."[11] Baur is the first scholar to suggest a Gnostic milieu for Ephesians, thus opening up an area of investigation which has come to blossom in the twentieth century[12].

Karl Reinhold Köstlin (1819—1894)

Among Baur's immediate followers were those whose investigations yielded conclusions somewhat different from his. Karl Reinhold Köstlin came to believe that Paulinism was in some respects closer to Jewish Christianity than Baur thought. Köstlin says that the relation of Judaism to Christianity expressed in Eph 2:11—22 is really not so far from Paul's understanding of it[13]. That is, neither Ephesians nor Paul views Christianity as a completely new religion over against Judaism. In Paul, the continuity and discontinuity between Judaism and Christianity are in balance.

Therefore Köstlin disagrees with Baur's judgment that Eph 2:12

---

[10] Paulus, II, 46. [11] Paulus, II, 10—11.

[12] Especially in the work of H. Schlier, E. Käsemann, P. Pokorny, see below pp. 178—184.

[13] Der Lehrbegriff des Evangeliums und der Briefe Johannis, Berlin 1843, 365—367.

contains concessions to Jewish Christianity which Paul would never have made[14]. Rather, the passage appeals to Gentile Christians who are in danger of cutting themselves off from the heritage of Israel by separating from Jewish Christians, which would amount to falling back into Gentilism. Köstlin's interpretation of Eph 2:11—22 presupposes that Gentile and Jewish Christians are in fact already united, whereas Baur said they had not yet achieved unity. Furthermore, Köstlin begins to isolate and describe Gentile Christianity as a factor in the early church distinct from Paulinism. Baur had made no distinction between Paul's theology and the theology of Gentile Christians.

Albrecht Ritschl (1822—1889)

Expanding on Köstlins's suggestions, Albrecht Ritschl, another pupil of Baur, gives a key position to Gentile Christianity as a factor in its own right. Ritschl breaks decisively with Baur in stating flatly: "The opposite of Jewish Christianity... is Gentile Christianity and not Paulinism... Over against a way of life, such as Jewish Christianity is, stands... not merely a doctrine, but rather another way of life."[15] Since he regards the history of the early church as more than the history of a doctrinal conflict and its resolution, Ritschl inquires more closely than did Baur into the matter of Jewish-Gentile fellowship. He concludes that close association, though practiced by moderate Jewish Christians with Gentile Christians, was limited because of Levitical purity laws. Yet "in comparison with the increasing numbers of heretical sects, the maintenance of association in discussion, hospitality, and worship between the two groups was very significant for their church unity"[16].

Later historical-critical studies of Ephesians generally agree with Ritschl in treating Gentile Christianity as a phenomenon distinct from Paulinism, and like Köstlin try to describe in closer detail the situation of the Gentile Christians to which the letter is addressed. With one exception they agree that the letter is written to Gentile Christians to persuade them of the crucial importance of unity with Jewish Christians.

---

[14] H. J. Holtzmann (Kritik der Epheser und Kolosserbriefe, Leipzig 1872, 209) says that the prerogatives of Israel named here do not go beyond those recognized by Paul in Romans 1:16; 2:10; 3:1,2; 9:4,5; 11:28,29; 15:8,9.

[15] Die Entstehung der Altkatholischen Kirche, Bonn 1857², 271.

[16] Die Entstehung, 256.

Heinrich Ewald (1803–1875)

Heinrich Ewald[17] puts forward the view that Ephesians was written shortly after the destruction of Jerusalem in 70 A.D. That catastrophe was a terrible expression of the hostility between Jews and Gentiles. The memory of it is reflected in the frequent mention of hostility in Eph 2:11—22. This event brought a sudden change in the church's life. The church had lost its home base, and was forced to live on Gentile soil. With the visible roots in Palestine gone, Gentile Christians were separated from Jewish Christianity and in danger of falling back into pagan ways. Ewald finds it natural that Gentile Christians should wonder what Paul would say in this situation. To meet this need, concludes Ewald, one of Paul's disciples wrote Ephesians.

Heinrich Julius Holtzmann (1832–1910)

Heinrich Julius Holtzmann, while not venturing so detailed a picture of the situation, agrees that there is a danger of the Gentiles' falling back into pagan ways. Holtzmann does not think, however, that Gentile Christians have separated from Jewish Christians. Ephesians was written rather to celebrate the fact that what Paul had struggled for has begun to be reality: a church including both Jews and Gentiles living in peace with one another. It also has the purpose of urging the Gentile Christians not to destroy the peace by a lapse into paganism[18].

Holtzmann calls Eph 2:11—22 the point at which the unique thought-world of Ephesians begins, in contrast to its extensive dependence on the writings of Paul and especially Colossians: "The most far-reaching and original of all the thoughts of our author lies in this passage, whereby Christ abrogates the Jewish people's cramping way of life, so hated by Gentiles, through his reconciling death, and in this way destroys the hostility together with its cause." Holtzmann finds that although the author's thought goes beyond Paul's teaching, it does not conflict with it because his thought is based on Paul's teaching about the law and reconciliation. To the affirmation of Gal 3:13 that Christ's atoning death has abrogated the law, Eph 2:14—15 adds the new meaning that thereby peace has been made between the two previously divided parts of mankind[19].

---

[17] Sieben Sendschreiben des Neuen Bundes, Göttingen 1870, 153—215.

[18] Kritik der Epheser- und Kolosserbriefe, Leipzig 1872, 304—305; so also O. Pfleiderer, Der Paulinismus, Leipzig 1890², 434—435.

[19] Kritik, 207—208.

This new sociological dimension is nevertheless expressed with the use of Paul's own terminology. Holtzmann observes that Eph 2:11—16 contains formulations which Paul uses in speaking of justification by God[20], or of reconciliation with God[21]. But the Ephesians passage, says Holtzmann, uses these terms in a different conceptual world from Paul's when it uses them to speak of the uniting of Jews and Gentiles[22]; at some points it becomes particularly obvious that the author uses terms that belong in another realm. For example, in Paul's vocabulary the word "reconcile" is used to refer to God's dealings with man. However, in the clause "that he might reconcile both in one body to God" (v. 16), it refers to the relation between Jews and Gentiles. Yet according to Holtzmann the addition of the words "to God" betrays the original meaning of the term[23].

Otto Pfleiderer (1839—1908)

Otto Pfleiderer, agreeing with Holtzmann that Eph 2:11—16 uses Pauline terms to express new concepts, points to the problem of the word "hostility" in vv. 15 and 16.—Commentators have often debated whether the hostility is between man and God or between Jew and Gentile; or whether it is both; or whether it has one meaning in v. 15 and another in v. 16.—Pfleiderer says the ambiguity is caused by the mixture of thought-worlds which Holtzmann has described. In v. 16 the word "hostility" seems to mean what Paul meant by it: hostility between man and God. But it therefore stands "in confusing misrelationship to the rest of the idea of the context, which has to do with the reconciliation, not of the sinful world with God, but of the Jews with the Gentiles[24]. According to Pfleiderer, the confusion is due to the fact that Paul's terminology is applied to a practical situation different from the one Paul faced: "No longer, as in the time of Paul, is the issue the possibility of Gentile Christianity, but the accomplishment of the complete unity of Gentile Christianity with Jewish Christianity, that is, the actualization of the universal church. In our letter the idea of cathol-

---

[20] E. g. ἐν τῷ αἵματι (in the blood) Eph 2:13, found in Rom 3:25; 5:9; I Cor 11:25.

[21] E. g. ἀποκτείνειν (to kill) Eph 2:16 in a metaphorical sense, as Rom 7:11; II Cor 3:6.

[22] Kritik, 93.

[23] Kritik, 94. Holtzmann's basic premise, that in Paul's vocabulary the word "reconcile" has to do exclusively with the relation of God and men, is challenged by I Cor 7:11 where it refers to the relation of husband and wife.

[24] Der Paulinismus, 450—451.

icity is for the first time raised to dogmatic definition and to a significance which governs the whole."[25]

The analysis of Holtzmann and Pfleiderer presupposes a gulf between the concepts of reconciliation between men and reconciliation with God. Like Baur, these scholars find unevenness and inconsistency in Eph 2:11—22. But instead of Baur's mixture of Paulinism and Jewish Christianity, they see a mixture of Paulinism and social Christianity. The term "social" to describe the new dimension which Ephesians adds to Paul is first used by Pfleiderer:

> The death of Christ has established peace between Jews and Gentiles through the removal of the social dividing wall of the ritual law, and thereby has created out of these two parts one new man and a new social fellowship, the mystical body of Christ or the church[26].

Albert Klöpper (1828—1905)

Albert Klöpper differs from the majority of historical-critical scholars about the situation to which Ephesians is addressed. The problem, says he, is not that the Gentile Christians are in danger of separating from the Jewish Christians. Rather, they are being treated as second class members of the church by Jewish Christians who want to fasten the demands of the ceremonial law upon them[27]. But the ceremonial law is what Christ has abolished (v. 15). The means of abolishing it is explained by Klöpper in a way different from any suggested by previous commentators:

> Since the Levitical ritual side of the law was applied by the scribes and Pharisees as the measure for judging Jesus, and he was condemned to death before their forum as a false Messiah, therefore the hostility of the law of commandments in ordinances acted against him also, and thereby forever lost its right[28].

---

[25] Der Paulinismus, 435.

[26] Das Urchristentum, Berlin 1902², II, 220. See also, Der Paulinismus, 450.

[27] Der Brief an die Epheser, Göttingen 1891, 17—23. Klöpper believes that the letter presupposes "some kind of co-existence" of Jewish and Gentile Christians among its recipients. Although the letter is addressed to Gentile Christians, the author counts on having Jewish Christian readers as well. Wanting to promote good relations among the two groups, he as a Jewish Christian disclaims in his letter those things which he knows some Jewish Christians claim as advantages over the Gentiles, and which hinder fellowship.

[28] Der Brief an die Epheser, 83n. A somewhat similar explanation had been suggested by Georg Schnedermann (Die Gefangenschaftsbriefe des Apostels Paulus, ed. Strack and Zöckler, Kurzgefaßter Kommentar zu den heiligen Schriften, Neues Testament, Nördlingen 1888, IV, 24). Schnedermann, however, does not think the ceremonial law alone is meant, but the entire law, looked at

According to Klöpper, Eph 2:11—22 portrays unity among men as the prerequisite of reconciliation with God, whereas in Paul's teaching unity among men is a result of the reconciliation of men with God. Klöpper therefore finds the Ephesians doctrine of reconciliation foreign to Paul's theology. Like most other historical-critical scholars, he sees Paul's theology as strongly centered on the individual's reconciliation with God, with unity among men as a relatively minor corollary. He therefore cannot conceive that the two dimensions might actually be much more integrally related, both in Ephesians and in Paul.

Hermann von Soden (1852—1914)

Hermann von Soden is not satisfied with the description of the situation given by other historical-critical scholars. For him the problem which the author of Ephesians faces is not the theological conflict of Paulinism versus Jewish Christianity, as Baur claimed. Nor is it quite what Ritschl asserted: a difference in way of life between Gentile Christians and Jewish Christians, expressed most specifically in the Levitical purity laws. As von Soden sees it, the obstacle is one of attitude: Jewish Christians and Gentile Christians are disinclined to integrate[29]. According to von Soden, the author's language about the two groups in 2:11 shows that the differences in doctrine and in religious practices have essentially faded. "The devaluation of the actual difference between the two groups expressed in the phrase 'in the flesh' and especially in the term 'so-called' goes far beyond any devaluation Paul made."[30] There is no longer conflict between Jewish and Gentile Christians about the place of Israel in God's plan, or about the law, and consequently there is no hostility between the two groups[31].

---

as a compilation of specific rules. "The law itself (Gal 2:19; 3:13) to which he was subject, caused his death, and through this its effect lost its validity, cf. Rom 7:4f., 7ff.; 8:3; Col 2:14. Actually Jesus died under the charge of Antinomianism John 5:16—18."

[29] Hand-commentar zum Neuen Testament, Freiburg and Leipzig 1893², III, 1, 85.

[30] Hand-commentar, III, 1, 120. Baur said Ephesians stresses the difference between Jews and Gentiles more than Paul; later scholars such as Holtzmann said Ephesians's view of the difference is the same as Paul's; now von Soden says Ephesians considers the difference to be less than Paul did.

[31] Because von Soden considers that these are not the issues which interest the author, he offers little comment on hostility (vv. 14, 16) and how it was ended, or on the law, and how it was abrogated (v. 15). He does say that the law is viewed "according to its weak and burdensome side", as "repeated editions of commands", and as that which caused hostility and separation.

Among the Gentile attitudes that form the chief hindrance to integration, von Soden finds particularly important one which previous interpreters have scarcely touched on:

a centrifugal individualism, which is understandable over against the challenge to Christians thrown together out of all circles and peoples, never educated to the social cohesiveness of the Jewish concept of community, to see themselves now as a people in close fellowship, a church[32].

Von Soden notes that especially vv. 12, 16, 19—22 of Eph 2 are directed against this "centrifugal individualism".

In his emphasis on reconciliation between Jewish and Gentile Christians, says von Soden, the author deliberately speaks also of reconciliation with God. Thus in v. 16,

the author does not speak of a reconciliation between the two groups, but rather, true to Paul, of a reconciliation of both with God. But what interests him about it is not, as in Col 1:22, this reconciliation itself, but the circumstance that for both those groups the means to it was one and the same, and that thereby between them, not between God and them as in Paul, there is peace[33].

The fact that there is peace betweeen the two groups is what the author continually holds up, because he wants to encourage his readers to live according to the peace that has been given—that is, for Gentile Christians to have fellowship with Jewish Christians. The dividing wall (v. 14) was not simply a religious barrier but the division "in all areas, religious, moral, social, which kept Jews and Gentiles from any fellowship in life". Nor is the wall broken down only within the church: "Through that which Christ has brought to men, the difference which split the world between Jews and Gentiles is ended." Therefore von Soden finds that the unity of the church is not the final goal of the author: the author's social consciousness is such that he hopes that through the unity of the church the unity of mankind will be realized: "Not to lead individual persons to the salvation of their souls, but rather to join mankind in a unified whole—this is the ideal about which the author is enthused."[34]

Like Klöpper, von Soden thinks that unity between Jews and

Such a view of the law, says von Soden, could not be held by a trained Palestinian Pharisee; it is the viewpoint of a Jew of the Diaspora where a Roman-Hellenistic culture conceived of law in this way ("Der Epheserbrief", JpTh 13. 1887, 435).

[32] Hand-commentar, 85—86.   [33] Hand-commentar, 124.

[34] Hand-commentar, 122—123; 85.

Gentiles has a different place in the theology of Ephesians than in the theology of Paul; Paul "never put as *the* purpose or even *a* purpose of the work of Christ to unite Jews and Gentiles"[35]. Nevertheless, von Soden considers the author of Ephesians justified in believing he was continuing the work of Paul. For Paul, "in his letters to the Romans and Philippians had already spoken like a universal apostle of Jews and Gentiles... If he had experienced the new development which came as a consequence of the year 70, he certainly would have written in the tone which the author of Ephesians felt called to sound"[36].

Bernhard Weiss (1827—1918)

We have seen that as the nineteenth century progresses scholars within the historical-critical group tend to see less difference than the pioneer Baur between Paul's thought and that of Ephesians. Therefore it is almost inevitable that one of them should raise the question, "Could not the difference be due to a development within the thought of Paul himself?" Bernhard Weiss asks this question and answers it affirmatively[37].

Weiss considers the treatment of the law and its abrogation in Eph 2:15 to be essentially the same as that contained in the undisputed letters of Paul. The only difference is that in Ephesians the abrogation of the law is not proclaimed, as in Galatians, polemically against the position that keeping the law is the way of salvation. The reason for the difference is that by this time in Paul's life the legalistic opposition had lost its power. Refuting it was no longer a genuine need.

The need was rather to find a new way of living together in mixed congregations. Weiss is convinced that the overcoming of the Jew-Gentile problem was of unique significance for the unity and mission of the church[38].

---

[35] Hand-commentar, 91.   [36] JpTh 13, 495.

[37] Lehrbuch der Biblischen Theologie des Neuen Testaments, Berlin 1888[5], 204. Although Weiss had misgivings about many of the conclusions of Baur and later historical-critical scholars, he was very much involved in their categories and ways of approaching problems. According to Weiss, the later development in Paul finds expression in the "Prison Epistles"; but, the beginnings of the later development are already present in his earlier writings, as is shown for example by the similarity of the account of the inclusion of the Gentiles into Israel in Eph 2:11—13 and the Gentiles as wild branches inserted into the cultivated olive tree of Israel in Rom 11:16—24 (Lehrbuch, 363).

[38] Lehrbuch, 435—437.

In the solving of the opposition between Gentiles and Jews the church becomes aware only in a primary and beginning way what its task is: namely to realize peace ... and so to be in its circle what Christ in the comprehensive sense is for the whole universe.

At this point Weiss's view of Ephesians comes close to that of von Soden, except that Weiss makes more of a distinction between the work of the church and the work of Christ.

Fenton J. A. Hort (1828—1892)

F. J. A. Hort agrees with Weiss that the changed situation of the church was the occasion for Paul to express new aspects of his thought about the relation of Jews and Gentiles in Ephesians[39]. Since Paul wrote Ephesians after he had completed his mission of carrying the Gentile collection to the Jewish Christians of Jerusalem, the sense of this completed token of unity helps to account for the tone of the letter.

Against the argument of Baur and many of his followers that Ephesians' emphasis on unity presupposes a stage in the centralization of doctrine and organization that came only after Paul's lifetime, Hort points out the fallacy of a simple identification of unity with centralized organization:

The unity of which it speaks has in itself nothing to do with organization, though no doubt a sense of it might be expected to help towards the growth of organization. The units of the one Church spoken of in the Epistle are not churches but individual men. From the first, each Christian community as soon as it was formed became as it were a school by which its members were trained in the life of mutual fellowship.

Philological Commentaries

Heinrich A. W. Meyer (1800—1873)

Whereas historical-critical scholars try to assess the specific value of Ephesians for a history of the early church, exegetes who take a predominantly philological approach deny the right to make such judgments. The question of truth, whether historical or theological, they do not consider to be part of the exegetical task, which is only to expound what the text itself says. In the preface to the first edi-

---

[39] Prolegomena to St. Paul's Epistles to the Romans and the Ephesians, London 1895, esp. 128—130.

tion of his commentary on Ephesians, H. A.W. Meyer terms his goal "pure objectivity", admitting how difficult this is, especially in commenting on Ephesians[40]. Meyer asserts that the arguments of Baur's school against Pauline authorship of Ephesians are answered "when the exposition, proceeding strictly objectively, shows in the passages in question only Pauline contents".

One such passage is v. 12 which Baur had contended makes an un-Pauline concession to Judaism, thus supporting Jewish Christian claims to a privileged position over Gentile Christians. Here Meyer insists on the crucial significance of the phrase "in that time": this designates the pre-Christian period of the Gentiles' lives. Only in that time were they in a position secondary to Jews; now since they are Christians the distinction no longer applies. Passages such as Rom 1:16; 3:1; Gal 3:13 show that Paul does teach a precedence of Jews over Gentiles before the latter became Christians; "but neither here nor elsewhere has he taught that the substantial content of Christianity is Judaism": in place of law as the way of justification Christ has opened the way to justification by faith.

Meyer also opposes the claim of many historical-critical scholars that the way in which vv. 14—16 affirm the uniting of Jews and Gentiles is un-Pauline:

> The uniting has come about as a lifting of both into a higher unity, vv. 16, 18, 21f; therefore this teaching is sufficiently explained from the designation as apostle to the Gentiles and the experience of the apostle himself, and out of his own universalism, which is also witnessed in other places. It does not need to have as its presupposition the sub-apostolic process of development of the church forming itself out of heterogeneous elements to unity.

What Meyer means by the "higher unity" into which Jews and Gentiles are lifted becomes somewhat clearer in his comment on the new man (v. 16):

> This man is neither Jew nor Greek ... but rather both parts have laid aside their previous religious and moral constitutions and without further difference have received the totally new being conditioned through the Christian faith. If καινόν (new) had not been added, one could wrongly imagine εἷς ἄνθρωπος (the one man) as an amalgam of Jew and Gentile.

---

[40] "In view of the difficulty and dogmatic sublimity of the letter the temptation to allow some influence on the interpretation from the doctrine of the church, or the speculation of the school, or one's own subjectivity lies very near ... The verdict of scripture can only be reached by the way of pure grammatical-historical exposition." (Der Brief an die Epheser, KEK, Göttingen 1843, x, xiii.) Other references are from Meyer's final editing, Göttingen 1867, 108—136.

This statement militates strongly against any sort of continuity of the church with Israel, since the "religious and moral constitution" of Israel had to be "laid aside" to make way for the church. Meyer also implies that there cannot be a unity which has room for differences: the differences must disappear, or the result is an amalgam. This assumption that unity demands the disappearance of differences is at least as old as Chrysostom[41] and is very strong in the nineteenth century.

Leopold Immanuel Rückert (1797—1871)

Like Meyer, Leopold Immanuel Rückert[42] describes the merger of Jews and Gentiles in the church as the overcoming of opposites by a higher unity. Interpreting the one new man (v. 16), Rückert says:

> Until now they were two, by essential marks so divided that a higher unity under which they could be joined was inconceivable. Gentile, Jew—true opposites. These differentiating marks are now put off however, no one is Jew any longer, no one Gentile, but rather the one like the other is a Christian. In this higher unity they fall together, are really one, and furthermore are something new which neither was before, and they cannot be thought of as two any longer. (Gal 3:28)[43]

The concept of "opposites" which are overcome by a "higher unity" suggests the influence of Hegel's dialectical view of history. If the conclusions even of scholars who explicitly disclaim philosophical presuppositions reflect Hegelian categories, it is not surprising that the terms "higher unity" and "unity above the opposites" are used frequently by other interpreters of the century[44].

---

[41] See above p. 33.

[42] Der Brief Pauli an die Epheser, Leipzig 1834, 101—129.

[43] Rückert also uses the term "higher unity" in commenting on "He has made both one" (v. 14).

[44] R. Stier (Die Gemeinde in Christo Jesu, Berlin 1848, I, 349) says that the idea of Judaism and Gentilism as two opposites reconciled in Christianity "comes in part from Hegelianism which puts the Gentiles on the same level with the Jews in contradiction to the Old Testament and the whole of scripture". The term "higher unity" also occurs in the interpretations of Eph 2:11—22 by Baur, Das Christentum, 116; Harless, 220, 223, 254; De Wette, 121; Klöpper, 85; Beck, 136; Wohlenberg, 11, 23; Schnedermann, 9; Henle, 116. Pfleiderer, Der Paulinismus, 438.

John Eadie (1810—1876)

John Eadie of Scotland, writing in a country where Hegel's thought had not been so throughly imbibed, asserts that according to v. 11, "Christianity does not obliterate difference of race"[45]. To explain his assertion, Eadie points out that Paul calls his readers "Gentiles"; it is not just that they *were* Gentiles, they are Gentiles now. They remain non-Israelites, but they now share in all that Israel has received. This is possible because Christ has made "peace between Jew and Gentile viewed as antagonist races". Yet Eadie says that the peace exists only within the church, for "the unconverted Jew and the unbelieving Gentile may be, and are, at enmity still". On the relationship of the believing Gentile and the unconverted Jew, Eadie makes no comment. Finally, although the word ἔχθραν signifies enmity between Jews and Gentiles, "the idea of enmity towards God would not be absent from the apostle's mind, for this enmity of race had its origin and tincture from enmity towards God".

Theological Commentaries

Interpreters following a more theological approach claim that the grammatical-historical method limits the exegete's task too much: it explains what the text meant to the people to whom it was written, but not what it means for readers today. Yet, so the argument of the theological group runs, the biblical authors believed that their writings had not just temporary, but eternal meaning. Commentators of this group use various methods to discern the deeper meaning: interpreting the passage in the context of the whole Bible; considering the church's understanding of the passage throughout the centuries; asking not only "what does the writer say?" but "why does he say it?". The latter question tends toward a rather psychological interpretation; this corresponds in some measure to the dominant theology of the century, which under the influence of Schleiermacher approached its task primarily by way of the believer and his religious feelings[46].

---

[45] A Commentary on the Greek text of the epistle of Paul to the Ephesians, New York 1861². Not all continental commentators think that the Christian has ceased to be a Gentile or a Jew. J. C. K. von Hofmann, for example, also holds that v. 11 addresses the readers as presently, not merely formerly, Gentiles (Der Brief an die Epheser, Nördlingen 1870, 78).

[46] For example, E. Haupt (KEK, 1902⁸, iii) says his work represents "the psychological exposition, which tries to understand not only what the author

While the great majority of theological commentators agree with the general consensus that the wall of Eph 2:14 was between Jews and Gentiles, two major theological commentators, Adolph Harless and Paul Feine hold that the wall was between men and God. The theological commentaries of the nineteenth century may be viewed as falling between these two men: Harless wrote in the early part of the century and later commentators often refer critically to him; Feine writes at the end of the century and surveys critically the work of commentators since Harless.

Adolph Harless (1806—1879)

Adolph Harless asserts that the theme of Eph 2:11—22[47] is Christ as the peace between men and God, and not as the peace between Jews and Gentiles.

> *He* is peace, and this peace, because it is *he,* is not the smoothing away of hate between Gentiles and Jews, but rather the peace of the *Reconciler,* because of whom both have access to the Father... This is the exclusive and main thought of the passage.

The whole of Harless' exposition of the passage is an argument for this position. Two chief elements in the argument are his interpretation of the dividing wall (v. 14) and of the phrase "making peace" (v. 15).

To show that the wall was between God and man, Harless first points out that it is defined by the appositive "the hostility". Therefore one must determine what this hostility is in order to find out what the wall is. Harless attempts to do this in the following argument. The hostility was erased by abrogating the law of commandments in ordinances (v. 15). Most commentators since Theodoret have considered that the law of commandments in ordinances was the ceremonial law[48]. Then they have naturally concluded that because the ceremonial law separated Jews from Gentiles, it was the cause of the hostility, and therefore figuratively a wall. But the purpose of the law's abrogation is, according to v. 16, re-

---

says, but also why, under the influence of the particular circumstances and his own individual characteristics, he says it in just this way; and which tries to understand the movement of ideas, and the transition from one idea to another".

[47] Commentar über den Brief Pauli an die Ephesier, Erlangen 1834, 197—268.

[48] Even many of the Reformers, says Harless, held that only the ceremonial law was abrogated, because they were fearful of lending support to the Antinomians if they should admit that the entire law was abrogated.

conciliation between men and God[49]. The abrogation of the ceremonial law could certainly not reconcile Gentiles to God, argues Harless, since the ceremonial law was never given to Gentiles and thus could not stand between them and God. Nor was the ceremonial law in itself a barrier between Jews and God.

The difficulty is solved, says Harless, when the hostility is seen as that of men against God, caused by the entire law. The dividing wall is the figure which represents this hostility. The hostility exists in Gentiles as well as Jews because the law which is written in the hearts of the Gentiles (Rom 2:15) is essentially the same as the Mosaic law. Harless finds additional evidence for his conviction that the hostility was between men and God in v. 16, where the word "hostility" is used in immediate connection with reconciliation to God.

As a second argument for his position, Harless points out that the verbs connected with uniting Jews and Gentiles are in the aorist tense whereas those connected with peace are in the present tense. From this fact, Harless concludes that the uniting of Jews and Gentiles was a past event only, and therefore not essentially related to the peace between man and God which continues in the present. "The peace as a consequence of which the birth of the new man comes about is . . . another thing entirely than the outward smoothing away of national hostilities."[50]

Harless' concern for the present value of the passage is one indication of his theological approach. Another is the amount of authority he attributes to earlier, and especially patristic, commentaries. For example, he is encouraged by the fact that Chrysostom, Theophylact and Oecumenius agree with his view that the "hostility" (vv. 14, 16) is exclusively between men and God. Harless relies

---

[49] The question is whether Harless is justified in limiting the meaning of "to reconcile" in v. 16 as he does. The only evidence Harless offers for such a limitation is Col 2:14: "the handwriting with its ordinances (τοῖς δόγμασιν) which was against us he took from between us (ἐκ τοῦ μέσου), nailing it to the cross." This must refer, says Harless, to the law as a barrier between men and God. He does not mention that other commentators such as Calvin think that Col 2:14 refers to the ceremonial law.

[50] W. De Wette raises the pertinent question of why Harless calls the resolution of national hostilities "outward". Do not the hostilities between Jews and Gentiles constitute a deep, spiritual, "inward" problem? According to De Wette, the peace spoken of in vv. 14, 15, and 17 is peace between Jews and Gentiles. The aorist tense is used to refer to Christ's death by which the peace was inaugurated; the present tense is used to show that the peace continues to depend upon the "higher unity" Christ has created (Kurze Erklärung der Briefe an die Colosser, an Philemon, an die Ephesier und Philipper, Leipzig 1847², 121).

heavily on Chrysostom, especially in the view that both Jews and Gentiles have been lifted to a better state. Although Chrysostom did not actually use the words "higher unity", Harless in his eagerness to claim Chrysostom's authority for the idea attributes the phrase to him: "It is a higher unity, says Chrysostom, in which they both become one."

Hermann Olshausen (1796—1839)

Harless' agreement with and defense of Chrysostom's position that the dividing wall (v. 14) was between men and God is severely criticized by Hermann Olshausen[51]. He attacks the key position of Harless, the assertion that "to reconcile" in v. 16 can only refer to reconciliation with God. Olshausen argues that the words "both in one body" which follow "to reconcile", as well as the previous "to create the two" show that the reconciliation of Jews to Gentiles is also meant. He further reasons that since the theme of the passage as a whole is clearly the relationship between Jews and Gentiles, v. 16 would not suddenly insert the thought of reconciliation to God. Besides, this would be unmotivated repetition, since reconciliation to God was the theme of chapter one. Against Harless' claim that the hostility (vv. 14, 16) was between man and God, Olshausen makes the counter claim that nowhere does the New Testament say that hostility against God is a result of the law.

Olshausen protests most vigorously against Harless' assumption that reconciliation with God and unity of Jews and Gentiles are essentially unrelated[52], and against Harless' relegation of Jewish-Gentile unity to an unimportant position by referring to it as "outward" in contrast to the "inner" reconciliation with God. A merely outward uniting, says Olshausen, would be "a purely negative removal of that which divided them". He contends that the uniting of Jews and Gentiles is not merely negative but positive; not merely outward, but inward. The basis for this contention can best be seen in his interpretation of the "new man" (v. 15).

Olshausen believes that calling the two groups, Jews and Gentiles, two persons is not simply using a figure of speech. The fact that the uniting of Jew and Gentile is called "creation" and that Christ does it "in himself" indicates that the term "one new man"

---

[51] Biblischer Commentar IV, Königsberg 1840, 187—205.

[52] De Wette agrees completely with Olshausen on this important point (Kurze Erklärung, 122): it is the specific purpose of the phrase "killing the hostility in himself" (v. 16) to "say clearly that reconciliation with God and the ending of racial hostility have taken place in one and the same act".

is not just personification. The biblical view of the corporate nature of man is involved here, and Olshausen attempts a brief explanation of it:

Just as single individuals coalesce in a people to a higher personality, so the peoples in the totality of the race to one man. That isolating view of mankind, according to which it forms a sum of absolutely separated individuals who are only placed next to one another, of whom each one stands and falls for himself, the holy scriptures do not know. Humanity is in Christ a living unity, filled and borne by one Spirit.

Christ's creation of the new man "in himself" must be understood in the light of Eph 1:10 which says that it is God's plan to unite all things "in Christ". Accordingly, in 2:15 "Paul presents Christ himself as the one true universal man, the representative of the race, in whom the two separated halves have returned to complete unity". Relying on his interpretation of Rom 5:12—21, which contrasts Adam and Christ as the representatives of the human race, Olshausen identifies the old mankind divided into Jew and Gentile with Adam; the new united mankind he identifies with Christ. Because the entire life and work of Christ was directed toward creating the one new man in himself, Olshausen maintains that the uniting of Jews and Gentiles cannot be called simply an outward matter.

In affirming the passage's emphasis on the social nature of man, Olshausen strikes a note which is rare in the early nineteenth century, but which is sounded later in the century by such men as Stier and von Soden on the continent, and by the English proponents of social Christianity, Maurice, Westcott and Gore.

Rudolf Stier (1800—1862)

Rudolf Stier[53] commends Olshausen's polemic against Harless' interpretation of the dividing wall as exclusively the barrier between man and God. On the other hand, Stier believes that Olshausen errs by interpreting some parts of the passage in terms of the Jew-Gentile dimension when they really refer to the God-man dimension. Recognizing that the question of how these two dimensions are related is basic in the exegesis of the passage, Stier proposes an answer in terms of typology.

The visible relation of Gentiles with Jews, says Stier, is in this passage the "historical type" of the relation of men with God. This is why the terms "near" and "far" are important for understanding

---

[53] Die Gemeinde in Christo Jesu, Berlin 1848, I, 289—412.

the passage. They refer not only to the visible relation of the Gentiles to Israel, but also to the invisible relation of men to God. To say that the Jew-Gentile relation is a "type" means that it is a sign or indicator, but also more than a mere sign, for it is "vitally, organically, historically, really so bound" with the God-man relation that "the hostility or tension between Israel and the Gentiles can only be taken away by reconciliation with God. And at the same time the opening of access (to God) for the Gentiles takes place only by their uniting with Israel".

According to Stier, Paul's thought in Eph 2:11—22 always moves from the type to that which the type signifies and whereof it partakes. Thus for example he speaks of hostility in v. 14 as an aspect of the Jew-Gentile relation and in v. 16 as an aspect of the God-man relation. This movement explains why the passage seems to speak of Jewish-Gentile reconciliation as a prerequisite of divine-human reconciliation. But because Paul proceeds from the type to its ground, from the visible to the invisible, he speaks first of Jewish-Gentile reconciliation.

Therefore, says Stier, to learn what Paul is saying about reconciliation in this passage, the Jewish-Gentile relation must be taken very seriously.

We must with lively imagination put ourselves in that time, when this difference between the two halves of mankind (yes, really like two kinds of men) was resolved by the one reconciliation of Christ for both—in order to understand the Apostle in his whole message, which so vitally and rightly grasps the innermost and most decisive, most revolutionary fact of history in its visible appearance.

The "most revolutionary fact of history" centers in the cross. The very shape of the cross indicates for Stier, as it did in the early days of the church for Irenaeus and Athanasius[54], that it has to do not only with men's relation to God, but with the relation of groups of men.

To bring together Israel and the Gentiles in God, that was, in the time of fulfillment, the great problem of the world-reconciling cross (v. 16). Just that was really the great knot which history, ruled by God's decision (positive leading of Israel and negative letting the Gentiles go their own way), had tied, which the cross stretching upward and downward and to both sides, solved.

For Stier the concept of the new man (v. 15) has a key position in the movement of Paul's thought from type to what is typified.

---

[54] See above, p. 24.

For the new man is, historically understood, the community formed
by the union of Jews and Gentiles (v. 14). But he is also the man
reconciled to God (v. 16). While the concept of the new man has
various aspects, they all begin from the center, Christ.

Because of the ἐν ἑαυτῷ (in himself) we believe that here the essential
concept proceeds completely from Christ, from himself as the first true
and really new man ... Christ himself is first of all ... the one true universal man, not merely as "representative", but really as root and origin
of the new race of men which is in him and from him.

Like many other commentators, especially in his century, Stier
considers the "new race of men" to be neither Jews nor Gentiles,
and cites Chrysostom with approval on this point. He does not
however call the new man a "higher unity", as many of his con-
temporaries do. Furthermore, Stier does not claim that this "new
race" exists concurrently with and superior to the races of Jew and
Gentile. For Stier believes that all mankind is included in the new
man. The creation of both halves of humanity into one new man
was the immediate purpose of Christ's work. The ultimate purpose
was "that he might reconcile both in one body to God". This purpose has been accomplished only in the case of those Jews and Gentiles who have actually become members of the church[55].

Stier says that the "historical process" proclaimed in Eph 2, by
which the church or "international Christianity" was then formed,
is itself a type for the future life of the church. In Stier's typologi-
cal view, the church today stands amidst the world as Israel once
stood amidst the Gentiles, and there exists today an analogous
hostility.

An analogy of the hostility as Paul meant it and as it existed up until
Christ's coming reproduces itself still wherever Christ has not yet made
everything new and spiritually free. We have before our eyes not only
the fact that the publicans and sinners in Christendom, who can be compared to the Gentiles, express and at the same time mask their hate toward the pious people; but also that the legally pious (even the Pietists,
insofar as they belong to this group) let out their unconquered ill-will
with proud pretense as hate of worldlings[56].

---

[55] B. F. Westcott goes a step further in saying the reconciliation of all men
to God was also accomplished by Christ, see below, p. 158.

[56] Similarly J. T. Beck (Erklärung des Briefes Pauli an die Epheser, Gütersloh 1891, 142): "Christ is the continuing peacemaker (therefore the present
tense ποιῶν εἰρήνην) between that Gentile and Jewish dichotomy, the lawless
worldliness and the legalistic forced piety, a dichotomy which goes through all
of history, even within Christendom, where the transformation into the unity
of the new humanity has not been accomplished through union with Christ."

The type which Eph 2 presents has relevance also for problems within the community of committed Christians.

In part, divisions, hostilities, oppositions, develop even within Christianity, whose solution by continual peace-making through vital contact with Christ remains the great task always on the way to fulfillment... In the Christian peoples and national churches the dividing walls must fall, the hostilities be killed.

Stier urges that efforts for union in the church today should rest on thorough knowledge of "that first great union". We know, says Stier, that in Paul's time the union of Jews and Gentiles was not fully realized, but Paul nevertheless believed it had already been given in Christ.

The great deep union of Gentile and Jewish Christians in the Apostle's time was far from completed. But he works at it, and points toward it, in that he takes up the problem, standing in Christ high above the division, and preaches tirelessly and powerfully that its solution has already taken place, so that it may also take place in the congregation before him. This way and no other do we have to work for union[57].

Adolphe Monod (1802—1856)

Unique in nineteenth century interpretation of Eph 2:11—22 is the way in which Adolph Monod[58] identifies himself with the Gentile Christians to whom the letter is addressed. Previous commentators in his century assume that Christianity is a new religion over against Judaism and Gentilism; and since they have been born into this new religion they think of themselves in a category apart from Gentiles or Jews. To describe this category Baur used the term "absolute religion"[59], expressing Christianity's essential independence from Israel.

In contrast, Monod affirms the continuity of Christianity with Judaism. He dwells on the concept of "the people of God" whose story begins in the Old Testament and continues through the New Testament. At one time the people of God was Israel alone; now we Gentiles are also part of God's people. The fact that we have been accepted into Israel ought to make us honor Israel highly:

---

[57] Westcott also says that the unity of all mankind, although already given in Christ, is not yet fully realized.

[58] Explication de l'épître de Saint Paul aux Éphésiens, Paris 1867, IV, 101—144.

[59] See above p. 132.

"Let us learn from this passage, then, the esteem which we ought to have for Israel—we who have been able to come to God only by becoming in Jesus Christ one with Israel, so that we ourselves are called 'the Israel of God' (Gal 4:16)."

Monod singles out the proclamation of v. 13 that the Gentiles who were "far" have become "near" as crucial for the understanding of the whole passage. He states that the kind of answers a commentator will get to the exegetical problems in vv. 14—22 depends to a large extent on his answer to the following question about v. 13:

Near to whom? to Israel, or to the God of Israel? V. 14 and following are among the most difficult of our epistle. And this difficulty is to a large extent due to the question which has just been indicated and which presents itself each time the words "peace", "hostility", etc. appear. Thence the rather great divergence among commentators according to the position they take on this point.

Monod finds that part of the cause for confusion lies in "the Apostle's thought and in the nature of the matter" but holds nevertheless that the context indicates which dimension is primary for a given passage. Since vv. 11—12 and 19—22, as well as the first part of Eph 3, especially v. 5, lift up the relation of Gentiles with Israel, Monod concludes that in Eph 2:13—15 Paul wants to speak primarily about this dimension, although reconciliation with God is in itself more fundamental.

Monod urges that the way in which Christ has united Jews and Gentiles is relevant for questions of church unity today. We cannot speak of one new man (v. 15) without constant reference to Christ, because without Christ we cannot understand the word "one" rightly:

Here is the secret of all true union, as much between groups as between individuals: it is not a question of the others' coming to us or of our going to them; but it is a matter for them and for us of going to Christ, in whom alone we can be effectively and really united. St. Paul says this, to be sure, of unregenerate men, who have to undergo a radical change. But this remark, modified according to the situation, applies to every union, among Christians as well.

Monod like Stier recognizes that there are divisions among men not only outside the church, but within it. Therefore we cannot simply say that if hostile groups of men today, like Jews and Gentiles in Paul's time, were to join the church, they would be united. The church is not in itself the one new man. Not only non-believers need to be made new; the various fragmented groups of Christians need to be made new in order that they may find unity with one another. They can be made new only as they move forward toward Christ, and in this way only can they find unity, not simply by moving toward one another.

Johann Chr. K. von Hofmann (1810—1877)

Like Monod, Johann Chr. K. von Hofmann[60] believes that Eph 2:11—22 strongly affirms the continuity of the church with Israel. For Hofmann, this continuity is expressed in the concept of "redemptive history", extending through both Old and New Testaments. The redemptive work of God centers in one people, which Hofmann calls "the community of redemption". In the Old Testament period this community was limited to the Jews, but now it is open to Gentiles as well. Hofmann says Paul's purpose in Eph 2:11—22 is to remind his Gentile readers "from what great separation from the Israelite community of redemption they now in Christ Jesus have been brought into the community of the apostles which is for both groups, and is one united community"[61].

Hofmann is one of the few nineteenth century commentators to state clearly that Gentiles remain Gentiles even after they have been united with Jews[62].

They are still non-Jews; what is past for them is their estrangement from the community of redemption, which was Israelite until in Christ Jesus it ceased being merely Israelite. To him they owe the fact that their exclusion from the redeeming gifts of Israel has ceased, while they have not ceased being non-Jews.

---

[60] Die Heilige Schrift Neuen Testaments, Nördlingen 1870, IV, 1, 76—108.

[61] In a later passage Hofmann charges Baur with being unwilling to grant that "the Apostle Paul teaches such a connection of the New Testament community with the Old Testament community that the Gentiles who were outside the latter were also thereby outside the area of salvation." But, argues Hofmann, if Paul did not teach this, he could not have taught for example that the gospel is "for the Jew first and also for the Gentile" (Rom 1:16), nor that the fatherhood of Abraham has come to include the believing Gentiles (Rom 4), nor that Israel has marvellous spiritual possessions (Rom 9:4), nor that Israel is the cultivated olive tree into which the Gentiles have been grafted (Rom 11:17—24). (Die Heilige Schrift, 286).

[62] J. Eadie, E. Haupt (KEK, Gefangenschaftsbriefe, 1902[8], 69n), and G. Wohlenberg (Die Briefe Pauli aus seiner ersten römischen Gefangenschaft, ed. Strack and Zöckler, Kurzgefaßter Kommentar, Munich 1895[2], II, 4, 22) also hold that the Gentiles remain Gentiles after their conversion. Wohlenberg gives a list of passages in which Paul addresses Gentile Christians as Gentiles: Eph 3:1; Rom 11:13; 15:27; 16:4; Gal 2:12, 14.

For Hofmann the unity of the community of redemption is not uniformity.

Hofmann's interpretation of the dividing wall (v. 14) is remarkably like that of Severian of Gabala[63]. It is important, says Hofmann, to note that φραγμός means that which surrounds something, marking it off from what is outside. The word μεσότοιχον means that which divides into two parts. When Paul says that the μεσότοιχον τοῦ φραγμοῦ is broken down, he means that only that aspect of the wall is ended which prevented Gentiles from entering the community of redemption. Correspondingly, the law as such is not abrogated, but that form of it which separated Jews from Gentiles. There still remains a wall in the sense of that which distinguished the community of redemption from the rest of the world. In this way Hofmann makes it clear that redemptive history continues, and that the community of redemption, the church, still has a unique function to perform. The death of Christ does not make the community of redemption equivalent to the entire world, nor does it make redemptive history identical with the whole history of mankind.

Hofmann spells out more fully than most other interpreters how Christ "ended the hostility in his flesh" (v. 14). His explanation depends on a unique interpretation of the phrase "in his flesh" according to which it designates the place where Christ has acted to end the hostility. It therefore does not simply mean "by his death" or "by his incarnation", which are the alternatives many commentators debate. Rather, it means that by the way in which he let his flesh be destroyed he ended the hostility.

So long as he remained in the life in which he stood from birth, so long did he remain limited to that people to which he belonged from birth. He could only remain in this life if he were the kind of savior his people wanted. As such he would have established an Israelite community of redemption which would have been hostile toward the Gentiles and would have regarded itself as justified by him in doing so. Correspondingly, the Gentiles would have retained their hostile attitude toward such a community of redemption. Now however he has let the fulfillment of his completely different mission as the savior cost his life in the flesh. Thereby the hostility against the Gentiles, which had its basis in Israel's unique position in redemptive history, is once for all done away with as far as the Israelite community of redemption which he established is concerned. Likewise the hostility of the Gentiles against this community of redemption, which otherwise would have been made firmer by the continuation of the separateness of Israel, was done away with for those among the Gentiles who became believers.

---

[63] See above p. 28.

It is significant that in the above explanation Hofmann calls the early church "the Israelite community of redemption". He thereby strongly emphasizes the continuity of the church with Israel: the church is Israelite in character, but it is no longer exclusively Israelite, since it is open to Gentiles. Christ established this community in order that in it all Jews and Gentiles might be reconciled to one another and to God. But this purpose has not yet been fully accomplished, since there are still many people outside the community of redemption[64]. Entrance into it depends on faith in Christ[65].

Hugh Oltramare (1813—1891)

Although Hugh Oltramare[66] shares the view of Hofmann that peace between Jews and Gentiles depends completely on their faith in Christ, he does not share Hofmann's emphasis on the continuity of the church with Israel.

Oltramare's interpretation of the new man (v. 15) illustrates a danger in considering individual conversion apart from the Christian community. According to Oltramare's description, the Gentile becomes a new man in Christ and the Jew becomes a new man in Christ—each individually and separately, before entering into relationship with the other: "Christ has made each of them a new man, equally Christian in the one case and in the other."[67] The result of Oltramare's reasoning is uniformity rather than unity. Differences are denied.

The two different personalities, the Jewish personality and the Gentile personality, are both wholly transformed by the union of the Jew and

[64] Beck takes the same position. He says that vv. 14—15a proclaim what is "objectively" accomplished by Christ on the cross; vv. 15—16, beginning with ἵνα (in order that) refer to the "subjective" result aimed for. "There is not, as in the historic νυνὶ ἀποκατήλλαξεν (he has reconciled) Col 1:22, the already accomplished "objective uniting" (Erklärung, 143).

[65] For this reason Hofmann considers Baur's view that the unity of Jews and Gentiles in Eph is a mere outward coalition based on removal of circumcision, completely mistaken. The unity depends on faith, which is certainly not merely an outward matter.

[66] Commentaire sur les Épîtres de S. Paul aux Colossiens, aux Éphésiens et à Philémon, Paris 1892, II, 349—417. Oltramare expresses his view unmistakably in such comments as, "Paul shows us peace between two peoples based on their conversion by union with Christ" and "this conversion of the one and the other is the foundation, and without it there is no peace possible between them".

[67] Similarly Beck, 144, speaks of "the transformation of the individual Jewish or Gentile man into the new spiritual man in Christ". (italics mine)

the Gentile with Christ into one new personality, the same for each one, that is the Christian personality[68].

The shift Oltramare has made from the text is evidenced by his speaking of "the union of the Jew and the Gentile with Christ", rather than "the union of the Jew with the Gentile in Christ".

The outcome of this interpretation of the new man is that after decrying the pride of the Jewish man in his law, which causes contempt for Gentiles, Oltramare finds a basis for the Christian man's pride—in the confidence that he is the new man.

> By the fact of the religious and moral ideal which we owe to Christ, we Christians feel that we are superior to the Jews, so that from every point of view we can judge the inanity of all the religious and moral apparatus which has the law for a basis. Their disdain cannot touch us, because our religious point of view is superior.

This is one of the few references to Jewish-Christian relationships in nineteenth century interpretation of our passage[69]. It illustrates the dangerous consequences for Christian-Jewish relations of the idea, very strong in the century, that the new man is *neither* Jew *nor* Gentile, instead of Jew *and* Gentile, and that Christianity is a higher unity which has left Judaism and Gentilism below and behind.

Erich Haupt (1841—1909)

Although Erich Haupt[70] shares with Oltramare the majority view that the new man (v. 15) is neither Jew nor Gentile, he differs in holding that the new man is Christ himself. Since Christ is the representative of all men, it can be said that in a secondary sense, all mankind is the new man.

Unique is Haupt's explanation that the term "new man" applies to Christ because of the way in which he abrogated the law. According to Haupt, Christ's crucifixion involves his expulsion from the Jewish community. Outside the community, he is no longer subject to the Mosaic law. Nor are those who believe in him, instead of in the law which cursed him[71]. Outside the community, Christ

---

[68] Beck, 141, also uses the term "personality": "the two personalities of the human race ... shall be transformed to one new personality."

[69] Another is that of G. Schnedermann, 25, who says that v. 19 assures complete equal rights of Gentiles with Jews and adds elliptically, "Important against modern overestimation of Israelite descent".

[70] Die Gefangenschaftsbriefe, KEK, Brief an die Epheser, 1897[7], 72—99.

[71] Haupt believes that the key to Eph 2:14—16 is Gal 3:13: "Christ

is no longer a Jew; neither is he a Gentile. He is the first of a third type: the "one new man" who is the beginner of a new, united humanity. However, Haupt says that because not everyone accepts unity in Christ, "it follows that 'peace' here refers exclusively to the resolution of differences among believers". In the later edition of his commentary, Haupt reverses his interpretation of "peace" (vv. 14, 15, 17). He no longer thinks that it is peace between Jews and Gentiles in the church, but peace with God. The chief reason he gives for this position is that v. 17 proclaims "peace to the far and peace" to the near. From this he deduces that the peace is not *between* the near and the far, but a peace offered equally to each[72].

Despite this reversal Haupt's interpretation does not essentially change in the second edition. He still maintains that the basic thought of the entire passage is that Gentiles are now equal to the Jews in their standing before God. He sees the passage more in terms of equal rights than of unity.

Brooke Foss Westcott (1825—1901)

Like Haupt, Brooke Foss Westcott[73] says that the new man (v. 15) includes all humans because Christ is the new man who as the head and representative of humanity makes the entire race a new man. Westcott, however, has different grounds than Haupt for calling Christ the new man. Haupt says Christ's death on the cross meant his ejection from the Jewish people, thus putting him outside of the divisive categories Jew or Gentile. Westcott says that Christ is the new man because of his birth. By becoming man, God's Son has made men new, and has made them one: "By the assumption of human nature He gave ideally new life to all who

---

redeemed us from the curse of the law, having become a curse for us—for it is written, 'Cursed be everyone who hangs on a tree'." According to Haupt, this verse means that Christ has not only made atonement for the guilt which the law has charged us with, but he has taken away the law itself, since it constitutes a curse. The essential agreement which Haupt sees between Galatians and Ephesians on this point is for him confirmation that Paul wrote Ephesians.

[72] Other reasons given (Epheserbrief, 1902[8], 76) are: peace is spoken of in v. 14 before there is any mention of hostility between Jews and Gentiles; vv. 14—16 tell of a complete union involving the abolition of the difference between Jews and Gentiles, giving no longer two parties but one, and yet peace is a term which can only be used for the relationship of two parties.

[73] St. Paul's Epistle to the Ephesians, London 1906, 34—41.

share it (II Cor 5:17).... The unity of humanity was gained by the Incarnation."[74]

Westcott faces the problem which is connected with the claim that all men have already been made one: the apparent disunity of men. He replies: "That which is complete in the Divine Act may be yet future in historic realisation" and then gives some quotations from other New Testament books which point to the tension between the already accomplished act and its historical realization[75]. So it is that Christ has already accomplished the twofold object announced in vv. 15 and 16: the uniting of Jew and Gentile into one man and the reconciliation of man to God. "This object He gained, though the result is not open to our vision. Humanity is in him 'one new man'. The enmity is slain, though we live among the fruits of its earlier vitality."

Westcott is anxious to show that Christ's accomplishment of his purpose does not mean that man has nothing to do. He points out that "the new man must be 'put on' (4:24) by those who are ideally included in him". Christ has given men the power to realize their unity: "By His life of perfect obedience, the virtue of which He offered to Jew and Gentile alike ... all men were made capable of a living unity."

Paul Feine (1859—1933)

In a detailed study of Eph 2:14—16[76], Paul Feine disagrees with the view of the majority of commentators that the dividing wall

---

[74] The Incarnation as the basis of the unity of mankind is a dominant theme among the group of nineteenth century English theologians who struggled to make the church aware of the social dimension of Christianity. Westcott identified himself with this movement, in which F. D. Maurice (see below pp. 164—165) had been the first major theologian. Westcott (Social Aspects of Christianity, London 1900[2], 9—10) states forcefully his conviction that all men are one in Christ: "In Christ all men are brethren ... Our relationship to one another does not depend on any remote descent: it is not imperiled by any possible discovery as to the origin or the antiquity of man ... The brotherhood of men seen in Christ is a question not of genealogy but of being. It rests upon the present and abiding fatherhood of God, Who in His Son has taken our common nature to Himself. We may acknowledge this God-made kinsmanship or we may neglect it; but none the less we all are not only brethren in constitution, brethren in death, but brethren in Christ, brethren for evermore."

[75] Other commentators such as Stier have said that according to Eph 2:11—22 unity is already given but not yet fully realized (see above p. 151). Westcott goes a step further in showing the presence of this tension in other New Testament passages: Hebr 2:8; I Cor 15:26.

[76] Theologische Studien und Kritiken 72, 1899, 540—574.

was between Jews and Gentiles. He observes that the generally accepted position involves treating the unity between Jews and Gentiles as a prerequisite of reconciliation with God. If this were really what vv. 14—16 imply, says Feine, then he would agree with Klöpper that they are not Pauline, since according to Paul unity between Jews and Gentiles depends on unity with God, and not the other way around.

Feine's approach to the passage is marked by theological preconceptions which he expresses, for example, in discussing v. 16: "It is obvious that a clear idea cannot be achieved if reconciliation with God and at the same time that of the Gentiles and Jews with one another are spoken of here, and reconciliation is really understood under the condition of actual incorporation into the church of Christ." Feine notes that Harless is the only commentator who interprets the dividing wall as between man and God, and that Harless's arguments are almost totally rejected by later commentators. Feine believes however that Harless is basically right, and that the majority opinion does not fit the immediate context of vv. 11—12, nor the wider context of Eph 1—3. If Eph 2:14—16 is rightly interpreted, says Feine, it is seen to be in agreement with Paul's theology.

Feine lays the groundwork for his case in an analysis of the construction of vv. 14—16. He says that the participial phrases "who has made us both one" and "who has broken down the dividing wall" modify αὐτός, that is, Christ, and not, as many interpreters assume, the nature of the peace mentioned in v. 14. Thus Feine contends that Christ's making both one, and his breaking the wall, are not the reasons he is our peace. Rather, he is our peace because he has "killed the hostility[77] in his flesh, the law of commandments in ordinances". Feine therefore outlines vv. 14—16 in the following way:

Christ is our peace because he, in his own person, has killed the hostility. Along with this main thought is also expressed in v. 14 what effect his act as peacemaker has brought about and in vv. 15 and 16 by what means he killed the hostility and what purpose led him in his action directed toward killing the hostility.

Having divided vv. 14—16 into a main thought and a secondary one, the way is open for Feine to argue that the main thought is peace with God.

---

[77] Following von Soden (Hand-Commentar, 123), Feine says that in v. 14 after the word "hostility" the thought is interrupted, and is resumed and completed in v. 16 by the phrase "having killed the hostility".

He proceeds by analyzing the train of thought in the context of vv. 11—19. The first part, vv. 11—13, introduces the idea that the Gentiles who were far from God have been brought near; this change has been effected, according to v. 13, in the blood of Christ. The second part of the passage, vv. 14—16, has the function of explaining how Christ's blood has caused the change; the fact that it is introduced with the word γάϱ (for, because) shows that this is its function. The following vv. 17—19 then return to elaborate on the idea begun in vv. 11—13.

Now, argues Feine, the idea that Christ has made peace between Jews and Gentiles does not fit, because it does not really explain why Christ's blood has brought the Gentiles into God's community. "The work of salvation itself, and accordingly the way and means and purpose of its accomplishment, is vastly more important than the consequence that it includes peace between both categories of men." In Feine's opinion, to say that "He is our peace" (v. 14) means "He is the peace between Jews and Gentiles" is "not to talk about the Savior who has come in the person of Jesus, but only about the union between Jews and Gentiles located in him". Because Feine assumes that peace between Jews and Gentiles is not really part of salvation itself, but only a by-product of the way in which salvation was accomplished, Feine can charge the majority of commentators with trying to make the secondary thought in vv. 14—16 into the primary one: the passage does not say "He is the peace of Jews and Gentiles", but "He is the peace of Christians". The proclamation that Christ is the peace of Christians, says Feine, follows naturally after the final phrase of v. 13, "in the blood of Christ": "In the blood of Christ is to be seen the basis for the peaceful status of Christians with God."

Feine does not deny that there is some reference in the passage to a unity between Jews and Gentiles. But since according to vv. 13 and 18 this unity is in Christ and in the Spirit, it must be unity in the ascended Christ. It is therefore not a matter of Christ's admitting Gentiles into unity with Israel. So Feine judges that Calvin was mistaken in saying that the Jews cannot have Christ as their reconciler unless they admit Gentiles to their fellowship. The unity of Jews and Gentiles is not fellowship in the flesh, contends Feine, because it is a spiritual fellowship. Feine argues that in the first three chapters of Ephesians Paul operates with the contrast of flesh and spirit, rather than law and gospel. As evidence he points to 1:3, which says that God has blessed the Christians "in every spiritual blessing". In 2:1—10 Paul says that Christians once "walked in the lusts of the flesh", but now "have been raised into the realms of heaven in Christ". There is every reason, says Feine, that this contrast between the low life in the flesh and the high life in the Spirit should be continued in vv. 11—22, since the passage begins with a "therefore", which shows that it depends on vv. 1—10. Thus it is that the phrases "in the flesh" and "in the world" are contrasted to "in Christ" and "in the Spirit". Since the change from life "in the flesh" to "life in the Spirit" is brought about "in the blood of Christ", vv. 14—16 have the function of showing how the blood of Christ has made the change:

The blood of Christ is the ground for his being in person our peace with God. He is this as the one who has made both parts of humanity into a unity and has torn down the dividing wall of separation. The present unity however is a spiritual one. The reason why this unity, which was created by the bloody death of Christ, did not exist before Christ, lay in the fact that Jews and Gentiles were in the flesh. Therefore the context demands that the words τὸ μεσότοιχον τοῦ φραγμοῦ λύσας (having broken down the dividing wall) refer to taking away this separation of humanity from God which resides in human σάρξ (flesh).

From this it follows that the word "hostility" (v. 14) refers to the hostility of men against God. According to Feine, v. 14 contains the same idea as does Rom 8:7, "the mind of the flesh is hostility toward God". By killing this hostility (v. 16), Christ intended to create all humanity into a new man (v. 15), no longer defined by the flesh. This purpose of Christ was "accomplished, whether the result has appeared yet or not".

No other commentator has worked out so detailed a defense of the view that the dividing wall is between man and God. In his emphasis on the contrast between flesh and spirit, on the wall between man and God, and on spiritual unity above and distinct from Israel, Feine resembles Chrysostom, whose interpretation he cites as precedent.

Theological commentators are thus divided: the minority, like Feine, think that Eph 2:11—22 is primarily about the new relationship to God which Christ has brought about; the majority think that the passage is primarily about the unity of the church.

Sermons and Practical Commentaries

In sermons and practical commentaries, there are very few men who do not emphasize the unity of the church. In this minority, however, is the most influential theologian of the century, Friedrich Schleiermacher.

Friedrich Schleiermacher (1768—1834)

In a sermon on Eph 2:19[78], Friedrich Schleiermacher argues that love for one's country is a key ethical imperative. He aims to disprove the opinion, which he says many educated people hold, that to be ethical we should try "by a sense of world-citizenship, to lift ourselves above the limitation which every smaller community unavoidably involves". Often, observes Schleiermacher, people suppose that the Christian faith, because it puts membership in the church above membership in the nation, supports such a view. On the contrary, says Schleiermacher, the Christian faith demands a whole-hearted participation in the life of one's own country.

According to Schleiermacher, Eph 2:19 proclaims that it is much better for the Gentiles to be fully participating members of the Christian Church, "fellow citizens of the saints and members of the household of God", than to be "strangers and sojourners", as most of them were in the Jewish synagogue.

Most of them had already been related to the Jewish Church, but in a subordinate way, not with the same rights as those who were members of that chosen people by birth. The Jewish Christians for the most part wanted to carry over this difference into the Christian Church and only rate as full members those who had been entirely incorporated into the Jewish Church. In opposition to this the apostle strove everywhere for a complete equality of all believers, whether gathered from the Jews or from the Gentiles, and this equality is what he wants to call their attention to as something important and worthy of thankfulness.

Thus for Schleiermacher, the right of the Gentiles to full participation in the church is the major theme, rather than unity with the Jews[79]. He grants that Paul speaks about participation in the one Christian Church, whereas today there are many churches. But Schleiermacher holds that the various churches arose for good reasons, and that Paul would encourage Christians today to devote themselves to their own churches.

The reasoning by which Schleiermacher connects full participation in one's church and full participation in one's nation is rather tenuous. From the fact that Paul uses political terms to explain that the position of the Gentiles is now far better than it was previously,

---

[78] Predigten, Berlin 1843², I, 218—233, "Wie sehr es die Würde des Menschen erhöht, wenn er mit ganzer Seele an der bürgerlichen Vereinigung hängt, der er angehört."

[79] Schleiermacher can therefore be numbered among those who interpret the passage in terms of equality rather than unity, of whom the first important commentator is Chrysostom.

Schleiermacher concludes that Paul would also consider it far better to be a full participant in one's nation than merely a resident who takes no vital part in the life of the nation as a whole—an attitude which Schleiermacher equates with being a "stranger and sojourner".

As his rationale for the continuing existence both of various churches and of various nations, Schleiermacher takes the saying of Jesus, "In my Father's house are many mansions." The mansions are the various peoples, each of whom presents a facet of the image of God. God can best be known therefore by his work in the lives of the various nations. But each individual can only learn to know God in this way when he first of all experiences God's work in his own people. And the individual can only act for God when he acts as a "member of God's household", therefore within his particular mansion or nation. Similarly the individual cannot love mankind as a whole; he must love his own people, for whom and with whom he can really accomplish something.

Schleiermacher's sermon is an interesting attempt to deal with the question of national loyalty on the basis of our passage. This question has been generally neglected by theologians, who have concentrated on the individual, the church and mankind as a whole. But Schleiermacher's appeal for civic responsibility reveals the uncritical acceptance of the disunity of the church which was widespread in the eighteenth and nineteenth centuries. His position could easily be used to justify the division of the church along national and ethnic lines, since he emphasizes that the best results are achieved in religion, as well as in other fields, when one works together with people with whom one has by nature much in common. Whatever the relative truth of his position may be, it completely neglects what many interpreters believe is the chief emphasis of Eph 2:11—22: that the church is and has been from its beginning the place where people who by nature have very little in common come together because they believe Christ has united them.

Nevertheless, Schleiermacher deserves much credit for being one of the first to call theology from its over-emphasis on the individual to an awareness of the importance of the social nature of man. This awareness is one of the chief characteristics of the work of a group of English theologians later in the nineteenth century, who however understand Eph 2:11—22 quite differently from Schleiermacher. We have already discussed the commentary of one of these men, B. F. Westcott. Now we come to writings of expressly practical purpose by two others, Frederick Denison Maurice and Charles Gore.

Frederick Denison Maurice (1805—1872)

In a sermon on Eph 2:15[80], Frederick Denison Maurice says that our passage proclaims a unity which holds together people who think differently theologically. Convinced that the major theme of the passage is unity of Jew and Gentile, Maurice focuses on what he believes is the essential difference between the two: their ways of thinking about God.

According to Maurice, the Gentile seeks God by investigating the natural world and his own experience; the Jew on the other hand believes that God has already shown himself, seeks man, and has given directions for life. The Apostle Paul, who is intimately acquainted with both these contrasting ways of thinking[81], does not suggest in Eph 2 that Jew and Gentile unite by means of some kind of compromise whereby each gives up some of his own ideas. Rather he indicates that each is incomplete without the other. Only together are they the new man.

They were incomplete, explains Maurice, because both their ways of thinking were unfulfilled. The true Jew, who believed that God had made himself known to Israel in order to make himself known throughout the whole earth, "must have been longing for a fellowship with all God's creatures which he had not yet realized". There was however a false Judaism—a growing tendency to limit God's activity to the past, and against it the true Jew could only hope that God would speak "to his age *more* directly, *more* personally than He had ever spoken before". This is what happened in Christ. The Gentile's thinking was also unfulfilled because he had been seeking God and not really finding him. But now he could see the Son of God as the Son of Man, sharing the sorrows and joys of men, and recognize that it was He for whom he had been seeking.

Maurice's personal history made him aware of the divisive power of theological differences. Alec Vidler explains that Maurice's father was a Unitarian minister, and that members of the family "broke away from their father's faith in different directions, some being drawn to Calvinistic nonconformity, others to the Church of England. This distressing state of division in his own family drove

---

[80] Sermons Preached in Lincoln's Inn Chapel, London 1891, I, 122—138.

[81] Maurice cites Acts 17 and Rom 3 as portraying the respective ways of thinking. In Acts 17 Paul acknowledges that the Gentiles seek after God. According to Rom 1—2, God has revealed himself to the Gentiles, but they have not known it and have sought God in their own ways, which end in idolatry. But according to Rom 3, the Jews "have oracles of God", for says Maurice, God has "by a whole course of discipline" made the Jews aware of his revelation.

Maurice to seek for a ground of unity between men other than that of their religious opinions"[82].

In the person of Christ, says Maurice, not in a set of theological propositions, Jew and Gentile found their theological unity. Christ is thus the unity of all kinds of theology, for every variety of religious thinking follows, in Maurice's view, one of the two ways represented by the Jew and the Gentile[83].

Innumerable as the forms of opinion and habits of feeling among us may seem to be, they do resolve themselves at last into these two capital divisions of which St. Paul speaks. If we search long, we shall not find any classification at once so scientific and so available in practice as that which he resorted to when he described the Jew and Gentile as forming the elements of the full Christian man.

From his conviction that both the Jewish and the Gentile ways of thinking are necessary in the new man, Maurice generalizes that variety is involved in Christ's unity: "He does not come to make a solitude and call it peace; He does not come to destroy all that is distinctive in nations or in individuals, for the sake of producing a dead uniformity."

Maurice himself worked ardently for the cause of unity and peace in the church and among all men, and the practical aim of his sermon is to provide help for his hearers in their work as peacemakers: "These recollections may be of some service to us, if we are heartily seeking in our own days to be Peace Makers, and so to be called the children of Him who is the Peace Maker."

Charles Gore (1853—1932)

The commentary of Charles Gore[84] deals not so much with the problem of theological differences as does Maurice's sermon, but more with the problem of a widespread popular misunderstanding of Christianity which treats it in an individualistic way that subordinates it to class, national and racial loyalties.

In commenting on v. 12, Gore points out that Paul speaks about redemption as communal and not simply individual, since he treats

---

[82] The Church in an Age of Revolution, London 1961, 84.

[83] On the problems involved in Maurice's explanation of the way in which Christ is the ground of human community, see R. Ahlers's Hamburg dissertation, Die Vermittlungstheologie des Frederick Denison Maurice, Hamburg 1967, esp. VII, C, "Jesus Christus demonstriert die göttliche Humanität", 218—229.

[84] St. Paul's Epistle to the Ephesians: a practical exposition, New York 1898, 102—129.

the "commonwealth of Israel" as the community of redemption under the old covenant, and proclaims the continuity of this community under the new covenant.

Under the old covenant it was to members of the commonwealth of Israel that the blessings of the covenant belonged. Under the new covenant St. Paul still conceives of the same commonwealth as subsisting ... and as fulfilling no less than formerly the same religious functions. True, it has been fundamentally reconstituted and enlarged to include the believers of all nations, and not merely one nation; but it is still the same commonwealth, or polity, or church; and it is still through the church that God's covenant dealings reach the individual.

This communal view of redemption, contends Gore, is not just Paul's idea, but that of the Bible as a whole, despite popular opinion to the contrary[85].

Gore thinks that when Paul speaks of the dividing wall (v. 14) he is alluding to the wall in the Jerusalem temple. For according to Gore, Paul is in prison in Rome in part because he was accused of having taken a Gentile, Trophimus the Ephesian, into the temple (Acts 21:27—29). Paul is therefore captive precisely because of the hostility between Jew and Gentile. Nevertheless, he knows that Christ has overcome the hostility, and that the church is called to demonstrate this truth—to be truly catholic. Gore notes that in the beginning of Eph 3 Paul claims that the task of teaching the catholicity of the church is his particular responsibility. The difficulty of this task Gore recognizes in its contemporary counterpart:

When we set ourselves to rehabilitate the sense of church membership, we feel at once the strength of the forces against us: we realize how much the feeling of blood-kinship in the family counts for, or the wider kinship of national life, or the common interests of our professions or our classes, compared to the feeble sense of fellowship which comes from a church membership which is so largely conventional. Most assuredly we feel the difficulty of what we have at hand. But we cannot feel it more intensely than St. Paul felt the difficulty involved in the very idea of a human brotherhood in which national distinctions were obliterated ... A society in which even the savage and brutal Scythians

---

[85] An attempt to correct popular opinion in this matter is made several years later by Sanday and Headlam, International Critical Commentary, Romans, Edinburgh 1902[5], 122—124: "It is and has been a popular religious idea that the primary aim of the gospel is to produce saved individuals; and that it is a matter of secondary importance that the saved individuals should afterwards combine to form churches for their mutual spiritual profit, and for promoting the work of preaching the gospel. But this way of conceiving the matter is a reversal of the order of ideas in the Bible. 'The salvation' in the Bible is supposed usually 'to reach the individual through the community'."

should have equal fellowship with Greeks and Jews, represented what had never been accomplished, and what the most sanguine might reasonably have thought impossible.

Gore points out that though the idea of the brotherhood of man is a common one, its difficulty is not realized until there is actual contact between peoples of different classes and races.

We have got into a habit of talking about the "brotherhood of man" as if it was an easy and obvious truth. All our experiences of our English relations with races of a different color to our own, nay all our experiences of class divisions at home, might have served to check this easygoing sort of language. If we will consent to pause and reflect on the actual difficulty of behaving or feeling as brethren should behave and feel towards men of other races and of other educations and habits than our own, we may be more inclined to believe that it is only through some fundamental eradication of selfish and inherent narrowness that it can be made possible; only when we begin to live from some center greater than ourselves. And that is the moral meaning of the constant doctrine of the New Testament that only through being reconciled to God can we be reconciled to one another.

This is the first specific mention of "races of a different color" in any commentary on Ephesians.

Gore charges that the popular idea that the church is formed by believing individuals who meet to develop and spread their faith defeats the purpose of God which Paul proclaimed not only in Ephesians, but throughout his writings.

We cannot but pause and ask, in view of all the moral discipline for men of various kinds which St. Paul sees to be involved in the simple obligation to belong to one Christian body (Philem. 16), what would have been his feelings if he had heard of the doctrine which cuts at the root of all this discipline by declaring that religion is only concerned with the relation of the soul to God, and that Christians may combine as they please in as many religious bodies as suits their varying tastes?

The individualistic view of the church which Gore opposes so vigorously is very firmly entrenched. A quotation from the commentary of William Neill[86] illustrates how obviously its presuppositions are expressed even in the interpretation of Eph 2:11—22. On v. 19 Neill says,

As the saints have interests to pursue, and enemies to contend with, which are common to them all in order that they may the more easily

---

[86] A Practical Exposition of the Epistle to the Ephesians, Philadelphia 1850, 93.

and completely compass the end of their holy calling, they are to be united; they are to form a community of brethren, bound together by the law of love, and to be distinguished from other societies by their evangelical principles and practice. This I take to be, substantially, what the apostle means by fellow-citizenship with the saints.

Neill begins with the individual Christian as the basic unit of Christianity. He then needs to find a rationale for the church, and seeks it in the interests and needs of the individual Christian, which are similar to those of other Christians. The fact that such reasoning appears even in a commentary on Ephesians, indicates its pervasiveness. To counter this view of the church, Gore emphasizes more than any previous commentator that it is not individual Christians who create the church, but God, and that its very nature is to reconcile different groups.

Although his commentary makes quite explicit the contemporary relevance of Ephesians, Gore, like most nineteenth century commentators, says nothing about the present relation of the church to Israel. We do find comments on this by two less well-known men.

Theophil Passavant (1787—1864)

On the basis of the ending of the hostility proclaimed in Eph 2:14, Theophil Passavant[87] speaks out against the hostility which Christians have often shown toward Jews. Passavant charges that the Gentiles who hated Jews in pre-Christian times

> have been imitated by very many peoples called Christian. But what has happened? Christian peoples of such a kind have been such a stumbling block for many heathen peoples and also for one another that many have not wanted to accept the faith of Christians, and still today do not want to accept it, nor to profess their gospel[88].

Passavant thus sees anti-Judaism as working against the mission of the church.

Heinrich Leonhard Heubner (1780—1853)

In contrast to Passavant, Heinrich Leonhard Heubner[89] takes a negative view of the Jews. He says v. 11 shows that while the Gentiles were physically uncircumcised, the Jews, though circumcised

---

[87] Versuch einer praktischen Auslegung des Briefes Pauli an die Ephesier, Basel 1836, I, 229—283.

[88] Passavant, 248.

[89] Praktische Erklärung des Neuen Testaments, Potsdam 1859, IV, 14—18.

physically, were not circumcised spiritually. He denies that the Jews had any more knowledge of God than the Gentiles when he states, "Outside of Christianity God remains only a general idea; we would know nothing more of God than the Gentiles." In limiting God to Christianity, Heubner implicitly denies the Old Testament roots of Christianity.

Although he says nothing explicitly about the contemporary relation of Christians and Jews on the basis of the passage, Heubner does speak about Christ and the peace of the nations, at least Christian nations: "Christ's death is the peace of the nations. Who can quarrel and war with others under Christ's cross?"

Summary

The great variety of nineteenth century interpretation may best be summed up with reference to several main themes: the unity of the church; Christianity as the "higher unity"; the relation of Christianity to Judaism; the unity of mankind.

The Unity of the Church

The historical-critical study of the New Testament which begins in the nineteenth century brings with it new interest in the problem of the unity of the church. Earlier commentators had recognized, to be sure, that Eph 2:11—22 proclaimed the unity of the church out of Jew and Gentile. But whereas they had assumed that the New Testament Church was in fact united from the very beginning, historical-critical scholars now question that assumption. Earlier commentators knew, for example, that Paul had to deal with the problem of party spirit in Corinth, but until the nineteenth century it was assumed that this and similar problems were of a more or less local nature. Now, however, Baur says these are not separate local problems, but the one central problem: two parties, the one essentially Jewish, the other essentially Gentile, each claiming to be followers of Christ. By making it the central task of New Testament scholarship to trace the path by which these two parties came together to form the Catholic Church, Baur, more than anyone else, may be said to have focussed the attention of New Testament scholarship on the question of the unity of the church.

To be sure, Baur sees the unity of the church as a historical question rather than a doctrinal one. Yet Baur does not limit his historical inquiry to the first century, for he sees the Catholic

Church of his time as in many respects a continuous development from the early Catholic Church which emerged at the end of the New Testament period. He is unalterably opposed to some of the characteristics of the Catholic Church of his time, and consequently very critical of the early Catholic unity, in which he sees the victory of some Jewish characteristics. The idea of unity itself he considers primarily a Jewish idea, and tends to identify it with a centrally organized system. Therefore he regards New Testament writings which emphasize unity, such as Ephesians, with a certain suspicion, for he believes that they depart to a greater or lesser degree from Paul's deep understanding of justification by faith in favor of an "outward unity". When Baur speaks of unity as "outward" (a term used by many commentators in the nineteenth century), he seems to say that visible unity is not only unessential to the gospel, but stands in a certain contrast to it. The unquestioned assumption of Baur that what is "inner" is truly Christian and what is "outward" is irrelevant or suspect may have its roots both in Pietism and in Idealism. So despite Baur's historical interest in church unity, he takes a rather negative view of it doctrinally. Insofar as his criticism is levelled against a unity made by men, it can serve a useful purpose, since all human institutions need to be criticized. But Baur's concept of unity as primarily organizational is a hindrance to an adequate interpretation of Ephesians.

Other historical-critical scholars give a needed corrective to Baur's view. Ritschl argues that historically viewed, unity is not simply identical with centralized organization made possible by doctrinal agreement, but that it has to do with the association of people of various traditions in daily life. After Ritschl, interpretations of Eph 2:11—22 tend to focus on questions of the social relationships of Jews and Gentiles. This is particularly true of von Soden, for whom Eph 2:11—22 upholds the importance of Christian community against the "centrifugal individualism" of the Gentiles. Weiss goes yet further when he speaks of the uniting of Jews and Gentiles as the event in which the church discovered its task.

Among theological commentators there is a major disagreement. Some, notably Harless and Feine, think the theme of the passage is the relationship of men to God, and therefore see little or no significance for the unity of the church. Others, however, look at Eph 2:11—22 as an authoritative source for the doctrine of the unity of the church. Stier sees the uniting of Jews and Gentiles as the original type from which we learn what the unity of the church is, and which serves as a model to guide all efforts to realize church unity. Monod emphasizes the necessity of renewed turning to Christ if unity is to be realized, since only in Christ are two made into one.

Practical interpretations consider Eph 2:11—22 in terms of some of the factors which stand in the way of contemporary church unity. For Maurice the chief factor dividing Jews and Gentiles was their theological difference which he finds divisive also for the church of his day. The way in which Eph 2:11—22 proclaims the uniting of Jew and Gentile indicates how men can hold different theological convictions and still be united. Gore feels that the disunity of the church can be traced primarily to social sources, such as class and race, and that these were factors which in the beginning of the church's life made unity between Jew and Gentile difficult. For Gore, Ephesians proclaims that belonging to a particular class or race is not so important as belonging to the church.

Christianity as the "Higher Unity"

Many nineteenth century writers use the term "higher unity" to describe the situation in which the hostility between Jew and Gentile was overcome. This term, rarely if ever used in previous centuries, seems to stem from Baur's view that Ephesians presents Christianity as "a unity standing above the antitheses" of Jew and Gentile. The need to see Jew and Gentile as antitheses out of whose struggle arises a higher unity is apparently influenced by Hegel's philosophy of history.

Baur's interpretation of Ephesians with the aid of Hegelian categories is patent in his interpretation of the new man (2:15): "As the distinction between Jews and Gentiles was cancelled in the unity of the new man, so Christianity stands above Gentilism and Judaism as the absolute religion." When Baur adds that the new man "has to put off more and more the old man which still clings"[90], a natural inference is that participation in Christian unity requires the rejection of membership in a particular racial or national community. Thus "higher unity" is usually conceived of as a "spiritual unity", in the sense that it is unrelated to the associations of everyday life.

The interpretation of the new man in terms of "higher unity" has been used to support the idea that the Christian is superior to other men, particularly to the Jew. Thus Oltramare says, "We are superior to the Jews."[91] Schnedermann makes the remark that v.

---

[90] Das Christentum, 117.

[91] Although Oltramare does not use the term "higher unity", he does hold that the new man supersedes both Jew and Gentile, see above p. 156.

19 is "important against modern overestimation of Israelite descent". Some commentators see the new man as the Christian who overcomes negative Jewish and Gentile traits; Beck says that the Jew represents slavery to the law whereas the Gentile represents irresponsible freedom[92].

Those commentators who do not use the concept of "higher unity" to describe the new man, usually regard Jews more favorably. Since they believe that after becoming a Christian a Jew remains a Jew and a Gentile remains a Gentile, they are inclined to consider Jew and Gentile as representing positive aspects of human life. Thus for Maurice the Jew and the Gentile represent two ways of thinking about God. For Gore, the difference between Jew and Gentile typifies all differences of nation and race. Passavant points out the harm, precisely to the mission of the church, that is caused by hostility against the Jews.

The Relation of Christianity to Judaism

Historical-critical scholars are keenly interested in determining what Eph 2:11—22 says about the relation of Christianity to Judaism. For Baur, the passage is ambiguous. On the one hand there is the strain, including the idea of the new man as "higher unity", according to which "Christianity stands above Gentilism and Judaism as the absolute religion . . . Since Christianity is the absolute religion, Gentilism and Judaism are negatively related to it"[93]. On the other hand the passage announces the inclusion of the Gentiles in Israel, which underscores the continuity of Christianity with Judaism. For Baur this strain is Jewish-Christian and marks the letter's divergence from true Paulinism. With some exceptions like Köstlin, who says that the strains of continuity and discontinuity with Israel are just as balanced in Paul as in Ephesians, historical-critical scholars agree with Baur.

Grammatical-historical commentators agree with Baur that Paulinism emphasizes discontinuity with Judaism. But unlike Baur, they find Ephesians so much in accord with Paul's theology on this and other points that they consider Paul the author.

Some theological commentators disagree with Baur's account of Paulinism. They believe that both Paul and Ephesians emphasize continuity with Judaism, and for this and other reasons consider

---

[92] But also Stier, who opposes the influence of Hegelianism, lets the Jew typify the person in all ages whose piety makes him look down on worldly persons, of whom the Gentile is the type, see above p. 150.

[93] Das Christentum, 117.

Paul the author. Most outspoken among these are Monod and Hofmann, who insist that there is just one people of God, whose history spans both Old and New Testaments.

The Unity of Mankind

The historical-critical scholar von Soden says that Ephesians has as its goal not only the unity of the church, but the unity of mankind. Some theological interpreters, notably Olshausen, Stier, Haupt, and Westcott, maintain that the passage proclaims the unity of mankind as already accomplished. They interpret Eph 2:11— 22 in light of other biblical passages which they believe show Christ as the head and representative of all mankind. These scholars therefore hold that the new man includes all humanity, whereas earlier commentators have usually taken the new man to be the church, or the individual Christian. The few who have said that the new man is Christ himself have spoken of him only as head of the church, not of the whole human race. The nineteenth century is the first period in which commentators explicitly say that the new man of Eph 2:15 includes all humanity.

But the fact that the unity of mankind as well as the unity of the church is usually considered to be a "higher" or "spiritual unity" means that it was not considered relevant to the relationships of different nations and races. This may help to answer the specific question: why is it that Eph 2:11—22 is nowhere discussed in connection with the crisis of the church in North America at the time of the Civil War? Several considerations would speak for its appropriateness at that time: the problem had to do with the relationship of two races, and Jew and Gentile had already been described as different races; many members of both races were also members of the church; divisions arose in the church itself because of disagreement on this issue of slavery. In some previous centuries when the unity of the church was at stake, Eph 2:11—22 was studied and interpreted in connection with the particular problem. During the Donatist schism, for example, Augustine as well as lesser known writers considered Eph 2:11—22 from the viewpoint of the contemporary division in the church. In the Reformation period, Musculus above all wrote about the problem of the unity of the church on the basis of this passage. Furthermore, some commentators on Eph 2 had clearly stated that the passage opposes discrimination in the church on the basis of race.

We might expect then that American Christians at the time of the Civil War, when the problem of race and the unity of the church were burning issues, would have turned to Eph 2:11—22. But although almost all publications of the time make abundant reference to the Bible, a fairly extensive search in books, periodicals and sermons revealed no mention of Eph 2:11—22 in connection with the problem of slavery. It is of course possible that our passage did play a part, but the fact that it was at best a very minor one deserves some comment. Several reasons why the passage was not discussed may be suggested.

The issue as it was seen at the time was that of slavery. The Bible was therefore thoroughly searched for material relating to slavery. Since slavery is mentioned often in the Bible, there were many passages for debate which fully absorbed the attention of scholars, preachers and laymen. George Bourne, for example, a Presbyterian minister who was one of the early outspoken opponents of slavery, and whose biblical arguments were used by many later writers, discusses over 30 passages in the Old Testament and over 25 in the New Testament[94]. But Eph 2:11—22 is not one of them. This is undoubtedly due to the fact that the passage does not mention slavery, or lend itself indirectly to a discussion of slavery any more than many other biblical passages.

A look at the table of contents of Bourne's book suggests another reason why our passage is not included. The headings "Pro-Slavery Perversions of the Old Testament" and "Pro-Slavery Perversions of the New Testament" reveal that Bourne regarded his task as the refutation of interpretations of these passages which had already been made by pro-slavery writers. Bourne's task was therefore primarily a negative one; this is to a large extent true for the whole period. Pro-slavery people, perhaps prompted by an uneasy conscience, first claimed the Bible for their position. Those who attacked their biblical arguments, because their task was essentially negative, appeared to the majority of pro-slavery people, especially those with a literal view of scripture, to be attacking the Bible itself.

Eph 2:11—22 is a passage which could have spoken positively of the church as uniting the races. The fact that it was not used is due in part to the theological climate in America, which was strongly individualistic, being influenced by elements in both Puritanism and revivalism which put great stress on individual conversion. As James Hastings Nicols says, "Most American theologians... inclined to the opinion that the Church did not belong to the essence of Christianity."[95] Though communication with European biblical

---

[94] A Condensed Anti-Slavery Argument, New York 1845.
[95] Romanticism in American Theology, Chicago 1961, 153.

scholarship was not widespread, there was some contact. But European historical-critical biblical scholarship in its early development was likewise not inclined to consider the church as belonging to the essence of the gospel. Like American theology, it usually saw church unity as an organizational matter, and therefore questionable.

What American commentators saw and concurred with in Eph 2:11—22 was the equality of all individuals before God, regardless of their backgrounds, rather than the reconciliation of differing groups in Christ. So the anti-slavery movement was concerned for equality and gave little thought to unity. The abolitionists were fighting for equality in earthly affairs—equality before men. Their opponents, the pro-slavery people, did not deny that men are equal before God, but they held that this equality had to do with a man's soul[96], and not with his earthly relationships. Therefore Eph 2, as understood at the time, must not have seemed to offer any help for the anti-slavery cause. The pro-slavery group would have had little trouble granting the existence of "higher unity" between blacks and whites, insofar as they could understand this as a unity above and apart from actual historical communities—as a spiritual unity which did not necessarily involve social fellowship between black and white. And this is the kind of unity which many nineteenth century commentators suggested when they spoke of the new man as neither Jew nor Gentile, thus taking an essentially individualistic view of the new man. This over-emphasis on the individual is linked with far-reaching rejection of the continuity of the church with Israel, partly because the sense of community, which is strong in Israel, is lost.

These may be some of the reasons why Eph 2:11—22 did not seem to offer any help in the anti-slavery cause. When they had won the battle over slavery, the abolitionists had little need for further biblical arguments against slavery. But the church and the nation were still inwardly divided after the Civil War. The war had been won, but the peace was not. The need was for reconciliation; for a deeper basis of unity than simply a cessation of hostilities. But those who had spoken from scripture on behalf of righteousness did not find words to speak in behalf of unity and reconciliation—perhaps because the "anti" set of mind was more conducive to opposition than to support, as the name of one reform organization of the time, "The Anti-Saloon League", suggests.

---

[96] Some pro-slavery writers attempted to show that according to the Bible, Negroes did not have souls and were not even men. This extremist group denied even equality before God.

Some theologians, hoping to avoid a split in the church over the slavery issue, attempted to keep their theological work from becoming involved with the slavery question. Charles Hodge, one of the leading Presbyterian theologians in America in the nineteenth century, held this position. He wrote the leading American commentary of the time on Ephesians[97], which contains not even the faintest reference to the relations of the races. Hodge's caution was of no avail; the Presbyterians split into northern and southern churches, and continue as separate denominations to this day.

Only later in the century, and then in England, did wrestling with the social problems posed by the Industrial Revolution lead Christians to look afresh at Eph 2, now with a new eye for the ways in which the Bible assumes and proclaims the unity of mankind. In commentaries on Eph 2, this development is most clearly seen in Charles Gore. Such development then takes its place as one strand in the twentieth century interpretation of our passage.

---

[97] A Commentary on the Epistle to the Ephesians, New York 1856 (reprinted 1858, 1866, 1873).

Chapter VIII

THE TWENTIETH CENTURY

*Developments in New Testament Research Influencing the
Interpretation of Eph 2:11—22*

Certain discoveries, crises and achievements, both within the
narrower realm of New Testament scholarship itself and within the
wider realm of the church's life in the world, have substantially
affected the interpretation of Eph 2:11—22 in the twentieth century. Developments in New Testament scholarship with bearing on
our passage include: advancements in the understanding of Gnosis[1]
made possible by the opening up of new sources[2]; increased use of
Jewish literature for elucidating the New Testament, a landmark
of which was the publication of Strack and Billerbeck's *Kommentar zum Neuen Testament aus Talmud und Midrasch*[3]; the discovery of the Dead Sea Scrolls; the application of form criticism to
the New Testament letters; increased knowledge of social, political
and economic conditions of New Testament times. Developments
within the church in the world which have caused scholars to
approach Eph 2:11—22 with new questions are: the rise of the
"Social Gospel"; the Kirchenkampf; the Jewish-Christian dialog;
the crisis in black-white relations.

Proponents of a Gnostic Background

Because studies of Gnosticism provide the most completely new
attempt at explaining the background of Ephesians, their application to our passage will be considered first. While the claim that
Ephesians must be understood in terms of a Gnostic background

---

[1] Some of the characteristics of Gnosis are mentioned in chapter 1, pp. 5—12,
21—22.

[2] Until the beginning of this century, virtually our only sources for Gnosis
were secondary: the anti-Gnostic writings of the church fathers. A survey of
the increase in number of accessible primary sources is given by R. Haardt,
Die Gnosis, Salzburg, 1967, 337—341.

[3] Munich 1922—1928, 4 vols. Index vols. 5, 6, ed. J. Jeremias, 1956, 1961.

had already been made by F. C. Baur[4], the first detailed study of
the relation of Gnostic texts to Ephesians was published by Heinrich Schlier in 1930[5]. Eph 2:11—22 figures prominently in
Schlier's work because the juxtaposition of the images of the wall,
the body, the new man and the building seems explicable to him
only on the basis of an underlying Gnostic myth which combines
these images. The myth, according to Schlier, is that of a cosmic
Redeemer, the Primal Man, who breaks down the wall separating
this world from the divine regions, after having gathered his members who had been imprisoned in this world into a new man, his
body, which the Gnostic texts also sometimes call a building[6].

Schlier's findings enable him to explain why Eph 2:11—22 has
caused interpreters so much difficulty: the author uses Gnostic
images for purposes not in accord with Gnosticism. The reason
scholarship has had such trouble deciding whether the wall was
between heaven and earth or between Jews and Gentiles is that
both dimensions are present. Schlier is now in a position to offer a
new solution to the question about how the two are related. The
vertical dimension is that of the Gnostic myth which forms the
background of the passage[7]. The author of Ephesians uses the language of this myth because it is part of the conceptual world in
which his readers live[8]. His purpose, however, is to proclaim not a
Gnostic myth, but an event in history: the abrogation of the law
which like a wall separated Jews from Gentiles and man from God.
The reconciliation of Jews and Gentiles is an event in redemptive
history[9].

Schlier's case for a Gnostic background of Ephesians was the
starting point of a controversy which is still under way[10]. Rather
than attempt an account of this controversy, we will deal here with
the question: what is at stake in the controversy? What difference

---

[4] See above p. 133.

[5] Christus und die Kirche im Epheserbrief, Tübingen 1930; repr. New York
and Nendeln, Liechtenstein, 1966.

[6] Schlier cites at many points the works of R. Reitzenstein, who first described the Gnostic Redeemer myth, esp. Das Iranische Erlösungsmysterium,
Bonn 1921.

[7] Christus und die Kirche, 18—23.   [8] Christus und die Kirche, Vorwort.

[9] Christus und die Kirche, 24n. See also Schlier's commentary, Der Brief an
die Epheser, Düsseldorf 1968[6], 133.

[10] A summary of this controversy is given by C. Colpe, "Zur Leib-Christi-
Vorstellung im Epheserbrief", Judentum, Urchristentum, Kirche, Festschrift
für J. Jeremias, Berlin 1960, 172—187; a list of literature since 1930 prefaces
the article. For a briefer account of the controversy, see P. Pokorný, Der
Epheserbrief und die Gnosis, Berlin 1965, 34—40.

does it make for our theological understanding of Eph 2:11—22 and thus for the mission of the church in the world whether its background is Gnostic or not?

Proponents of the Gnostic background for Ephesians hold that there is a basic consequence for the question: how can the gospel be communicated? They argue that there is no communication of the gospel unless it is proclaimed in language its hearers can understand. The hearers of the Ephesian letter were Gentile Christians whose intellectual world was formed to a significant extent by Gnosis. In order to make genuine contact with them, the author had to confront Gnostic ideas, deal with its concepts, use its language. The interpretation of Eph 2:11—22 is thus seen as a particularly clear example of the way in which the gospel must be communicated today: in confrontation with current forms of thought, however foreign these forms may seem to the gospel.

Opponents of the so-called "Gnostic interpretation" do not deny that the gospel must be proclaimed in language people can understand. They do deny however that only Gnostic language could be understood by the recipients of the letter. For example, Ernest Scott maintains that the recipients knew a great deal about the temple in Jerusalem and would readily understand imagery based upon it[11]. And Franz Mussner argues that the circumstances of Paul's arrest would have been made known to the readers by Tychicus. Since the immediate cause of the arrest (Acts 21:27—30) was the charge that Paul took a Gentile into the temple, the readers would have immediately recognized the allusion to the wall in Eph 2:14[12].

In Schlier's judgment Mussner's argument is purely speculative. Such far-fetched explanations are, in Schlier's eyes, motivated by a desire to avoid admitting that the passage has a Gnostic background. But, he asks, what valid reason can there be for anxiety about accepting a Gnostic background? Schlier reiterates that doing so by no means makes Paul a Gnostic. Rather, Paul puts a new, Christian interpretation on material with which his readers are already familiar. This is how human language operates, says Schlier, in continual reinterpretation of people's presuppositions,

[11] The Epistles of Paul to the Colossians, to Philemon and to the Ephesians, MNTC, London 1948[7], 171. Paul Ewald (Die Briefe des Paulus an die Epheser, Kolosser und Philemon, KNT, Leipzig 1910[2], X, 138) had taken the opposite position that Gentile Christians in Asia Minor could hardly be expected to have been familiar with the details of the Jerusalem temple. Others in agreement with Ewald include: M. Dibelius, An die Epheser, HNT, Tübingen 1913, III, 2, 105; Schlier, Brief an die Epheser, 127.

[12] Christus, das All und die Kirche, Trierer Theologische Studien, 5, Trier 1968[2], 5, 84.

whether in our case these are Jewish or Hellenistic or Gnostic presuppositions. And why should that which holds for the Jews not hold for the Gnostics? That the Old and New Covenants are related in the one great redemptive economy of God as promise and fulfillment does not mean that the Apostle of the New Covenant, who is the Apostle of the Gentiles, could only think and speak from Jewish presuppositions and only in confrontation with questions which come from there. What he says is neither Jewish, nor Greek, nor Gnostic, but Christian. But that *to* which he says it is the question of those persons whom he addresses. Consequently the way he says it is conditioned by the images, the concepts, and in some circumstances the literary forms of Jews, Greeks and also Gnostics[13].

Schlier makes his point cogently and persuasively. Yet his argument seems to imply that the Christian substance of Paul's message is equally independent of Judaism, Hellenism and Gnosticism. But this is the very point at issue. Schlier's opponents maintain that part of the Christian substance of Paul's message is its rootage in Israel, and that the background of Ephesians is therefore to be sought there first of all.

Leaving this controversy about how the gospel is communicated, let us look at a second and even more important reason Schlier gives for the significance of Paul's use of Gnostic concepts. He believes that although Paul combats Gnosis, at one point he can make common cause with it: like the Gnostics Paul wants to make clear that his message has cosmic dimensions[14]. The gospel includes the very being and structure of the universe. Schlier considers this highly significant for contemporary theology, since it shows that a theology which concentrates only on God's Word and man's reception of it in faith is not sufficient. The breaking of the dividing wall marks an ontological change in the world. For Schlier, the ontological is identified with the sacramental; thus he argues that this passage shows the necessity of a theology which does justice to both Word and sacrament.

This exposition is theologically especially important. It implies namely not only a fundamental difference between the New Testament and Gnosis, but also between the New Testament and every conception of Christianity which lets the Christian life be founded on the moral (that

---

[13] Brief an die Epheser, 133n.
[14] E. Schweizer ("Die Kirche als Leib Christi in den Paulinischen Antilegomena", Neotestamentica, Zürich 1963, 304) has pointed out, however, that it was not necessary to borrow Gnostic terms in order to express a cosmic dimension, since there were also non-Gnostic traditions which used cosmic language.

is, only in "Word") and not on the ontic (that is, the sacrament). The sacramental church knows ultimately only apostles, prophets, teachers who appear on earth. The church of the sacrament, and the sacrament that does not let itself be absorbed in the "Word", is not only sign but effective sign, is founded not in the Word, but on the body of Christ on the cross[15].

The theological issue involved here has been particularly important in Schlier's own life. His conviction of its validity helped him decide, in the middle of his scholarly career, to become a Roman Catholic.

According to Schlier's conviction about the sacramental meaning of the broken wall, the separation of Jews and Gentiles no longer exists, regardless of what any particular Jew or Christian may think about the matter. It follows further that for Schlier the new man includes all humanity; mankind is made new in Christ[16].

Other scholars, convinced of the validity of Schlier's case for the Gnostic background of Ephesians, express their own ideas of its significance. Karl Ludwig Schmidt[17] relies strongly on Schlier's conclusions for his treatment of the church in Ephesians. Schmidt says that after discovering the source of the imagery, the question of why and how this particular imagery was used must be considered. Schmidt suggests two closely related reasons for the use of Gnostic imagery: it offered a way to emphasize the very close connection between Christ and his church, and to show the immense significance of Christ. These thrusts were needed to counter false teaching and division, specifically between Jewish Christians and Gentile Christians. According to Schmidt, Jewish Christians claimed a privileged position because Christ was from their land and their blood. Against this very earthly claim, Ephesians had to present the heavenly church. The Gentiles, on the other hand, ignoring land and blood, were attracted by Gnostic speculations about such things as a mythical marriage of Christ with Sophia, the principle of wisdom. Against this belief, Ephesians says that the only bride of Christ is the actual fellowship of believers.

Ernst Käsemann judges that the Gnostic Redeemer myth was admirably suited to show how creation and redemption are joined in Christ, since the basic feature of the myth is the identity of the Primal Man and the Redeemer: "Christ as Primal Man in whom everything has its existence, is creation itself; and Christ as Redeemer and Complete Man who is all in all, is the church itself.

---

[15] "Die Kirche im Epheserbrief", Die Zeit der Kirche, Freiburg 1956, 162n. 5. See also Brief an die Epheser, 130, 133, 144n. 2.

[16] Brief an die Epheser, 133—135. [17] "ἐκκλησία", TWNT III, 514—515.

Thus in Christ, church and creation are identical." This universal view of the church shows how impossible it is to think of the church simply as a group of men who voluntarily band to-gether[18].

Käsemann takes Schlier's thesis about the dividing wall (Eph 2:14) a step further. He says that in Gnosis the φραγμός (partition) originally referred to the flesh. Flesh is the "cosmic" wall that se-parates God and man. In Gnosis "flesh" is understood as the power of matter; in Pauline thought it is the power of worldliness fallen into sin. Christ's death on the cross then, is treated as a kind of circumcision in which this flesh is gotten rid of. This circumcision is also spoken of as baptism[19].

More recently, Käsemann has emphasized the ways in which Ephesians combats Gnosticism. As he pictures the situation to which Ephesians speaks, Gentile Christians have begun to feel that they can ignore the historical rootage of the church in Israel, and conse-quently push aside and despise Jewish Christians[20]. In place of the Jewish heritage they are tempted to put the timeless myths of Gnos-is, which would lead to a dissolving of Christian community. In-dividuals would then simply band together with other individuals who accepted the same myth. Against this temptation Ephesians maintains that the church is creation redeemed[21]. As such, it reaches not only throughout space—the cosmos, which is what the Gnostics were interested in—but also throughout history in a "con-tinuity of grace". In order to emphasize the historical dimension, Eph 2:11—22 uses the concept of the people of God. "It is the indelible character of the church to be constituted out of Jews and Gentiles."[22]

In Käsemann's view, Ephesians is so concerned with the nature of the church and its unity that it tends to make Christology sub-ordinate to ecclesiology. Thus it displays an element of early ca-tholicism, which is the chief feature distinguishing it from Paul's

---

[18] Leib und Leib Christi, Tübingen 1933, 156—158.

[19] Leib und Leib Christi, 139—141. John of Damascus interprets the pas-sage in this way, see above p. 37.

[20] Käsemann (RGG II, 517) points out that Paul had already felt the need to warn against such tendencies. See also "Eph & Acts", Studies in Luke-Acts, ed. Keck and Martyn, Nashville 1966, 291 and Paulinische Perspektiven, Tübin-gen 1969, 190—191.

[21] "Predigt-Meditation über Eph 2:17—22", Exegetische Versuche und Be-sinnungen I, Göttingen 1960, 280—283.

[22] Studies in Luke-Acts, 291; see also Exegetische Versuche I, 280.

theology[23]. When Schlier not only attributes this dominance of ecclesiology to the maturest thought of Paul, but also claims an ontological grounding for it, Käsemann protests[24].

Helmut Merklein rejects Käsemann's charge that Ephesians subordinates Christology to ecclesiology. To substantiate his position, Merklein devotes an entire book to Eph 2:11—18, because he is convinced this passage reveals the fundamental structure of the theology of Ephesians[25]. Merklein grants freely that the passage puts ecclesiology before soteriology. The fact that reconciliation of Jews and Gentiles comes before their reconciliation with God shows this. But this does not mean, as Käsemann charges, that Ephesians subordinates Christology to ecclesiology. The unity of the church out of Jews and Gentiles depends on Christ's death on the cross. So ecclesiology depends on Christology. Merklein concludes that the unique aim of Ephesians is to reorient a cosmic Christology so that it is related to the concrete life of the church.

Petr Pokorny believes that the concrete problem in the church life dealt with by Ephesians is tension between Jews and Gentiles caused by the threat of Gnostic heresy[26]. For the Gentile Christians are, or are about to be, involved in Gnosis, whereas the Jewish Christians are not. To be sure, both Gentile and Jewish Christians in Asia Minor at this time have spiritualist, syncretist leanings which make them susceptible to Gnosis. But the Jewish Christians have more resistance because of their strong Old Testament monotheist rootage. Furthermore, they consider themselves the core of the community. The Gentile Christians, to compensate for their inferiority feelings, reach out to a form of Judaistic Gnosis.

According to Pokorny, Eph 2:11—22 is sharply polemical against this Gnosis. For whereas in the Judaistic Gnosis keeping certain regulations was supposed to contribute to the uniting of the separated parts of the god-man, thus bringing peace, in Eph 2:15 these regulations are the very wall which must be torn down that there may be peace[27]. Whereas Gnosis uses the word "cornerstone"

[23] "Paulus und der Frühkatholizismus", Exegetische Versuche II, Göttingen 1964, 239—252, esp. 245—247.

[24] "Das Interpretationsproblem des Epheserbriefes", Exegetische Versuche II, 253—261. Käsemann sees in this interpretation the way which led Schlier from Protestantism to Catholicism.

[25] Christus und die Kirche: Die theologische Grundstruktur des Epheserbriefes nach Eph 2:11—18, Stuttgart 1973.

[26] Der Epheserbrief und die Gnosis, Berlin 1965, 20—21. Pokorny does not, however, share Käsemann's view that Ephesians subordinates Christology to ecclesiology.

[27] Pokorny, 115.

to refer to the "inner" man, Eph 2:20 uses it of Christ in connection with the building which is the community. This brings out the social nature of Christianity against the individualism of Gnosis[28].

Henry Chadwick[29] finds that Ephesians uses Gnostic concepts not as polemic, but as apologetic. The basic problem to which Ephesians is directed, says Chadwick, is not so much the group relations of Jews and Gentiles in the church as it is the credibility of the Christian faith. The difficulty was that Christianity was a new religion with no history, and the presupposition of antiquity was that what is oldest is true. Thus an important feature of Christian apologetic was the claim that Christianity was not a new religion, but an old one. Ephesians is a kind of early apologetic, which makes use of Gnostic terminology in order to "underscore the apologetic claim to universality".

Hans Conzelmann, like Chadwick, thinks that tension between Jewish and Gentile Christians is no longer the problem at the time of the writing of Ephesians. He sees Eph 2:11—22 as a theological meditation on the "founding of the church's unity" in the reconciliation of Jews and Gentiles[30]. The Gnostic background serves to express in thought-forms familiar to the readers that the church not only had its beginning in Christ, but that in the present he holds the church in unity.

In order to illustrate some of the specific differences in interpretation which may be related to the acceptance or rejection of the Gnostic interpretation, we will look briefly at debated points between Käsemann and Percy, and between Schlier and Mussner.

Käsemann, in a review[31] of *Probleme der Kolosser und Epheserbriefe*[32], charges that the basic error of Percy's book is his rejection of a Gnostic background. The Gnostic background, according to Käsemann, enabled the author of Ephesians to transpose Paul's apocalyptic expectation of the unity of Jews and Gentiles expressed in Rom 11 into affirmations about the present unity of the church. Since Percy rejects this Gnostic background, says Käsemann, he also rejects the thesis that the central concern of Ephesians is the unity of the church.

Percy replies that Käsemann's interpretation from Gnostic concepts keeps him from seeing that the "peace" of Eph 2:14 should be interpreted in light of the abrogation of the law in v. 15. This

---

[28] Pokorny, 116. Pokorny agrees completely on this point with P. Vielhauer, Oikodome, Karlsruhe 1940, 91, 174.

[29] "Die Absicht des Epheserbriefes", ZNW 51, 1960, 145—153.

[30] NTD 8, Göttingen 1965, 67—70.   [31] Gnomon 21, 1949, 342—347.

[32] Lund 1946.

way of interpreting it fits perfectly with Paul's great theme that the Gentiles now have access to God on the same basis as Jews, that is, without regard to the law. Equal standing before God, rather than unity, says Percy, is the real theme of the passage[33]. The only reason that the passage speaks of peace between Jews and Gentiles is that the citation of Isa 57:19 called forth the idea[34].

A charge similar to that of Käsemann against Percy is made by Schlier against Mussner. Schlier claims that a desire to avoid the Gnostic god-man concept is responsible for Mussner's rather unusual interpretation of "one new man" in v. 15[35]. For Mussner, "one new man" does not refer to the unity of Jew and Gentile but to the quality of the new life of each[36].

If the charges of Käsemann and Schlier are right, then Percy and Mussner miss the central concern of Eph 2:11—22—the unity of the church out of Jew and Gentile—because they reject a Gnostic background. But as we shall see below, other modern exegetes who reject a Gnostic background uphold the unity of Jew and Gentile as the central concern of the passage.

Recently the concept of the Gnostic Redeemer myth as a possible background of various New Testament passages has been subjected to thorough examination. Such works as those of Carsten Colpe[37] and Hans Martin Schenke[38] have concluded that the Gnostic Redeemer myth is post-Christian and cannot legitimately be treated as background material for the New Testament. This does not of course prove that Ephesians does not contain Gnostic concepts. But it does seem unlikely that the author of Ephesians had in view the system of concepts which modern scholars have called the Gnostic Redeemer myth. Those exegetes who make use of Gnosis in interpreting our passage now do so in a more careful and qualified way than previously. Pokorny's writings provide an example of recent work of this type. So the question is far from closed, and the debate continues.

---

[33] Zu den Problemen des Kolosser- und Epheserbriefes", ZNW 43, 1950—51, 187—188, 191.

[34] Probleme der Kolosser- und Epheserbriefe, 282—283.

[35] Brief an die Epheser, 134n. 1. Mussner himself says that his interpretation of the new man is important for his controversy with the "Gnostic" interpretation (Christus, das All und die Kirche, 88—91).

[36] Christus, das All und die Kirche, 87. Similar, basically individualistic interpretations of the new man are presented by Percy, ZNW 43, 191—193, and E. Best, One Body in Christ, London 1955, 153—154.

[37] Die Religionsgeschichtliche Schule, FRLANT 60, Göttingen 1961, esp. 199—208.

[38] Der Gott "Mensch" in der Gnosis, Berlin 1962, 155—156.

Proponents of an Old Testament-Rabbinic Background

The most vocal opponents of a Gnostic background for Eph 2:11—22 are those scholars who propose an Old Testament and rabbinic background. Frequently they focus on the Old Testament concept of corporate personality as a more probable background than the Gnostic Primal Man-Redeemer. According to the concept of corporate personality, Christ represents men and incorporates them in himself, as he does in Rom 5:12 and I Cor 15:12 where Paul considers men in Adam as contrasted to men in Christ[39].

One of the chief advocates of the corporate personality concept against the Gnostic Redeemer myth in the interpretation of our passage is Ernst Percy. Percy says that the ideas expressed in Eph 2:14—18 "in no way go beyond the Old Testament concept of the father of the people, who includes all his progeny in himself"[40].

For Percy, the corporate personality concept is the key to what he regards as the decisive question about the passage: how does Christ abrogate the law? Percy answers that after Christ's death the law no longer applied to him, in accordance with Rabbinic teaching that death frees a person from the law. Since Christ is the representative who includes his followers in himself, they are also freed from the law by his death. The idea of representation in-volved here—that one person can act in the place of and for the sake of many—is the crucial feature missing in the Gnostic concept. The Gnostic Redeemer includes men in himself, but he does not act in their place[41].

Percy believes that Eph 2:16 is extremely important for under-standing what Paul means by being "in Christ". "Nowhere else does the entire content of this thought, central for the whole theol-ogy of the Apostle (II Cor 5:14), come forward so clearly as right here in Eph 2:16." Relating this to freedom from the law, Percy cites Rom 7:4, "You have died to the law through the body of Christ." Since the law is no longer valid for those who are in Christ, it no longer functions as a wall between Jews and Gentiles who are in him. Christ and those Jews and Gentiles who are includ-

---

[39] The concept of corporate personality was used to interpret the New Testament concept of the body of Christ by T. Schmidt, Der Leib Christi, Leipzig 1919, 223—224. On the concept in the Old Testament, see H. W. Robinson, "The Hebrew Conception of Corporate Personality", Werden und Wesen des alten Testaments, ed. J. Hempel et al, Berlin 1936, 49—62. On rabbinic thought about mankind in Adam, see W. D. Davies, Paul and Rab-binic Judaism, London 1955[2], 36—57.

[40] Probleme der Kolosser und Epheserbriefe, 285n.

[41] Der Leib Christi, Lund 1942, 41—43.

ed in him are the new man (Eph 2:15) and have died to the Old Age and are alive to the New Age.

Stig Hanson[42] interprets our passage similarly in terms of corporate personality[43] with particular stress on the disunity of mankind in Adam after the Fall as the problem for which Ephesians sees unity in Christ, the second Adam, as the answer.

Advocates of an Old Testament and rabbinic background also claim the building image in vv. 20—22 as evidence for their view. They point out that building imagery is found not only in Gnostic texts, but also in Jewish texts, as Vielhauer's work shows[44]. Hanson argues that the concept of the people of God is basic to Eph 2:11—22, and it is about the people of God that the Old Testament uses the terms "to build" and "house" (Ruth 4:11; Jer 24:6; 31:4; 42:10). In later Jewish literature, says Hanson, the term "to build" has cosmic connotations and alludes to the heavenly as well as the earthly Jerusalem and its temple.

Another advocate of Judaic sources for the building imagery of Eph 2:20—22 is R. J. McKelvey[45] who has done a detailed study of the image of the temple in the New Testament. McKelvey says that Eph 2:20—22 is inspired by "the world-shrine of Isaiah and the intertestamental writers". In particular, McKelvey cites the vision in Enoch 90:29—34 in which the Lord provides a new temple to house both Jews and Gentiles. McKelvey believes that the cosmological dimension is not due to Gnostic influence, but can be explained by "the rabbinic identification of the cornerstone in Zion as the embryo of creation".

Franz Mussner considers the most impressive evidence for an Old Testament and rabbinic background to be the parallel of the Jewish concept of new creation to the new man of Eph 2:15, the latter being central for the whole section 2:13—18[46]. Mussner relies on material gathered by Erich Sjöberg in which Jewish texts speak of the Gentile proselyte as "a new man", and in which Israel itself in decisive moments in history and worship is spoken of as "created into a new being"[47]. As the proselyte to Judaism is "created" into a "new man", "brought near", and placed "under the wings of the

---

[42] The Unity of the Church in the New Testament, Uppsala 1946, 145.

[43] As do R. Shedd, Man in Community, Grand Rapids, Michigan 1964, 132—138; V. Warnach, Die Kirche im Epheserbrief, Münster 1949, 16; H. von Mühlen, Una Mystica Persona, Munich 1967, 132—134.

[44] Oikodome, 10, 15—21, 114.   [45] The New Temple, Oxford 1968, 118—120.

[46] Christus, das All und die Kirche, 94—96.

[47] Sjöberg, "Wiedergeburt und Neuschöpfung im palästinensischen Judentum", StTh 4, 1950, 44—85.

Shekinah", so Eph 2 speaks of being "created" into a "new man" (v. 15), "brought near" (v. 13) and given "access to the Father" (v. 18)[48].

Mussner's interpretation of the new man of Eph 2:15 follows the analogy of the proselyte. That is, the new man is the Christian. This man is new not because two men formerly separated have been brought together to form him, but because a new quality of life has been given him[49].

Mussner holds that the dividing wall (v. 14) is best understood by reference to Jewish sources which speak of the law metaphorically as a wall. For example, the apocryphal Letter of Aristeas, 139, says that "Moses surrounded Israel with an impenetrable fence and an iron wall" so that they "would not have any fellowship with other peoples"; Mussner also cites rabbinic texts which call the Torah a fence around Israel and the traditions of the fathers a fence around the Torah[50]. The metaphor of the wall, says Mussner, also alludes to the wall in the temple keeping Gentiles from the inner parts.

Like Mussner, J. J. Meuzelaar's understanding of Eph 2:11—22 depends on a framework from Jewish proselytism[51]. The terms "near" and "far" (vv. 13, 17), "new man" (v. 15), "strangers and sojourners" (v. 19) are all well attested in rabbinic thought about Gentile proselytes, with which Paul was familiar. Thus when Paul announces that Gentiles have been united with Jews "in the blood of the Messiah", he is saying that the regulations about proselytes have been abrogated by Christ. Proof of this is the claim in v. 19 that the Gentiles are "no longer strangers and sojourners". "How could anyone think that they were strangers and sojourners'?" asks Meuzelaar, and answers that only the categories of proselyte-thought could account for it. According to these categories, Gentile Christians have not fulfilled the requirements of proselytes and are still strangers and sojourners. But Paul claims that because they are in the Messianic community they are "fellow citizens of the saints and members of God's household". These terms were also used in Judaism of proselytes. The proselyte shared in the holiness

---

[48] N. A. Dahl ("Christ, Creation and the Church", The Background of the New Testament and its Eschatology, ed. W. D. Davies and D. Daube, Cambridge 1956, 436) finds the terminology of Jewish proselytism to be a background, but not necessarily the only background, of Eph 2:11—22.

[49] E. Best (One Body in Christ, London 1955, 154) interprets the new man in essentially the same way.

[50] Mussner suggests that "ordinances" δόγμασιν in v. 15 probably refers to the traditions of the fathers.

[51] Der Leib des Messias, Assen 1961, 60—69.

of Israel as soon as he converted to Judaism. In Eph 3:6 Paul says that in the Messiah the Gentiles share all that is promised to Israel. Meuzelaar finds this verse very significant for the idea that Jews and Gentiles are united in one body (v. 16). For the word σύσσωμα (co-body) occurs there, which suggests that there may have been a tradition in which the image of the body referred to Israel. Meuzelaar cites examples from Philo to show that there was in fact such a tradition. Philo says that the High Priest prays and sacrifices for the people "so that all parts of the people, like members of a body, may be led together to one and the same fellowship". Proselytes should be regarded as members of the people "so that despite different members there exist only one being".

In these quotations from Philo, the image of the body has an ethical purpose: to urge people to live together in unity. According to Meuzelaar, the place in Greek thought from which the image of the body arose was ethics. Meuzelaar's study aims to show that this is its place in Paul's thought also. Paul takes the image of the body from Greek ethical thought, where it is often used, and is thus familiar to his readers. He rejects, however, the naturalistic basis it has there, and puts in its place redemptive history; in this way the image is used for the practical purpose of furthering unity and fellowship within the Christian community, above all between Jews and Gentiles[52]. Meuzelaar claims that Paul's use of the image of the body for a practical ethical purpose proves that the image does not have a Gnostic source: "Precisely for this reason the idea of the body in Paul cannot be explained Gnostically. Where Gnosis has transformed the figurative concept of the body into a cosmic myth, the practical purpose of the idea of the body has been lost."[53]

Another interpretation of Eph 2:11—22 against a background of Jewish proselyte practice, probably the most detailed interpretation of its kind, is that of Harald Sahlin[54]. The basic difference between Sahlin's interpretation and those of Mussner and Meuzelaar is that Sahlin says all the Jewish terms, such as "the commonwealth of Israel", "near", "far", must be understood as referring only to

---

[52] Meuzelaar, esp. 168—174.

[53] Käsemann ("Epheser 2, 17—22", Exegetische Versuche I, 280—283) would agree that for Paul and for the author of Ephesians the concept of the body has a practical purpose. But he says that this is the purpose which the New Testament has given it. He finds that the opposite of what Meuzelaar postulates is the case: Gnosis has not "transformed the figurative concept of the body into a Gnostic myth" but the New Testament has transformed the cosmic myth of Gnosis into the figurative concept of the body with a practical purpose.

[54] Die Beschneidung Christi, SBibUps 12, Lund 1950.

the "true Israel", that is, the Christian Church[55]. For Israel's place as the elect people is taken by the Christian Church. The passage is therefore about Gentiles being baptized into the Christian Church. This is described in analogy and contrast to the Jewish initiatory rite of circumcision.

The shedding of the convert's blood in circumcision is replaced by Christ's shedding of blood (v. 13), which may refer either to Christ's crucifixion or to his circumcision or to both, according to Sahlin. For when a person is baptized, he participates in all that happens to Christ. Baptism thus makes the distinction between circumcised and uncircumcised obsolete[56]. This distinction, which caused the age-long hostility (v. 14) between Jew and Gentile, is based on the law of commandments in ordinances (v. 15) and is symbolized by the dividing wall in the temple in Jerusalem. All three concepts, the wall, the hostility, and the law, refer to circumcision. In the new temple (v. 21) there is no dividing wall. The new temple is identical with the new man (v. 15): the Israel of God which is the Christian Church. The saints (v. 19) are all the baptized. Thus according to Sahlin, the inclusive new temple replaces the exclusive temple in Jerusalem.

A. G. Lamadrid[57] approaches the theme of peace in Eph 2:11—22 by studying Old Testament passages on peace[58], especially Messianic passages which speak of peace[59] and the coming of the Gentiles to Israel[60]. Lamadrid concludes that the concept of peacemaking in the Bible is a way of describing redemptive history. Biblical teaching about peacemaking has the special quality of emphasizing both the vertical and the horizontal dimensions of salvation. According to Lamadrid, the biblical doctrine of peacemaking is given its most mature statement in Eph 2:11—22. This doctrine becomes the basis of the statement in the Constitution on the Church of Vatican II that the church is "a kind of sacrament or sign of intimate union with God, and of the unity of all mankind"[61].

Eduard Schweizer[62] mediates between those who advocate an

---

[55] So also Hanson, 142; Vielhauer, 124.

[56] G. Vermes (Scripture and Tradition, Leiden 1961, 178—192) lends support to Sahlin in a broader study of the relation of baptism to circumcision.

[57] "Ipse est pax nostra", Estudios Bíblicos XXVIII (1969), 209—261; XXIX (1970), 101—136; 227—266.

[58] E. g. Is 52:7; 57:16—19; Ps 85.

[59] E. g. Is 9:1—6; 11:1—9; Mic 4—5; Jer 23:5—6.   [60] E. g. Is 49:6; 66:11—12.

[61] The Documents of Vatican II, New York 1966, 15.

[62] "Die Kirche als Leib Christi in den Paulinischen Antilegomena". Neotestamentica, Zürich 1963, 294—316.

Old Testament and rabbinic background for Eph 2:11—22 and those who advocate a Gnostic background. Like Schlier, he believes that Ephesians interprets ideas about the cosmos in a historical way; but he holds that these ideas do not come from Gnosis, but are part of a "cosmic theology" held by some circles in the early church. This theology has roots in Judaism, particularly in the idea of Adam as collective humanity and of the wisdom of God as a more or less personified being filling the universe; it also has roots in Hellenistic thought about the cosmos as "makro-anthropos". The fact that an indelible characteristic of this theology is its conception of the reconciliation of the entire universe shows that it is not Gnostic, since Gnosis holds to an ultimate separation of the higher and lower spheres. The author of Ephesians corrects this "cosmic theology" by interpreting it in terms of the cross of Christ, the reconciliation of Jews and Gentiles, and the task of preaching the gospel to all nations[63].

Schweizer points out that the interpretations by way of Gnosticism and Judaism have come closer to one another than they once were[64]. Schlier and others now emphasize the Jewish character of the early Gnosis which they see behind Ephesians. On the other hand, later Judaism picked up some ideas which are at least similar to Gnostic ones.

The whole question of the traditions which lie behind Eph 2:11—22 has been investigated by Derwood Smith[65]. He analyzes each of the phrases and concepts which Schlier claims are of Gnostic origin. Convinced that the quest for their background must be broadened, Smith examines not only the Gnostic material adduced by Schlier but also potentially relevant traditions in Greek philosophy, hellenistic Judaism and rabbinic literature. This broad net yields sources other than Gnostic which are at least as plausible, and usually more so, than those Schlier claims.

---

[63] J. Gnilka (Der Epheserbrief. Freiburg 1971, 151 152) agrees with Schweizer.

[64] The probability of the closeness of the two positions was early expressed by N. Dahl (Das Volk Gottes, Oslo 1941, 260). He says Schlier's statement that "in concepts and language Ephesians is a product of the Hellenistic-Oriental (Syriac) environment" should be modified to read "that this environment presents above all a 'Hellenistic-Oriental' (Gnostic) Judaism". Recently Käsemann has asked why both the Jewish concept of corporate personality and the Gnostic myth of the god-man cannot be contributing factors to the concept of the body of Christ (Paulinische Perspektiven, Tübingen 1969, 180—181).

[65] Jewish and Greek Traditions in Ephesians 2:11—22, unpublished Yale doctoral dissertation, 1970; see also "The Two Made One", Ohio JRS VI, 1 (1973) 34—54.

Smith concludes that the background of Eph 2:11—22, far from being a unified Gnostic myth, is actually composed of a variety of Jewish and Greek concepts which reinterpret each other as they are combined to express the author's message. Many of the same concepts are picked up by various Gnostic writers, sometimes from Ephesians, but more often quite independently; these writers reinterpret the concepts to fit their own mythologies. This is the reason for the parallels between gnostic literature and Ephesians which so impress Schlier, but which do not reveal the place where Ephesians fits into the history of these concepts.

In making a convincing case against a Gnostic background for Eph 2:11—22, Smith shows that the immediate background of the passage can be found in Jewish traditions about proselytes, in Greek philosophical traditions about overcoming divisions, and in Jewish cosmological traditions. Each of these areas has been put forth by other scholars, as we have seen above, but no one else has dealt with them all simultaneously with reference to Eph 2:11—22.

Markus Barth gives reasons similar to Smith's for rejecting Gnostic traditions as a background for Eph 2:11—22[66]. Barth, however, puts primary emphasis on Old Testament roots which with "features of apocalyptic and rabbinic interpretation suffice to demonstrate the public and cosmic character of Christ's coming and work as it is preached in Eph 2". Barth considers the quotation from Isaiah 57:19 to be very important, since it appears in vv. 13 and 17, and since Paul interprets it and applies it throughout the passage. The peace spoken of in Isaiah, "given by God *to* those far and near", is also "a peace between the two. Peace is not simply a matter of the soul or of individuals only; if it is peace from and with God, then it is also peace among men. Only by changing man's social relations does God also change man's individual life"[67].

Studies Based on the Dead Sea Scrolls

When the Dead Sea Scrolls were discovered at Qumran, it seemed to many scholars that we now had abundant early documentary evidence of a kind of Judaism, which if not Gnostic, showed great affinity with Gnosticism. This view has had to be corrected. There is a growing consensus that the views of Qumran can be distin-

---

[66] Ephesians, Anchor Bible 34, Garden City, N. Y. 1974, 285—86.
[67] Barth, Eph., 278.

guished from those of Gnosis, and that the scrolls should be considered as part of the literature of Judaism, although it may reasonably be argued that they provide material which shows development in the direction of Gnosticism[68].

Karl Kuhn finds similarities in the language and style of Ephesians with the literature of the form of Palestinian Judaism exhibited by the Qumran texts[69]. For Kuhn this is strong evidence against Schlier's Gnostic thesis.

Mussner carries the investigation begun by Kuhn into the area of "important recurring themes, concepts and patterns of thought"[70]. He is convinced that there are close connections, especially in Eph 2, between Ephesians and Qumran: "We find here a thematic association of ideas, which is also evidenced in the Scrolls. This intensifies the belief that the thematic material of Ephesians has its roots in a tradition that is represented at Qumran, and which is far removed from later Gnosticism."

In Qumran, Mussner finds the theme of the bond between the community and heaven, and the theme of unity expressed in the same passage:

To those whom God hath chosen hath he given as an eternal possession ... an inheritance in the lot of the saints, and hath united their community with the sons of heaven to be a congregation of unitedness and an assembly of the sacred building (1 QS 11: 7f).

In Ephesians, the bond between the community and heaven is claimed when v. 18 says that both Jews and Gentiles "have access to the Father", and v. 19 speaks of being "fellow citizens with the saints"[71]. The theme of unity is expressed in Eph 2:16, where Jews and Gentiles are said to be reconciled "in one body" with God. Mussner agrees with J. Maier[72] that in Qumran the concept of unity is probably always connected with that of the temple.

The theme of the community as temple and as city is frequent in Qumran. The community is a "house of holiness for Israel", a "precious cornerstone" whose "foundations shall not tremble" (1 QS 8:4—10)[73]. It is "a fortified city and unshakable through a high

---

[68] Wilson, 3.

[69] "The Epistle to the Ephesians in the light of the Qumran Texts", Paul and Qumran, ed. J. Murphy-O'Connor, London 1968, 115—131.

[70] "Contributions Made by Qumran to the Understanding of the Epistle to the Ephesians", Paul and Qumran, 159—178.

[71] Mussner now thinks "saints" refers to the angels, whereas earlier he said it referred to Jewish Christians.

[72] "Zum Begriff yhd in den Texten von Qumran", ZAW 72, 1960, 148—166.

[73] McKelvey, 47, calls this passage "the fullest expression of the spiritual

wall", with "the foundation on a rock" (1 QH 6:25—27). With such passages, Mussner compares the building imagery of Eph 2:20—22. He admits that the church is also described as a building in other New Testament passages, but finds the unique parallel with Qumran in the connection of the building with the heavenly world. For the church, as for Qumran, the earthly temple at Jerusalem was no longer the place of meeting with God. This is the reason why there was within Christianity a tradition about the community as the spiritual temple on which the author of Ephesians could rely.

On the theme of new creation, Mussner quotes 1 QH 11:8b—14 and 1 QH 3:19—23; an excerpt of the former is:

> And thou hast cleansed man from sin because of thy glory ... that he may be joined with the sons of thy truth and the lot of thy saints; to raise from the dust the worm of the dead to (an eternal) community ... that he may be renewed ... with all that shall be.

Mussner finds a similar pattern in both Qumran passages: 1) deliverance from sin or corruption; 2) lifting or re-creating from dust; 3) entrance into the heavenly community. Mussner believes that the same pattern can be discerned in the structure of Eph 2: i) deliverance through grace from a state of death caused by sin, and elevation into the heavenly region (2:1—11); ii) the transformation into one new man (2:13—17); iii) entry into the heavenly community in the spiritual temple of the church (2:18—22).

Another concept common to Eph 2:11—22 and Qumran is that of entrance into the community as "coming near" (e. g. 1 QS 6:16, 22). This is closely identified with coming near to God, such as in the phrase "in thy mercy dost thou permit me to draw near" (1 QS 11:13). The idea and language are probably drawn from the temple tradition. Similarly, Eph 2:13 speaks of those far-off coming near. Here too, being included in the community is closely identified with coming near to God. According to Mussner the similarity between Qumran and Ephesians at this point is explained by the fact that both see the community as the true temple of God.

Bertil Gärtner's investigation of Eph 2:11—22 in the light of the temple symbolism of Qumran coincides with Mussner's at some points and supplements it[74]. Gärtner, like Mussner, observes that

temple concept in Qumran". He states: "The discovery of the Qumran scrolls has demonstrated that the idea of the community as a temple did indeed exist before New Testament times and that it is not necessary to go outside Palestinian Judaism to look for it."

[74] The Temple and the Community in Qumran and the New Testament, Cambridge 1965, 60—65.

in Judaism access to God is associated with the temple tradition. Gärtner then remarks that the temple "was originally the property of the chosen people; no stranger might come before the face of Jehovah". With this idea Gärtner compares the insistence of the Qumran text 4 Q Flor on the strict conditions for entrance into the new, pure, spiritual temple: "That is the house where there shall not enter (anyone whose flesh has a) permanent (blemish) or an Ammonite or a Moabite or a bastard or an alien or a stranger forever." Of particular interest here are the terms alien and stranger, which are related to the words "strangers" and "sojourners" of Eph 2:19. As Eph 2:19 contrasts "strangers and sojourners" to "fellow citizens with the saints", so 4 Q Flor contrasts "strangers" and "sojourners" to God's "holy ones" who are within the house forever. At this point Gärtner quotes the passages also quoted by Mussner, 1 QS 9:7f and 1 QH 3:21ff, which depict the Qumran community as united with the angelic community of heaven. Gärtner has thus added another element to the cluster of ideas which Ephesians seems to have in common with Qumran.

The exclusiveness of the Qumran community, documented by Gärtner, is the theme which Otto Betz uses to trace the background of the dividing wall image in Eph 2:14[75]. Betz shows that the Qumran emphasis on exclusiveness comes from the struggle for the preservation of a consecrated people in the Sinai tradition of the Old Testament. According to the Sinai tradition, God commanded Moses to "set bounds around the mountain and consecrate it" (Ex 19:23). He was also to "set bounds around the people" (Ex 19:12). The protecting boundary is an important idea in Judaism, as is evidenced in the Talmud, and objectified by the boundary wall in the temple. The boundary came to be understood as a metaphor for the law, as in the Letter of Aristeas, 139.

In the Old Testament there is a warning against any attempts to break through this boundary: God will "break out" against those who dare to "break through". In Qumran there is a great deal of emphasis on the idea that those who have broken in, disobedient and unworthy claimants to be God's people, will be destroyed when God comes.

This threatening exclusiveness is what the dividing wall in Ephesians symbolizes. To break it down, Christ had to pay the price prescribed, "in his flesh" (2:14) by death "through the cross" (2:16):

---

[75] "The Eschatological Interpretation of the Sinai Tradition in Qumran and in the New Testament", Revue de Qumrân 21, Feb. 1967, 89—107.

This was a Messianic action, a deed of realized eschatology. It became necessary because the Law was not able to procure "shalom", wholeness and peace. By turning a certain group of people into a holy nation, it created boundaries and barriers, differences and distinctions, hatred and contempt. Eschatological sanctification had to be unifying and universal.

Qumran research has made illuminating contributions to our understanding of Eph 2. However, few would now claim that the Qumran literature provides the whole background for such concepts in our passage as the new man and the dividing wall.

Form Criticism

Pioneer work in applying form criticism to Ephesians has been done by Gottfried Schille[76]. His contention is that the author of Ephesians quotes passages from early Christian liturgy. These passages, having been composed earlier than the rest of the letter, enable us to look behind the letter itself into the ideas of the early Christian community.

Schille begins with an analysis of Eph 2:14—18, which he observes has long been recognized as an excursus[77]. After listing formal elements which indicate that this excursus is a quotation, he gives reasons for believing that the quotation is a hymn which has the character of a confession of faith[78].

Typical of a confession of faith are the "we"-style and the use of many participles and relative clauses. Furthermore, the function of the quotation is to confirm the claim made in v. 13 that the readers, who were far from the commonwealth of Israel, have been brought near in Christ. What could better perform this function than an affirmation with which his readers are already familiar because they use it regularly in their common worship?

Schille then proceeds to analyze the contents of this hymn. Recognizing the mixing of vertical and horizontal dimensions which

---

[76] Frühchristliche Hymnen, Berlin 1965; based on his dissertation of 1953, "Liturgisches Gut im Epheserbrief".

[77] Schille, 24. He calls to witness Haupt, Ewald and Dibelius.

[78] Bengel's opinion that the verses have a hymn-like quality (see above p. 120) has often been cited by commentators. K. Staub ("Die Gefangenschaftsbriefe", Regensburger Neues Testament VII, Regensburg 1959, 136) calls the verses "The Hymn of Peace". K. Wengst (Christologische Formeln und Lieder des Urchristentums, Bonn 1967, 178) agrees that the quotation is a hymn; J. Sanders ("Hymnic Elements in Eph 1—3", ZNW 56, 1965, 218) a hymn or part of a hymn; E. Käsemann (Exegetische Versuche I, 280) "a liturgical piece". Wengst, Sanders and Käsemann conclude from their form-critical analyses that the quotation includes only vv. 14—16.

long vexed interpreters, he accepts Schlier's thesis about the presence of language from a Gnostic Primal Man-Redeemer myth. But Schille's solution of the problem is more complicated than Schlier's. Whereas Schlier distinguishes between the Gnostic myth on the one hand and the transforming use of it by the author on the other, Schille posits three stages: the Gnostic myth; the church's use of it in composing a hymn about Christ's reconciling man with God; and finally, the author's interpretation of this hymn to proclaim reconciliation between Jews and Gentiles. Schille believes that the glosses which the author uses to interpret the hymn can be identified on literary grounds. They are "the hostility" (v. 14), "having killed the hostility in himself" (v. 16), "to you" (v. 17) and "both in one spirit" (v. 18)[79].

According to Schille, the hymn belongs to the type "Redeemer-song"[80], which probably has its roots in the Oriental hymn-type, of which there are many examples in the Old Testament, especially in the Psalms. Schille lists other examples of this type in the New Testament and other early Christian literature. He believes that the Redeemer-song is a creation of the Christian community[81], and probably the earliest type which it produced. The occasion for using this type of hymn was baptism[82].

Joachim Gnilka, building on the form-critical work of Schille, clarifies its implications for the theology of Ephesians[83]. The original hymn, as reconstructed by form criticism, was about Christ as the peace of the entire universe. The author of Ephesians was in hearty accord with this theme. However, the hymn as it stood told of the overcoming of a rift in the universe in such a general way that it sounded unhistorical, even mythological. That portrayal of peace was too vague and impersonal, too easy a peace. It did not correspond to the Hebrew shalom, which is a personal, historical, vital peace.

---

[79] K. Wengst, 177—178, includes the clause "having killed the hostility in himself" in the original hymn but considers the end of v. 14 and the beginning of v. 15, "the hostility, having in his flesh abrogated the law of commandments in ordinances", as interpolation. J. Sanders, 217—218, agrees with Schille that both references to "hostility" are glosses. In addition, he considers "through the cross" (v. 16) an interpolation, a "Paulinism"; he cites interpolations about the cross in similar cases (Phil 2:8; Col 1:20). Sanders then concludes that "making peace" probably also drops out on formal grounds.

[80] Wengst, 180, terms it a "Reconciliation-song". Pokorny (Epheserbrief und Gnosis, 14, 20), following Schille, calls Eph 2:14—18 a "Redeemer-song"; however, he thinks that the song is a creation of the author of Ephesians.

[81] Schille, 50—52.   [82] Schille, 43, 102.

[83] "Christus unser Friede — ein Friedens-Erlöserlied in Eph 2:14—17", Die Zeit der Kirche, Freiburg 1970, 190—207.

The author of Ephesians, by adding some interpretive phrases to the hymn, and by setting it in the context of the relation of Jews and Gentiles, has given concrete form to the peace of which the hymn sings. Peace now has a personal and historical dimension. Its reality is exemplified in the church as formerly hostile groups are reconciled. The author shows that this peace is not easy by emphasizing its dependence on the cross; to realize the peace of Christ is difficult, requiring involvement and sacrifice.

An interesting elaboration of the hymn thesis has been developed by E. Testa[84]. Testa theorizes that Eph 2:14—16 is the third strophe of an early Jewish-Christian hymn, the first two strophes of which are Col 1:15—17 and 18—20. The theme of the hymn is "Jesus, the Universal Peacemaker". The first strophe tells of the unity of creation in Christ: "In him all things are held together" (Col 1:10). The second strophe tells of the unity in redemption through Christ: "He has made peace through the blood of his cross" (Col 1:19). The third strophe, Eph 2:14—16, combines both aspects of the theme and relates them to the historical event of Jews and Gentiles being united in the church. Testa gives the following kinds of evidence to support his thesis: the similarity of ideas, language and style in Col 1:15—20 and Eph 2:14—16; the existence of early Christian hymns such as the Odes of Solomon with similar theme and structure; the prevalence of the theme of Christ as universal peacemaker in Jewish-Christian literature.

Testa believes that the hymn, and especially its last strophe Eph 2:14—16, aimed to correct two heresies prevalent among Jewish Christians: Gnosticism and Ebionitism. The Gnostics held that the world is eternally divided between upper and lower realms; corresponding to this is a division between the enlightened persons who have knowledge of the upper realm and the unenlightened who have knowledge only of the lower realm. Against this, the hymn proclaims the unity of the cosmos, and thus the basic unity of humanity. The Ebionites claimed that Jesus as the Messiah of Israel had kept the Jewish law, and that his followers must do so also. Therefore they separated themselves from Gentile Christians. Against this heresy, the hymn proclaims that the law as a divisive factor is abrogated, and therefore Jews and Gentiles are united.

Markus Barth agrees with the growing concensus that Eph 2:14—18 is a hymn, but notes that this does not necessarily disprove Pauline origin:

---

[84] "Gesù Pacificatore Universale", Studii Biblici Franciscani Liber Annuus 19 (1969) 5—64.

Only if decisive elements or the whole content of this passage, the unification of Jews and Gentiles through the death of Christ, were absent from or flatly contradictory to genuine Pauline writings, would it be necessary either to consider the whole of Ephesians as non-Pauline or to call the hymn of 2:14—18 a pre- or post-Pauline product. But many authentic Pauline passages affirm precisely this unification[85].

Although increasing numbers of scholars have been exploring the possibilities in viewing Eph 2:14—22 or parts of it as a hymn, others have remained unconvinced. A warning against the tendency to find hymns in too many New Testament passages has been sounded by Reinhard Deichgräber[86]. He does not agree that Eph 2:14—18 is a hymn, "certainly not . . . a hymn which had already been composed and was available for the writer to quote".

Deichgräber's chief objection is that the section has a prosaic, not a poetic character: the lines into which Schille divides the section would be too long for poetry; the sentence construction is prose-style, vv. 14—16 consisting of one long sentence. Further, Deichgräber notes that the "we"-style is used fairly often in Ephesians, chiefly where the writer wants to identify with his readers; but, in the Christ-hymn of the New Testament, "we"-style is rarely used. Finally Deichgräber questions whether vv. 14—18 could ever have been an independent hymn as Schille claims, since the word "both" in vv. 14 and 15 requires some previous mention of two realms or two groups, such as Eph 2:11—13 provides[87].

Since Schille's work, several studies have appeared which, while not so thoroughly guided by the form-critical method, also seek to understand Ephesians by connecting it with the liturgy of the early church. These studies stress more than Schille does the continuity between Jewish liturgy and early Christian liturgy.

On the basis of similarities to Jewish liturgy, expecially that of Qumran, J. C. Kirby[88] develops the thesis that Ephesians is actually the substance of the Pentecost worship service used by the church in Ephesus, with some epistolary additions to put it into the form of a letter. According to this thesis, the first three chapters are in essence a lengthy *Berakah,* or blessing. Within this blessing, 2:11—22 is a distinct unit, which was probably independently com-

[85] Ephesians, Anchor Bible 34, 261—262.

[86] Gotteshymnus und Christushymnus in der frühen Christenheit, Studien zur Umwelt des Neuen Testaments 5, Göttingen 1967, 165—167.

[87] Similar criticisms are made by W. Weifel in his review of Schille's book, ThLZ 90, 1965, 118—121. A more detailed study by Helmut Merklein (Zur Tradition und Komposition von Eph 2:14—18), Biblische Zeitschrift 7 (1973) 79—102) develops and widens Deichgraber's critique.

[88] Ephesians: Baptism and Pentecost, London 1968.

posed[89]. Because Kirby believes that the whole passage 2:11—22 has the form of an elaborate chiasmus, he rejects Schille's thesis that only vv. 14—18 are an independent piece[90].

Content-wise, Eph 2:11—22 makes use of some of the Jewish teaching on proselyte baptism in order to expound on the meaning of Christian baptism[91]. In doing so, it offers a Christian *midrash* or commentary on Isa 57:19. The proclamation of the passage that in the church the deepest division of mankind—that between Jews and Gentiles—has been brought to an end is "so central ... to the thought of the epistle that all the moral exhortations are directed toward it"[92].

Related to the studies which consider Eph 2:11—22 as part of early Christian liturgy are those which treat the passage as dependent on the liturgy, though not necessarily actually a part of it. These studies follow the form-critical method insofar as they try to link the passage with a particular situation.

Charles Perrot, on the basis of detailed study of Jewish lectionaries, argues that the background of Eph 2:11—22 is the synagogue service in which the Torah reading was Ex 21:1—22:21, part of the "Book of the Covenant"[93]. Among the variety of subjects treated in these chapters, the liturgy concentrates on that of the Gentiles who live in the land of Israel. The prophetic readings for the service, Is 56:1—9 and 57:19, speak about the relation of Gentiles to Israel. Besides the quotation of Is 57:19 in Eph 2:17, "peace to the far and to the near", Perrot lists a number of parallels in the language of Eph 2:11—22 and the lectionary readings. For example, the two categories of Gentiles named in Ex 21:8 and 22:20 would explain why Eph 2:19 mentions two categories, "strangers and sojourners". And the statement in Eph 2:12 that the Gentiles were "alienated from the commonwealth of Israel" is reminiscent of the exclamation of the Gentile in Is 56:3, "Surely the Lord will separate me from his people!" Perrot concludes that Eph 2:11—22 is a *midrash* on the lectionary readings which gives them a radically new interpretation in the light of Christ.

R. Storer also approaches Ephesians by way of the Jewish lec-

---

[89] Kirby, 189.   [90] Kirby, 156—157, 169.

[91] Kirby 157—159. Kirby's interpretation of the passage is similar to that of Sahlin, see above pp. 189—190, although Sahlin's work was not available to him.

[92] Kirby, 140—141.

[93] "La lecture synagogale d'Exode 21:1—22:23 et son influence sur la littérature neo-testamentaire", A la Rencontre de Dieu, Mémorial A. Gelin, Le Puy 1961, 223—239.

tionary[94]. He suggests that Ephesians may be connected with the book of Ruth, which was one of the assigned readings in the Jewish liturgy for Pentecost. Storer lists a number of ideas which the two books have in common, three of which occur in Eph 2:11—22: bringing near the Gentile who was far off (Eph 2:11; Ruth 2:11); breaking a dividing wall so that Jew and Gentile might be joined Eph 2:14; Ruth 4:12)[95]; making out of two, one (Eph 2:15 to which Storer compares the uniting of Ruth and Naomi, and of Ruth and Boaz). Storer also presents a list of verbal parallels between the LXX version of Ruth and Ephesians. He believes that the book of Ruth would naturally have a special appeal for Gentile Christians, and that the hypothesis of its influence on Ephesians should be pursued further.

The possibility that study of Jewish liturgy may shed new light on the New Testament is the driving force behind a renewed interest in the study of the Targums, which arose from the Jewish liturgy. It is possible that the Targums "were for a time the common property of the synagogue and the early Christian Church"[96]. Although study of relationships between Targums and New Testament is only in its beginning stages, R. Le Déaut has investigated the dominant themes in a Targum Passover text and called attention to the fact that the theme of the creation of the new man found there is also in Eph 2:15[97].

The studies by Perrot, Storer and Le Déaut are necessarily fragmentary, since there are many unanswered questions about Jewish liturgical materials. One of the difficult problems is dating. It cannot yet be shown conclusively that the Jewish liturgies discussed are earlier than Ephesians.

The Sociological Dimension

Another relatively new field of research is the study of culture in the New Testament period in its social, political and economic as well as religious dimensions as an aid to interpretation of scripture. Although comparatively few scholars have engaged in this work, several of them have touched on Eph 2:11—22.

[94] "A Possible Link between the Epistle to the Ephesians and the Book of Ruth", Studia Evangelica IV, 1, ed. F. L. Cross, Berlin 1968, TU 102, 343—346.

[95] Ruth 4:12 does not actually mention a wall, but only refers to Perez, son of Tamar, whose story is told in Gen 38. Storer undoubtedly has in mind the patristic exegesis which links Gen 38:29 with Eph 2:14, see above p. 32.

[96] P. Nickels, Targum and New Testament: a Bibliography, Rome 1967, v.

[97] La Nuit Pascale, Rome 1963, 254, 256.

A study which attempts to see the early church in a broad cultural context is *Jew and Greek: a Study in the Primitive Church* by Gregory Dix[98]. According to Dix, the conflict of the Syriac and Greek cultures played an important role in world history for several millennia. These cultures were based on theological ideas which differed profoundly from one another. Yet Eph 2:11—22 makes the remarkable statement that this conflict, which it calls "hostility" (vv. 14, 16) has ceased between those members of both cultures who are within the Christian fellowship: Ephesians "reports, and at first hand, one of the decisive turning-points of human history—the emergence in history of the Catholic Church"[99]. After surveying the history of the racial hatred of Jew and Gentile and their reconciliation in the early church, Dix concludes: "This is not an aspiration, but an appeal to facts which they all know. It is St. Paul's account of the history of the Apostolic Age as he had known it from within."[100]

Bo Reicke makes use of research into the social, political and economic background of the early church in order to give a more detailed picture of the situation which Eph 2:11—22 tries to meet[101]. The Gentile Christians, mostly from the working classes of the large industrial cities of Asia Minor, are inclined to rebel against authority and those who persecuted them. To compound their Gentile aggressiveness, they are now susceptible to a kind of exclusive pride toward outsiders characteristic of militant Jewish nationalism. Eph 2:11—12 reminds them that they too were once outside "the commonwealth of Israel" in order to dissuade them from pride and hostility toward unconverted Gentiles, and to encourage them to take part in the mission to them.

The description of the Gentile Christians in Asia Minor by Pokorny is similar to that of Reicke[102]. They were city-dwellers, laborers in the large workships, craftsmen, shopkeepers, and slaves. They were suspicious of imperial authority, influenced by the general low state of morality which accompanied an economic upsurge, and inclined to riotous enthusiasm. Pokorny differs from Reicke in holding that for the problems of their existence among people of other religions, Gnosis offered a syncretistic solution. But the two scholars come out quite close together in their conclusion

---

[98] Westminster 1953.   [99] Dix, 1.   [100] Dix, 60.

[101] Diakonie, Festfreude und Zelos (Uppsala Universitets Årsskrift 1951:5) Uppsala 1951, 317—318.

[102] Epheserbrief und Gnosis, 22—24. Like Reicke, Pokorny believes that New Testament scholarship has neglected the study of the texts in relation to their social and political environment. (See above, pp. 183—184.)

that Eph 2:11—22 calls the Gentile Christians to responsibility in the mission of the church.

The recognition of the significance of the social environment for the early church is part of a more general awareness of the social dimension which has made itself felt in Christian theology. We have seen that in the late nineteenth century a few interpretations of Eph 2:11—22 demonstrated a new social consciousness—notably those of Maurice, Westcott and Gore[103]. Their influence can be seen in some of the comments on our passage by a practical commentary, *The Speaker's Bible*[104], which says that in Paul's missionary activity he was demonstrating that the dividing wall had been broken,

giving conscious unity to the highly heterogeneous elements in the lower strata of the population. He was building up a vigorous corporate life, informed by a common religious inspiration, in the great cosmopolitan centers of the Empire. Jews and Greeks, Romans, Thracians, Dacians, slaves and free men, coloured men and white men, people of all religions or none, educated and illiterate, who jostled one another in the streets of the great towns like Ephesus and Corinth, suddenly found themselves one family, actuated by one purpose, bound by a new and higher allegiance, bought with a price by one common Redeemer. They were one man in Christ Jesus.

Universal brotherhood in Christ is presented in *The Speaker's Bible* as the answer to contemporary problems of international conflict, sectarianism, class strife, and above all racial injustice[105], which it points out becomes increasingly serious as technological development brings people physically closer together.

In its desire to point out the social relevance of our passage, *The Speaker's Bible* interprets some verses in terms of a highly questionable version of evolutionary theory. Thus the new man (v. 16) is the hope for universal brotherhood, for he will appear in the course of the evolutionary process by which God has already brought man "from the slime of animalism towards the purity of a more spiritual life". This "steady climb" proceeds by "the fusion of existing types in a higher and nobler unity", just as Christ used both Jew and Gentile "in creating a new man—the Christian" who was "neither a Jew nor a Gentile".

Perhaps the most serious danger of this interpretation is its sug-

---

[103] See above pp. 157—158, 164—168.

[104] Ed. J. Hastings, Aberdeen 1925, VIII, 103—111.

[105] *The Speaker's Bible* is ahead of its time in predicting that the race problem would become one of the chief world problems.

gestion that Jews may be on a lower level of the evolutionary process than Christians. Although this was surely not the intention of *The Speaker's Bible*, its formulations at best do not oppose the modern form of racial prejudice against the Jews which was already widespread at that time. In its attempt, laudable in itself, to communicate the meaning of the passage to modern man by using current modes of thought, *The Speaker's Bible* gravely compromised its message of the unity of mankind.

Thus in the United States, one of the factors which kept the Social Gospel movement from accomplishing much for social justice was the uncritical acceptance by some of its leaders of current forms of evolutionary thought according to which the Negro race was at a slightly lower stage in the evolutionary process than the white race[106].

This charge can probably not be made against the outstanding theologian of the Social Gospel movement, Walter Rauschenbusch. Yet although he was far ahead of his time in attacking social injustice, he said relatively little about racial injustice. The following characterization of Ephesians illustrates how even he links Ephesians with an evolutionary view of history; the effects of this linkage are to be traced through the nineteenth century into the present.

When Christianity came on the stage of history, there were two distinct types in possession, the Gentiles and the Jews, with a deep and permanent cleavage between the two. Christianity added a third genus, and Christians were profoundly convinced that they were to assimilate and transform all others into a higher unity. The Epistle to the Ephesians is a tract reflecting on this aspect of the mission of Christ. Rom 9—11 is a philosophy of history, forecasting the method by which this process of absorption and solidification was to come about... The evolution of religion has always been intimately connected with the evolution of social organization. When tribes were amalgamated into a nation, tribal religions passed into a national religion. In the Roman empire nations were now being fused into a still larger social unity. The old national religions were incapable of serving as the spiritual support for this vaster social body. There was a crying need for an international and purely human religion[107].

A more careful interpretation of Ephesians is given by E. F. Scott[108], a New Testament scholar influenced by the Social Gos-

---

[106] See J. Russell, God's Lost Cause, London 1968, 79—83.

[107] Christianity and the Social Crisis, New York 1908, 114.

[108] The Epistles of Paul to the Colossians, to Philemon and to the Ephesians, London 1848[7], 167—180.

pel Movement. He sees in New Testament times, as in the modern world, a growing interest in the idea of the solidarity of mankind.

In that age too, the idea of human solidarity had become hardly less real than in our own day. Stoicism had given it a philosophical basis in the doctrine that all men are one in so far as they all share in the one principle of Reason. The Roman Empire had imposed a visible unity by bringing all races under a common government and culture. Thoughtful men were demanding, as they are now, that religion should prove itself equal to a new task. Instead of dividing men as heretofore, might it not be made the instrument of reconciliation[109]?

According to Scott, in Eph 2:11—22 Paul presents the grounds on which he believes the solidarity of mankind rests. Christ is "the proto-type of a new humanity (a new man Eph 2:15) in which the old divisions were fused ... Christ was the Adam of a new type of human beings". Eph 2:10 says that God's purpose is to unite all men in him. That this is not just an ideal is shown by the fact that Jews and Gentiles, formerly deeply antagonistic, now live in fellowship in the church. "Out of a divided humanity God has made a new, united humanity through Christ. This is to be the beginning of a world-wide process of reconciliation."

It is noteworthy that Scott sees the reconciling of divided mankind as the task of the church.

First it is shown that God's great purpose is to unite all things, and that this is the meaning of the church. Then the Christian duties are examined in the light of this object for which the church exists. If the church is to unify the world it must first be united within itself[110].

Scott's scholarship has helped him to see the place of the church in Ephesians, whereas *The Speaker's Bible* and Rauschenbusch virtually by-pass the church.

The significance of the church in Ephesians is strongly emphasized in an address by Wilhelm Zoellner at a meeting of theologians on the nature of the church sponsored by the Faith and Order Movement in 1930[111]. Zoellner makes the judgment that in the past Christian thinking was in the main too individualistic. A lack of understanding for the significance of group life could result in individualistic interpretation of even so church-oriented a writing as Ephesians.

---

[109] Scott, 131.   [110] Scott, 124.

[111] "Die Kirche nach dem Epheserbrief", Die Kirche im Neuen Testament in ihrer Bedeutung für die Gegenwart, ed. F. Siegmund-Schultze, Berlin 1930. 13—45.

Everything that was said and intended about fellowship, about the church in Ephesians, was without hestitation applied to the individual. The individual was the constitutive element, the whole resulted from the simple addition of individuals. Therefore everything that could be said about the whole must also be valid for the individual. The individual was in a sense there before the whole, and the whole had therefore no essential meaning for the individual. A glance at the commentaries, for example, even that of Ewald ... confirms this ... That many plurals ... refer to the congregation and that not everything which is said in the plural can be directly applied to the individual in the same sense; this at least one could have learned from Ritschl, who to be sure did not always get so far with his plural as to consider the church, but who at least recognized better the relationship of the community to the individual in the sense of the New Testament.

Zoellner declares that the problem with which Ephesians deals is not a problem of the individual, but the problem of whether or not to have separate churches for Jewish Christians and for Gentile Christians. Therefore "Christ is our peace" (Eph 2:14) does not mean here that Christ is our peace with God, which is the way it is characteristically interpreted when the context is not rightly understood[112]. Rather it means that Christ is the peace "beyond all the clefts which have arisen here on earth between the great communities of peoples and between their basic cultural streams".

In his stress on the social dimension of Ephesians, Zoellner by no means wishes to reduce the gospel to human relations. On the contrary, he believes that much confusion has arisen because the ideas of unity and brotherhood, which originally belonged to the church, have become secularized. Consequently a secular internationalism in the form of Communism has arisen as an alternative to the internationalism of the church. Yet this secular internationalism does not really overcome the divisions among men, since it champions one class, the workers, over others. As a reaction against the Marxist form of internationalism, a new German nationalism has arisen. In this situation, the task of the church is to put the cross between two ideologies as Paul put the cross between Jews and Gentiles as their reconciliation (Eph 2:14—16). For the deepest cause of divi-

---

[112] From a more unexpected quarter, the Pietist commentator F. Rienecker (Praktischer Handkommentar zum Epheserbrief, Neumünster 1934, 243), comes a similar charge: the full significance of the cross of Christ according to Eph 2:11—22 "has often not been sufficiently recognized ... The blood of Christ has not only redeeming, sin-destroying, purifying power for the individual believer, but it means at the same time ... unity and fellowship between God and man on the one hand and between man and men on the other, which has never been considered in such a way in any previous age".

sion between them is the claim each makes on the basis of its achievements. But at the cross our claims disappear, since we see that we depend ultimately on God's peace, not on our achievements. Zoellner does not consider it by any means his original discovery that Ephesians is peculiarly relevant for contemporary problems of church and society. It is rather a ferment already at work in the church. He compares the new understanding of Ephesians with the new understanding of Romans at the time of the Reformation.

There was a time when one could say that the letter to the Romans was rediscovered. That was the time of the Reformation ... Dare one say today that Ephesians has been rediscovered as the letter about the church; that is, that we begin to read it with other eyes than the commentators did not too long ago?

In answer to his own question, Zoellner cautions against speaking too quickly of a new beginning. Yet there is evidence of commentators reading Ephesians with new eyes.

In later decades there are increasing numbers of comments on the social significance of Eph 2:11—22 based on closer attention to the text in the light of its historical situation. One result of this closer reading is a greater emphasis on the particular function of reference to Jews and Gentiles. Thus Schlier says that "the prototype of every hostility of men with each other" is the hostility between Jews and Gentiles spoken of in Eph 2[113]. John Mackay speaks of the reconciliation between Jews and Gentiles proclaimed in Eph 2:11—22 as a pattern for the reconciliation of other hostile groups: "It is the will of God that the corporate unity into which formerly antagonistic groups are brought when the peace of God reigns in all hearts should be patterned upon this first and most decisive reconciliation."[114]

C. H. Dodd in his address "Christianity and the Reconciliation of the Nations"[115] attempts to suggest some specific ways in which reconciliation today can be patterned on the reconciliation of Jews and Gentiles as portrayed in Eph 2:11—22. The abrogation of the law (v. 15) means that both parties gave up self-righteous claims to moral superiority; a large step toward peaceful solution of international conflicts is the acknowledgment by both sides of responsibility for the evil which exists. The peace which Eph

---

[113] "Die Kirche im Epheserbrief", Die Zeit der Kirche, Freiburg 1956, 162.

[114] God's Order: The Ephesian Letter and This Present Time, New York 1953, 114.

[115] London 1952.

2:11—22 speaks of came by the acceptance of a larger community; giving up some national sovereignty for the sake of the larger community of nations is an essential for world peace. The change that brought peace between Jews and Gentiles in the early church was a fundamental change of mind, not just a change of techniques, leadership, organization; so today, important and essential as techniques, politicians, organization are, even more urgent is "rethinking our inherited ideas upon such questions as the true ends of human society, the nature and relations of freedom, justice and law, and the true content of human welfare".

Paul Minear points out that statements in Eph 2:11—22 about concrete groups, Jews and Gentiles, serve to guard against a false individualizing or spiritualizing of the concept of the body of Christ.

The references to circumcision and uncircumcision are absolutely necessary to make clear the kind of hostility and alienation which have been overcome in the one body. They are necessary if the reader, in hearing of the body, is to visualize something more than an endless number of anonymous individuals who enter a haven of peace. Rather, it was important, at least to Paul, that readers visualize two *men* becoming one, two men whose alienation had been religiously grounded and buttressed, two societies and two historical traditions whose hostility had attained the most massive kind of sociological inertia. This association gave to the miracle of the one body a tremendous social and historical weight. And it gave to the goal of unity also a tangible, earthy concreteness. The whole parade of analogies gave an immediate historical relevance to the "one Body" of the cross, making clear the impact of this body on all the societal structures of the world[116].

The passage's opposition to individualistic misunderstandings of the gospel is the basic theme of a sermon on Eph 2:11—22 by Eduard Thurneysen. He emphasizes the essential role of Israel in the passage.

Israel was involved and is involved from the beginning when it comes to God's acting in the world, because God does not want to create a little private peace for individual men, but wants to have a people that will light the way for all peoples. All the promises to Israel aim at the world of nations. We are so slow to understand this. God does not want to rescue only a few souls out of this unpeaceful world . . . World-wide and indivisible is the peace of God . . . East and West are reconciled in the blood of Christ . . . Let's not let ourselves be stirred up against one another by our politicians and newspaper writers. Away with the iron curtains, away with all ideological dividing walls and fences[117]!

---

[116] Images of the Church in the New Testament, Philadelphia 1960, 235.
[117] "Es geht um Israel!", Basler Predigten 28, 8 Dec. 1964, 11—12.

Eminent among those who lift up the social dimension of Ephesians is Markus Barth. His writings on Ephesians are always alert to this. For example, Barth says about the "new man" (2:16):

Above all, the joining of "the two" into "one new" whole reveals that neither of the two can possess salvation, peace, life without the other. Jews need Gentiles, Gentiles need Jews, man needs fellow man, if he will be saved at all. Under the rule of Christ no one "comes into heaven" except in the company of fellow men ... Thus the "one new man" is created to be a social being. New existence is social existence[118].

Although the whole thrust of his work is toward the implications of Ephesians for the mission of the church amidst the social problems of today's world, Barth warns against deriving social meaning from Eph 2:11—22 without recognizing the primary place of the reconciliation of Jews and Gentiles. He says about the breaking down of the dividing wall:

We observe that it is *not* related primarily to the partition between races and classes, nations and neighbors, ages and cultures.
It may well seem to us that political and social, racial and moral, sexual and spiritual, educational and psychological tensions and contrasts deserve more attention than—of all things!—the relationship between the church and Israel.

Lest he seem to have gone over to the camp of those who want to keep religion out of social problems, Barth hastens to add that he does not retract what was said about these other dimensions:

But we have to realize at this point that in the letter to the Ephesians, Paul does not from the outset generalize what he says about "the one new man". In this epistle the "workmanship of God" (2:10), the "one new man" (2:15 cf. 4:24) is said to be created only of ... these two: Jew and Gentile (2:11-22). That both Jews and Gentiles are divided also into male and female, young and old, owners and slaves, is not forgotten by Paul. But social peace, between the sexes, between young and old, and between different classes, is no substitute for that unique peace which ended the hostility between the insiders and the outsiders of God's house. According to Eph, social peace in any realm and in any form is a consequence of the peace which was made between Jews and Gentiles[119].

In the same vein, Helmut Gollwitzer says:

The fact that we have not heard a voice like that of Ephesians, or have heard it falsely, has not only had evil effects for the Jews living among

---

[118] Ephesians, Anchor Bible 34, 311.
[119] The Broken Wall, Chicago 1959, 124—125.

us. The consequence of our letter is this: if the time of this dividing wall is past, behind which God's law stood, how much more is the time of all other walls past, behind which stand only human laws[120].

Because the consequences have not been drawn from the broken wall, says Gollwitzer, we have misused the Christian message to sanction our own walls of nation, class and race.

The fundamental connection between participation in society and the individual's inner life is illuminated in an essay on Eph 2:11—22 by the psychotherapist Ann Belford Ulanov[121]. Ulanov observes that "in social oppression of any kind, personal repression and projection are always operating". But she goes on to say that working for individual mental health is not the answer, since it results in setting up a new wall between the sick and the healthy:

> Once more, as in the Temple of old, we have a privileged sanctuary to which only a few are admitted, those with the right sign—the circumcised, the analyzed. Any personal value—a concern for racial equality, for peace, for the end of sexual discrimination—if elevated to absoluteness can become a tyranny that only forces us into new kinds of divisive hostility. Against this tyranny of human standards stands the person of Christ. The bond of peace is a person, not a doctrine.

Although an emphasis on the social relevance of Eph 2:11—22 is one of the characteristic features of twentieth century expositions, some interpretations point in a more individualistic direction. Ernst Percy says that Eph 2:11—22

> is not primarily concerned about the unity between Jews and Gentiles, but about the unity between individual members of the community without regard to their ethnic descent; the ethnic contrast between Jews and Gentiles belongs apparently for the author, as for his readers now, completely to the past[122].

J. C. G. Kotzé, a South African theologian, deals with the problem of individual and group in an address, "The Meaning of Our Unity in Christ"[123]. He takes a very definite stand opposing the significance of Eph 2:11—22 for group relationships. "To transfer this conception of unity to the relations between peoples is definite-

---

[120] "Bibelarbeit über Epheser 2, 11—22", Der Friede Gottes und der Friede der Welt, ed. F. Lorenz, Berlin 1967, 29. The point Gollwitzer makes about God's law and human laws was made earlier by Bayne (see above p. 107) and moved Sewall to challenge American slavery laws.

[121] "The Two Strangers", Union Seminary Quarterly Review 28, 1973, 273—283.

[122] Probleme der Kolosser und Epheserbriefe, 284.

[123] Ecumenical Review VII, 4, Jul. 1955, 321—337.

ly wrong", says Kotzé. His reason for taking this position is that "peoples as a whole have not been saved, but only individuals out of the peoples".

Yet Kotzé does not deny the reality of group life. On the contrary, he considers it important that making saved Jews and saved Gentiles "one in a Christian sense does not destroy their identity as peoples". But according to Kotzé, the identity of a people is a natural fact, whereas unity in Christ is a spiritual fact. Kotzé's use of the categories "natural" and "spiritual" allows him to say that the spiritual has no necessary relevance for the natural: "Because unity in Christ is not dependent on race or culture, it is not denied when believers with such great differences at the natural level are organized into their own church groups." Kotzé does warn against the dangers involved in dividing Christians into separate churches according to race or culture, but his warning sounds weak after he has interpreted the passage in a way which justifies segregation.

Yet it is understandable that the present situation in South Africa makes it very difficult to interpret Eph 2:11—22 otherwise. Most theologians there take the Israel of the Old Testament as the pattern of a people whose identity God commanded them to keep in order to fulfill their mission, just as South Africans must now keep their identity. If this command is abrogated, then the theological basis for segregation is gone. Therefore they believe that "the unity between Jews and Gentiles of which Eph 2:11—22 (3:6) speaks is only a spiritual one, without any blotting out of natural barriers"[124].

Those who deny that Eph 2:11—22 has relevance for problems in society do so on the grounds that the passage applies only to Christians. Most of these interpreters would agree, however, with the majority view that the passage deals primarily with the unity of the church; but they often limit this unity to a spiritual sphere separate from visible fellowship, as does Kotzé[125].

---

[124] G. Menzel, Die Kirchen und die Rassen, Wuppertal 1960, 47.

[125] A minority, among whom Ewald and Percy are most prominent, believe that the passage deals primarily with equality of access to God. Ewald, 133, states: "What Paul really says about the Gentile Christians... is that they stand with completely equal rights along with the born Jews." Percy ("Zu den Problemen des Kolosser- und Epheserbriefes", ZNW 43, 1950—1951, 187) claims to have proved "that Eph 2:11—22 does not have to do primarily with the uniting of Jews and Gentiles in the one Christian Church, even though this thought is an important member in the complex of ideas presented in this section. Rather it says that the Gentiles participate in salvation in the same way as the Jews do."

Developments in the Church and its Relation to the World Motivating Attention to Eph 2:11—22.

The Ecumenical Movement

The struggle to understand what the unity of the church is, and to express that unity in practice is the task to which the Ecumenical Movement is committed—a movement which more than any other has spurred study of Ephesians in the twentieth century. This movement is of course closely related to the increased social awareness just discussed, and has in turn contributed to it.

The connection between the Ecumenical Movement and Ephesians is exhibited in the report by W. A. Visser't Hooft, General secretary of the World Council of Churches in its second assembly at Evanston in 1954. He says that the impulse behind the Ecumenical Movement was the recognition that the true nature of the church was being obscured by divided churches.

For how could they "make all men see what is the plan of the mystery" (Eph 3:9), how could they convince men that "the dividing wall" had been broken (Eph 2:14), so long as they kept on living isolated from one another? The churches had to speak and act more together in order to show that the church is dependent on God alone and not dependent on men. For only in their togetherness can they express clearly how their fellowship in Christ reaches beyond the dividing walls of nation, race, class or culture[126].

The problems which have chiefly absorbed the attention of the Ecumenical Movement have been differences in theological tradition between the churches. Dealing with these differences has given Christians a fresh awareness of the difficult problems which the contrasts between the theologies of Jewish Christianity and Gentile Christianity posed in the early church. J. Willebrands suggests that the unity these two groups had for a time, described by Paul as "two in one body" (Eph 2:16), is a historical example of the church's living with great diversity of tradition, yet in unity, and is thus a helpful guideline for contemporary ecumenical efforts[127].

Edwin Roels, noting that the passages in which Paul speaks of the unity of the church always mention the new relationship of Jews and Gentiles, puts forth the thesis that "the Jew-Gentile relationship will presumably form the key to an understanding of at least the Pauline, if not the total Scriptural emphasis upon the uni-

---

[126] Hauptschriften II, Stuttgart 1967, 114.
[127] Oecuménisme et Problèmes Actuels, Paris 1969, 124—126.

ty of the Church". Accordingly, Roels regards Eph 2:11—22 as "the pivotal point in Paul's message of unity"[128]. Although Roel's purpose is to deal with the theology of mission in Ephesians, he becomes deeply involved in discussing the unity of the church as well. This parallels the experience of the Ecumenical Movement: missionary work has stimulated the church's thought about unity, and conversely, efforts toward unity have been fruitful for missionary thought and practice.

The connection between the unity of the church and mission is seen by Ferdinand Hahn as basic to the understanding of Eph 2:11—22[129]. The unique feature of the passage is its proclamation that unity between Jews and Gentiles has already been created in the death of Christ. But this unity has its "concrete realization" through the apostles and their preaching. Therefore the one church out of Jews and Gentiles is said to have them as its foundation (Eph 2:20). And therefore mission and unity are involved together in the very being of the church.

The conviction that the churches today are likewise called to "realize concretely" the unity already given in Christ has motivated the Ecumenical Movement in its attempts to remove barriers which divide groups of Christians from one another. These attempts have shown that not only theological traditions divide the church, but also barriers of nation, race and class. These barriers used to be known in the Ecumenical Movement as "non-theological" factors, but in recent years this term has been felt to be inappropriate since these factors ought to be dealt with theologically.

The Kirchenkampf

The struggle of the church in Germany in the 1930's showed in an especially striking way that much needed to be done in thinking through the unity of the church with relation to race and nation. The problem which focused attention upon biblical passages about the relation of Jews and Gentiles, including Eph 2:11—22, was that posed by the so-called "Aryan paragraph"[130]. This was a reg-

---

[128] God's Mission, Franeker 1962, 114.

[129] Das Verständnis der Mission im Neuen Testament, Neukirchen 1963, 133—134.

[130] Text of the "Aryan paragraph", some historical background, selections from the controversy about it in *Der Ungekündigte Bund*, ed. D. Goldschmidt & H. J. Kraus, Berlin 1962, 194—214; additional documents, *Die Evangelische Kirche in Deutschland und die Judenfrage*, Geneva 1945; largest collection of

ulation introduced in 1933 according to which Jewish Christians were denied the right to serve as pastors in the church[131]. It was an indication of a desire for more radical measures which would separate Jewish Christians into separate congregations. Those church leaders who accepted the Aryan paragraph claimed that it was a practical organizational matter. Those who opposed it insisted that it had to do with the biblical concept of the church.

Dietrich Bonhoeffer was among those who spoke out early against all proposals for segregating Jewish Christians. In a mimeographed flyer written in August 1933, before the Aryan paragraph was accepted by the General Synod of the Evangelical Church in Prussia, Bonhoeffer cites Eph 2 as the first reason why the exclusion of Jewish Christians from fellowship in congregations with Gentile Christians violates the nature of the church:

> The exclusion of Jewish Christians from church fellowship destroys the substance of the church of Christ: for first of all it revokes the work of Paul which was based on the conviction that through the cross of Christ the fence between Jews and Gentiles has been broken, that Christ has made out of the two one (Eph 2), that here (namely in the Church of Christ) there is neither Jew nor Gentile ... but all are one[132].

Opposition to the Aryan paragraph grew rapidly, although it represented only a very articulate minority. In order to bring as much light as possible into the increasingly heated conflict, the church asked theological faculties to give written opinions on the question. The first to do so, the Marburg faculty, said in presenting their opinion against the Aryan paragraph that the unity of Jews and Gentiles in the church is most fully developed in Ephesians:

> He who does not acknowledge with the Apostles and Reformers the full unity between Jewish and non-Jewish Christians in the church, as the Ephesians letter develops it most impressively in the New Testament, and who does not want to actualize this unity fundamentally in the constitution of the church, deceives himself when he confesses that for him the holy scriptures are God's Word and Jesus Christ is God's Son and the Lord of all men[133].

---

sources, *Die Bekenntnisse des Jahres 1933*, ed. K. D. Schmidt, Göttingen 1934. See also K. Meier, *Kirche und Judentum: Die Haltung der evangelischen Kirche zur Judenpolitik des Dritten Reiches*, Göttingen 1968.

[131] The "Aryan paragraph" was part of a law instituted April 7, 1933, by the new National-Socialist government as part of its program to keep "non-Aryans" from public office.

[132] "Der Arierparagraph in der Kirche", Gesammelte Schriften II, ed. E. Bethge, Munich 1959, 62–63.

[133] "Gutachten der Theologischen Fakultät der Universität Marburg zum

Supporters of the Aryan paragraph charged that it was a misuse of the New Testament to regard it as decisive for a problem the like of which did not exist in New Testament times. Among the supporters was George Wobbermin, professor in Göttingen, who published a critique of the Marburg statement and of a similar statement by a group of New Testament scholars. Wobbermin insisted that in contrast to the New Testament question about the relation of Jews and Gentiles,

the present German Jewish question is a racial question. The New Testament does not know the concept and problematic of race and the racial question. The statements admit that, too; but they do not face the unavoidable conclusion that the present German Jewish question cannot be answered adequately from the New Testament alone[134].

Since the New Testament does not speak to this question, argued Wobbermin, we must deal with it on the basis of more general theological considerations, using the best modern thought on the subject to meet the existential situation.

Wobbermin's article received a thorough answer in an article by Rudolf Bultmann[135]. Bultmann maintained that the question can only be answered from the New Testament concept of the church and the confessional statements of the Reformation. He reaffirmed the position of the Marburg faculty that according to passages like Gal 3:28 ("There is neither Jew nor Greek, there is neither slave nor free, there is neither male nor female; for you are all one in Christ Jesus."), no classifications of people, whether based on modern or ancient concepts can be used to separate members of the church. Thus Bultmann and the Marburg faculty emphasize that Eph 2 speaks with Gal 3 about overcoming all kinds of human divisions, not only the religious ones to which Wobbermin wanted to limit it.

A great many other voices were involved in the controversy over the Aryan paragraph. In summarizing what the controversy tells us about the interpretation of Eph 2:11—22, a few representatives are chosen. Although the supporters of the Aryan paragraph did not interpret Eph 2, their position can be inferred from their criticisms of the interpretation of their opponents. Wobbermin seems a suitable representative of the supporters of the Aryan paragraph, since he concerned himself with church unity to the point

Kirchengesetz über die Rechtsverhältnisse der Geistlichen und Kirchenbeamten", ThBl 12, 1933, col. 293.

[134] "Zwei theologische Gutachten in Sachen des Arier-Paragraphen—kritisch beleuchtet", ThBl 12, 1933, 358.

[135] "Der Arier-Paragraph im Raume der Kirche", ThBl 12, 1933, 359—370.

of being active in the Ecumenical Movement[136]. His position is an example of a view of the unity of the church according to which unity is not denied by separation according to human groupings.

Against the claim that Eph 2 is about the fellowship of Jewish and Gentile Christians, Wobbermin argues that the equality of all kinds of men before God is not affected by the way the church is organized.

It is correct that according to those statements of Paul the relationship of the individual to God ultimately is absolutely independent from all distinctions of the human sphere. Therefore pastoral care and fellowship in the Lord's Supper must be granted to all baptized persons without exception. In this direction lies the goal of the Ecumenical Movement. But in the Aryan paragraph it is completely and exclusively the human sphere which is involved[137].

Opponents of the Aryan paragraph reject this separation of the divine and human spheres. The statement of a group of New Testament scholars argues that

out of the fundamental equality of all men before God follows for the New Testament ... the complete equality of believers within the community, which is the Body of Christ, and into which the believer is received by baptism. In the community worldly distinctions cease (I Cor 12:13)[138].

Closely related to the emphasis on equality within the community is the assertation that Eph 2:11—22 deals with visible—not just invisible—unity. This assertion forms an important part of the conclusion of the New Testament scholars quoted above: "According to the New Testament the Christian Church is a church out of 'Jews and Gentiles', who are visible together in one community."[139] The statement of the Marburg faculty likewise speaks emphatically for the necessity of visible unity.

---

[136] Wobbermin took part in the 1930 meeting of theologians called by the Faith and Order Movement to discuss the nature of the church according to the New Testament. He presented there the grounds for his later position on the Aryan paragraph ("Der Schriftgemäße Begriff der Kirche", Die Kirche im Neuen Testament, ed. F. Siegmund-Schultze, Berlin 1930, 83): "From the soteriological-eschatological viewpoint the church is invisible. The Body of Christ belongs in the sphere of that which is invisible and eternal, not in the sphere of that which is visible and temporal (II Cor 4:18). In the latter sphere belongs the sociological form of the church, that is, church order and constitution."

[137] ThBl 12, 1933, 358.

[138] "Neues Testament und Rassenfrage", ThBl 12, 1933, 295. The presence of Schlier's name among the signers of the document is particularly interesting in light of his intensive work on Ephesians.

[139] ThBl 12, 1933, 296.

One dare not say that this unity only applies for the invisible church, while in the visible church the walls which divide men in society generally must be recognized and maintained. The visible church must form itself so far as it is possible on earth according to the image of the invisible, if its faith in the invisible is true. "Spots and wrinkles" may be borne on her body as inescapable signs of earthly weakness (Eph 5:27). But consciously to cripple the body is sin against the Spirit which is given her. To put up with any imperfection in the church otherwise than out of patience for weakness—and it is not maintained that taking away the rights of Christians of Jewish descent in the German Evangelical Church is so intended—means to make a virtue out of the lack of faith and love, and abrogates the gospel of the rule of God and the justification of the sinner out of grace in faith[140].

The question of how much "imperfection in the church" may be allowed when the fellowship of Jewish and Gentile Christians is involved had been raised in connection with the early church by Harnack several decades before the controversy over the Aryan paragraph. Harnack asks whether Paul may have had to tolerate for a time the existence of separate Jewish Christian congregations. He says that he sees no way of denying that Paul did so. But Harnack would clearly be in agreement with the Marburg statement in seeing it as a matter of patience with weakness, not a matter of principle, to allow separate congregations for Jewish and Gentile Christians[141].

In answer to the argument that there were separate congregations of Jewish Christians in New Testament times, the Marburg faculty replies that the separation was on doctrinal, not racial grounds. The separated congregations were those of Jewish Christians who required as a basis of entrance the observance of the law. And most important, they were not forced by the Gentile Christians to be separate, but stayed separate by their own conviction, the practice of which excluded other Christians. Dietrich Bonhoeffer points out that excluding Jewish Christians from full fellowship in the Christian community meant doing essentially the same thing as those separatist Jewish Christians did. They demanded as a basis for entrance into full fellowship with them something else besides faith in Christ—the Old Testament law. The Aryan paragraph likewise requires for entrance into fellowship something else besides faith in Christ—the Aryan law[142].

---

[140] ThBl 12, 1933, 292.

[141] Die Mission und Ausbreitung des Christentums, 1924[4], I, 69.

[142] This is the chief thesis of his address, "Die Kirche vor der Judenfrage", Gesammelte Schriften II, 44—53; the idea appears more summarily in "Der Arierparagraph in der Kirche", 63.

The contention that separate congregations for people of different races was the practice in some other countries is flatly dismissed as "backsliding" by the Marburg statement:

The quite sporadic examples of small non-European church formations with racial limitations on church membership one meets in Asia, Africa, and America (in which cases moreover the difference between Jews and Aryans is not involved) are to be judged as backward or backsliding formations in which the Christian message and its demands are broken[143].

The fact that the Marburg faculty underestimates the extent of racial separation in non-European churches, as for example the black and white congregations of the United States, does nothing to disprove their argument that the Christian message demands the visible unity of the church.

In his book *Die Evangelische Kirche und die Judenchristen*, Gerhard Jasper[144] says that to deny the visible fellowship of Jewish and Gentile Christians is to do the opposite of what Eph 2:11—22 requires: "Think of the complete homelessness of the Jewish Christians who are rejected by the community of their people, and whom the church then also refuses a home, in contradiction to Eph 2:11 ff."

Jasper's plea for Jewish Christians "rejected by ... their people" conflicts with the statement of the Erlangen faculty who support the Aryan paragraph on the grounds that one's membership in a particular people is a divine command for his loyalty to that people: "The biological tie to a particular people, which is a destiny we cannot escape, is to be acknowledged by Christians in attitude and deed." The Erlangen statement claims that the Reformers not only recognized national characteristics but actually promoted them. Furthermore, the foreign missions policy of the Lutheran Church had always been to let the peoples of various lands develop their churches in accordance with their own respective cultures. From these observations, the Erlangen statement concludes that the church must be true to "her task of being the people's church of the Germans"[145].

In reply to such views, the Bethel Confession says that the break-

---

[143] ThBl 12, 1933, 293.

[144] Göttingen 1934, excerpted in Die Evangelische Kirche in Deutschland und die Judenfrage, Geneva 1945, 105—109.

[145] "Theologisches Gutachten über die Zulassung von Christen jüdischer Herkunft zu den Ämtern der deutschen evangelischen Kirche", ThBl 12, 1933, 321—324.

ing down of the dividing wall marks the beginning of the universality of the church:

By the crucifixion and resurrection of Christ Jesus the fence has been broken down between Jews and Gentiles (Eph 2). In the place of the covenant people of the Old Testament steps not another nation, but the Christian Church from and in all peoples[146].

The first draft of the Bethel Confession had gone yet a step further when it said that the presence of Jewish Christians in the church today, with all the rights that Gentile Christians have, is living testimony to the reality of Eph 2:

When the Jewish Christian is not set apart in the church in some legalistic way, he is in her a living reminder of the faithfulness of God and a sign that the fence between Jews and Gentiles has been broken down and that the Christian faith dare not be falsified in the direction of a national religion or a type of Christianity congenial to the nature of a particular people[147].

This earlier form of the Bethel Confession notes the significance of the difference between Jews and Gentiles within the unity of the church. The final form quoted above emphasizes the church's universality.

Those who spoke for the universality of the church were often accused of denying that human differences had any meaning in the church. It was said that they made the church irrelevant to life, where the diversity of nation, culture, race, sex are significant. Put theologically, the charge was that they disregarded the orders of creation[148]. But there is certainly no lack of statements which acknowledge that the church does take account of human differences. Bonhoeffer speaks most strongly of all about the importance of human differences in the church. In doing so, he turns the argument of the German Christians against themselves. For he says that

---

[146] "Das Bekenntnis der Väter und die bekennende Gemeinde", Bekenntnisse des Jahres 1933, 127.

[147] "Erstform des Betheler Bekenntnisses", Bonhoeffer's Gesammelte Schriften, 117. The same idea is expressed in almost identical language by Gerhard Jasper, Die Evangelische Kirche in Deutschland und die Judenfrage, 106.

[148] This charge may have had partial justification with respect to some of the interpretations of the universality of the church according to Eph 2. Sometimes the overcoming of differences in the church was described in rather strong terms—as for example in Käsemann's opinion (Leib und Leib Christi, 156) that according to the Deutero-pauline writings, "the church is based—and this distinguishes her from heresy—on the destruction of all earthly-historical individuality in baptism".

the church needs human differences, and that therefore different kinds of people must not be kept apart from one another.

> The given order of race is so little disregarded as that of the sexes, of class, etc. . . . In the church Jew remains Jew, Gentile Gentile, man man, capitalist capitalist, etc. . . . But the call of God draws and gathers all to one people, to the people of God, to the church to which they all belong in the same way and with one another. The church is not the fellowship of people of the same kind, but rather precisely of strangers, who are called by the Word[149].

In his study of the church, written several years before, Bonhoeffer had presented grounds for this position from social philosophy and biblical theology. There he discusses the nature of the church's unity as requiring diversity and in doing so draws upon Eph 2:11—22:

> It is not made possible by uniformity, similarity, kindred souls, nor is it to be confused with unity of attitudes. It is much rather real just at the place where the apparently hardest contrasts exist . . . There, where Jew and Greek conflict in the complete difference of their psychological structure, their sensibility and their knowledge, precisely there by God's will is unity set: "here is neither Jew nor Greek, here is no slave nor free, here is no man nor woman: for you are all one in Christ Jesus." (Gal 3, 28) Out of two men he has created one new man in himself and has made peace (Eph 2:15); it remains however a peace which is beyond all understanding. For the contrasts remain, they even become sharper[150].

According to Bonhoeffer, Eph 2 does not say that Christ made the two one by leaving the two behind: both Jew and Gentile are needed for the unity of which Eph 2 speaks.

Although few scholarly commentaries on Ephesians were produced in Germany during the 1930's, it was constantly being interpreted in the heat of controversy. Those who based their case against the Aryan paragraph on the New Testament concept of the church believed that Eph 2:11—22 deals with the relation of Jewish and Gentile Christians to one another, not only their relation to God; with visible, not only invisible unity; with diversity in unity.

The question of separate Jewish Christian and Gentile Christian congregations has not yet found a complete answer which is generally accepted. There is still disagreement among scholars about the

---

[149] Gesammelte Schriften II, 63.

[150] Sanctorum Communio, ThB 3, Munich 1960³, 140. The same point is made by Gollwitzer, see below pp. 229—230.

situation in the early church. Whereas Harnack said that Paul may have tolerated separate Jewish congregations in the same geographical area, although not accepting separation as a principle, Alfred de Quervain says flatly: "Paul did not permit Jewish Christians to form their own congregations alongside Gentile Christian ones." On this basis then Quervain answers the question for today: Paul has "taken away from us every ground to let the church of Jesus Christ fall apart into various churches according to nations, according to the descent of the members"[151]. The view that Jewish Christians should have separate congregations Quervain condemns as meaning "the dissolution, the destruction of the community of Jesus Christ out of Jews and Gentiles, the rebuilding of the dividing wall by Christians, the dividing wall which has been removed by Christ's death"[152].

Against persistent contemporary tendencies in various places to form separate Jewish Christian congregations, Karl H. Rengstorf[153] argues that the picture of the early church we get from the New Testament is "the picture of a fellowship, which, with all its tensions here and there, feels itself sick and denatured as soon as this fellowship breaks or threatens to break". Among the reasons he gives for Jews and Gentiles to remain together in the same congregation is that the church is the community of the Messiah. Because the scriptures promised that the Gentiles would come to the Messianic community, the early Jewish Christians accepted the entrance of Gentiles despite the difficulties it caused. The Jewish Christians overcame their hesitations as they sought to obey the Messiah, whose work Rengstorf describes by quoting from Eph 2:

In his death and resurrection he maintained the grace of God against the law and thereby created for Jew and Gentile a completely new situation. Since he is *the* Way, he bound both to himself. And so he is "our peace, who has made both one and has broken down the fence that was between, in that he took away the hostility through his flesh...; for through him we both have access in one Spirit to the Father."

The Faith and Order Commission of the World Council of Churches in its study-report "The Church and the Jewish People" discusses the question of separate Jewish Christian congregations and on the basis of Eph 2 decides against separation:

We are not advocating separate congregations for them. History has shown the twofold danger which lies in this: the danger of discriminat-

---

[151] Kirche, Volk, Staat, Zürich 1945, 294.   [152] Quervain, 311—312.
[153] "Die Eine Kirche aus Juden und Heiden", Viva Vox Evangelii, Festschrift für H. Meiser, Munich 1951, 231—240.

ing despite all intention to the contrary, and the danger that such separate congregations tend to evolve sectarian traits. But more important
than these considerations is that in Christ the dividing wall has been
broken down and Jew and Gentile are to form one new man; thus any
separation in the church has been made impossible.

But the report at the same time recognizes the importance of diversity in unity:

> However, without detracting in any way from what has just been said,
> we should remember that there is room for all kinds of peoples and cul-
> tures in the Church. This implies that Jews who become Christians are
> not simply required to abandon their Jewish traditions and ways of
> thinking; in certain circumstances it may therefore be right to form
> special groups which are composed mainly of Jewish Christians[154].

That Jewish Christians are discussed in a report on the church
and the Jewish people illustrates the fact that the question of the
relationship of Jewish and Gentile Christians cannot be separated
from the larger question of the relationship of the church to Israel.

The Church's Relation to Israel

It has often been observed, with regret, that the church only became sensitive and articulate about discrimination against the Jews
under Hitler's government when this discrimination directly affected the church's own members. Then theologians in increasing
numbers began to rethink not only the relationship of Jewish and
Gentile Christians, but also the whole question of the relationship
of Israel and the church. In this rethinking a fresh study of Romans
9—11 played an important role, and continues to do so in connection with the new Jewish-Christian dialog that has developed since
World War II. Only in the last two decades, however, has Eph
2:11—22 received much attention as a source for understanding the
relation between Israel and the church. The main single study devoted to this aspect of Eph 2:11—22 is *Israel und die Kirche im
Brief des Paulus an die Epheser*[155], by Markus Barth. In his preface Barth says: "That not only Rom 9—11 but also Eph 2 is a
locus classicus for the discussion about Israel was for me a big sur-
prise."[156]

---

[154] Faith and Order Studies 1964—1967, Geneva 1968, 73.

[155] ThEx 75, Munich 1959; the chief themes of this study are restated in
Jesus, Paulus, und die Juden, ThSt(B) 91, Zürich 1967, 76—78.

[156] J. C. Coetzee, Volk en Godsvolk in die Nuwe Testament, Potchefstrom,
South Africa 1965, 211, observes that studies on "Israel in the New Testa-

Barth begins with the concept of the new man (v. 15). He submits that the new man is not constituted by the abolition or denial of differences between Jews and Gentiles, as commentaries have usually claimed when they said that the new man is Jesus Christ himself, or the individual "Christian personality" or the group made up of individuals having this new type of personality. Rather, the new man is constituted by the ending of the hostility between Jew and Gentile and by their common worship of the Father[157].

Although Barth opposes traditional interpretations of the new man, he is not alone in his protest. We have seen that Bonhoeffer considered the idea of the new man in Eph 2:15 as scriptural evidence for his strong emphasis on the place of differences within the church. And Jacob Jocz says:

> We doubt whether there is a parallel in any ancient literature, be it gnostic or otherwise, to the "Ephesian" concept of the "new man": a combination of Gentile and Jew. This is the very point of the *novum* of the messianic age: the new man is Jew and Gentile united[158].

Gregory Baum takes Eph 2:11—22 as Paul's treatment of the way both Jews and Gentiles in the church have complete equality and unity without losing their identities[159]. And Jakob Meuzelaar makes the judgment that "an 'abolition of all differences in the body of Christ' has in the past . . . again and again led to the 'Christian' view that the Jew as Jew no longer has a right to existence"[160].

The view that the new man is a unity of Jew and Gentile which includes their difference, championed by Barth and shared by a minority of scholars, has received its most serious criticism by Ernst Percy. In a review of Barth's *Israel und die Kirche*, Percy argues that Paul's concept of the new man involves dying with Christ to this age and rising with Christ to the new age where people are no longer put into categories.

> There can be no doubt that the expression "one new man" in Eph 2:15 denotes the new existence which has been created in Christ—in his death

---

ment" have not considered Eph 2, and welcomes Barth's writing as "pioneer work in this area".

[157] Israel und die Kirche, 11—12. Barth expounds the significance of differences within the unity of the "new man" in Eph., Anchor Bible 34, 292 and 310—311.

[158] A Theology of Election: Israel and the Church, London 1958, 124.

[159] Is the New Testament Anti-Semitic?, Glen Rock, N. J. 1965, 316—322.

[160] Der Leib des Messias, 86.

224

and resurrection—as representative of Jews as well as of Gentiles, and which means freedom from sin, death and law and thereby also the ending of the difference between Jews and Gentiles[161].

Percy must then face Barth's argument that the fact that Paul addresses the letter explicitly to Gentile Christians, while referring at times to himself and other Jewish Christians as "we" shows that Paul himself recognizes a continuing difference[162]. Percy's answer is that the "we" does not refer to Jewish Christians, but simply to those who have been members of the church for some time in contrast to new converts[163].

It is doubtful whether Percy has adequately faced the evidences that Paul's letters recognize a valid difference between Jews and Gentiles in the church. Furthermore, Paul's portrayal of dying and rising with Christ does not mean dying to the differences in this world, but rather dying to the powers which make these differences grounds for pride, discrimination, hostility[164].

From the position that Eph 2:11—22 presents Israel as having continuing significance for the church, Barth takes a further step. He points out that nowhere does the passage limit the sense in which Israel is to be understood. Many commentators would agree with Barth that the "commonwealth of Israel" (Eph 2:12) denotes the historical-ethnic community of the Jews as God's chosen people[165], and not only the faithful remnant[166], a spiritual ideal[167], the true Israel[168], or the Christian church[169]. But they

---

[161] ThLZ 86, 1961, 200—201. [162] Israel und die Kirche, 10.

[163] ThLZ 86, 200. See Die Probleme der Kolosser- und Epheserbriefe, 266n.16.

[164] R. Tannehill (Dying and Rising with Christ, BZNW 32, Berlin 1967, esp. 70—74) points in this direction.

[165] So Schlier, Der Brief an die Epheser, 120; Robinson, 57; Dahl, Kurze Auslegung des Epheserbriefes, Göttingen 1965, 33—34. Dibelius, 68, thinks that the writer does not intend to limit "commonwealth of Israel" to the Jewish community, but has the Christian Church in mind also. Mussner (Christus, das All und die Kirche, 77n) maintains against Dibelius that vv. 11—12 refer only to the time before the coming of Christ; therefore, "commonwealth of Israel" refers only to the Jewish community. Barth would not quarrel with Dibelius or others who speak similarly, such as K. L. Schmidt, Die Polis in Kirche und Welt, Zürich 1940, 20; E. Gaugler, Der Epheserbrief, ed. M. Geiger and K. Stalder, Zürich 1966, 103. Barth's point is only that Israel as a whole is included. [166] So J. C. Coetzee, 217.

[167] So H. Ockenga (Faithful in Christ Jesus, New York 1948, 124) says it is a "spiritual commonwealth of God ... separate from an earthly kingdom strictly connected with the twelve tribes of Israel". [168] So Vielhauer, 124.

[169] So Hanson, The Unity of the Church in the New Testament: Colossians and Ephesians, Uppsala 1946, 142; Sahlin, 10.

have assumed that at some point the passage has ceased speaking of Israel in this sense and has begun to speak of the Christian Church. Barth challenges this assumption. He argues that Paul proclaims to Gentile Christians that they have a new relationship with Israel. In the area where these Gentile Christians live are all kinds of members of Israel, including some who believe that Jesus is the Christ. Paul does not tell the Gentile Christians that their new relationship is only with those Jews who believe Jesus is the Christ, or only with the Israel of past times, or only with a "spiritual" Israel, but rather with all of Israel.

The Gentile Christians are exhorted not to forget, but to remember (2:11) that all they have received from God, and still receive, they share with Israel. No word says that they only share it with Jewish Christians. Rather it is clear that "in Christ" they have been united with Israel as a whole and come before God—unhindered by what they hear of reliance on physical circumcision[170].

Therefore Barth cannot follow those commentaries which say that Eph 2:11—22 is about the uniting of Gentile Christians with Jewish Christians. It is rather about the unity of the church out of Jews and Gentiles with Israel.

Barth grants that this view poses difficulties for us, and asks what the grounds are on which Paul could make the claim that the church is united with Israel. Judging such grounds as their common humanity, or historical continuity inadequate, Barth maintains that Paul sees their unity grounded in Christ. Christ is the Messiah of all Israel, not just a part of it, and it is in him that the church is united with Israel.

André Lacocque interprets the unity which the church has with Israel in a way similar to Barth's. As Lacocque puts it, Eph 2:11—22 views Christ as the representative of Israel[171]. Therefore when the

---

[170] Israel und die Kirche, 19. Barth reaffirms this position in Eph., Anchor Bible 34, 270.

[171] La pérennité d'Israël, Geneva 1964, 68. In direct contrast is the view presented by Haupt at the end of the nineteenth century (see above p. 156) that Christ was able to abrogate the law and thus to unite Jews and Gentiles only by *ceasing to be a Jew*. Likewise Rienecker, 249, says that Jesus's crucifixion means his expulsion from Israel; outside of Israel there is no wall separating Jesus from the Gentiles so he forms a new community of Jews and Gentiles which only those Jews who are outside of Israel can join. A. Schlatter (Die Briefe an die Galater, Epheser, Kolosser und Philemon, Stuttgart 1949², 182) also says that Christ unites Jews and Gentiles by ceasing to be a Jew, but not because of his expulsion from Israel: his death ends his fleshly life, which includes his Jewishness.

Gentile Christians came to him, they came to Israel. Israel's vocation was to be a mission to the Gentiles; this mission was what Christ accomplished.

Other interpreters point to the Jewish Christians as representatives of all Israel. They argue on the basis of the Old Testament concept of the remnant, maintaining that it is not an exclusive concept, but that the function of the remnant is to represent all of Israel. So the Jewish Christians are now the remnant representing Israel as a whole[172]. They are the "first fruits", the promise of the future day when all Israel will recognize Jesus as the Messiah. A typical spokesman for this idea is J. Rennes[173]. He describes the unity of Jews and Gentiles within the church as the eschaton experienced in advance. Whereas Rom 9—11 treats the relation of Jews and Gentiles in a historical, eschatological way, Eph 2:11—22 treats the representative realization of the eschaton in the church. In Rennes's opinion, Eph 2:11—22 therefore condemns all anti-Judaism more clearly than Rom 9—11. The ending of the hostility (Eph 2:14) applies first to the Jewish Christians, and through them to those Jews who are still unbelieving.

Percy's first objection to the view that the church is united with Israel as a whole is based on his concept of the new man (Eph 2:15). According to Barth's account, says Percy, only the Gentiles become new, the Jews remain as before. This contradicts what Eph 2:15 says about both becoming new[174]. But Percy argues here from his own essentially individualistic view of the new man, and does not take into consideration that the unity of Jew and Gentile is itself new.

More serious is Percy's second objection: that the peace of which Eph 2:14 speaks exists only in Christ. This sounds very much like what Barth says, but Percy means it in quite a different way: only those people who by faith are in Christ are included in the peace[175]. Hendrik van Oyen makes essentially the same objection. He argues that in Eph 4 "faith as response to revelation is presented as the decisive mark of the community. ('One Lord, one faith, one baptism') Thereby it does not matter in the least whether Jews or Gentiles are involved"[176].

---

[172] G. Baum, 346, cites as a New Testament parallel I Cor 7:14 where Paul says that the unbelieving husband is consecrated through his believing wife.

[173] "Christ Notre Paix", Foi et Vie 63, 4 (1964) 274—275.

[174] ThLZ 86, 1961, 199.   [175] ThLZ 86, 1961, 200—201.

[176] "Eine theologische Absage an die Judenmission?", Christlichjüdisches Forum 22, Feb. 1960, 2—3.

According to Barth, the idea that the peace of Eph 2:14 includes only those who have faith in Christ would make Christ's work dependent on man's faith. Barth argues that Christ brought peace before Jews, or Gentiles, had faith in him; so it is "impossible to make their faith a condition of this unity"[177].

The position which Barth takes is expressed also in the commentary of Hans Asmussen[178], written shortly after World War II.

This passage does not have to do with the creation of faith among individual Jews and Gentiles, but rather with a deed of Christ which lies *before* faith. *Before* faith God swept old realities out of the world and placed there new realities, corresponding to the way in which instead of the sins and lusts in which the unbelievers walked, he created new works in which the believers can now walk (Eph 2:10).

Asmussen indicates what is at stake in the interpretation of the unity of Jews and Gentiles when he alludes to the recent persecution of the Jews.

The reconciliation meant here is not a reconciliation of individuals. For now history will consist of God's struggling with both for the acceptance of this reconciliation. And the recent past shows that this struggle is not yet ended.

A final objection of Percy to Barth's interpretation must be considered. Percy points out that according to Eph 2:15 the creation of the new man depends on the prior abrogation of the law. But if a Jew enters into fellowship with Gentiles on the basis that Christ has abrogated the law, then he is no longer a Jew, but a Christian[179].

Barth, however, does not believe that the Old Covenant itself is abrogated. That would take away the ground of Israel's existence. What Christ has done in breaking down the wall (Eph 2:14) is to make powerless the separating, enslaving, accusing and merely provisional functions of the law, *not* the Old Covenant itself. As evidence for this interpretation Barth points on the one hand to the absence of any polemic against the Old Covenant in Ephesians, and on the other hand to the emphasis in Eph 2:11—22 on the indissoluble bond by which the election of the Gentiles depends upon the election of the Jews. Barth contends that these features of Eph 2:11—22 ought to be a warning against isolating and absolut-

---

[177] Israel und die Kirche, 19.
[178] Der Brief des Paulus an die Epheser, Breklum 1949, esp. 51—53.
[179] ThLZ 86, 1961, 201.

izing passages elsewhere in the New Testament which contrast the church and Israel[180]. Nor is Ephesians alone in providing this warning; very similar testimony is made in Rom 9—11.

Eph 2:11—22 emphasizes that which is described in Rom 11 as the grafting of the wild olive branch, representing the Gentiles, into the cultivated tree, representing Israel[181]. Just as the discussion of the relation of Jews and Gentiles in Rom 9—11 leads into the ethical instruction of Rom 12, says Barth, so Eph 2:11—22 is the heart of the theological basis for Eph 4, which is devoted specifically to ethics[182].

The doctrinal teaching of Eph treats the uniting of Jews and Gentiles which has been planned in eternity, carried out on the cross, and witnessed in the gospel. The ethics of Eph urges us to live according to the unity so created in all situations in dealings with every fellow man[183].

On the basis of his interpretation of Eph 2:11—22 Barth concludes that the Christian attitude toward the Jews should not be missionary in nature, but should rather be a dialog; and that Christian theology flourishes in the context of brotherhood with the Jewish people.

Barth's interpretation of Eph 2:11—22 is a challenge to the frequently repeated characterization of the church as the "third race"[184]. This term appears often in twentieth century commentaries on Ephesians, perhaps as a result of Adolf von Harnack's study of the idea[185]. In recent years a number of interpreters have

---

[180] Israel und die Kirche, 15—16.

[181] Israel und die Kirche, 26. Other scholars in this century who stress the similarity between Eph 2:11—22 and the olive tree image of Rom 11 are Lacocque, esp. 87; Rennes, Foi et Vie 63, 4, 274—275; L. Cerfaux, La Théologie de l'Église suivant Saint Paul, Paris 1965³, 54; G. Baum, 318. Schlier objects to this view on the grounds that Ephesians speaks of "the togetherness of Jews and Gentiles in one body of Christ, a heavenly city and holy temple, but not the absorption of the Gentiles in Israel. Even 2:11 ff. does not speak of the insertion of the Gentiles into Israel" (Die Zeit der Kirche, 164n).

[182] So also Kirby, 141.   [183] Israel und die Kirche, 17.

[184] See Ephesians, Anchor Bible 34, 310, where Barth explicitly rejects this term.

[185] Die Mission und Ausbreitung des Christentums, Leipzig 1924⁴. Harnack devotes a whole chapter to "The Message of the New People and the Third Race", 259—289, and considers the two terms virtually equivalent. For him Ephesians is evidence of the concept that the Christians are the "higher unity of a third people". Apparently the term "third race" was used more by the enemies of Christianity than by Christian writers. According to Harnack, the term is first found in Tertullian (ad. nat. I, 8, 20) who says, "We are called the third race", but rejects the term. Harnack grants that he can find only one

challenged the legitimacy of the idea of the "third race". Lacocque argues against the idea very vigorously. Beginning from the conviction that Eph 2 proclaims the restoration of the fundamental unity of the human race, Lacocque asks how "the one people of one God" is to be described:

> Would it be a hybrid nation where neither Jew nor Gentile could be recognized? This is in fact the solution which has traditionally been chosen. Even if we do not say so, we act as if "Israel" designated a deicide people, a tragic personification of Judas Iscariot, as if Jesus was the founder of a new religion and the church a new sort of people from the ashes of the old, an "idea", a "spirit" surging at last from the material, fleshly order. *Hegel* has triumphed, and from the antithesis Israel/the nations, a new synthesis is born: the church. In doing this we pass by the Pauline message according to which the church *is* Israel. It is not a third term; it is, in reality, the eschatological extension and promise of Israel to the nations[186].

Gollwitzer points out that the translation of Eph 2:11—22 in the Luther and Zurich Bibles may reflect and support the highly questionable idea of the third race. They say "at one time you were Gentiles", as though the readers are no longer Gentiles since they have become Christians. This translation, says Gollwitzer, supports the idea that there are three groups of men: the Jews, the Gentiles and the Christians,

---

instance where a Christian writer uses the term to describe Christians, but he believes the *idea* is present in many passages, especially where Christians are described as a new people. A. Oepke (Das Neue Gottesvolk, Gütersloh 1950, 266—267) agrees with Harnack. Other scholars in the twentieth century who use the term "third race" to interpret Eph 2:11—22 include F. Synge, St. Paul's Epistle to the Ephesians, London 1941, 23; J. Lichtenberger, "Situation et Destinée d'Israël à la lumière de Romains 9—11 et d'Éphésiens 2, Foi et Vie 64, 6 (1965) 504; Gaugler, 111—112. Chadwick (ZNW 51, 147) uses the term, but immediately qualifies it: "The Christians are a third race, but not in the sense of a discontinuity toward the people of the Old Covenant." Cerfaux, 210, speaks of a "new race (as opposed to Jews and Gentiles)"; Hanson, 122, of "an entirely new race"; Best, 154, of "three faces of men: Jews, Gentiles, and Christians".

[186] "Israël, pierre de touche de l'oecuménisme", Verbum Caro 48, 1958, 339. Meuzelaar, 15, says that to guard against misunderstanding "body of Christ" as "a new race over against Judaism and Gentilism", it is important to realize that the concept of Israel in the Old Testament was not a closed one. "When one takes no notice of the 'openness' of the concept Israel in Judaism, then there arises in the opinion of scholars a sharp contrast between the people of the New Covenant and the people of Israel, between the Christian ecclesia and Judaism."

the last as a new, third group into which the Jews and Gentiles are destined to dissolve. "Jew" and "Gentile" is then a characteristic of the past, which one leaves behind, or at least should leave behind and overcome in order now to be only Christian ... But Paul and Ephesians do not think this way. Just as the difference between man and woman or (in the thought of that time) the difference between master and slave was not abolished by Christ, so a man did not stop being a Jew or a non-Jew when he became a Christian. Not the difference, but ... the hostility between these two human groups is put aside by Christ. Christians do not replace Jews and Gentiles; rather, Israel and the nations, previously deeply divided, are joined together by Christ in his body and life[187].

If the church is not a third race[188] which supersedes Jews and Gentiles, then should the fact that both Judaism and the Christian Church exist separately be seen as a split in the people of God? Is this not then the original and deepest ecumenical problem? This question has been discussed with increasing frequency in the last two decades. During the preparations for the Evanston Assembly of the World Council of Churches in 1954, the theme of which was "Christ, the Hope of the World", Karl Barth submitted a text entitled "The Hope of Israel" which concluded with the words: "The problem of the unity of the church with Israel is the first problem of ecumenical unity."[189] And Amos Wilder concludes an article: "The unity of the Church depends upon a prior understanding of the mystery of Israel and of the meaning of the Elect people of God throughout the Bible."[190]

In the literature on the relation of Israel to the Ecumenical Movement, two authors who deal specifically with Eph 2:11—22 are Andre Lacocque and Jean-Paul Lichtenberg. Lacocque insists that there is only one Israel[191], the people of God, and that according to Eph 2, the wall which in God's plan of redemption separated the people of God from the Gentiles has now been broken

---

[187] Gollwitzer, 24.

[188] A. Wilder ("The Church and Israel in the Light of Election", Studia Evangelica IV, Berlin 1968, 347) believes that the church's view of itself as the third race came as a result of Judaism's understandable reconstruction of itself after 70 A.D. and the ensuing excommunication of Christians from the synagogue. The third race idea is thus according to Wilder a distorted one, deriving more from the feelings of the times than from the gospel.

[189] Freiburger Rundbrief, Oct. 1955, 26—27.

[190] Studia Evangelica IV, 347. B. Lambert (La Problème oecuménique II, Paris 1962, 595—652) devotes a chapter of his comprehensive study on ecumenics to this problem.

[191] Verbum Caro 48, 331—343.

down. To say that there are now two Israels, a spiritual one which is the church and a fleshly one which is Judaism is to put a Platonic scheme in place of non-dualistic Hebraic, biblical thought. It is to raise again the dividing wall which according to Eph 2 Christ has broken down. The truth is that there is only one Israel. This Israel is not simply the Christian church, as some commentators claim[192]. Rather, Israel includes both Jews and Christians.

On the basis of Eph 2:11—22, Jean-Paul Lichtenberg[193] disagrees with Lacocque's view that Israel includes both Jews and Christians. Lichtenberg argues that the passage describes only the unity that exists within the Christian Church. Insofar as this unity includes both Jews and Gentiles who believe in Jesus as the Christ, it is a kind of preview of the future time when all Jews will accept Jesus Christ. But this "realized eschatology" exists only in the church. The Jews who are not baptized Christians are, for the present time, excluded, and should therefore not be considered as part of the people of God today.

Those scholars who take Lichtenberg's position believe that the church's attitude toward Israel should be a missionary one with the goal of converting individual Jews[194]. Those scholars who take the position of Barth and Lacocque believe that the church is called not to a mission *to* Israel, but to brotherly conversation *with* Israel[195]. Shortly after the Evanston Assembly of the World Council of Churches, F. Ernest Johnson interviewed several leading American theologians about whether Jewish people are a missionary concern or an ecumenical concern. One unnamed theologian, a leader in the Ecumenical Movement, answered that on the basis of Eph 2:14 the church dare not put the Jews in a special theological category apart from other people who are not Christians. Of course, the theologian said, our approach must be one of love, and that means taking into account how their unique experience affects their attitude to the gospel. But this approach is just as valid for a person belonging to any other religious tradition. According to this theologian,

The presuppositions on which it rests are universal, and ought to be; for Jesus "broke down the wall of partition between Jew and Gentile"

---

[192] E.g. Hanson, Sahlin, see above p. 224.

[193] Foi et Vie 64, 6 (1965) 488—509.

[194] So H. Schlier (Freiburger Rundbrief 8, Oct 1955, 32) cites Rom 11:23 and I Cor 9:20 as indications that we should not work to realize unity with Israel, but to rescue some of the members of Israel.

[195] A. de Kuiper considers the two alternatives in his dissertation, Israel tussen Zending en Oecumene, Wageningen 1965.

once and for all, as Paul insisted even against strenuous opposition in the early Church, which for a time clung to a view which some in effect hold even today[196].

Judging from his reply, this speaker interprets the broken wall of Eph 2:14 to mean that the Jews have ceased to be in any sense the elect people of God. There may be more theologians in America than in Europe who are willing to take this position[197]. Long before the current awakening of interest in the relation of the church to the Jewish people, the commentary of a European theologian, Paul Ewald, cautioned that the broken wall does not mean the end of the religious uniqueness of Israel[198].

Whether the relation of the church to Israel is to be considered an ecumenical or a missionary concern was one of the issues which was discussed during the Second Vatican Council. The version of the statement on the Jewish people which was first presented to the Council in session was included in the Decree on Ecumenism. Many of the Council fathers questioned the legitimacy of discussing the Jewish people in this context. After a stormy series of arguments, the final version of the statement was included in the Declaration on the Relation of the Church to the non-Christian Religions[199].

From the basic preparatory study on through to its approval by the Council, all the versions of the statement on the Jews made reference to Eph 2:11—22. The first version of the text, after declaring that all Christians are included in the calling of Israel, proceeds to say:

And the church, New Creation in Christ which she is (cf. Eph 2:15), can never forget that she is the spiritual continuation of that people with whom the merciful God in gracious condescension made the Old Covenant.

---

[196] "The Jewish Question as an Ecumenical Problem", ER VII, 1955, 288—229.

[197] But probably not many theologians in America would agree with the extreme position of H. Ockenga in his interpretation of Eph 2:11—22. Ockenga, 125, says that Paul, designating the unbaptized Jews "as the so-called citizens of the Commonwealth of Israel ... speaks of them with utmost scorn". Ockenga concludes: "We hold it to be utter folly and anti-Biblical to teach that the Jews are the chosen people of God today."

[198] Die Briefe des Paulus an die Epheser, Kolosser und Philemon, Leipzig 1910², 137.

[199] A detailed history of the text is presented by J. Oesterreicher in LThK, Das Zweite Vatikanische Konzil II, Freiburg 1967, 414—478.

In truth, the church believes that Christ, our peace, with one and the same love embraces Jews and Gentiles (cf. Eph 2:14) and that he has made both one. She rejoices that the uniting of both in one body (Eph 2:16) announces the reconciliation of the whole earth in Christ[200].

When a revised shortened version of the statement on the Jews was presented in the third session of the Vatican Council under the title "On the Jews and the non-Christian Religions", a great debate ensued. For two days one Council father after another rose to demand a stronger, better statement. Two of the speakers, Cardinal Frings and Bishop Hengsbach, regretted that the text did not make more use of the "extraordinarily beautiful and grand theology" of Ephesians. Cardinal Frings named the passage about Christ's "tearing down the dividing wall between Jews and Gentiles" as the classical scriptural passage for the relation between the people of the Old and New Covenants[201].

There were also opposing voices which critized the text and the Council for neglecting to consider all that the Bible and the tradition has to say about the matter. Monsignor Carli, Bishop of Segni, published a lengthy article after the third session of the Council arguing that according to the witness of the Bible and the church fathers Judaism was responsible for the death of Christ, and is rejected and cursed by God[202].

In reply to Monsignor Carli's article, Rector Heinrich Spaemann pointed out that a basic theme of the Bible is God's faithfulness to his covenant with Israel. "The covenant-faithfulness of God to Israel, which was revealed and carried out on the cross, redeemed us *with* Israel." Declaring that this is the theme of Eph 2:11—22, Spaemann noted that Monsignor Carli had completely neglected this passage in his survey of biblical passages about the Jews. But, says Spaemann, "this text has decisive significance as a guideline for our attitude to Israel". Spaemann goes on to discuss the passage in terms of ethical motivation:

The peace of which it speaks is entrusted to us for its actualization. According to the order of salvation as it began to take effect with the death and resurrection of Jesus, the spreading of his peace into human hearts, including those of the Jews, is partly dependent on the witness of the church, for which purpose he gives her his Holy Spirit. Those who receive peace have to proclaim it, act it, give it further. That this giving it further now takes place to Israel through us Gentile Christians, as the

---

[200] LThK, Konzil II,426.   [201] LThK, Konzil II, 443.
[202] Freiburger Rundbrief 16—17, July 1965, 31—37, contains an account of the contents of the article together with an explanatory introduction.

co-heirs of Abraham in a final transposition of the original order... presupposes that we not only recognize the faithfulness of Jesus to his people, but also, that we let our hearts be filled by it. So may we, with all consistency and at the same time with the still more binding humility of him who is allowed, completely undeserving, to step into the heritage of the older brother, make the faithfulness of Jesus visible for the Jewish people[203].

In a later publication, Spaemann reveals even more clearly how much his interpretation is oriented toward the future[204]. There he says that Christ's purpose "to create us, Jews and Gentiles, in his person into one new man... is not concretely realized; ... we are not yet the one new man". Spaemann calls upon his fellow Christians to move forward toward the new man, for "when the dividing wall, the hostility which Christ fundamentally broke down in his death on the cross has finally fallen... then the decisive step will have been made for the overcoming of hostility among all men".

As the statement on the Jewish people was finally promulgated by the Vatican Council on Oct. 28, 1965, the substance of Eph 2: 14—16 is given in connection with the image of the olive tree in Rom 11:

The Church cannot... forget that she draws sustenance from the root of that good olive tree onto which have been grafted the wild olive branches of the Gentiles (cf. Rom 11:17—23). Indeed, the Church believes that by His cross Christ, our Peace, reconciled Jew and Gentile, making them both one in Himself (cf. Eph 2:14—16)[205].

In an address given after the Vatican Council, the Jewish scholar Ernst Ludwig Ehrlich quoted with approval the Council's references to Rom 9—11 and Eph. 2. Ehrlich asked that the church not isolate statements about the Jews in the gospels from the context of the entire New Testament. For the New Testament understanding of the Jews, says Ehrlich, Rom 9—11 and Eph 2 are basic[206].

---

[203] Freiburger Rundbrief 16—17, July 1965, insert VIId.

[204] Die Christen und das Volk der Juden, Munich 1966, esp. 49, 59. Also future-oriented is the comment of R. Laurentin (LThK, Konzil II, 432) made while the Vatican II discussion was in progress: "There is a deep solidarity, yes a certain unity of Israel and the church in the expectation of becoming one at the end of time. 'Christ has made the two peoples (Jews and Gentiles) one, in that he has torn down the dividing wall, in order to unite both in his person to one single new man'" (Eph 2:14—15).

[205] The Documents of Vatican II, ed. W. Abbot and J. Gallagher, New York 1966, 664.

[206] Was bedeutet das Zweite Vatikanische Konzil für uns? ed. W. Schatz, Basel 1966, 194.

Blacks and Whites

The relation of Jews and Christians as well as that of blacks and whites is often considered under the heading of "race relations". Visser 't Hooft explains why this is possible:

From the point of view of the Church, anti-Semitism is not merely and not even in the first place a question of race relations. The specific connexion between the Christian church and the Jewish people, their common heritage, their agreement in essential convictions and their disagreement in no less essential points are above all religious and theo-logical matters which transcend the biological and sociological realm. But in the case of National Socialism the Churches confronted a form of anti-Semitism which based itself on the absolutizing of race, and they were forced not only to redefine the Christian attitude to the Jewish people, but also to formulate their convictions concerning the race problem as a whole[207].

Although German theologians did formulate their convictions about the race problem as a whole, their arguments were always directed toward the specific question of the relation of Jews and Gentiles. Formally at least they were dealing with the same question which the New Testament deals with. The problem of hostility between blacks and whites, however, is not present in the New Testament; it is a modern question. How is Eph 2:11—22 related to this modern question? This is a problem which is handled by interpreters in various ways.

One group says that Eph 2:11—22 does not relate to the race question at all. They treat the difference between Jews and Gen-

---

[207] The Ecumenical Movement and the Racial Problem, Paris 1954, 35—36. Because of the experience German theologians have had with the race problem under National Socialism, K. Beckman (Die Kirche und die Rassenfrage, ed. K. Beckmann, Stuttgart 1967, 74) feels they have a special responsibility to help with the world-wide race problem. "For Germany and German evangelical theology there is the burning question whether it is willing, ready, and in a position to make a positive contribution to the world problem of the race question, which will decisively affect the future of the world . . . For theology this will raise the further question about the connection of the Jewish question and the race question, in particular for Germany, about the connection of the struggle of the Confessing Church and possible solutions today. Can for example the present generation of theologians in South Africa in its vigorous confrontation with the Apartheid politics of the government, gain guidelines from the themes of the German Church struggle? The question is not to be answered here; it did not originate with us, but is asked by a group of South African theologians." More information about the group of South African theologians who are studying the German Church struggle is presented in the same volume in an article by S. Groth, "Die Kirchen und Missionen in Süd- und Südwestafrika", 36—37.

tiles strictly as a religious difference. A representative of this group is Edwin Roels, who after a careful exegesis of Eph 2:11—22[208] says that "the race problem as such as it presently exists is not considered by Paul either in Ephesians or anywhere else". In itself Roels's statement could hardly be denied. Yet Roels deduces from it that there is no New Testament imperative which has to do with the relationship of various races in the church; it is "in the sphere of the practical and not in the sphere of absolute musts".

It is entirely conceivable, therefore, that in the whole complex of relationships which constitute the church's life, certain factors of language, culture, race, etc. would make separate organizations not only permissible, but desirable.

Roels says that he is not arguing for segregation, and that the unity of believers in Christ is more important than any differences. Yet he believes that "practical considerations might make separate organizations more desirable" on the basis of blood and ethnic ties[209].

Roels can take this position because throughout his study of Eph 2:11—22 he has consistently interpreted the difference between Jews and Gentiles as a religious distinction only. The dividing wall (Eph 2:14) was an "essential religious distinction". The enmity (2:14) is another name for this distinction; it designates a condition, and not "the kind of sentiment usually associated with strong prejudicial race hatred or even with the very word 'anti-Semitism'". Christ's breaking the wall means "the complete obliteration of that religious distinction which existed in the Old Testament". The frequent mention of peace (vv. 14, 15, 17) "emphasizes the new religious unity of Gentile and Jew in the one Christ". In other Pauline passages which tell of different groups which have been united in Christ (Gal 3:28; Col 3:10—11; I Cor 12:13), Roels notes that the distinction between Jew and Gentile "of all the distinctions mentioned, is the only one specifically religious, moreover, . . . the only distinction which is essentially obliterated".

At the opposite extreme from those who see the difference between Jews and Gentiles as a purely religious one are those who see the difference as an entirely racial one. Members of this group, convinced that Eph 2:11—22 is relevant to black-white relations, draw fairly direct lines from the text to the modern race problem.

---

[208] God's Mission, Franeker 1962, 117—132.

[209] Roels, 136. The position that separate organizations on the basis of race is a "practical" matter was steadfastly opposed by the Confessing Church of Germany, see above pp. 216—220.

Where these lines come out depends partly on the particular concept of race the interpreter holds.

One of the first to make more than a brief reference to Eph 2:11—22 in discussing the black-white problem was Homes Rolston. Addressing an audience most of whom had been brought up to accept segregation, he made a bold attempt to communicate to them what St. Paul's teaching has to say to the race problem[210]. Rolston finds Eph 2:11—22 the central passage which shows Paul's conviction that the church unites races.

> The epistle in which Paul attempts most seriously to explain the power of Christianity to break down the barriers between Jew and Gentile is the Epistle to the Ephesians. It is not by accident that this passage is found in the epistle in which Paul presents most clearly his conception of a universal church. The power of Christianity to unite men of different races is closely related to its power to build a world church.

Rolston then quotes the whole of Eph 2:11—22 and comments that the wall which separated Jews and Gentiles was the law as the way of salvation. For it was their adherence to the law as the way of salvation that kept the Jews a distinct people. Christ abolished this wall by offering a new way of salvation—through faith in him. When men accept faith in Christ alone, without any additional requirements, as the way of salvation, then the unity of the church is maintained. For it is the adherence to the same way of salvation that constitutes the new man; the one new man means that "the church must be the same among all races and among all nations". This can only be the case "when the church in each race breaks all entangling alliances with the culture of the race within which she moves and builds her message of salvation on faith in Jesus Christ and on this alone". The attempt by the Jews to have Christ *and* the law, and by the Gentiles to have Christ *and* Greek culture is what threatened the unity of the church.

It is significant that Rolston does not say that the new man is Jew and Gentile together, but rather Jew and Gentile, each of whom holds the same faith. Thus Rolston speaks of "the church in each race", rather than the church which unites races. This view is important for the way in which Rolston applies Paul's "teaching concerning race" to the situation of the southern United States.

Basic to Rolston's approach is the analogy he draws between the white race today and the Jewish race before the time of Paul. Just as the Jews protected their racial identity because they were con-

---

[210] "The Order of Race—Jew and Gentile", The Social Message of the Apostle Paul, Richmond, Virginia 1942, 125—151.

vinced that they had a unique contribution to make to the world, so the white race has protected its identity. Although he qualifies it in various ways, Rolston lets this analogy stand. Perhaps in his situation Rolston could not have been expected to follow the analogy through and say that in Eph 2:11—22 Paul proclaims that the time of protecting racial identity is past, since Christ has abolished the law as the way of salvation, which had kept the Jews a distinct people.

Rolston does make the following strong statement: "It is doubtful if Paul would ever have agreed to the idea of race churches." Yet Rolston understands only too well the predicament of his hearers. Separate churches for whites and blacks are already in existence and this situation cannot be changed immediately. Accepting that fact, Rolston nevertheless sees it as a judgment on the church in the United States: "A Christianity that is not vital enough to build churches that bridge effectively the chasms of class within the white race could hardly be expected to build churches that bridged the deeper chasm of race." Rolston urges that Christians of both races should "come together in Christ and realize in Him a unity that goes deeper than the divisions of race". Rolston does not suggest how this is to be done, but probably he would encourage interracial activities among Christians outside the segregated framework of the church.

Although Rolston took an important step forward, he did not openly challenge two traditionally accepted ideas which have delayed racial justice. He speaks of "the fact that Christianity is primarily a message of personal redemption" in a way which could be taken to mean that individual redemption may not necessarily be connected with social redemption. And, having shown the white man's effort to keep his race distinct, he does not mention the system of oppression this effort has caused, nor call for its abolition on the basis of the unity which Paul proclaims.

Like Rolston, Harold Ockenga treats the Jews as one race among other races. He calls Eph 2:11—22 "a racial discussion and a revelation involving racial conditions"[211]. Thus he moves directly from the relation of Jews and Gentiles to the relation of blacks and whites. The broken wall (2:14) means that

the church breaks down all human divisions and partitions. No special place in this economy of the Church is given to Jews or Gentiles. In our day it is not to the Jew first or to the Gentile first... The truth of the Church declares that there are no privileges given to men. It strikes

---

[211] Faithful in Christ Jesus, 123.

hard at all the super-racial theories of our day. There is no such thing as a super-race before God. The color line must be removed among believers. That does not mean that all classes and races of men have the same opportunity, but it does mean that they are equal in value before the Lord[212].

A categorical call from the pulpit for the removal of the color line among Christians was not a frequent occurrence in the 1940's when Ockenga preached this sermon, although the Federal Council of Churches and some denominations had already announced their intention to work for a "non-segregated Church and a non-segregated society"[213]. Yet Ockenga does not spell out what he means by the removal of the color line. He only says that it "does not mean that all classes and races of men have the same opportunity". As a description of the contemporary situation in church and society in the United States, the statement is correct. But up until this sentence Ockenga had not been describing the situation; he had been demanding that it be changed. A conflict in Ockenga's thought is expressed here which is more openly revealed by a later passage in his volume of sermons on Ephesians where he speaks of the importance of maintaining racial limits.

Then let us recognize that the freedom or liberty which we prize as an ideal must be within certain limitations. The first limitation is race. Race distinctions are honorable and are recognized by God in scripture. The Lord distinguished among Shem, Ham and Japheth with a Divine purpose in mind. The Lord distinguishes between the descendants of Shem and the descendants of Japheth just as much as he distinguishes between the descendants of Japheth and the descendants of Ham[214].

Since the Lord distinguishes between the races, argues Ockenga, "to attempt to abolish racial distinctions would be folly and is impossible". What does Ockenga mean by an "attempt to abolish racial distinctions"? In the same paragraph he says that God "will hold the sons of Japheth responsible for the rule which He committed to them over their brethren". According to this, the distinction between white and black seems to involve rulership of white over black. Apparently this is Ockenga's interpretation of Gen 9:25—27 where Noah's anger at Ham issues in a curse of Ham's

---

[212] Ockenga, 148. Writing in the time when Hitler's ideas of Aryan superiority were condemned by using the phrase "super-race", Ockenga alleges that white racism stands under the same condemnation.

[213] For a summary of Protestant pronouncements on race relations in 1945 to 1947 see F. Loescher, The Protestant Church and the Negro, Philadelphia 1948, App. I, 132—143.

[214] Ockenga, 232.

son Canaan, according to which he is to be "a servant of servants" to Japheth and Shem[215]. Yet Ockenga himself has said that since Christ broke down the wall (Eph 2:14) there is "no special place in this economy of the Church".

Rolston and Ockenga have in common that they treat the Jewish people as a race, and they regard race as a part of the natural order. Ockenga emphasizes that the natural order is God's creation, and that it must not be disregarded. From what he considers the nature of God's created order he derives the ethical command to maintain the identity of the white race. Rolston refers to the natural order simply as a way of understanding how the present racial situation came to exist. Neither Ockenga nor Rolston explains how the concept of natural order relates to the command seen in Eph 2:11—22 to end racial discrimination.

Most writers who discuss the relevance of Eph 2:11—22 for the contemporary race problem do not treat the Jew-Gentile problem as simply a racial matter, but find other ways to relate the problem of Ephesians's time to the problem of today. Some point out that the Jew-Gentile problem is the closest approximation in the Bible to the black-white problem of today. This approach is taken by Everett Tilson[216], an American theologian who has worked intensively on the relation of biblical studies to the race problem. He notes that according to any of the modern definitions of race, the tension between Jews and Gentiles was not a race problem, since the Jews were of the same racial stock as many of the people around them whom they called Gentiles. Nevertheless, he believes that the Jew-Gentile problem of New Testament times is "closely related, alike in basic character and practical consequen-

---

[215] This interpretation of Gen 9:25—27 has long been held by a considerable number of whites, including ministers, as Ockenga's sermon shows. An earlier version of this interpretation, used as an argument for slavery, was opposed as early as the seventeenth century by S. Sewall, see above p. 107. Ockenga, far from defending slavery, insists that "there is no reason for degradation or oppression or exploitation" in race distinctions. Yet if one uses Gen 9:25—27 as authority for white rule, one must accept the reason Gen 9:25—27 gives for the subordination of Ham's descendants, namely a curse on Canaan because of the sin of his father Ham. But to count a trespass of Ham against those regarded as his descendants today is impossible when one believes that "God was in Christ reconciling the world to himself, not reckoning their trespasses against them" (II Cor 5:17). The role of Gen 9:25—27 in discussions of slavery is frequently touched upon by D. B. Davis, The Problem of Slavery in Western Culture, Ithaca, New York 1966; see index under "Ham" and "Canaan".

[216] Segregation and the Bible, Nashville 1958, esp. 78—91.

ces" to the modern race problem. He agrees with Visser 't Hooft who says "the 'race problem' with which the Churches have to deal is not so much a biological as a sociological problem in which theological, cultural and psychological factors all play their part"[217]. Considered in this way, Tilson believes that the Jew-Gentile problem faced by the early church, despite many differences, has also many similarities to the present black-white problem. So he quotes Eph 2:11—22 as a "plea for a 'non-segregated church'".

Similar to the question of whether white churches will admit black Christians into their church membership on a completely equal basis with white members is the question of whether Jews would admit Gentiles into the people of the covenant without making them become Jews. Tilson says that the attempt at a compromise represented by the position of James and his party (Acts 15:24—29) "demonstrated the impossibility of invigorating a world movement within the framework of a nationalistic faith". Tilson paints the alternatives before the church starkly.

> Would it cling to the law and remain a Jewish sect? Or would it surmount the law and become a world faith? Unable to do both, it did the latter. It spurned the segregation of Gentiles in favor of separation from the Jews ... it drove such a wedge between the two religious systems, Jewish and Christian, that the followers of both had to choose "the Law or the Gospel, Sinai or Calvary, Moses or Christ".

A danger in Tilson's method of relating the Jew-Gentile problem to the race problem becomes visible at this point: the Jews are seen as representing that which is to be rejected, that is, racial discrimination. In trying to bring blacks and whites closer together, Tilson runs the risk of pushing Christians and Jews further apart. For while it is true that Judaism is closely related to the Jewish nation, its scriptures contain the strongest kind of attack on "nationalistic faith". And to stress that one's decision must be either "the Law or the Gospel" suggests an absolute dichotomy between the two which is difficult to maintain in light of the positive statements about the law in the New Testament, especially by Paul e. g. Rom 3:31, 7:10, 12.

On the grounds that "the Jew-Gentile question represents the New Testament's nearest approximation to a race problem", Tilson says that the decisive question for the practice of the church amid racial tensions today is whether Jews and Gentiles were members on an equal basis of the same congregations in the early

---

[217] The Ecumenical Movement and the Racial Problem, 8.

church. As evidence that this was the case, Tilson cites Acts 11:20; 13:1 and 13:43—48, and adds that Paul indicates the same practice in Rom 2:17 and 11:13.

D. P. McGeachy is convinced that the Jew-Gentile problem and the black-white problem are similar in that each involves the major dividing wall of its time. In a sermon on Eph 2:11—22[218], McGeachy says that the difficulty between Jews and Gentiles "was the most important 'dividing wall' troubling the early church"[219]. Surveying the contemporary divisions in the United States, McGeachy goes on to say, "In the midst of this fragmented mess, the tension between people of different races is the most obvious and painful of our separations." McGeachy then points out emphatically that according to Eph 2 racial separation means separation from God.

Both the cause and the result of this wall's existence can be found in the ominous words of our text: "without God in the world." When there is no vertical relationship there can be none that is horizontal; if I do not love God with all my being, then I cannot love my neighbor as myself. And the converse is true: if I hate my brother, then I am a liar if I say I love God (I John 4:20).

As McGeachy reminds us, race prejudice is a form of hatred. This subjective aspect of the race problem is the chief connection with the Jew-Gentile problem of Eph 2:11—22 in the eyes of some commentators. T. O. Wedel stresses that despite the many objective differences between the two problems, the taboos, the deep-seated feelings are very similar[220]. For interpreters like Wedel, the fact that the word "hostility" occurs twice is indicative of a keen awareness on the part of the author of Ephesians of the intensity of feeling between Jews and Gentiles.

The attempts to show the relevance of Eph 2:11—22 for the race problem mentioned so far tend to look for parallels between the situation of the white race today and the Jewish people of biblical times. On this basis, they usually follow either of two lines. One is

---

[218] "The Maker of Peace", The Unsilent South, ed D. W. Shriver, Richmond, Virginia 1965, 125—130.

[219] McGeachy puts the problem of divisions in historical persepective by adding: "As time has passed, other divisions have loomed large on the human scene, like that which caused the schism of the Reformation. As this has happened, Eph 2: 12—14 has flashed from many facets, like a gem growing richer with age. Today it continues to cast light on the principal divisions that separate us from one another and from God."

[220] Exposition of Ephesians in the Interpreter's Bible, New York 1953, X, 649.

to justify the desire of the Jews to protect their racial purity as a way of accepting the idea that the white race should protect its racial purity. The other is to condemn the racial exclusiveness of the Jews, thereby condemning racial discrimination in the church today.

Another method for relating Eph 2:11—22 to the race problem, instead of working on the basis of a parallel between the Jewish race and the white race, draws a parallel between Christ and the Christians. Christians are called to do today in the conflict between black and white what Christ did in the conflict between Jew and Gentile. Daisuke Kitagawa takes this approach when he relates Eph 2:15—16 to the race problem by making the church its subject instead of Christ. In the conflict between blacks and whites, Christians

are called to the way of the Cross, to "create ... one new man in place of the two, that so making peace, they might reconcile us both to God in one body through the Cross, thereby bringing the hostility to an end" (Eph 2:15—16)[221].

As Kitagawa explains it, this method views the Christians as a "third race", or "marginal race". Constituting the "third race" are those of both races "who trust each other despite the barrier of race" and who are consequently "ostracized by both whites and Negroes". They are not simply to accept ostracism, for their vocation is to reconcile the two races. "It is for this purpose that Christians have been chosen as a *third race* whose destiny is no other than to be 'Suffering Servants' of the Lord." It should be observed that Kitagawa's term "third race" has a different content from the term as it appears in early Christian literature and modern commentaries.

Different from any of the previous methods is that which emphasizes the election of the Jews, and therefore the basic uniqueness of the Jew-Gentile problem. Instead of drawing parallels from New Testament times to the race problem today, this approach says that the relationship between Jews and Gentiles today is fundamental, and all group relationships must be seen within that framework. This approach emphasizes that both white and black Gentiles are by birth outsiders compared to the Jews, who remain God's elect people. This approach calls out anew to all Gentiles, white and black, the appeal of Eph 2:11, that they should remember that they were once separated from the people of God, but now have been included by Jesus Christ.

---

[221] The Pastor and the Race Issue, New York 1965, 65.

Nils Dahl says that it is important to note that Ephesians was written to Gentile Christians, for after centuries of church history Christians today commonly take it for granted that the church is almost completely Gentile. They forget then that only by the breaking of the wall did they become part of the church, and that putting up walls against any group denies the essence of the church. Eph 2:11—22 reminds us, says Dahl, that

it is not to be taken for granted that we as non-Jewish Christians read the Old Testament scriptures, or that the history of Israel is our own history, or that we know the Jew Jesus of Nazareth as our savior. We are the church only by virtue of God's mysterious action with humanity, because the dividing wall was broken and because the gospel of Christ was brought by Paul and others to the Gentiles. Our text places us before the difficult question whether the reality of our churches, as we experience them, still corresponds to the true nature of the church. Are not the nature of the church and Christ's reconciling work denied wherever and whenever boundaries of nations and races, of social classes and customs make church fellowship and the fellowship of the Lord's Supper impossible[222]?

James Daane also urges the church to remember that she is predominantly Gentile when he sums up Eph 2:11—22 and its relevance for the race problem in the following way:

The basic separation between men is posited by God's elective action and falls between Gentiles and Jews, and specifically on this Jew, God's Elect. But by the death of God's *Elect,* the two are made one in Christ, the enmity is resolved by the reconciling power of his Cross, and thus peace is made ... At the Cross is disclosed the truth about race and election. Here it is revealed that the non-elect is not the Negro but the Gentile, whatever his race or color. Yet how often Christian people have gone to the Old Testament to find biblical support for the specious argument that the Negro is a lesser people by virtue of a divine curse ... Had he gone to the Cross for his answer, the Gentile Christian would have discovered that it is not the Negro who is the "lesser breed" but the Gentile, white or Negro, yellow or red ... At the cross the Gentile Christian can learn that there is no theological justification for anti-Jewish or Negro prejudice. On the contrary, he can learn there that in the eyes of God white and Negro are on the same side of the line, and that if either is to enter into the truth of Christianity it is by participating and sharing in the election, the glory and the inheritance of the Jews. For without this participation, the Gentile, whatever his color, is, in biblical language, "no people"[223].

---

[222] "Bibelstudie über den Epheserbrief", Kurze Auslegung des Epheserbriefes, Göttingen 1965, 39.

[223] The Anatomy of Anti-Semitism and Other Essays on Religion and Race, Grand Rapids, Michigan 1965, 40—42.

Daane goes on to say that the reason the church in the United States has done so little about the race problem is that she has not understood her own nature. She can only understand herself if, as a church consisting mainly of Gentiles, she remembers that she was once "without God and without hope in the world":

If only she will recognize this, then she may be moved by those theological and religious considerations that lie far deeper than the color of skin, and she may read the signs of the time as a call to repentance and reform. The liberal American churches had their social gospel and the evangelical churches their Bible, yet both long remained insensitive to the most obvious blight and the greatest social injustice on the American social scene. Indeed, if the Church can recognize that the reduced social status of the American Negro is for the Church something far greater than a gross social injustice, namely a violation of every fundamental truth of her faith and confession, then there is hope that the Church can and will act in accordance with her nature[224].

Markus Barth likewise insists that only when the church understands her nature as founded on the reconciliation of Jews and Gentiles in Christ will she see herself as a place where divisions among peoples are being healed. The peace made by Christ between Israel and the Gentiles dare not be seen as only a parallel to peace between blacks and whites or other hostile groups, but as its source: "only the peace between Jews and Gentiles, which makes both together have peace with God and free approach to God (2:16—18) is the source from which peaceful coexistence at all levels of life is to be drawn."[225] From this position Barth draws the corollary that the peace between Jews and Gentiles is the standard by which all efforts for peace, including those for racial peace, are to be judged.

This same peace also is the standard by which to test all efforts to peace, whether they be honest or escapes from the basic issues. Whether it be Hitler's attempt to establish a pure Germanic race, or Russia's purge of party ranks, or the concern in certain American circles for the conservation of the white race, or the flaming patriotism of some Arab nations, the text for the sincerity and good intentions of the movement

---

[224] Daane, 49.

[225] J. Verkuyl (Break Down the Walls: a Christian Cry for Racial Justice, Grand Rapids, Mich. 1973, 48) agrees with Barth and comments: "To confess Christ is to witness to the conquest of separation, segregation, apartheid, and of all ghettoes. We build all sorts of walls to serve as barriers between people and races, but our comfort is this: none of these walls has any status with God. God's work in Christ cannot be undone."

is always to be found in the way it treats the Jews, politically, socially, and culturally[226].

Barth does not mean that any position Jews take is automatically right. But any movement which is in principle anti-Semitic is automatically wrong. It violates the peace between Jews and Gentiles which Christ has made and which is the basis and norm for peace among all groups.

We have discussed various ways of relating Eph 2:11—22 to the modern race problem. There are dangers connected with seeing the difference between Jews and Gentiles as either purely religious or purely racial. Most theological depth seems to be in the interpretation which goes from Eph 2:11—22 to the black-white problem by way of the nature of the church as the people of God consisting of Jews and Gentiles reconciled in Christ.

Summary

As we have seen the twentieth century has introduced many new approaches to Eph 2:11—22. Most of them point to our passage as the theological center of the letter. The agreement on its centrality is one of the reasons why debate about the exegesis of Eph 2:11—22 is so vigorous.

Debate begins with the scholarly question of whether the language of the passage has more affinity with Gnosticism or with Judaism. The opposing viewpoints have come somewhat closer together since there is now wide agreement that the language of Ephesians has similarities to that of Qumran. More recent research indicates that the background of Eph 2:14—18 is to be found in hellenistic Judaism.

Whatever their views about the conceptual background, the majority find that the central theme of Eph 2:11—22 is the unity of the church out of Jews and Gentiles. There has been a shift in the way this unity is understood. In the first 30 years of the century, emphasis was put on the concept of the body of Christ as the expression of unity. But interpreters tended to see this unity as something apart from, or in contrast to, the historical communities and traditions from which men came. In the church as "the third race", the Jew was no longer a Jew and the Gentile was no longer a Gentile.

---

[226] The Broken Wall, 126.

The roots of this way of thinking began to be evident in the nineteenth century. The concept current then was "the higher unity". In many ways this concept is the equivalent of "the third race". It has contributed on the one hand to both religious and racial pride, and on the other to apathy about divisions within the church, since it held that "outward" unity was not relevant.

The "third race" concept, although perhaps originally intended in a metaphorical sense, is indicative of a tendency to think about the difference between Jews and Gentiles in racial rather than religious terms. While examples of this can be found in earlier centuries, it became firmly entrenched in the nineteenth and twentieth. Thus George Wobbermin could say in the 1930's in Germany that discrimination against Jewish Christians was not a religious but purely a racial matter.

Contributing to this racial thinking were ideas about biological evolution which assigned human groups to various positions on an evolutionary scale. Furthermore, evolution came to be seen as a key concept not only in biology, but in the history of ideas, culture and religion as well. It seemed to fit very well with Hegel's philosophy of history.

When biblical scholars adopted the historical-critical method, they strove to be objective as they located Ephesians in the development of man's religious life and thought. But influenced by current concepts of history, they were predisposed to read Eph 2 in terms of "a higher unity". Thus it was that historical-critical commentaries were the first to use this term, and the ones who used it most often. Their influence soon affected virtually all interpretation.

The struggle of the church in Germany with National Socialism forced a re-thinking of the idea of unity. Wrestling with the question of the relation of the church to Israel involved a rediscovery of the concept of the people of God, a concept by which the church is seen in historical perspective. Scholars became aware of the danger which lies in an emphasis on the church as the body of Christ if this concept is not held in close connection with the concept of the people of God. As Paul Minear has pointed out, an exclusive concentration on the idea of the body of Christ has sometimes been used as a support for anti-Semitism[227]. The unique importance of Eph 2:11—22 lies in the fact that it contains both concepts—the people of God and the body of Christ.

---

[227] Images of the Church in the New Testament, 234.

At least some of the scholars who claim a Gnostic source for the body concept in Ephesians now stress that the author uses the concept of the people of God in order to combat the mythical, a-historical associations of the Gnostic concept of the body. These scholars interpret the concept of the body of Christ (Eph 2:14—16) in such a way as to emphasize its difference from and tension with the concept of the people of God. The tension is most vividly emphasized by those who, on the basis of form criticism, maintain that vv. 14—16 are a hymn of the early church. For if this analysis is correct, then the hymn itself which contains Gnostic concepts was composed by the early Christian community, whereas the frame of the hymn which contains Jewish concepts is from the hand of the author of Ephesians.

On the other hand, those interpreters who claim a Judaic background for the entire passage interpret the body concept in ways which emphasize its consonance with the concept of the people of God. They believe that the two concepts were not as divergent in their origins as they have become in the history of Christian thought. They therefore seek the roots of the concept of the body of Christ in late Judaism and in the Old Testament.

Despite their differing convictions about the sources of the concept of the body of Christ, both groups of scholars agree on the importance of the fact that Eph 2:11—22 as it now stands holds both concepts—the body of Christ and the people of God—together. The passage thus proclaims that the church is not only a new creation, which the concept of the body of Christ emphasizes; it also exists in continuity with the redemptive work of God in history, which the concept of the people of God emphasizes.

The concept of the people of God includes the recognition of the course this people has taken through history: a course which includes first Jews, then Jews and Gentiles. In conjunction with the concept of the body of Christ, it reminds us not only that the body of Christ includes both Jews and Gentiles, but that these two groups do not simply forget their histories when they become parts of the body of Christ. This is why Eph 2:11 explicitly calls on Gentiles to remember their history. Since the identity of both Gentiles and Jews depends on their remembering their history, this means that they do not simply lose their identities in the body of Christ.

When theology neglected the concept of the people of God, it thereby forgot that the body of Christ reconciled both groups: Jews and Gentiles. Consequently theology lost sight of the church as the reconciler of groups. Reconciliation was then seen as having to do

with the relation of man to God, and in a secondary sense, of one man to another; but the group, be it nation or race or class, was hardly given consideration. When groups made their presence felt, then theology tried to cope with them under the heading of the doctrine of creation.

This was the situation in Germany in the twenties. For various reasons, the group—people, nation, race—became increasingly important. But because exegesis had declared these factors irrelevant to the new man in Christ, they did not seem to most theologians to have any relation to the unity of the church. And so it was possible to say, when the Aryan paragraph was introduced, that having congregations for people of different races was an organizational matter and did not involve the doctrine of the church. The minority of theologians who did say that the doctrine of the church was involved, helped to change the course of interpretation of Eph 2:11—22. They saw that the contemporary problem had an essential similarity to the New Testament problem: shall Jewish and Gentile Christians have table fellowship in the same congregation as complete equals?

When Gentile interpreters were so dramatically reminded how important the question of the place of the Jews in the church is, they were at the same time reminded that they themselves are Gentile Christians, and that Eph 2:11—22 is addressed specifically to them. In the past 25 years, interpreters of the passage have frequently pointed this out. There is less of a tendency than in earlier times to read the passage from a detached viewpoint, as simply a record of the past. Thus the awareness of the presence of the Jewish people is a kind of bridge for the interpreter to New Testament times. Because the presence of Jewish people reminds us that the church is made up of two different groups, it is also the bridge to the meaning of Eph 2:11—22 for the inclusion in the church of other differing groups, such as black and white. Modern interpreters point out more frequently than earlier ones that in the light of Eph 2:11—22 church unity does not mean uniformity.

CONCLUSION

The starting point of this history of interpretation of Eph 2:11–22 was the contemporary problem of racial hostility. This starting point was chosen not only because the problem is an urgent one, but because a number of interpreters in recent years have claimed that Eph 2:11–22 is relevant to the race problem, while others have denied any such relevance. Looking at commentaries from other countries and centuries has been a way of asking how these opposing viewpoints hold up in light of a broad range of commentaries. Further, if the passage is relevant to the contemporary race problem, how is that relevance to be expressed? What guidance, warnings, suggestions come through Eph 2:11–22 to the church as it faces racial hostility?

The study has shown that the twentieth century is not the first in which commentators have claimed that Eph 2:11–22 is relevant to problems of racial hostility. In the Reformation period a number of interpreters, both Roman Catholic and Protestant, say that according to Eph 2:11–22 people of all races are to be accepted in the fellowship of the church without any discrimination. The specific examples of people of different races which they name are Jews and Turks. Of course the term race did not have quite the same meaning for commentators of that period as it does today. Nevertheless, race is understood both then and now as something given by a person's natural descent, which cannot be changed.

Why is it that commentators of the Reformation period spoke against racial hostility on the basis of Eph 2:11–22 at a time when religious hostility would seem to have absorbed all their attention? Probably because they had become aware of faith as something much stronger than the bonds of race and culture. Since Constantine, Christianity was widely regarded as something given by birth. Therefore it was difficult to believe that a person born in a Jewish or Turkish family could really become a Christian, and there was prejudice and discrimination against Jewish and Turkish Christians. The factor of natural heritage was regarded as more important than the factor of common faith. Thus, although the medieval church stressed unity, as its commentaries on Eph 2:11–22 indi-

cate, in the minds of the vast majority this unity rested more on natural and cultural factors than on faith.

Partly in reaction against a merely cultural Christianity, the medieval mystics emphasized the relation of the individual to God. Their commentaries do not see Eph 2:11–22 as proclaiming the unity of the church, but the breaking of the barrier between men and God. These commentaries stand in the tradition which stretches from Chrysostom to some modern commentators and is present in commentaries of the most varied kinds, including many Pietist, Rationalist, and some historical-critical works. This tradition says that men now stand on a completely equal basis before God, since Christ has opened a new way to God, the way of faith; but it does not say anything about the relation of human groups to one another. Although there are few representatives of this tradition among present-day commentators, there are a number who hold a position which is related, at least in its consequences. They claim that Eph 2:11–22 is about a spiritual unity which does not need to press for visible unity and which is therefore not affected when Christians in the same city are segregated according to race, class or tradition. According to this kind of interpretation, the form which the church takes in the world is theologically irrelevant. The inadequacy of this opinion was dramatically exposed in the time of the church struggle in Germany, when its proponents accepted discrimination against, and even segregation of, Jewish Christians.

The majority of commentators today hold that Eph 2:11–22 is about concrete fellowship between Jews and Gentiles in the church. Twentieth-century developments in New Testament research point in this direction. Even Gnostic and form-critical studies serve to throw into sharper relief the passage's concern for the visible unity of the church. Both those who conclude that the passage has a Gnostic background and those who add that it contains a piece of early liturgy agree that the author of Ephesians wants to teach Gentile Christians that they cannot sing of Christ's reconciling them to God without singing of his reconciling them to the Jews.

Some interpreters, while agreeing that Eph 2:11–22 is about the visible unity of Jews and Gentiles, maintain that this has nothing to do with race, since the difference between Jews and Gentiles was a religious, not a racial one. These interpreters point out that the concept of race is a uniquely modern one, foreign to the New Testament. They remind us that Eph 2:11–22 has little to do with race in the sense in which the word is used by modern geneticists, for in this sense many of the Gentiles whom the Jews knew would be classified in the same race with them. In the ancient world, words which are often today translated by "race" referred to a people distinguishable from others primarily by such factors as language, culture, religion and common history. Today the biological component usually plays a more important role than it did in ancient times, or even until the nineteenth century. Yet geneticists themselves have difficulty agreeing on an exact definition of the word, and the very fact that we can still use the word "race" to translate γένος, for example, suggests that the two are not totally unrelated.

But the difference between the concept of race in the ancient world and today is not the only, or even the most serious objection to the use of the term "race" in interpreting Eph 2:11—22. For it is doubtful if even according to the ancient conception of race Jews could properly be so categorized, since they understood themselves as determined by God's election, and not by natural descent. Thus Gentiles whom God called could become Jews if they accepted circumcision and all that it involved. Therefore Judaism cannot be considered a purely racial matter. On the other hand, the ceremonial laws, and in particular the requirement of circumcision, kept many Gentiles from becoming converts to Judaism. Furthermore, there is some question as to whether a convert was as complete a Jew as a person of Jewish parentage. The question of what category Jews should be understood by has always been a difficult one, not only for Gentiles but for Jews themselves. Finally, to use the concept of race today in describing the Jews seems especially dangerous, since under the Third Reich Jews were defined in racial terms in order to eliminate them.

The category of race is however not absolutely essential to describe the problem which is the starting point of this investigation. "People" and "nation" are often used by commentators and could serve as well. But a number of recent interpreters point out certain phenomena connected with racial hostility today which are similar to phenomena involved in the relations between Jews and Gentiles in New Testament times. For example, in both cases there are taboos which have the purpose of keeping a psychological and sociological distance between the two groups, especially to prevent intermarriage. These measures presuppose that members of the two groups live in the same city or narrow geographical area, for if they were separated by geographical boundaries, the boundaries of law and custom would not be necessary. Together with these practices go such attitudes as stereotyped thinking, mistrust and scapegoating. Phenomena such as these suggest that Eph 2:11—22 has relevance for the problem of racial hostility. This does not mean that the passage can be used as a proof-text to determine exactly what must be done in any particular situation involving people of different races. Nor does it mean that the passage can be taken in isolation from the rest of the Bible as containing in itself all there is to say about the church and race. But the interpretation of Eph 2:11—22 provides material for the doctrine of the church and for social ethics.

One of the issues which has come up again and again throughout the history of interpretation is: what role do racial differences play within the church? Some exegetes say that racial differences have absolutely no significance in the church. In the new man (v. 15) Jews cease to be Jews, Gentiles cease to be Gentiles. Other exegetes oppose this view finding that neither Jews nor Gentiles lose their identity on entering the church. The significance of this issue can be seen especially clearly in considering the encounter of blacks and whites. Blacks today are discovering the importance of accepting wholeheartedly their identity as blacks. They point out that whites have usually spoken of unity in the church in a way that has ignored racial differences. In doing so whites have demeaned black identity. Blacks reject categorically any kind of church unity which does not first respect their identity as blacks[1]. If the arguments of Bonhoeffer, Barth and Gollwitzer in favor of understanding the unity of the new man as including group differences are valid, then the insistence on black identity as a condition of reconciliation is in accord with Eph 2:11—22.

The more similarities we see between the Jew-Gentile hostility of New Testament times and black-white hostility today, the more persistent becomes the question: why, when Ephesians sees the church as the community in which the deepest hostility between men was healed, does the church today by and large not seen itself as the community in which the hostility between whites and blacks is healed? Events of the past two decades have made increasingly clear how urgent the problem of racial hostility is. The response of the church to the historical movement often referred to as "the racial revolution" has tended to polarize. On the one hand is the attitude that when the church "gets mixed up in race relations" it turns aside from its task of preaching the gospel and administering the sacraments. When a person who is concerned about the contemporary race problem encounters this attitude, he sooner or later becomes tempted to believe that the best, or perhaps the only way to

---

[1] See for example James Cone, Black Theology and Black Power, New York 1969, especially "Reconciliation", 143—152.

work for racial reconciliation is outside the church. On the other hand there is the attitude according to which the church must either see itself completely as a channel for the racial revolution, or it will be, if it is not already, totally irrelevant.

If we look at both these attitudes in the light of the early church, we see first of all that the church's missionary nature meant preaching to Gentiles as well as to Jews and that this preaching involved an invitation to become part of the Christian community. So the church was by its very nature involved in the problem of the relation of Jews and Gentiles, which was a social as well as a religious problem. The church had no choice about whether or not to become involved in the "race problem" of its time. It *was* involved. The question was, how would it be involved? Would there be separate congregations? Would the unity between Jews and Gentiles be only an invisible one, or would it also be visible? Paul's struggle was for the latter way. The victory of this way is proclaimed in Ephesians 2:11—22.

Similarly the church today does not have a choice about whether or not to be involved in the race problem. It *is* involved—not just some exceptional members, not just some "radical leaders who are out of touch with the people", but the whole church is involved. The question is, how is it involved? Has it not been involved for the most part in supporting racism in contradiction to its nature as described in Eph 2:11—22? For Eph 2:11—22 challenges the idea that the unity of the church is of such a nature as not to be affected by racial discrimination. The uniqueness of the passage indeed lies in its proclamation of the interrelatedness of Christ's work of reconciling men to God and to one another. Furthermore, it points out that neither reconciliation among men nor reconciliation with God is only an individual matter; it involves the relationship of groups as well. This suggests that a Christological approach to the relations of groups such as races and nations ought to be more thoroughly explored. Traditionally, theology has either regarded differences of race and nation as irrelevant to its work, or else it has dealt with them under the doctrine of creation. By contrast, a Christological approach would consider as a clue to the meaning of the contemporary racial revolution Christ's reconciliation of Jew and Gentile. It would consider the implications of the fact that the life and death and resurrection of Jesus Christ and the beginnings of his church took place amidst forces of group hostility similar to those of today.

The early church was revolutionary in that it broke out of the established structures which separated Jews and Gentiles. The early church did not set out self-consciously to be revolutionary; it was revolutionary by nature. When the church views herself in the light of Eph 2:11—22 then it is impossible for her to be conformed to the divisions which exist in society. It is her nature to be the place where divisions are healed, and so to be the servant of this healing in the world also. For Eph 2:11—22 does not limit its statements to the church. According to many commentaries, the breaking of the wall is an event in the world, not just in the church. For Christ is Lord, not only of the church but of the world. If the author of Ephesians could interpret Christ's work in one of its aspects as the reconciliation of hostile groups to one another, then we can see the breaking of centuries-old barriers of race in the contemporary world as part of his work today.

SELECTED BIBLIOGRAPHY

(Abreviations in the body of the work as well as in the bibliography are taken from *Religion in Geschichte und Gegenwart,* third ed.)

Sources for Chapter I

The First Three Centuries

Clement of Alexandria: Stromata I—IV. GCS 15. ed. O. Stählin. Leipzig 1906.
    Excerpta ex Theodoto. SC 23. ed. F. Sagnard. Paris 1948.
Cyprian of Carthage: Ad Quirinium testimoniorum libri III. CSEL 3, 1. ed. G. Hartel. Vienna 1868.
Epistula ad Floram. SC 24. ed. G. Quispel. Paris 1949.
Hermas: Hirt des Hermas. Die Apostolischen Väter I. GCS 48. ed. M. Whittaker. Berlin 1956.
Hippolytus: Exegetische Fragmenta. GCS 1, 2. ed. H. Achelis. Leipzig 1897.
    In Danielem. GCS 1, 1. ed. G. N. Bonwetsch. Leipzig 1897.
    Refutatio omnium haeresium. GCS 26. ed. P. Wendland. Leipzig, 1916.
Ignatius: Ad Ephesios. Ad Smyrnaeos. Die Apostolischen Väter I. ed. K. Bihlmeyer. rev. of Funk. Tübingen 1956.
Irenaeus: Sancti Irenaei Episcopi Lugdunensis Libri quinque adversus haereses. ed. W. W. Harvey. Cambridge 1857.
    Contre les Hérésies III. SC 34. ed. F. Sagnard. Paris 1952.
    Contre les Hérésies IV. SC 100. ed. A. Rousseau et al. Paris 1965.
    Contre les Hérésies V. SC 152. ed. A. Rousseau et al. Paris 1969.
    Démonstration de la prédication apostolique. SC 62. ed. L. Froidevaux. Paris 1959.
Justin Martyr: Apologia. Dialogus. Die ältesten Apologeten. ed. E. J. Goodspeed. Göttingen 1914.
Origen: Commentarii in Romanos. MPG 14.
    The Commentary of Origen upon the Epistle to the Ephesians (from catenae). ed. J. A. F. Gregg. JThS 3 (1901—1902) 405 ff.
    Commentarii in Ioannem. GCS 10. ed. E. Preuschen. Leipzig 1903.
    In Librum Iesu Nave homiliae. GCS 30. ed. W. Baehrens. Leipzig 1921.
    Commentarii in Canticum Canticorum. GCS 33. ed. W. Baehrens. Leipzig 1925.
    Commentarii in Matthaeum series (Latin). GCS 38. ed. E. Klostermann. Leipzig 1933.
    Commentarii in Matthaeum. GCS 40. ed. E. Klostermann. Leipzig 1935.
    Fragmenta zu Matthaeus. GCS 41. ed. E. Klostermann. Leipzig 1941.
Tertullian: Adversus Marcionem. CSEL 47. ed. E. Kroymann. Vienna 1906.

Sources for Chapter II

From the Fourth Century to the Close of the Patristic Age

Adamantius: De recta in Deum fide. GCS 4. ed. W. H. van de Sande Bakhuyzen. Leipzig 1901.

Ambrose of Milan: Expositio evangelii secundum Lucam. CSEL 32, 4. ed. K. Schenkl. Vienna 1902.

Ambrosiaster: Commentarius in epistolam ad Ephesios. CSEL 81, 4. ed. H. Vogels. Vienna 1969.

Arnobius the Younger: Commentarius in Psalmos. MPL 53.

Athanasius: De incarnatione verbi Dei. MPG 25.

Augustine: Tractatus in Iohannem IX. MPL 35.

    Ennarationes in Psalmos. MPL 37.

    Sermones. MPL 38.

    Adversus Iudaeos. MPL 42.

    Sermo ad Caesariensis ecclesiae plebem. MPL 43.

    Contra Faustum. CSEL 25. ed. J. Zycha. Vienna 1891.

    Contra Parmenianum Donatistam. CSEL 26.

    Contra litteras Petiliani. CSEL 52.

    Sermones post Maurinos reperti. Miscellanea Augustiniana I. ed. G. Morin. Rome 1930.

Pseudo-Basil: De baptismo. MPG 31.

Cyril of Alexandria: Glaphura in Genesim. MPG 69.

    Commentarius in Ioannem. MPG 74.

Ephraem of Syria: Commentarii in epistolas D. Pauli nunc primum ex armenio in latinum sermonem a patribus Mekitharistis translati. Venice 1893.

Epiphanius: Panarion haereticorum. GCS 31. ed. K. Holl. Leipzig 1922.

Eusebius of Caesarea: Quaestiones evangelicae ad Stephanum. MPG 22.

    Demonstratio evangelica. GCS 23. ed. I. A. Heikel. Leipzig 1913.

Euthymius Zigabenus: Commentarii in epistolas S. Pauli et catholicas. ed. N. Kalogeras. Athens 1887.

Gregory of Nyssa: Contra Eunomium. MPG 45.

Ishoda'ad of Merve: The Commentaries of Ishoda'ad of Merve V, 2. ed. M. D. Gibson. Cambridge 1916.

Jerome: Commentarii in epistulam ad Ephesios. MPL 26.

    Commentariorum in Hezechielem. Corpus Christianorum: Series Latina 75. ed. F. Glorie. Tournai 1964.

    Tractatus in Psalmos. Corpus Christianorum: Series Latina 78. ed. G. Morin. Tournai 1968.

John Chrysostom: Adversus Iudaeos homiliae. MPG 48.

    Expositio in Psalmos. MPG 55.

    Homiliae in Matthaeum. MPG 57.

    Homiliae in epistulam ad Ephesios. MPG 62.

John of Damascus: In epistolam ad Ephesios commentarius. MPG 95.

Marius Victorinus: In epistolam Pauli ad Ephesios commentarius. MPL 8.

Oecumenius: Commentarius in epistolam ad Ephesios. MPG 118.

Optatus of Mileve. Contra Petilianum Donatistam. CSEL 26. ed. C. Ziwsa. Vienna 1893.

Pelagius: Pelagius's Expositions of Thirteen Epistles of St. Paul II. ed. A. Souter. Cambridge 1926. (Texts and Studies IX. ed. J. A. Robinson.)

Photius of Constantinople: Pauluskommentar aus der griechischen Kirche. NTA 15. ed. K. Staab. Münster 1933.

Rufinus of Aquileia: Apologia. MPL 21.

Severian of Gabala: Catenae graecorum patrum in Novum Testamentum VI. ed. J. A. Cramer. Oxford 1842.

Pauluskommentare aus der griechischen Kirche. NTA 15. ed. K. Staab. Münster 1933.

Theodore of Mopsuestia: Theodori Episcopi Mopsuesteni in epistolas B. Pauli commentarii I. ed. H. B. Swete. Cambridge 1880.

Theodoret of Cyrus: Interpretatio in Psalmos. MPG 80.

Quaestiones in Genesim. MPG 80.

Interpretatio epistolae ad Ephesios. MPG 82.

Pseudo-Primasius: In epistolam ad Ephesios commentaria. MPL 68.

Theophylact: Commentarius in epistolam ad Ephesios. MPG 124.

Sources for Chapter III

The Western Middle Ages

Abelard, Peter: Commentarius Cantabrigiensis in epistolas Pauli e schola Abelardi II. In epistolas ad Corinthios I et II, ad Galatos et ad Ephesios. ed. A. Landgraf. Notre Dame 1939.

Anselm of Laon, school of: Glossa Ordinaria. MPL 114.

Atto of Vercelli: Expositio in epistulam ad Ephesios. MPL 134.

Bruno, founder of the Carthusian order: Expositio in epistolam ad Ephesios. MPL 153.

Dionysius the Carthusian: In omnes B. Pauli epistolas. Opera omnia XIII. ed. Carthusian monks of Montreuil-sur-Mer 1901.

Gregory the Great: Expositio in librum Iob, sive Moralium Libri XXV. PL 76.

Haymo of Auxerre: Expositio in epistolam ad Ephesios. PL 117.

Herve of Bourg-Dieu: Commentarius in epistolam ad Ephesios. PL 181.

Lanfranc: Commentarius in epistolam ad Ephesios. PL 150.

Rabanus Maurus: Ennarationes in epistolam ad Ephesios. PL 112.

Sedulius Scotus: Collectanea in epistolam ad Ephesios. PL 103.

Thomas Aquinas: Super epistolas S. Pauli lectura II. ed. P. R. Cai. Rome 1953.

Sources for Chapter IV

The Reformation

Annotationes in Veterum Testamentum et in Ephesios. Amsterdam 1710. (Author uncertain. First edition probably 16th century.)

Beza, Theodore: Annotationes Maiores in Novum Domini Nostri Jesu Christi Testamentum II. Geneva 1594.

Brenz, John: Kommentar zum Briefe des Apostels Paulus an die Epheser. ed. W. Kohler. Heidelberg 1935.

Bucer, Martin: Praelectiones in epistolam D. Pauli ad Ephesios. Heidelberg 1561. "Judenratschlag." Opera Omnia I, 7. ed. R. Stupperich. Gütersloh 1964.

Bugenhagen, John: Annotationes in epistolas Pauli. Basel 1525.

Bullinger, Heinrich: In omnes apostolicas epistolas. Zurich 1537.

Cajetan, Thomas de Vio: Epistolae Pauli et aliorum apostolorum ad graecam veritatem castigatae. Paris 1540.

Calvin, John: Commentarius in epistolam Pauli ad Ephesios. CR 51. Sermons sur l'épître aux Éphésiens XII—XV. CR 51.

Clarius: Critici Sacri. ed. N. Gürtler. Frankfurt a. M. 1695².

Erasmus: Querela Pacis undique gentium eiectae profligataeque. Opera omnia IV. Leyden 1703.
Novum Testamentum iuxta Graecorum lectionem. Opera omnia VI. Leyden 1705.
Paraphrases in Novum Testamentum. Opera omnia VII. Leyden 1706.

Flacius Illyricus, Matthias: Glossa compendiara in Novum Testamentum ex versione Erasmi. Basel 1570.

Gwalther, Rudolf: Archetypi homiliarum in epistolas S. Pauli ad Galatas, Ephesios, et al. Zurich 1609.

Hemming, Nicolas: Commentaria in omnes epistolas apostolorum. Leipzig 1571.

Luther, Martin: Die Deutsche Bibel VII. Weimar 1931.
Matthäus 18—24 in Predigten ausgelegt (1537—1540). WA 47.
Wider das Papstum zu Rom. WA 54.

Maior, Georg: Ennaratio epistolae Pauli ad Ephesios praelecta. Wittenberg 1561.

Marlorato, Augustino: ed. Novi Testamenti Catholica. Geneva 1585⁴.

Megander, Caspar: In epistolam Pauli ad Ephesios commentarius. Basel 1534.

Melanchthon, Philipp: Commentarii in Psalmos (118:22). CR 13.
Loci Communes von 1521. Melanchthons Werke in Auswahl II, 1. ed. H. Engelland. Gütersloh 1952.

Musculus, Wolfgang: In epistolas Apostoli Pauli, ad Galatas et Ephesios, commentarii. Basel 1561.

Naclantius, Jacob: Enarrationes in D. Pauli epistolas ad Ephesios notae. ed. John Piscator. Herborn 1588.

Rollock, Robert: In epistolam S. Pauli apostoli ad Ephesios commentarius. Geneva 1593².

Salmeron, Adam: Disputationum in epistolas D. Pauli III. Cologne 1604.

Sasbout, Adam: In omnes D. Pauli ... epistolas explicatio. Antwerp 1501.

Stapulensis, Jacob Faber. In omnes D. Pauli epistolas commentarii V. Cologne 1531³.

Zanchius, Hieronymus: Commentarius in epistolam Sancti Pauli ad Ephesios I. ed. de Hartog. Amsterdam 1888 (first ed. 1594).

Zegerus: Critici Sacri V. ed. N. Gürtler. Frankfurt a. M. 1695².

Zwingli, Ulrich: "De Peccato Originali Declaratio." CR 92.
"In catabaptistarum strophas elenchus." CR 93.

Sources for Chapter V

The Seventeenth Century

Balduinus, Frederick: Commentarius in omnes epistolas Beati Apostoli Pauli. ed. J. Olearius. Frankfurt a. M. 1691.

Bayne, Paul: An Entire Commentary upon the whole Epistle of St. Paul to the Epesians. Edinburgh 1866 (first ed. 1643).

Boyd, Robert: In epistolam Pauli Apostoli ad Ephesios praelectiones. London 1652.

Calixtus, Georg: In epistolam Pauli ad Ephesios. Braunschweig 1653.

Calov, Abraham: Biblia Novi Testamenti illustrata II. Dresden and Leipzig 1719 (first ed. 1672).

Cappellus, Ludwig: Critici Sacri V. ed N. Gürtler. Frankfurt a. M. 1695².

Cocceius, Johannes: Exercitatio de principio epistolae ad Ephesios cum commentario in totam epistolam. Opera Omnia IV. ed. J. H. Cocceius. Amsterdam 1673.

Crell, Joannis: Opera omnia exegetica. Bibliotheca fratrum Polonorum. Amsterdam 1656.

Crocius, Johannes: Commentarius in epistolam S. Pauli Apostoli ad Ephesios. Kassel 1642.

Estius, Wilhelm: Commentarius in omnes D. Pauli et catholicas epistolas. Biblia Maxima XVI. ed. John de la Haye. Paris 1660.

Goodwin, Thomas: An Exposition on the First and part of the Second Chapter of the Epistle to the Ephesians and Sermons preached on several occassions. Works I. London 1681.

Grotius, Hugo: Annotationes in epistolas apostolicas et Apocalypsin. Opera Omnia Theologica II, 2. Amsterdam 1679.

Hammond, Henry: A Paraphrase and Annotations upon the New Testament. London 1698⁶.
Novum Testamentum cum paraphrasibus et adnotationibus H. Hammondi. transl. J. Clericus. Amsterdam 1968.

a Lapide, Cornelius: Epistolae D. Pauli. Antwerp 1614.

Schlichting, Jonah: Commentaria posthuma II. Bibliotheca fratrum Polonorum. Amsterdam 1656.

Sewall, Samuel: The Selling of Joseph. repr. American Issues I. ed. W. Thorpe et al. Chicago 1944.

Sources for Chapter VI

The Eighteenth Century

Bahrdt, Carl Friedrich: Briefe von Paulus. Die neuesten Offenbarungen Gottes III. Riga 1773.

Baumgarten, Siegmund Jacob: Auslegung der Briefe Pauli an die Galater, Epheser ... Thessalonicher. ed. J. S. Semler. Halle 1767.

Bengel, Johann Albrecht: Gnomon Novi Testamenti. Tübingen 1742.

Bruckner, Jacob, ed. „Englisches Bibelwerk." Die Heilige Schrift des alten und neuen Testaments IV. Leipzig 1762.

Calmet, Augustin: Commentaire litteral VIII. Paris 1726.

Chandler, Samuel: A paraphrase and notes on the Epistles of St. Paul to the Galatians and Ephesians. ed. N. White. London 1777.

Ernesti, Johann August: „Fortsetzung des Artikels: D. Zachariae paraphrastische Erklärung paulinischer Briefe." Neueste Theologische Bibliothek II, 1. Leipzig 1772.

Fende, Christian: Des hocherleuchteten Apostels Pauli vortrefflicher Brieff an die Ephesier. Frankfurt a. M. 1727.

Grynaeus, Simeon: Das Neue Testament in einer erklärenden Übersetzung II, 1. Basel 1775.

Hahn, Phillipp Matthäus: Erbauungs-Stunden über den Brief an die Epheser. Stuttgart 1845.

Hedinger, Johann Reinhard: Die Epistel an die Epheser in Das Neue Testament ... mit Summarien etc. Bremen 1707².

Koppe, Johann Benjamin: Novum Testamentum Graece perpetua annotatione illustratum VI. ed. T. C. Tychsen. Göttingen 1791².

Krause, Friedrich August Wilhelm: Der Brief an die Epheser. Frankfurt und Leipzig 1789.

Lange, Joachim: Apostolisches Licht und Recht. Halle 1729.

Locke, John: A Paraphrase and Notes on the Epistles of St. Paul to the Galatians, Romans, Corinthians, Ephesians. London 1707.

Michaelis: Johann David. Paraphrasis und Anmerkungen über die Briefe Pauli an die Galater, Epheser ... Philemon. Bremen und Göttingen 1769².

Roëll, Hermann Alexander: Commentarii in epistolam S. Pauli ad Ephesios II. Utrecht 1731.

Schoettgen, Christian: Horae Hebraicae. Dresden and Leipzig 1733.

Spener, Philip Jacob: Erklärung der Episteln an die Epheser und Colosser. Halle 1706.

Starke, Christoph: Synopsis bibliothecae exegeticae in Novum Testamentum. Biel 1748³.

Wettstein, Johann Jakob: Η ΚΑΙΝΗ ΔΙΑΘΗΚΗ. NT graecum. Amsterdam 1752.

Zachariae, Gotthilf Traugott: Paraphrastische Erklärung der Briefe Pauli, an die Römer ... Epheser ... I. Tübingen 1781.

Zinzendorf, Nikolaus Ludwig von: Sieben Letzte Reden. Hauptschriften II. Hildesheim 1963.

Sources for Chapter VII

The Nineteenth Century

Bauer, Ferdinand Christian: Historisch-kritische Untersuchungen zum Neuen Testament. ed. Klaus Scholder. Stuttgart-Bad Cannstatt 1963.
Die Tübinger Schule und ihre Stellung zur Gegenwart. Tübingen 1859.
Das Christentum und die christliche Kirche der drei ersten Jahrhunderte. Tübingen 1860.

262

Vorlesungen über Neutestamentliche Theologie. ed. F. F. Baur. Leipzig 1864.
Paulus, der Apostel Jesu Christi. ed. E. Zeller. Leipzig 1866—67[2].

Beck, J. T.: Erklärung des Briefes Pauli an die Epheser. ed. J. Lindenmeyer. Gütersloh 1891.

Dale, R. W.: The Epistle to the Ephesians: Its Doctrine and Ethics. London 1887.

De Wette, Wilhelm Martin Leberecht: Kurze Erklärung der Briefe an die Colosser, an Philemon, an die Ephesier und Philipper. Leipzig 1847[2].

Eadie, John: A Commentary on the Greek text of the epistle of Paul to the Epesians. New York 1861[2].

Ewald, Heinrich: Sieben Sendschreiben des Neuen Bundes. Göttingen 1870.

Feine, Paul: „Ephesians 2: 14—16." ThStKr 72 (1899) 540—573.

Flatt, Johann Friedrich von: Vorlesungen über die Briefe Pauli an die Galater und Epheser. ed. M. C. F. Kling. Tübingen 1828.

Gore, Charles: St. Paul's Epistle to the Ephesians: a practical exposition. New York 1898.

Harless, Gottlieb Christoph Adolph: Commentar über den Brief Pauli an die Ephesier. Erlangen 1834.

Haupt, Erich: Die Gefangenschaftsbriefe. KEK 8. Göttingen 1897[7].
Die Gefangenschaftsbriefe. KEK 8. Göttingen 1902[8].

Henle, Franz Anton: Der Epheserbrief des hl. Apostels Paulus. Augsburg 1890.

Heubner, Heinrich Leonhard: Praktische Erklärung des Neuen Testaments IV. ed. A. Hakn. Potsdam 1859.

Hodge, Charles: A Commentary on the Epistle to the Ephesians. New York 1858.

Hofmann, Johann Christian Konrad von: Der Brief Pauli an die Epheser. Die heilige Schrift Neuen Testaments IV, 1. Nördlingen 1870.

Holtzmann, Heinrich Julius: Kritik der Epheser und Kolosserbriefe. Leipzig 1872.
Lehrbuch der Neutestamentlichen Theologie. Freiburg und Leipzig 1897.

Hort, Fenton John Anthony: Prolegomena to St. Paul's Epistles to the Romans and the Ephesians. London 1895.

Klöpper, Albert: Der Brief an die Epheser. Göttingen 1891.

Köstlin, Karl Reinhold: Der Lehrbegriff des Evangeliums und der Brief Johannes. Berlin 1843.

Maurice, Frederick Denison: Sermons Preached in Lincoln's Inn Chapel I. London 1891.
The Gospel of St. John. London 1894.

Meyer, Heinrich August Wilhelm: Kritisch-exegetisches Handbuch über den Brief Pauli an die Epheser. KEK II, 8. Göttingen 1843.
Kritisch-exegetisches Handbuch über den Brief an die Epheser. KEK II, 8. Göttingen 1867[4].

Monod, Adolphe: Explication de l'Épître de Saint Paul aux Éphésiens. Paris 1867.

Neill, William: A Practical Exposition of the Epistle to the Ephesians. Philadelphia 1850.

Newland, Henry Garrett: New Catena on St. Paul's Epistles. London 1860.

Olshausen, Herman: Biblischer Commentar über sammtliche Schriften des Neuen Testaments IV. Königsberg 1840.

Oltramare, Hughes: Commentaire sur les Épîtres de S. Paul aux Colossiens aux Éphésiens et à Philémon II. Paris 1892.

Passavant, Theophil: Versuch einer praktischen Auslegung des Briefes Pauli an die Ephesier. Basel 1836.

Pfleiderer, Otto. Der Paulinismus. Leipzig 1890².

Das Urchristentum. Berlin 1902².

Ritschl, Albrecht: Die Entstehung der Altkatholischen Kirche. Bonn 1857².

Rückert, Leopold Immanuel: Der Brief Pauli an die Epheser. Leipzig 1834.

Schleiermacher, Friedrich: Predigten I. Sämmtliche Werke II. Berlin 1834.

Schmidt, Woldemar: Kritisch-exegetisches Handbuch über den Brief an die Epheser. KEK 8. Göttingen 1878⁵.

Schnedermann, Georg: Die Gefangenschaftsbriefe des Apostels Paulus. Kurzgefasster Kommentar zu den heiligen Schriften. ed. H. Strack and O. Zöckler. Neues Testament IV. Nördlingen 1888.

Schwegler, Albert: Das Nachapostolische Zeitalter. Tübingen 1846.

Soden, Hermann von: Die Briefe an die Kolosser, Epheser, Philemon; Pastoralbriefe. Hand-commentar zum Neuen Testament III, 1. Freiburg und Leipzig 1893².

"Der Epheserbrief." JpTh XIII (1887) 403–435, 452–498.

Stier, Rudolf: Die Gemeinde in Christo Jesu: Auslegung des Briefes an die Epheser. Berlin 1848.

Weiss, Bernhard: Lehrbuch der biblischen Theologie des Neuen Testaments. Berlin 1888⁵.

Westcott, Brooke: St. Paul's Epistle to the Ephesians. London 1906.

Wohlenberg, Gustav: Die Briefe des Paulus: An die Epheser, an die Kolosser, an Philemon, an die Philipper. Kurzgefasste Kommentar zu den heiligen Schriften II, 4. ed. H. Strack and O. Zöckler. Munich 1895².

Sources for Chapter VIII

The Twentieth Century

Abbot, T. K.: A Critical and Exegetical Commentary on the Epistle to the Ephesians. ICC. Edinburgh 1964⁵.

Abbot, W. and Gallagher, J.: ed. The Documents of Vatican II. New York 1966.

Allan, John A.: "The 'In Christ' Formula in Ephesians." New Testament Studies V (1958–1959) 54–62.

Asmussen, Hans: Der Brief des Paulus an die Epheser. Breklum 1949.

Barry, F. R.: A Philosophy from Prison. New York 1926.

Barth, Markus: The Broken Wall. Chicago 1959.

Israel und die Kirche im Brief des Paul an die Epheser. Munich 1959.

Jesus, Paulus, und die Juden. ThSt (B) 91. Zurich 1967.

Ephesians. Anchor Bible 34. Garden City, N. Y. 1974.

Bauer, Walter and other New Testament scholars in Germany. „Neues Testament und Rassenfrage." ThBl 12 (1933) 294–296.

Baum, Gregory: Is the New Testament Anti-Semitic? Glen Rock, N. J. 1965.

Beckmann, Klaus-Martin, ed. Die Kirche und die Rassenfrage. Stuttgart 1967.

Rasse, Kirche, und Humanum. Gütersloh 1969.

264

Benoît, Pierre: "L'unité de l'Église selon l'Épître aux Éphésiens." Analecta Biblica XVII, 57—77. Rome 1963.

Best, Ernest: One Body in Christ. London 1955.

Betz, Otto: „The Eschatological Interpretation of the Sinai Tradition in Qumran and in the New Testament." Revue de Qumrân 6 (1967—68) 89—106.

Bonhoeffer, Dietrich: „Die Kirche vor der Judenfrage." Gesammelte Schriften II. ed. E. Bethge. Munich 1959.
„Der Arierparagraph in der Kirche." Gesammelte Schriften II.
„Erstform des Betheler Bekenntnisses." Gesammelte Schriften II.
Sanctorum Communio. ThB 3. Munich 1960³.

Bultmann, Rudolf: „Der Arier-Paragraph im Raume der Kirche." ThBl 12 (1933) 359—70.

Cerfaux, Lucien: La Théologie de l'Église suivant Saint Paul. Paris 1965³.

Chadwick, Henry: „Die Absicht des Epheserbriefes." ZNW 51 (1960) 145—153.

Coetzee, J. C.: Volk en Godsvolk in die Nuwe Testament. Potchefstrom, S. A. 1965.

Colpe, Carsten: „Der Leib-Christi-Vorstellung im Epheserbrief." Judentum, Urchristentum, Kirche. BZNW 26. Berlin 1960.

Conzelmann, Hans: „Der Brief an die Epheser." NTD 8. Göttingen 1962.

Daane, James: The Anatomy of Anti-Semitism and Other Essays on Religion and Race. Grand Rapids, Mich. 1965.

Dahl, Nils Alstrup: Das Volk Gottes. Darmstadt 1963².
"Christ, Creation and the Church." The Background of the New Testament and its Eschatology. ed. W. D. Davies and D. Daube. Cambridge 1956.

Dahl et al: Kurze Auslegung des Epheserbriefes. Göttingen 1965.

Davies, W. D.: Paul and Rabbinic Judaism. London 1955².
Christian Origins and Judaism. London 1962.

Deichgräber, Reinhard: Gotteshymnus und Christushymnus in der frühen Christenheit. Studien zur Umwelt des Neuen Testaments 5. Göttingen 1967.

Deimel, Ludwig: Leib Christi. Freiburg 1940.

Dibelius, Martin: An die Kolosser, Epheser, An Philemon. HNT 12. reworked by H. Greeven. Tübingen 1953.

Dix, Gregory: Jew and Greek: a Study in the Primitive Church. Westminster 1953.

Dodd, C. H.: "Christianity and the Reconciliation of the Nations." London 1952.

Ehrlich, Ernst Ludwig: „Was bedeutet das Zweite Vatikanische Konzil für uns Juden?" Was bedeutet das Zweite Vatikanische Konzil für uns? ed. W. Schatz. Basel 1966.

Ewald, Paul: Die Briefe des Paulus an die Epheser, Kolosser und Philemon. Kommentar zum Neuen Testament X. Leipzig 1910².

Fischer, Karl: Tendenz und Absicht des Epheserbriefes. Göttingen 1973.

Gärtner, Bertil. The Temple and the Community in Qumran and the New Testament. Cambridge 1965.

Gaugler, Ernst: Der Epheserbrief. Auslegung Neutestamentlicher Schriften 6. ed. M. Geiger and K. Stalder. Zurich 1966.

Gnilka, Joachim: Der Epheserbrief. Herders Theologischer Kommentar zum Neuen Testament X, 2. Freiburg 1971.

„Christus unser Friede — Ein Friedens-Erlöserlied in Eph. 2:14—17." Die Zeit Jesu, Festschrift für Heinrich Schlier. Freiburg 1970.

Gollwitzer, Helmut: „Bibelarbeit über Epheser 2:11—22." Der Friede Gottes und der Friede der Welt. ed. F. Lorenz. Berlin 1967.

Grosheide, F. W.: De Brief van Paulus aan de Efeziers. Kampen 1960.

„Gutachten der Theologischen Fakultät der Universität Marburg zum Kirchengesetz über die Rechtsverhältnisse der Geistlichen und Kirchenbeamten." ThBl 12 (1933) col. 291—294.

Hahn, Ferdinand: Das Verständnis der Mission im Neuen Testament. Neukirchen 1963.

Hanson, Stig: The Unity of the Church in the New Testament: Colossians and Ephesians. Uppsala 1946.

Hastings, J.: ed. The Epistle of Paul to the Ephesians. The Speaker's Bible VIII. Aberdeen 1925.

Jocz, Jacob: A Theology of Election: Israel and the Church. London 1958.

Johnson, F. Ernest: "The Jewish Question as an Ecumenical Problem." ER VII (1955) 228 ff.

Johnston, George: „The Church and Israel: Continuity and Discontinuity in the New Testament Doctrine of the Church." JR 34, 1 (Jan 1954) 26—36.

Käsemann, Ernst: Leib und Leib Christi. BHTh 9. Tübingen 1933.

Review of Percy's Die Probleme der Kolosser und Epheserbriefe. Gnomon 21 (1949) 342—347.

Review of Mussner's Christus, das All und die Kirche. ThLZ 81 (1956) 585—590.

„Epheserbrief." RGG II, 517—520.

„Epheser 2:17—22." Exegetische Versuche und Besinnungen I. Göttingen 1960.

„Paulus und der Frühkatholizismus." Exegetische Versuche II. Göttingen 1964.

„Das Interpretationsproblem des Epheserbriefes." Exegetische Versuche II.

"Ephesians and Acts." Studies in Luke-Acts. ed. Keck and Martyn. Nashville 1966.

Paulinische Perspektiven. Tübingen 1969.

Kirby, J. C.: Ephesians: Baptism and Pentecost. London 1968.

Kitagawa, Daisuke: The Pastor and the Race Issue. New York 1965.

Kotzé, J. C. G.: „The Meaning of Our Unity in Christ." ER VII, 4 (Jul. 1955) 321—337.

Kuhn, Karl Georg: „The Epistle to the Ephesians in the Light of the Qumran Texts." Paul and Qumran. ed. J. Murphy-O'Connor. London 1968.

Lacocque, André: „Israël, pierre de touche de l'eocuménisme." Verbum Caro 48 (1958) 331—343.

La pérennité d'Israël. Geneva 1964.

Lamadrid, A. Gonzáles: „Ipse est pax nostra." Estudios Biblicos XXVIII (1969) 209—261 and XXIX (1970) 101—136; 227—266.

Le Déaut, R.: La Nuit Pascale. Rome 1963.

Lichtenberg, Jean-Paul: „Situation et Destinée d'Israël à la lumière de Romains IX—XI et d'Éphésiens II." Foi et Vie 64, 6 (Nov.—Dec. 1965) 488—518.

266

Mackay, John A.: God's Order: the Ephesians Letter and This Present Time. New York 1953.

McGeachy, D.P.: „The Maker of Peace." The Unsilent South. ed. D. W. Shriver, Jr. Richmond, Virginia 1965.

McKelvey, R. J.: The New Temple. Oxford 1968.

Masson, Charles: L'Épître de Saint Paul aux Éphésiens. Commentaire du Nouveau Testament IX. Neuchatel and Paris 1953.

Meuzelaar, Jacobus Johannes: Der Leib des Messias. Assen 1961.

Minear, Paul: Images of the Church in the New Testament. Philadelphia 1960.

Mühlen, Heribert von: Una Mystica Persona. Munich 1967.

Mussner, Franz: Christus, das All und die Kirche. TThS. Trier 1968².

"Contributions made by Qumran to the Understanding of the Epistle to the Ephesians." (Engl. transl.) Paul and Qumran. ed. J. Murphy-O'Conner. London 1968.

„Die Geschichtstheologie des Epheserbriefes." Analecta Biblica XVIII, 59—63. Rome 1963.

„Kirche als Kultgemeinde nach dem Neuen Testament." Praesentia Salutis. Düsseldorf 1967.

Nauck, Wolfgang: „Eph 2, 19—22 — ein Tauflied?" EvTh 13 (1953) 362—371.

Ockenga, Harold J.: Faithful in Christ Jesus. New York 1948.

Oesterreicher, Johannes: „Erklärung über das Verhältnis der Kirche zu den nichtchristlichen Religionen." Das Zweite Vatikanische Konzil. LThK Suppl. II. Freiburg 1967.

Oyen, Hendrik van: „Eine theologische Absage an die Judenmission?" Christlich-jüdisches Forum 22 (Feb. 1960).

Percy, Ernst: Der Leib Christi in den paulinischen Homologumena und Antilegomena. Lund und Leipzig 1942.

Die Probleme der Kolosser- und Epheserbriefe. Lund 1946.

„Zu den Problemen des Kolosser und Epheserbriefes." ZNW 43 (1950—1951) 178—194.

Review of Barth's Israel und die Kirche. ThLZ 86 (1961) 200—201.

Perrot, Charles: „La lecture synagogale d'Exode XXI, 1—XXII, 23 et son influence sur la litterature neotestamentaire." A la Rencontre de Dieu, Mémorial Albert Gelin. Le Puy 1961.

Peterson, Erik. „Die Kirche aus Juden und Heiden." Theologische Traktate. Munich 1951.

Pokorný, Petr.: Der Epheserbrief und die Gnosis. Berlin 1965.

de Quervain, Alfred: Kirche, Volk, Staat. Ethik II, 1. Zurich 1945.

Rauschenbusch, Walter: Christianity and the Social Crisis. New York 1908.

Reicke, Bo.: Diakonie, Festfreude und Zelos. Uppsala universitets Årsskrift 1951:5. Uppsala 1951.

Rengstorf, Karl Heinrich: „Die Eine Kirche aus Juden und Heiden." Viva Vox Evangelii. Festschrift für H. Meiser. Munich 1951.

Rennes, Jean: „Christ Notre Paix: note sur Éphésiens 2." Foi et Vie 63, 4 (1964) 274—275.

Rienecker, Fritz: Praktischer Handkommentar zum Epheserbrief. Neumünster 1934.

Robinson, J. Armitage: St. Paul's Epistle to the Ephesians. London 1928².

Roels, Edwin D.: God's Mission: the Epistle to the Ephesians in Mission Perspective. Franeker 1962.

Rolston, Holmes: The Social Message of the Apostle Paul. Richmond, Virginia 1942.

Sahlin, Harald: Die Beschneidung Christi. SBibUps 12. Lund 1950.

Sanders, J.: „Hymnic Elements in Ephesians 1—3." ZNW 56 (1965) 214—232. The New Testament Christological Hymns. Cambridge 1971.

Schille, Gottfried: „Der Autor des Epheserbriefes." ThLZ 82 (1957) 325—334. Frühchristliche Hymnen. Berlin 1965.

Schlatter, Adolf: Die Briefe an die Galater, Epheser, Kolosser und Philemon. Stuttgart 1949².

Schlier, Heinrich: Christus und die Kirche im Epheserbrief. Tübingen 1930.
Der Brief an die Epheser. Düsseldorf 1968⁶.
Response to K. Thieme's „Der ökumenische Aspekt der christlich-jüdischen Begegnung." Freiburger Rundbrief 8 (Oct. 1955) 32.
Die Zeit der Kirche. Freiburg 1956.

Schmidt, Karl Ludwig: Die Polis in Kirche und Welt. Zurich 1940.
Ἐκκλησία. TWNT III.

Schweizer, Eduard: „Die Kirche als Leib Christi in den Paulinischen Antilegomena." Neotestamentica. Zurich 1963.

Scott, Ernest Findlay: The Epistles of Paul to the Colossians, to Philemon and to the Ephesians. Moffatt NTC. London 1948⁷.

Smith, Derwood: Jewish and Greek Traditions in Ephesians 2:11—22. Unpublished Yale doctoral dissertation 1970.
„The Two Made One." Ohio Journal of Religious Studies VI, 1 (1973) 34—54.

Spaemann, Heinrich: Response to Mon. Carli. Freiburger Rundbrief 16—17 (July 1965) insert VII d.
Die Christen und das Volk der Juden. Munich 1966.

Staab, K.: „Die Gefangenschaftsbriefe." Regensburger Neues Testament VII. Regensburg 1959.

Stefanovic, Dimitrije: „Die Einheit der Heilsgemeinde: Eph 2:11—22." ThBl 9 (1930) 334—336.

Storer, R.: „A Possible Link between the Epistle to the Ephesians and the Book of Ruth." Studia Evangelica IV, 1. ed. F. L. Cross. Berlin 1968.

Strack, H. and Billerbeck, P.: Kommentar zum Neuen Testament aus Talmud und Midrasch. Munich 1922—1928. Index vols 5 (1956) 6 (1961). ed. J. Jeremias.

Synge, F.: St. Paul's Epistle to the Ephesians. London 1941.

Testa, E.: „Gesù Pacificatore Universale." Studii Biblici Franciscani Liber Annuus 19 (1969) 5—64.

„Theologisches Gutachten über die Zulassung von Christen jüdischer Herkunft zu den Aemtern der deutschen evangelischen Kirche." ThBl 12 (1933) 321—324.

Thornton, Lionel: The Common Life in the Body of Christ. London 1950³.

268

Thurneysen, Eduard: „Es Geht um Israel!" Basler Predigten 28, 8 (Dec. 1964).

Tilson, Everett: Segregation and the Bible. Nashville 1958.

Ulanov, Ann Belford: „The Two Strangers." Union Seminary Quarterly Review 28 (1973) 273—283.

Verkuyl, Johannes: Break Down the Walls. transl. L. Smedes. Grand Rapids 1973.

Vielhauer, Philip: Oikodome. Karlsruhe 1940.

Visser 't Hooft, W. A.: Report of the General Secretary, Second Assembly of World Council of Churches, 1954. Hauptschriften II. Stuttgart 1967.

The Ecumenical Movement and the Racial Problem. Paris 1954.

Wedel, T. O.: Exposition of Ephesians. Interpreter's Bible 10. New York 1953.

Wengst, Klaus.: Christologische Formeln und Lieder des Urchristentums. Bonn 1967.

Weifel, Wolfgang: Review of Schille's *Frühchristliche Hymnen*. ThLZ 90 (1965) 118—121.

Willebrands, J.: Oecuménisme et Problèmes Actuels. Paris 1969.

World Council of Churches. Die Evangelische Kirche in Deutschland und die Judenfrage. Geneva 1945.

„The Church and the Jewish People." Faith and Order Studies 1964—1967. Geneva 1968.

Zerwick, Max: Der Brief an die Epheser. Düsseldorf 1962.

Zoellner, W.: „Die Kirche nach dem Epheserbrief." Die Kirche im Neuen Testament in ihrer Bedeutung für die Gegenwart. ed. F. Siegmund-Schultze. Berlin 1930.

Secondary Literature

Ahlers, Rolf: Die Vermittlungstheologie des Frederick Denison Maurice. Hamburg 1967.

Altaner, Berthold and Stuiber, Alfons: Patrologie. Freiburg 1966⁷.

Bardenhewer, Otto: Geschichte der altkirchlichen Literatur. Darmstadt 1913—1932.

Bea, Augustine Cardinal: Die Kirche und das Jüdische Volk. Freiburg, Basel, Vienna 1966.

Bengsch, Alfred: Heilsgeschichte und Heilswissen: eine Untersuchung zur Struktur des theologischen Denkens im Werk „Adversus Haereses" des Hl. Irenaeus von Lyon. Leipzig 1957.

Blumenkranz, Bernard: Die Judenpredigt Augustins. Basel 1946.

Les auters chrétiens latins du moyen age sur les juifs et le judaisme. Paris 1963.

Bonner, Gerald: St. Augustine of Hippo. Philadelphia 1963.

Bourne, George: A Condensed Anti-Slaverery Argument. New York 1845.

Brennecke, Gerhard: „Inter-group Relations — the Church amid Racial and Ethnic Tensions." ER VII, 1 (Oct. 1954) 49—55.

Bultmann, Rudolf: „The Transformation of the Idea of the Church in the History of Early Christianity." transl. S. M. Gilmour. Canadian Journal of Theology I, 2 (Jul. 1955) 73—81.

Colpe, Carsten: Die Religionsgeschichtliche Schule. FRLANT 60. Göttingen 1961.

Cone, James: Black Theology and Black Power. New York 1969.

Corwin, Virginia: St. Ignatius and Christianity in Antioch. New Haven 1960.

Danielou, Jean: Théologie du Judéo-christianisme. Tournai 1958.

Davies, W. D.: Paul and Rabbinic Judaism. London 1955².

Davis, D. B.: The Problem of Slavery in Western Culture. Ithaca, New York 1966.

Dumond, D. L.: Antislavery: the Crusade for Freedom in America. Ann Arbor 1962.

Ebeling, Gerhard: Kirchengeschichte als Geschichte der Auslegung der heiligen Schrift. Tübingen 1947.

Geiger, Wolfgang: Spekulation und Kritik: Die Geschichtstheologie Ferdinand Christian Baur. Munich 1964.

Goldschmidt, D. and Kraus, H. J.: ed. Der Ungekündigte Bund. Stuttgart 1962.

Grant, Robert: A Short History of the Interpretation of the Bible. New York 1963.

Greenslade, S. L.: Schism in the Early Church. New York 1953.

Greer, Rowan: Theodore of Mopsuestia: Exegete and Theologian. London 1961.

Grolle, J. H.: „Dialogue between the Church and Israel." The Student World 52, 1 (1959) 87—93.

Haardt, Robert: Die Gnosis. Stuttgart 1967.

Harnack, Adolf von: „Der Kirchengeschichtliche Ertrag der exegetischen Arbeiten des Origenes." TU 42, 4. Leipzig 1920.
  Die Mission und Ausbreitung des Christentums. Leipzig 1924⁴.
  The Mission and Expansion of Christianity. transl. J. Moffatt. New York 1961.

Hennecke, E.: New Testament Apocrypha. ed. W. Schneemelcher. transl. R. M. Wilson. London 1963.

Heussi, Karl: Kompendium der Kirchengeschichte. Tübingen 1960.

Hübner, Eberhard: Schrift und Theologie: eine Untersuchung zur Theologie Joh. Chr. K. von Hofmann. Munich 1956.

Jonas, Hans: Gnosis und spätantiker Geist I. Göttingen 1934.
  The Gnostic Religion. Boston 1958.

Judge, E. A.: „Contemporary Political Models for the Interrelations of the New Testament Church." The Reformed Theological Review XXII, 3 (Oct. 1963) 65—76.

Karig, Werner: Des Caius Marius Victorinus Kommentare zu den paulinischen Briefen. Marburg 1924.

Koch, Karl: Studium Pietatis: Martin Bucer als Ethiker. Mainz 1960.

Kotze, J. C. G.: Principle and Practice in Race Relations According to Scripture. Stellenbosch, S. A. 1962.

de Kuiper, Arie: Israel tussen Zendig en Oecumene. Wageningen 1964.

Ladner, G. B.: „The Symbolism of the Biblical Corner Stone in the Medieval West." Mediaeval Studies IV. Toronto 1942.

Laeuchli, Samuel: The Language of Faith. Abingdon and Nashville 1962.

Lambert, Bernard: Le problème oecuménique. Paris 1962.

Lauras, Antoine: „Deux images du Christ et de l'Église dans las prédication augustinienne." Augustinus Magister. Congrès International Augustinien II, 671—675. Paris 1954.

Lawson, John: The Biblical Theology of Saint Irenaeus. London 1948.

Locher, Gottfried W.: „Calvin spricht zu den Juden." ThZ 23, 3 (May-June 1967) 180—196.

Loescher, Frank: The Protestant Church and the Negro. Philadelphia 1948.

Lubacs, Henri de: Exégèse médiévale. Les quatre sens de l'Ecriture. 1959—1964.

Maier, J.: „Zum Begriff yhd in den Texten von Qumran." ZAW 72 (1960) 148—166.

Marsch, Wolf-Dieter and Thieme, Karl: ed. Christen und Juden: Ihr Gegenüber vom Apostelkonzil bis heute. Mainz und Göttingen 1961.

McNally, Robert: The Bible in the Early Middle Ages. Woodstock, Virginia 1959.

Meier, Kurt: Kirche und Judentum: Die Haltung der evangelischen Kirche zur Judenpolitik des Dritten Reiches. Göttingen 1968.

Menzel, Gustav: Die Kirchen und die Rassen. Wuppertal 1960.

Merklein, Helmut: Christus und die Kirche: Die theologische Grundstruktur des Epheserbriefes nach Eph 2:11—18. Stuttgart 1973.

Das kirchliche Amt nach dem Epheserbrief. Munich 1973.

„Zur Tradition und Komposition von Eph 2:14—18." Biblische Zeitschrift 17, 1 (1973) 79—102.

Munck, Johannes: Paulus und die Heilsgeschichte. Copenhagen 1954.

Nichels, Peter: Targum and New Testament: a Bibliography. Rome 1967.

Nicols, James: Romanticism in American Theology. Chicago 1961.

Norris, Richard A.: God and World in Early Christian Theology. New York 1965.

Oepke, Albrecht: Das Neue Gottesvolk. Gütersloh 1950.

Oxford Society of Historical Theology. The New Testament in the Apostolic Fathers. Oxford 1905.

Pagels, Elaine: The Gnostic Paul. Philadelphia 1975.

Peterson, Erik: „Das Problem des Nationalismus im alten Christentum." ThZ 7, 2 (Mar.-Apr. 1951) 81—91.

Pfisterer, Rudolf: Im Schatten des Kreuzes. Hamburg 1966.

Quasten, Johannes: Patrology. Utrecht 1950—1960.

Rathke, Heinrich: Ignatius von Antiochien und die Paulusbriefe. TU 99. Berlin 1967.

Ratzinger, Joseph: Volk und Haus Gottes bei Augustin. Munich 1954.

Reuss, Edward: Die Geschichte der Heiligen Schriften II. Neues Testament. Braunschweig 1874[5].

Russell, Jean: God's Lost Cause. London 1968.

Sanday, William and Headlam, Arthur: A Critical and Exegetical Commentary on the Epistle to the Romans. Edinburgh 1902[5].

Schelkle, Karl: Paulus, Lehrer der Väter. Düsseldorf 1956.

Schenke, Hans-Martin: Der Gott „Mensch" in der Gnosis. Göttingen 1962.

Schmidt, Kurt Dietrich: Die Bekenntnisse und grundsätzlichen Äußerungen zur Kirchenfrage des Jahres 1933. Göttingen 1934.

Schmidt, Traugott: Der Leib Christi. Leipzig 1919.

Schrenk, Gottlob: Gottesreich und Bund im älteren Protestantismus. Gütersloh 1923.

Schwab, Paul J.: The Attitude of Wolfgang Musculus toward Religious Tolerance. Scottdale, Penna. 1933.

Schweitzer, Albert: Geschichte der Paulinischen Forschung von der Reformation bis auf die Gegenwart. Tübingen 1911.

Shedd, Russell: Man in Community. Grand Rapids, Michigan 1964.

Sjöberg, Erich: „Widergeburt und Neuschöpfung im palastinensischen Judentum." StTh 4 (1950) 44—85.

Sleeper, C. Freeman: Black Power and Christian Responsibility. Nashville 1969.

Smalley, Beryl: The Study of the Bible in the Middle Ages. Notre Dame 1964[2].

Souter, Alexander: The Earliest Latin Commentaries on the Epistles of St. Paul. Oxford 1927.

Spicq, Ceslaus: Esquisse d'une histoire de l'exégèse latine au Moyen Age. Paris 1944.

Staedke, J.: „Die Juden in historischen und theologischen Urteil des Schweizer Reformator Heinrich Bullinger." Judaica II (1955) 236—256.

Strecker, Georg: „Christentum und Judentum in den beiden ersten Jahrhunderten." EvTh 16 (1956) 458—477.

Tannehill, Robert: Dying and Rising with Christ. BZNW 32. Berlin 1967.

Tischendorf, Constantin von: Novum Testamentum Graece II. Leipzig 1872[8].

Turner, Cuthbert H.: „Greek Patristic Commentaries on the Pauline Epistles." Dictionary of the Bible, extra vol., 484—531. Edinburg 1947[8].

Vermes, Geza: „Baptism and Jewish Exegesis." NTS 4 (1958) 308—309.
   Scripture and Tradition. Leiden 1961.

Vetus Latina: 24, 1. Ad Ephesios. ed. H. Frede. Freiburg 1962—64.

Vidler, Alec: The Church in an Age of Revolution. London 1961.

Westcott, Brooke F.: Social Aspects of Christinaity. London 1900[2].

Wickert, Ulrich: Studien zu den Pauluskommentaren Theodors von Mopsuestia. BZNW 27. Berlin 1962.

Wilde, Robert: The Treatment of the Jews in the Greek Christian Writers of the First Three Centuries. Washinton D. C. 1949.

Wilder, Amos N.: „The Church and Israel in the Light of Election." Studia Evangelica IV, 1. ed. F. L. Cross. Berlin 1968.

Willis, Geoffrey: St. Augustine and the Donatist Controversy. London 1950.

Wilson, R. McLachlan: Gnosis and the New Testament. Oxford 1968.

Wingren, Gustaf: Man and the Incarnation: a Study in the Biblical Theology of Irenaeus. transl. R. Mackenzie. Edinburgh 1959.

Wobbermin, George: „Zwei theologische Gutachten in Sachen des Arier-Paragraphen — kritisch beleuchtet." ThBl 12 (1933) 358 f.
   „Der Schriftgemäße Begriff der Kirche." Die Kirche im Neuen Testament. ed. F. Siegmund-Schultze. Berlin 1930.

INDEX OF MODERN AUTHORS